A Tropical Plains Frontier

A Tropical Plains Frontier

The Llanos of Colombia
1531–1831

Jane M. Rausch

University of New Mexico Press
Albuquerque

Library of Congress Cataloging in Publication Data

Rausch, Jane M., 1940-
A tropical plains frontier.

Bibliography: p.
Includes index.
1. Colombia—History—To 1810. 2. Colombia—History—War of Independence, 1810–1822. 3. Colombia—History—1822–1832. 4. Llanos—Colombia—History. 5. Indians of South America—Colombia—History. 6. Indians of South America—Colombia—Missions—History. I. Title.
F2272.R29 1984 986.1 84-13072
ISBN 0-8263-0761-2

Manufactured in the United States of America.
Library of Congress Catalog Card Number 84-13072.
International Standard Book Number 0-8263-0761-2.
First Edition.

For the People
of the Llanos
Past and Present

Contents

Maps

Illustrations

Tables

Preface

Historians have long been intrigued by the role of frontier regions in national development. Nearly one hundred years after Frederick Jackson Turner delivered his seminal paper, "The Significance of the Frontier in American History," they continue to debate the merits of his concept of a "moving frontier."[1] Of the Latin Americanists who have responded to the call of Walter Prescott Webb in *The Great Frontier* to examine the impact of border zones of the former Spanish and Portuguese territories, Silvio Zavala and José Honório Rodrigues agree that there was no counterpart to the North American West, but they suggest that more data are needed on individual regions before the final assessment can be made.[2] More recently, Alistair Hennessy, in his comprehensive monograph *The Frontier in Latin American History,* concluded that "one of the most extraordinary features of Spanish American life is the persistence of frontier conditions through the centuries since the Conquest," and that despite the dearth of research on this phenomenon, "the heart of the Latin American historical experience is the interplay between metropolis and frontier."[3]

One persisting frontier worthy of greater consideration is that of the vast tropical plains, the Llanos of Colombia, which extend east of the Andean Cordillera for 253,000 square kilometers. Cut by fast-flowing rivers that join the Orinoco to the east, the Llanos are alternately lands of flood and drought. Strips of rain forest stand along the rivers, but the predominant vegetation is tall, tropical bunch grass that supports herds of wild cattle and horses, descendants of animals introduced by the Spanish. Comprising the present Department of Meta, the Intendencias of Casanare and Arauca, and the Comisaría of Vichada, the region today accounts for one-fifth of Colombian territory but less than 2 percent of the population of 25,600,000.

Until the beginning of the sixteenth century, Indian cultivators and foragers occupied the Llanos to the limits of the region's potential, given the exploitative techniques available to them. They engaged in widespread trade and warfare. The grasslands were a conduit of cultural contact, diffusion and migration between the Andes, the Caribbean coast, the Amazon Basin, and the Guiana Highlands. The arrival of the Spanish, in 1531, dramatically altered these precontact relationships. Within decades the Llanos of San Juan and San Martín, south of the Meta River, and the Llanos of Casanare and Arauca, to the north of it, became an eastern frontier of the Andean settlements of New Granada—a region geographically isolated by the steep mountain slopes but symbolizing potential mineral and agrarian wealth.

Spanish interest in the Llanos, intense at the outset, quickly dissolved, after hundreds of conquistadors explored its grassy tracts without discovering the fabled kingdom of El Dorado. Their successors were *encomenderos,* administrators, slave hunters, ranchers, and missionaries, who subjugated the Indians and formed tiny enclaves of Hispanic life in the tropical wilderness. By the eighteenth century the Provincia de los Llanos, with its capital at Santiago de Las Atalayas, was a modest territorial unit within the Viceroyalty of New Granada. The mission emerged as the principal institution of imperial rule, and miscegenation between Spanish and Indians produced a cowboy subculture—the llaneros—who in the Wars of Independence formed the nucleus of Simón Bolívar's victorious army.

Much of the explanation for the decline of the Llanos in the nineteenth century appears to lie in the impact of this devastating war. By mid-twentieth century, with the exception of the area around Villavicencio, south of the Meta River, the region remains undeveloped. Despite the control of tropical diseases and other advances of modern technology, the severe climate and geographic isolation continue to postpone the integration of the Llanos into national life. The few hundred thousand settlers who have crossed the Andes to live there since World War II do not appear to be the avant-garde of millions of people who would follow in the path of the pioneers.[4]

Although parts of the Llanos have been under continuous Hispanic settlement since the sixteenth century, they have received little attention from historians. Colombian scholars have traditionally focused upon the Andean interior and the Caribbean coast. Their predilection for military, political, ecclesiastical history, and biography has done little to challenge the assumption that the sparsely populated and remote eastern regions have never played an important part in national cultural development.[5] A review of the extensive bibliography of Llanos sources compiled by María Teresa Cobos reveals that with some notable exceptions, geographers and anthropologists have undertaken the most significant investigations.[6] Often these scholars complain that the absence of reliable historical information about the plains presents major problems for scientific documentation.[7] To these voices are added pleas from officials and residents of Meta, Casanare, and Arauca, who urge the government to sponsor studies of Llanero life in order that Colombians may become more aware of the true nature of this forgotten part of their country.[8]

The study that follows presents an analysis of a Spanish American plains frontier by tracing the history of the Llanos of San Juan and San Martín, Casanare, and Arauca and the interrelation of these regions with the core highland settlements in New Granada from the sixteenth century to 1831. Its purpose is to illuminate an unexplored theme of Colombian history as a whole and to provide data for scholars concerned with comparative world frontiers. The research is based on a review of manuscript collections and published sources at the Archivo Histórico Nacional, Archivo del Congreso, the Biblioteca Nacional, and the Biblioteca Luis Angel Arango, in Bogotá, the Fundación John Boulton and the Biblioteca Nacional, in Caracas, and the University of Massachusetts Library, in Amherst. In addition, visits were made to the Llanos cities of Villavicencio, San Martín, Puerto López, Yopal, Arauca, and San Fernando de Apure.

Two limitations of the research design deserve comment. First, it is obvious from a glance at a map of South America that the Llanos form a greater portion of Venezuela than they do of Colombia. Indeed, my original idea was to write a comparative history of the plains frontiers of both countries from the sixteenth century to the present. After making four trips to Caracas and Bogotá between 1974 and 1976, during which I collected data and discussed the project with colleagues, I realized that the scheme was too ambitious to be completed within a reasonable length of time. I decided then to concentrate on the Llanos of New Granada, choosing the colonial era because it had traditionally been cited as the "golden age" of Casanare, and carrying the narrative through the breakup of Gran Colombia. Fortunately, the Llanos of Venezuela have attracted the talents of several able scholars, including José Antonio de Armas Chitty, Marco-Aurelio Vila, and Miquel Izard. The final chapter, which draws some broad comparisons between the Llanos of New Granada and Venezuela, leans heavily upon their work.

Second, historians from Turner to Hennessy have found *frontier* an elusive concept to define. To the dispair of his critics, Turner repeatedly interchanged *West* and *frontier* in his writing and used the word at different times to mean "a migrating region," "form of society," "state of mind," and "stage of society," rather than a place.[9] Recognizing this difficulty, Hennessy jettisons precise definitions to adopt Richard M. Morse's broader view: "The Frontier is not a line or a limit or a process either unilateral or unilinear. We must in fact, speak not of a frontier but of multiple, complex frontier experiences, transactions and mutations."[10] This approach, however, tends to transform the concept into a capacious umbrella, under which almost everything in Latin American history can be subsumed.[11]

For the purpose of this study, I have chosen to regard frontier as a geographic area where the edge of Hispanic settlement meets the wilderness. The wilderness is not empty but inhabited by native Americans. Thus, the frontier is also a zone of interpenetration between two previously distinct societies, and the geographic characteristics of the area set the limits for human activity there. The Spanish intrude into the area from their principal center of operation, or metropolis, in this case the Andean highlands.[12] They established institutions designed to incorporate the land and people into their empire. Over the course of centuries the interplay of cultures and of people with the environment produces a regional identity and has an impact on the metropolis. Because of the nature of the available sources, my primary concern has been with the Spanish side of the frontier, but the Indian contribution is an integral part of the story. As Charles Gibson wrote of the Spanish borderlands of the United States, "The outstanding differences between borderlands society and the society of central Mexico and Peru, were differences of degree and emphasis, and they depended more on Indian society than on Spanish society."[13]

The country known since 1886 as the Republic of Colombia had a variety of names during the period covered in this volume. Under Spanish rule, it was first the Presidency and later the Viceroyalty of the New Kingdom of Granada (Nuevo Reino de Granada). Between 1819 and 1830, it united with Ecuador and Venezuela to form the short-lived nation of Colombia which modern historians call Gran Colombia. In 1832 it became simply New Granada (Nueva Granada). To avoid confusion, I refer to its inhabitants as New Granadans in the sections on the colonial and independence eras and as Colombians in those dealing with the twentieth century.

Many institutions and people have contributed to this project since its inception in 1973. Generous grants from the National Geographic Society, the American Philosophical Society, and the University of Massachusetts Graduate Research Council facilitated the research, and I am grateful for their support. In all the archives and libraries where I studied, I received unfailing courtesy and much assistance. Among the directors and staffs of those institutions, a special word of thanks goes to Alberto Lee López and Pilar Moreno de Angel of the Archivo Histórico Nacional, Jaime Duarte French of the Biblioteca Luis Angel Arango, Manuel Pérez Vila of the Fundación John Boulton, and Pauline P. Collins of the University of Massachusetts Library.

I want to acknowledge the help and support of the late John L. Phelan, who served as my major professor at the University of Wisconsin and whose courses and published works on Latin American history provided a starting point for my thoughts about the frontier. Juan Manuel Pacheco, Rogerio Guáqueta Gallardo, J. Noé Herrera, Miquel Izard, Susan Berglund, Raymond E. Crist, David Bushnell, John W. Loy, Juan C. Zamora, Erika Brieke, and Gerald and Dorothy McFarland all gave generously of their time and wisdom. Frank Safford read the entire manuscript and provided a valuable critique. Beatriz de Muñoz and Guillermo Ramírez invited me to their *hatos* in Meta and Casanare so that I might experience life in the plains at first hand. Guillermo patiently explained many Llanero expressions and customs that otherwise would have remained incomprehensible to me.

I am indebted to Patricia Cutts for her fine maps and to Kate Jones for her careful preparation of the manuscript. Finally, I am especially grateful to my husband, Marvin D. Rausch, an extraordinary scientist with a humanistic bent. His love of travel and his unflagging encouragement and support have made it possible for me to complete this work. For its errors and shortcomings, I alone am responsible.

Jane M. Rausch
Amherst, Massachusetts
July 1983

A Tropical Plains Frontier

1 *The Llanos on the Eve of Discovery*

On December 7, 1882, four horsemen galloped along the streets of Bogotá, enveloped by the cool darkness of early dawn. In the lead, Ernst Röthlisberger silently bid goodbye to civilization and allowed the thrill of adventure to overwhelm his apprehension of Indian attacks and yellow fever. Accompanied by three students, the Swiss history professor set forth across the rugged Eastern Andean Cordillera to visit one of the least-known regions of Colombia—the Llanos Orientales, or eastern tropical plains.

The travelers climbed steadily, following the steep trail that ascended the rim of mountains to the southeast of the Sabana of Bogotá. At an altitude of 10,313 feet above sea level, they reached the Boquerón of Chipaque, the principal pass through the Cordillera that marks the continental divide. To the west, mountain streams tumbled down rocky crests to meet eventually with the Magdalena River. To the east the panorama, when not hidden as it was then by dense fog, would reveal innumerable folds and peaks of the Andes. Down these slopes ran tributaries of the Río Negro, which join the Meta and Orinoco rivers in the Llanos to flow thousands of miles to the Atlantic Ocean. Also hidden by fog was the precarious trail cutting down the mountain wall in a northeasterly direction. Undaunted and spurred on by an icy wind, the party descended.

Within an hour Dr. Röthlisberger and his companions halted at Chipaque, a pleasant town at 8,240 feet, surrounded by fertile fields of corn and pasture. Here they exchanged their horses for mules, whose surefootedness was better suited to the narrow path to come. Now the trail followed the left bank of the Cáqueza River. At times it sloped gently; at times it was broken by deep ravines through which gushed mountain streams. Each twisting turn brought new, breathtaking views of virgin wilderness, which, as the descent continued, took on an increasingly tropical character. By afternoon they reached the village of Cáqueza at 5,600 feet, picturesquely situated high above the river, at the base of rocky mountains. They were soon climbing again, following the old Spanish road. When twilight forced a halt, they camped in the broad valley where the Cáqueza River meets the Río Negro.

Back in the saddle on the second day, the travelers faced the most dangerous pass of their journey. A little beyond Quetame, they encountered a deep gorge created by the raging waters of the Río Negro. Looking into the chasm, they saw the remains of an iron bridge. Constructed in the United States some years before and installed at great expense across the gorge, the bridge had proven too short for the gap and collapsed one day into the river below. Now a cable with a basket suspended provided contact with the other side. Fortunately for the travelers, the river was shallow enough to permit their mules to swim across it, and they avoided the delay of two or three days usually experienced at this point.

With the winding Río Negro ever visible hundreds of feet below, they continued along a new road, carved into the mountain by government engineers. It was less than a meter in width and interrupted frequently by landslides and waterfalls. Precarious wooden bridges, sometimes no more than three logs laid side by side, allowed passage over these obstacles. To summon the courage to cross such makeshift contraptions, Dr. Röthlisberger and his companions placed complete faith in their mules which negotiated them with painfully slow caution. The landscape became more tropical. In clearings within the rain forest, they saw huts clinging to the mountain slopes here and there, adjoined by plots of *yuca,* corn, *plátanos,* and bananas. After such a demanding journey, they welcomed the sight of Susumuco, where they spent the night at a friend's hacienda.

The morning of December 9, the travelers began the final segment of the trip. Steadily descending, the trail still had its share of dizzy precipices as it passed through forests and followed rivers. By afternoon, ninety-three miles from Bogotá but fully eight thousand feet below the capital in altitude, they arrived at the last outcropping of the Andes, the Alto of Buena Vista. Dr. Röthlisberger dismounted and stood at the edge of the eminence. To his right he could see below him streams flowing out from the mountain gorges to the plains. To the left the cordillera lost itself in the bluish horizon. The true spectacle lay before him—stretched

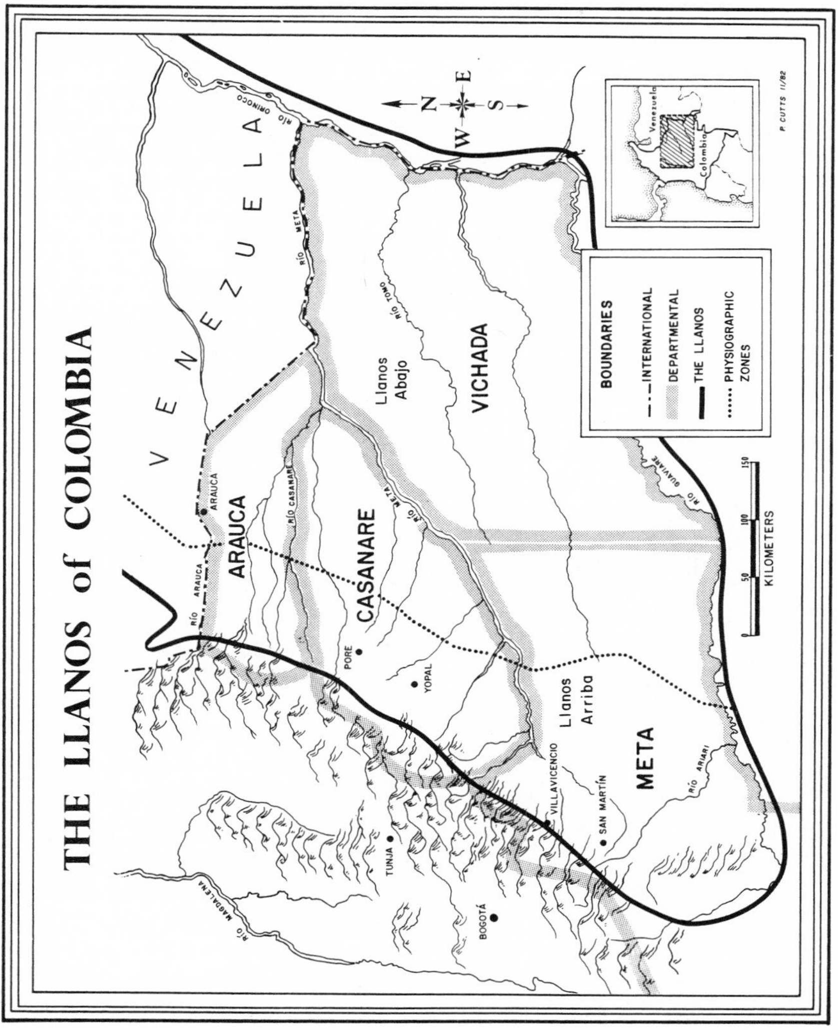

THE LLANOS of COLOMBIA
VENEZUELA
RÍO ORINOCO
RÍO META
ARAUCA
RÍO ARAUCA
ARAUCA
CASANARE
RÍO CASANARE
PORE
YOPAL
RÍO TOMO
Llanos Abajo
VICHADA
RÍO META
Llanos Arriba
VILLAVICENCIO
SAN MARTÍN
META
RÍO ARIARI
RÍO GUAVIARE
TUNJA
BOGOTÁ
RÍO MAGDALENA
N
E
S
W
BOUNDARIES
INTERNATIONAL
DEPARTMENTAL
THE LLANOS
PHYSIOGRAPHIC ZONES
0 50 100 150
KILOMETERS
Venezuela
Colombia
P. CUTTS 11/82

out in all their glory, a perfect semicircle with a radius of thirty leagues—the Llanos.

"How can I describe my astonishment and rapture," he wrote in his memoirs, "when all of a sudden, I saw the boundless plains spread out before me?" The countless rivers cut slowly through the grassland, like silver ribbons unwinding in the distance fringed with dense virgin forest. Three colors intermingled in the landscape—the silver-gray of the waters, the lush green-gray of the pastures, and the flecks of forest which, like dark shadows, variegated the predominant green. Röthlisberger continued:

> No greater contrast can be imagined than that between the intricate massiveness of the Cordillera, rising to the region of perpetual snow, and this uniform tropical plain. Great and majestic in its solitude and mystery is the ocean; greater and more impressive are the Llanos. The ocean waves are rigid and dead, an image of Dread and of blind Might, but the Llanos have movement of color and endless diversity. They are the image of Life—Life that preaches to man not his puny impotence, but awakens in him Hope, such as aroused the companions of Columbus on hearing the magic cry, "Land! Land!"[1]

Ernst Röthlisberger's personal discovery of the Llanos merits recounting in detail, because nearly everyone who has traveled there across the Eastern Cordillera since the sixteenth century has experienced the same euphoria.[2] Although today a paved highway has substituted a four-hour drive by automobile for the three-day mule excursion, travelers, on completing the perilous course through the mountains, still find in their first view of the plains a vision of hope, of a new frontier, of El Dorado. It is only after living for several years, months, or even weeks in this tropical grassland that they become disillusioned, embittered and beaten by what, in spite of modern technology, loom as insurmountable natural obstacles. Then, at best, the Llanos seem a melancholy wasteland, at worst, a green hell. A review of the topography, climate, vegetation, and fauna of the region explains the paradox which it presents to the European, while a description of the pre-Columbian peoples who lived there reveals that the native Americans came to terms with the environment long before the arrival of the first conquistadors.

The Colombian Llanos are located between the latitudes of 3 degrees and 7 degrees north. Sloping eastward from the Andes, they merge imperceptibly with the Venezuelan Llanos at elevations near sea level. The Arauca River serves as their northern boundary. The southern limit is the

Guaviare River, at the edge of the Amazon jungle. Many other rivers run through the plains. The largest is the Meta, which can be navigated by steamships at certain times of the year to its confluence with the Orinoco.[3] The vast area of approximately 253,000 square kilometers makes up one-fifth of the total territory of Colombia and comprises the present-day Department of Meta, the Intendencias of Arauca and Casanare, and the Comisaría of Vichada (see map 1).[4]

Textbooks sometimes refer to the Llanos as a "featureless grassland plain," and it is true that, except where it is fringed by the Andes to the north and west and by the Guiana Highlands to the east, the entire region forms a hollow basin with an altitude averaging between one hundred and five hundred meters. Closer investigation reveals, however, that diversity rather than uniformity is the rule. As geographer Dieter Brunnschweiler has pointed out, the Llanos are not all plains, not all grass and, least of all, featureless.[5]

Physiographically there are two well-defined zones. the llanos arriba and the llanos abajo. The llanos arriba are the higher plains near the Andean foothills. These plains consist of great alluvial fans formed by streams flowing east from the Andes. Wide belts of fine-grained, moisture-retentive alluvium lie around the base of the sloping fans. This soil supports clumps of rain forest and is ideal for the cultivation of rice, sugarcane, coffee, tobacco, corn, cotton, bananas, and other crops. The llanos abajo lie *más allá,* or farther to the east. These are the true plains where the relief is so level that there is rarely three hundred feet of difference between adjacent high and low points. Only coarse grasses will grow on the infertile, weathered soil, and modern agricultural activity is limited to cattle grazing.[6]

Of historical importance is the geomorphological distinction between the high plain, rising several meters south of the Meta River, and the substantially lower alluvial overflow plain, north of it. Throughout the colonial period, the southern plain, known as the Llanos of San Juan and San Martín, remained relatively isolated. Development took place only after the completion of a passable road between Bogotá and Villavicencio, at the turn of the nineteenth century. By contrast the Llanos of Casanare, to the north, and its subregion, the Airico de Macaguane (present-day Arauca), were more accessible. Here the Spanish established Santiago de las Atalayas, capital city of the Provincia de los Llanos. Casanare became the center of missions and cattle raising. During the Wars of Independence, it served as a bastion of patriot resistance and nurtured the heroic struggle that culminated in Bolívar's triumph at Boyacá, on August 7, 1819.

A North American viewing the Llanos from the Alto of Buena Vista is struck by their apparent similarity to the Great Plains. After traveling through the grasslands, he soon realizes that their location in the low latitudes, the presence of the mountain barrier to the west, and the trade wind patterns combine to produce a climate inconceivable in the temperate zone. Nowhere, even in Colombia, a country of meteorological extremes, are the seasons so marked as in the Llanos. The annual dry season, or summer, extends from December to the end of March. Some rain falls during this period, but it has little effect because of high evaporation rates and rapid runoff.[7] Within weeks the rivers shrink to streams and the lakes turn into stagnant pools, before disappearing completely. Dust covers the vegetation, the trees lose their leaves, and the ground cracks as if there had been an earthquake. While the land bakes and the grass turns brown, animals travel far in search of food; many die of thirst.[8]

Relief comes with the advent of the rainy season. Precipitation begins in April and continues until the end of November. Peaking in June and October, the rain sometimes falls without interruption for days. The flooding rivers create vast seas, leaving only small islands of dry land. Wild animals seek refuge on these islands, but frequently they starve to death or drown. Even horses cannot pass through the inundated areas; the human inhabitants are forced to rely on dugout canoes for transportation. Total annual accumulation ranges from 72 inches in the llanos abajo, near the Orinoco, to 184 inches near the base of the Andes.[9] Despite the contrast between the dry and wet seasons, the air temperature is remarkably stable, due to the buildup of cloud cover toward a maximum in the rainy season, the high sun period of the year. The plains are subjected to the permanently hot thermal regime of the *tierra caliente*. Annual mean temperature is 80°F, with daily fluctuations from 70°F to 86–93°F.[10]

These climatic conditions influence the vegetation, which includes many varieties of savannas and forest. In his comprehensive study of northern South American vegetation, J. S. Beard defines savanna as "a virtually continuous ecologically dominant stratum of more or less xerophytic herbaceous plants, of which grasses and sedges are the principal components with scattered shrubs, trees or palms sometimes present." The essential factor that distinguishes the savanna from forest, woodlands, *páramo,* and swamp is that the herb stratum is ecologically dominant.[11] The entomologist Marston Bates identified three types of savannas in the Llanos. The *serranía* is the country highly dissected into ridges by gorges, characteristic of south banks of the larger rivers. The hills often have fantastic shapes. A sedge *(Bulbostylis)* of low grazing value protects the very steep slopes from obvious erosion. The infertile soil is a gravel layer over clay, with occasional outcrops of a reddish rock. More common are gently rolling savannas with extensive marshy areas, called *bajos*. When sheets of shallow open water accumulate in the bajos, they are called *esteros*. A third kind of savanna is *sural*—a marshy terrain of bunch grass which presents a reticulate pattern of deep ditches surrounding mounds a meter or two in diameter. As the top of the mound is more than a meter above the surrounding ditch, surales, which frequently occur in Casanare, are difficult to traverse. Bates notes that a man either on foot or mule must decide whether to follow the endless twisting of the boggy ditches or to jump from mound to mound. Both are awkward expedients that generally end in complete frustration, and there are substantiated stories of man and mule firmly stuck in a narrow, deep ditch between two sural mounds.[12] Regardless of type, on well-drained portions of savanna, the ground covering is long-stemmed strawgrass *(Trachypogon vestitus)* and creeping guarátare *(Axonopus purpussi)*. In poorly drained areas, bunchgrasses *(Andropogon* and *Leptocoryphium)* predominate.[13]

There are four kinds of forests in the Llanos. Foothill forests cover the lower slopes of the Andes at altitudes of five hundred to twelve hundred meters. Like all classic rain forests, they have little or no underbrush because of the heavy canopy of many layers of tree heights. Below five hundred meters, and extending from the base of the mountains for fifteen to twenty kilometers, is the piedmont forest, nurtured by a rainfall of four to five meters annually. Since the 1920s this forest has been completely cleared from around Villavicencio, but stumps still litter the pastures, and the original forest pattern can be seen a few kilometers from the trails.[14] Savanna forests fill the valleys of the serranías and the depressions of the rolling grasslands. Unlike the rain forests, they are stands of *moriche* palms, with an admixture of other trees and shrubs. In marshy areas an algae-filled sludge covers the ground and there is a dense undergrowth of spider ferns. Finally, on the flood plains of major rivers such as the Meta, Guaviare, and Casanare, are gallery forests, physiognomically and floristically more closely related to the rain forests than to the savanna palm groves. Gallery forests have many large-crowned trees which form an unbroken canopy over a multi-storied undergrowth.[15] All four types of forest have products of potential value: palm oil and wine; medicinal substances such as quinine; balsams, rubbers, brazilwood dye; tonka beans, used in perfumes; and flavorings such as vanilla and sarsaparilla.[16]

Throughout the Llanos the boundary between forest and savanna is abrupt. There is no thinning out of trees in the savanna or islands of grass within the forest. This sharp division may be evidence that the plains exist not because prehistoric people cleared trees away, but because they are a natural plant formation "representing a vegetational climax caused by and in equilibrium with ambient climate."[17] While acknowledging that destruction by human and natural fires, soil ill-adapted to forest growth, and poor drainage in some areas may have impeded the development of forests, Brunnschweiler argues that the critical factor in savanna formation is moisture deficiency, due to the alternating wet and dry seasons. The lack of rain for a three-month period, when coupled with the high daytime temperatures and evaporation rates, leads to an acute soil water shortage in all sites except those where water is provided by other than atmospheric means. Forests can grow only along the rivers and in the marshy depressions where there is water present above or at root level even during the drought period.[18]

There is a notable poverty of macrofauna on the savanna. While the forests swarm with wildlife, including armadillo, tapir, capybara, jaguar, rabbits, and monkeys, the coarse, unpalatable pasturage of the grasslands limited the larger animals to deer and anteaters until the Europeans introduced horses, mules, and cattle. On the other hand, cats, mice, and two dozen species of birds, among which are *moriche* orioles, savanna hawks, parrots, burrowing owls, and white and scarlet ibises, abound. The rivers teem with fish, amphibians, and reptiles, not the least of which are crocodiles, anacondas, stingrays, and electric eels. But the richest life in the savanna proper is in the realm of microfauna—the larger insects of myriad genera and species. There are horseflies, ticks, fleas, and gnats. Within a ten-mile radius of Villavicencio, Bates counted 150 mosquito species, compared to 125 known in all of North America.[19]

As this cursory description suggests, the Llanos are not a tropical paradise. The extremes of the seasons and the hordes of insects turn them into an incubator of disease. Until the development of vaccines and DDT, the white and mestizo population suffered fevers, malaria, and tuberculosis, as well as malnutrition. Since 1978 petroleum has been produced in Casanare, but known deposits are not extensive.[20] Other valuable minerals have not been discovered in quantities that would make them profitable to exploit. Cattle thrive in some areas, but the difficulty of getting them to market places ranchers at a disadvantage compared with those in more accessible Colombian regions. The barrier presented by the Eastern Cordillera discouraged any kind of large-scale food production until the boom period of the last thirty years.

Perhaps it is the vastness of the Llanos that fosters the persistent illusion of fabulous wealth, yet there is contradiction in the grandeur of their nature. The rising sun, so breathtakingly beautiful at dawn, becomes a relentless killer during the day, scorching the plains, drying up the water, and leaving humans and animals alike in an agony of thirst. The storm, majestic in its passage across the skies, changes fertile savannas into desolate swamps and leaves the inhabitants without protection or shelter. In his famous novel *La vorágine* (Bogotá, 1924), José Eustasio Rivera dramatizes this paradox. The book's protagonist, Arturo Cova, is a young poet who, after seducing his girl friend in Bogotá, elopes with her to Casanare. At first the tropical landscape has only a magical attraction for Cova: "The freshness of early dawn greeted us as we drank our coffee, a subtle fragrance of lush grasses, plowed earth, newly cut timbers . . . An unexpected joy swelled our veins, while our spirits, flowing amply like the pampas felt grateful for life and existence."[21] Later he confesses: "I even felt like imprisoning myself forever in those fascinating plains, living with Alicia in a smiling home, which I myself would build on the banks of a river of opaque waters, or on one of those verdant knolls where a seagreen pool sleeps in the shadow of a palm."[22]

Unfortunately, Cova's subsequent adventures shatter his idyllic vision. Crossing from plain to plain, river to river, he learns of the terrors of this devastating environment. While camping by a waterhole and indulging in romantic meditation, he comes upon a hideous water snake. A round-up of cattle stops abruptly when one of the cowboys is gored and left headless.[23] The Llanos become a feverish, grotesque nightmare, and when Cova reaches the jungle, he finds that the human personality breaks down completely. "This sadistic and virgin jungle casts premonitions of coming danger over one's spirit. Vegetable life is a sensitive thing, the psychology of which we ignore. In these desolate places only our presentiments understand the language it speaks. Under its influence, man's nerves become taut and ready to attack, ready for treachery and ambush. Our senses confuse their tasks, the eye feels, the back sees, the nose explores, the legs calculate and the blood cries out. 'Flee! Flee!' "[24]

The literary critic Jean Franco describes *La vorágine* as a "cry of horror and surprise at the hostile world that Cova finds outside the civilized fringe of urban society."[25] Rivera exaggerates Cova's dilemma with poetic license, but the young man's disillusionment is shared by many Europeans and highland Colombians who, coming to the plains with a romantic idea of taming the wilderness, are unable to cope with the demands placed upon them by a starkly different land. Yet scientists remind us that the

Llanos are not hostile, they are merely disinterested.[26] People can and have come to terms with this environment. Certainly the native Americans were able to do so. On the eve of discovery, numerous interdependent and related societies of farmers and nomadic hunter-gatherers made their homes throughout the forests and savannas.

Until recently few archaeologists had concerned themselves with prehistoric settlement in the Llanos because of limited interest and the difficulty of carrying out research. Vegetation and erosion have destroyed many sites. Deep river deposits and jungles hide others. There are few surface features to guide scholars in a search for prehistoric remains; once located, the sites yield only the most limited information. Unlike the Inca ruins in the high Andean valleys, these sites include no stone buildings and walls, no terraced agriculture, no golden pots or jewels. The sites that have been uncovered offer, instead, thousands and thousands of potsherds that must be laboriously pieced together in order to tell their story.[27] In addition, the natural attraction of archaeologists to the so-called higher civilizations that played pivotal roles in the Spanish conquest makes it easy to understand why they have neglected the Llanos.

Lack of knowledge, in turn, reinforces an interpretation of pre-Columbian history that views the tropical lowland cultures as passively molded by their environment and by influences radiating from the more advanced Andean area. Best expounded by Julian Steward and Louis C. Faron, in *Native Peoples of South America* (New York, 1959), this model emphasizes the negative aspects of the tropical environment, the relatively short time depth of human existence there, the resistance to change by aboriginal people, and their failure to develop complex precontact sociopolitical and economic units.

More recent studies, however, have challenged this position by arguing strongly that lowland culture development was not late, simple, or dependent upon highland stimulus.[28] No preceramic sites have been found yet in the Llanos, but Rouse and Cruxent, on the basis of investigations in similar regions of Venezuela, have postulated that people may have reached the plains between 15,000 and 5,000 B.C. and may have survived by hunting large mammals such as mastodons, which roamed the savannas until desiccation caused them to become extinct.[29] These scholars, in Venezuela, and Reichel Dolmatoff, in Colombia, have found evidence of a relatively early and widespread agriculture in the tropical lowlands. They postulate that manioc cultivation and ceramic complexes may have appeared by approximately 1,000 B.C.[30] Their findings bear out geographer Carl Sauer's earlier hypothesis that manioc may first have been domesticated in Venezuela.[31] Prehistoric earthworks have been reported in widely scattered localities in lowland South America, including sites in the northwestern llanos of Venezuela and the foothills of the northwestern llanos of Colombia. This evidence would seem to indicate that the populations of these areas were much larger than previously supposed.[32]

In his analysis of the hunting economies of the tropical forest zone, Donald Lathrap argues that from 2,500 B.C. until the arrival of the Europeans, the dominant historical pattern was the struggle of tropical-forest villagers to occupy the fertile areas along the rivers and to push out weaker peoples, who were then forced to become nomads on the savannas. In contrast to the riverine groups, who were sedentary populations engaged in intensive root-crop farming, fishing, and hunting, the people relegated to the elevated regions between the major rivers were organized in widely dispersed, mobile social units. Lack of agricultural potential on the plains and insufficiency of aquatic resources to supply protein limited the size of these groups, since they were dependent on terrestrial hunting. Thus, "most of the primitive groups inhabiting the tropical forest upland away from the major flood plains can be interpreted as the wreckage of evolved agricultural societies forced into an environment unsuitable to the basic economic pattern. This condition forced them to rely on hunting. A more intense hunting led to more nomadism, a decline in agricultural productivity and a still greater dependence on wild food."[33]

The current emphasis on regional strife and environmental factors in shaping tropical plains cultures does not completely preclude the importance of contacts with the high Andean civilizations. Paul Kirchhoff's study of the Guayupe and Sae, who lived on the slopes and foothills of the Eastern Cordillera, shows that their culture mixed tropical forest features with traits associated with the circum-Caribbean peoples. The Guayupe and Sae fought and traded with the Chibchas, absorbing aspects of that culture in the organization of their villages, warfare, and religion.[34] The Swedish anthropologist Sven Lovén has noted that the Chibcha trade network extended to the Meta River, although the route they used to cross the Cordillera is still not known. The Achaguas, located on the headwaters of the Orinoco, Río Negro, and Meta, exported tropical foods to the highlands in exchange for salt, gold, and fine cotton blankets.[35] On the other hand, Robert and Nancy Morey have demonstrated that the Orinoco River was a major avenue of commerce throughout northern South America. Llanos Indians traded with groups in the Andes, but also with one another and with peoples on the island of Trinidad, the Atlantic coast, and the Guiana highlands. They manufactured *quiripa,* strings of shell disks, which were used in and outside the plains as a form of money. Articles exchanged included foodstuffs, tropical dyes, curare, cooking pots, slaves, turtle eggs and oil, dogs, birds, and fish. The Llanos, in pre-Columbian times, were more than a frontier of Andes civilization. They were a fertile field of cultural contacts, diffusion, and migration between the mountains and the Caribbean coast, the Amazon Basin and the Guiana hills.[36]

Preconquest history remains a topic worthy of future investigation, and it is hoped that more scholars will turn their efforts to filling in the tantalizing gaps of knowledge. For the purposes of this study, it is more appropriate to focus upon the major groups of cultivators and hunter-gatherers that inhabited the plains on the eve of European discovery—the Achagua and Sáliva in the Llanos of Casanare; the Betoy, Jirara, and Tunebo in the Airico de Macaguane; the Guayupe and Sae in the Llanos of San Juan and San Martín; and the Guahibo in all three regions (see map 2).[37]

The Arawak-speaking Achagua were the most numerous and culturally most complex group. They occupied the major streams and the best hunting and fishing areas of the Llanos of Casanare, extending into Barinas, Barraguan, and the Llanos of Apure, in Venezuela. Adjoining them along the Orinoco, Guaviare, Vichada, and Meta rivers were the Sáliva, a related people who spoke a Tairoan language. Both groups practiced slash-and-burn agriculture. Along the fertile river banks they grew yuca *(Manihot utilissima),* sweet potatoes, yams, maize, beans, and gourds.[38] They hunted birds, monkeys, deer, and turtles; captured ants and grubs; and fished with bows and arrows. Other Indians sharing this large territory were primarily foragers, living in the less-productive regions.

The Achagua resided in small, kinship-based hamlets, characterized by a single communal dwelling and a separate men's clubhouse, which was often, but not invariably, surrounded by a palisade. The Indians were divided into animal-named lineages, each localized in a single house community and probably exogamous.[39] Each communal house, or village, had a chief, called a *cacique* by the chroniclers, who was subject to a more important chief with authority over several hamlets. These clusters of hamlets comprised the larger kinship unit to which all belonged. The more powerful chief appears to have been important only in activities which involved more than one hamlet, such as warfare.[40]

Men took three or four wives, of whom each had equal rights and cultivated her own fields. The men held drinking bouts in their clubhouse, from which women were barred. Daily tasks were divided by sex. Men made baskets, mats, and wooden articles; cleared the fields for farming; hunted, fished, and assisted in gathering wild foods. Women fashioned

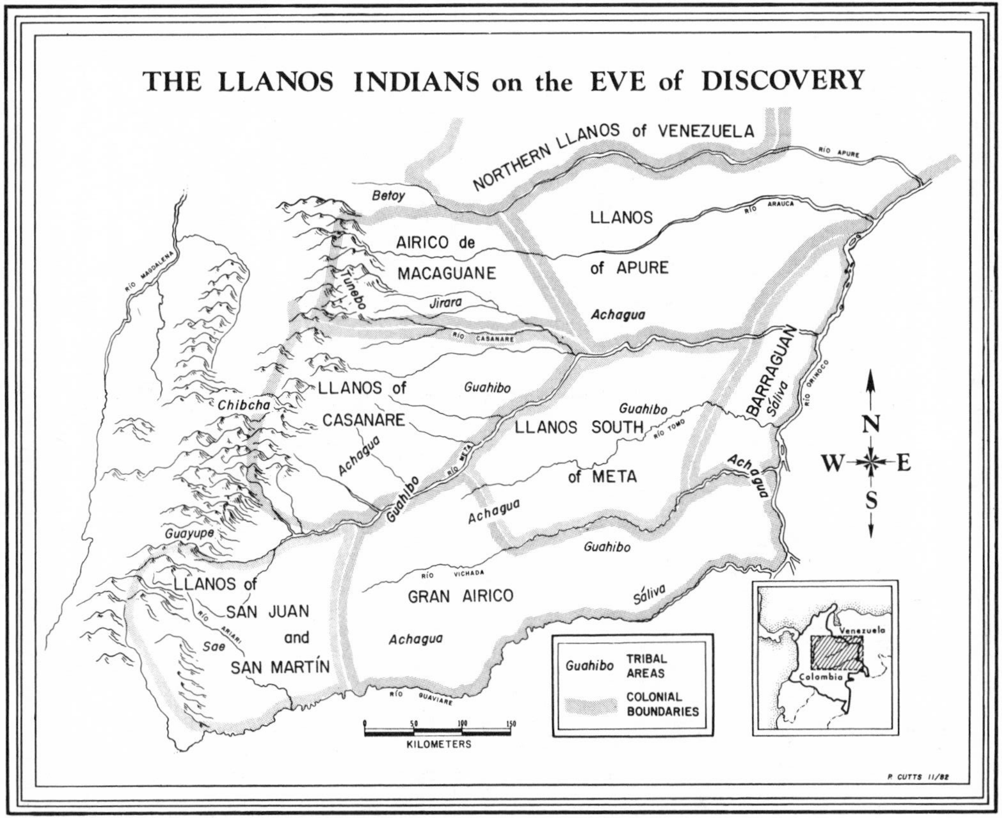
THE LLANOS INDIANS on the EVE of DISCOVERY
NORTHERN LLANOS of VENEZUELA
RÍO APURE
RÍO ARAUCA
LLANOS
of APURE
Achagua
Betoy
AIRICO de
MACAGUANE
Tunebo
Jirara
RÍO CASANARE
LLANOS of
CASANARE
Guahibo
Chibcha
Achagua
Guahibo
RÍO META
BARRAGUAN
Sáliva
RÍO ORINOCO
Guahibo
LLANOS SOUTH
RÍO TOMO
of META
Achagua
Achagua
Guayupe
Guahibo
RÍO VICHADA
GRAN AIRICO
Sáliva
Achagua
LLANOS of
SAN JUAN
and
SAN MARTÍN
RÍO ARIARI
Sae
RÍO GUAVIARE
RÍO MAGDALENA
N
W
E
S
Guahibo TRIBAL AREAS
COLONIAL BOUNDARIES
0 50 100 150
KILOMETERS
Venezuela
Colombia
P. CUTTS 11/82

cord hammocks, nets, and pots; fetched firewood and water; cultivated the fields; cooked and prepared the manioc bread called *casabe,* and painted their husbands' bodies. Both sexes wore their hair long to the waist. Clothing consisted of hemp cord skirts for women and breechclouts for men.[41]

Further social differentiation is evident in the display of wealth and the keeping of slaves. Men and women wore the strings of shell beads known as quiripa to show their affluence. In some hamlets the rich often hired the poor as servants, paying them well. Slavery was more developed than among most llanos groups. Even before European contact, the Achaguas were raiding neighboring tribes. They also traded for slaves, both to resell and to use themselves. Their language had distinctive words for male slave *(macogerrí)* and for female slave *(macegetua).* After the conquest the term *maco* was used throughout the plains to designate a slave.[42] The Achaguas also traded craft articles, food stuffs, dogs, birds, and jaguar skins, for salt from the highlands and palm oil, palm fruits, fish, and meat from the Guahibos, to the east. Specialists among them manufactured quiripa. The Sálivas were well-known traders in yellow and red dyes and yuca graters.[43]

Achagua religion incorporated beliefs in a supreme god and in gods of the fields, wealth, earthquakes, madness, and fire. They worshipped lakes. Men used dance masks on certain religious occasions, from which women were excluded. The Sáliva sculptured figures of so-called demons, which their shamans consulted as oracles. Cane flutes and drums provided music for their ceremonies. The Indians believed in divination and witchcraft. They used *yopo,* a narcotic snuff made of certain leaves. They drank *berria,* an intoxicating drink made of casabe fermented with honey and water, and *chicha,* a brew of fermented manioc. The Achaguas practiced female infanticide and buried their dead in sealed graves. At a Sáliva funeral special paraphernalia and trumpets were used. The body was buried and subsequently disinterred, cremated, and the ashes drunk with chicha. Both groups moved their villages on the death of an occupant.[44]

Warfare was widespread in the Llanos before the arrival of the Europeans. Missionaries from the sixteenth to the eighteenth centuries portray the Achagua and Sáliva as victims in these struggles, but accounts of the first expeditions into their territory describe them as being very warlike—fighting with lances, darts, poisoned arrows, shields, and clubs. Major reasons for battle were to capture female slaves and to loot villages and gardens. The Achagua attacked in surprise raids. War leaders were so-called captains, who were able to attract a following in proportion to their success on such raids. To make themselves brave in battle, the warriors drank a potion in which they mixed the dried heart of a vanquished opponent. After they killed their enemies, they made flutes of the arm and leg bones.[45]

Located north of the Achagua, between the Casanare and Apure rivers, in the Airico de Macaguane, were three other farming tribes—the Betoy, Jirara, and Tunebo. The Betoy were the most numerous and spoke a language now considered to be Tucano. The Jirara included several subgroups—Arauca, Airico, Burro, Ele, and Situfo. The Tunebo lived on the western fringes of the Airico de Macaguane, largely in the mountains. These peoples used slash and burn agriculture to grow manioc, maize, pineapples, and peppers, but relied more heavily than the Achaguas on hunting, fishing, and gathering for their subsistence.[46]

The Betoy, Jirara, and Tunebo lived in small, scattered communities that consisted of a single communal house. Betoy houses were small shelters, easily abandoned after a death, but each hamlet did have a male clubhouse that was used for festivals and for the accommodation of guests. The Jirara built long, narrow houses about thirty feet wide and two hundred feet long. Tunebo family hamlets were located as many as forty miles from each other. Local exogamy was practiced. In all these groups, the headman was the oldest male of the community.

Tasks were divided by sex. Men hunted, fished, and cleared the fields. Women planted, weeded, harvested, and prepared meals. The Tunebo were monogamous, and there was little polygamy among the others, because female infanticide created a shortage of women. A Betoy mother would bury her newborn daughter alive unless prevented by her relatives, because she believed that a woman's life was very hard and painful. Nudity was characteristic, although the headmen wore bark cloth garments. Both sexes painted their bodies for decoration and for protection against the sun and insect bites.[47]

These groups made cooking vessels, bark cloth, and calabash containers. They traded, using the quiripa currency. They were more nomadic than the Achaguas, although they moved for the same reason—the death of an occupant of the hamlet. Believing that sickness and death contaminated all, they would seek a new village site, traveling in dugout canoes and on foot, carrying all their goods on their backs.

The Betoy and Jirara believed in a sun god and other mythological beings. They had no priests or idols, but shamans acted as so-called medicine men and could send demons to cure the sick. Flutes and drums provided music. Chicha was drunk on all social occasions and the shaman used yopo. The Tunebo had a sacred lake where they went to consult a large snake about their problems. This lake was so famous that it even attracted tribes from the highlands.[48]

For purposes of warfare, Jirara hamlets could unite behind a prominent chief. Such leaders were advised by a council of adult men. Like the Betoy, they used clubs, bows and arrows, axes, and lances. Destruction of the enemy, rather than taking captives, appears to have been their aim. The Jirara were a continual problem after the sixteenth century for the Spanish, who called their attacks *gritos* because they uttered so many shouts on going into battle.[49]

South of the Achagua, along the forested slopes of the Eastern Cordillera and in the fertile flood plains of the Llanos of San Juan and San Martín, lived the Guayupe and the Sae. Their language was Arawakian, but their proximity to the Chibchas (Muiscas) in the highlands caused them to adopt circum-Caribbean cultural traits.[50] Like other rain-forest farmers, their principal crop was bitter manioc (yuca), but they also grew maize, sweet potatoes, beans, peanuts, chili peppers, cotton, and tobacco. Both groups fished. The Guayupe hunted deer and peccaries, but the Sae did not hunt, because they believed that wild game should not be eaten.

These Indians lived in fairly large villages of from one hundred to four hundred people.[51] Each hamlet consisted of several houses and a special building used for ceremonial purposes, all constructed around a plaza. The houses were big enough to accommodate several families. It is probable that each village had more than a single lineage. Every hamlet had a headman with a special stool and lance as his insignias of office. He was installed in a ceremony during which the people carried him around on a litter, an Andean practice. Men and women both went naked, except for females among the Guayupe, who wore a pointed piece of bark in front, hanging from a string tied at the waist. Generally both sexes wore their hair long, but on the Meta River, women shaved their heads completely.[52]

The Guayupe and Sae could speak the Muisca language and knew well the Chibchas, who came down from the Sabana of Bogotá to purchase cotton in exchange for gold objects. They also were acquainted with highland tribes who lived to the south of the Chibchas. From these people they obtained twenty-two-carat gold in thin leaves and sheets, jewels, and silver bells.

The Guayupe and Sae made deerhide moccasins and leggings from a leaf fiber of the *palmicha* tree which they wore for protection against the high, tough grass that covered the savannas. In order to travel on land more easily, they burned this grass several times a year. They used canoes for river transportation.[53]

The sun and the moon played a prominent role in their religion. Both groups placed considerable emphasis upon the transmigration of human souls to animals. They esteemed and feared their shamans, believing that they could take the form of jaguars or bears to kill their enemies. At religious ceremonies the men danced. They took yopo and tobacco to provoke visions.

Guayupe and Sae were quite warlike and had a special group of so-called war captains to organize the men into fighting squadrons. Weapons included short wooden hurling spears, long lances, three-edged clubs tied to the wrist, bows and arrows, and, in some tribes, slings. The warriors wore protective armor made of tapir hides and carried shields large enough to protect their whole bodies—both Andean characteristics. They attacked in orderly formation with shouting and trumpets, having first worked up their courage by drinking yuca and corn beer. Some groups built palisades of wooden posts tied closely together with lianas. The Guayupe initially made valiant efforts to repel the Spanish expeditions that entered their territory.[54]

The Achagua, Betoy-Jirara-Tunebo, and Guayupe-Sae were all cultivators who controlled the forested rivers and lived in the fertile agricultural areas on the Andean slopes and the llanos arriba. Farther east, in the llanos abajo, where the pure grasslands could not support a sedentary population, the Indians were by necessity foragers, dependent on hunting and gathering. Some of them, as Lathrap has suggested, may have practiced agriculture originally, but on being driven out of the choice riverine areas by stronger groups, they adopted a new mode of subsistence.

Among the foragers the Guahibo, also known as Chiricoa, were the most important.[55] They were found throughout the Llanos of Casanare, the Llanos of San Juan and San Martín, and to a lesser degree in the Airico de Macaguane. Their language was distinct from Arawak or Carib. They hunted deer, peccaries, jaguars, pumas, mice, and snakes with bows and arrows and other devices. To entice armadillos out of their dens, they used pointed sticks. Sometimes they burned the grass close to the rivers so that the fresh sprouts would attract deer and other animals. Famous for eating "everything that exists above and everything underground," they supplemented their meat diet with roots, palm fruit, wild vegetables, fruits, insects, and grubs.[56]

The Guahibo were true nomads. They had no dwelling of any kind and never spent more than two or three days in the same place. At night they slung hammocks between trees in the open air or slept on the bare ground. They traveled in bands of six or eight families, led by a chief who was succeeded in office by his son. Headed by captains, subgroups within the kinship-based band separated for hunting but joined together in launching attacks on other tribes.

A Guahibo band on the move was an extraordinary sight. The Jesuit missionary Joseph Gumilla, who observed such treks in the early eighteenth century, wrote that across plains covered with grass taller than their own height, the Indians carried all their belongings on their backs, organized in six well-defined sections. First came the unmarried young men, walking single file amd armed with bows, arrows, and lances. Their task was to break a path for those who followed. When the leader tired, his legs bleeding from the tough blades of grass, he ceded his place to the next man and took a position in the rear of the entire band, where walking was easy. Second came the married men, carrying their weapons and young children; then the old people who could still walk and the physically weak. The fourth group consisted of married women carrying large baskets filled with domestic utensils, each usually with one child on top of this load and another clinging to her breast, and accompanied by other children old enough to walk. In the fifth group the strongest men carried the sick and aged of both sexes in large baskets on their backs. Finally came the rear guard of warriors and those from the first tier who had become tired. Gumilla added that neither childbirth nor death were reasons to stop. The mother-to-be simply dropped out of line, had her baby on the road, and returned to the march. The Indians quickly buried their dead or left them exposed to animals.[57]

As soon as the band arrived at a river, the men would hunt or fish, while the women gathered plant foods. The Guahibo collected turtles, turtle eggs, and caymans. They valued the palm fruit for its meat and oil, which they extracted and traded to other Indians, who used it on their hair. They also made weapons, hammocks, mortars, rafts, garments, calabashes, baskets, and cooking vessels. Short and muscular, both sexes wore their hair cut short or shaved off. The men went naked, but some women wore Achagua-style aprons made of palm thread.

As the largest and most powerful foraging tribe, the Guahibo aroused the fear and scorn of the cultivators, who said that "they learned their way of life from the monkeys and other animals."[58] Since hunting and gathering alone could not support their population, they adopted the twin strategies of trading with and raiding their neighbors. Frequently a band would descend upon a village for the purpose of bartering, bringing palm oil, hammocks, calabashes, and slaves captured or stolen from other tribes. They traded these commodities for chicha, tobacco in powder form, snail shells, and agricultural produce. An exchange of news accompanied the trading, for the villagers welcomed the nomads as carriers of information picked up in their wanderings; they, in turn, queried the cultivators about events that had taken place since their last visit. The Guahibo would also indulge in begging and stealing, so that on leaving a village, laden with goods, they would fall upon the surrounding fields and take whatever else they wanted. Their superior numbers made them bold, and their insolence in dealings with other tribes was notorious.[59]

The Guahibo were excellent fighters. Under the leadership of their chief, the men of a band would attack with perfect discipline, using bows, arrows, and clubs with skill. If they had limited their aggressive actions to raiding villages for food prior to contact, with the arrival of the Europeans and the expansion of the slave trade, the Guahibos quickly turned to this avenue for grain. Relentlessly they pursued the Achagua and Sáliva, their former trade partners and close associates, capturing their children to sell as slaves to the Spanish and the Caribs, to the east. In the seventeenth and eighteenth centuries, as a result of their depredations, some tribes completely disappeared and others lost control over their native lands. The balance of power among llanos societies was disrupted. By the nineteenth century the people who dominated the savanna were no longer the formerly powerful cultivators, but the Guahibo, the only group mobile enough to defend itself against the Spanish and Caribs and adaptable enough to adjust to the changes which took place after European contact.[60]

How many people were living in the Llanos on the eve of discovery? Throughout the New World such a question has generated heated debate, widely varying estimates, and no satisfactory answers. A paucity of historical accounts, the incompleteness of available data, and the rapid decline of Indians due to overwork, disease, dislocation, and warfare under Spanish rule complicates the problem. Historians tend to take a conservative view, suggesting a population considerably under 100,000, while some anthropologists have insisted that the plains supported many times that figure.

In 1964 Jaime Jaramillo Uribe published a systematic analysis of the demography of preconquest Colombia. In "La población indígena de Colombia en el momento de la conquista y sus transformaciones posteriores," he reviews previous estimates of the aboriginal population, which vary from well under one million to five or six million. Next, dividing New Granada into four subregions (Eastern Cordillera, Atlantic Coast, Central and Western Highlands; and Chocó and Llanos Orientales, lumped together as peripheral lowlands), Jaramillo proceeds to assess for each area statistics offered by the chroniclers, censuses, and tribute roles as well as the impact of disease, mistreatment, and social dislocation on the population during three centuries of Spanish rule. With regard to the Llanos, Jaramillo emphasizes the dispersed and nomadic nature of the Indian societies, their low birth rates, practices of infanticide, and limited access to food resources. He points out that none of the missions established there reached one thousand neophytes and that the only sizable groups were the Achagua and the Guahibo. Jaramillo calls metaphorical the statement by Padre Juan Rivero that the Indians in Casanare were as "numerous as grains of sand along a river," preferring the more sober description by another Jesuit, Joseph Gumilla, of enfeebled tribes along the Orinoco and in the plains. Finally, and erroneously, he cites a census in 1810 that shows only 8,077 Indians remaining in the region.[62] On this evidence, Jaramillo concludes that the population of the Llanos Orientales subregion, taken together with that of the Chocó Pacific Lowlands, where many of the same conditions existed, was no more than 100,000, or one-ninth of the total of 900,000 which he suggests for all of New Granada.[63]

Until recently anthropologists following Steward's theory that Amazon territory was marginal to the development of civilization in the Andes also maintained that few people could have lived in the tropical lowlands. In 1966, however, William Denevan challenged this view, arguing that Greater Amazonia "could potentially support and actually did support a relatively large number of people at a Tropical Forest level of culture and economy."[64] Denevan asserted that the number of Indians in any region was a function of the availability of good soils and rich wild life. He constructed a habitat density formula to calculate the populations in the different habitats afforded by the Amazon Basin, northeast Brazil, the Brazilian savannas, and the Colombian and Venezuelan llanos at the time of contact.[65] For the Llanos, which he classified as lowland savanna, Denevan suggested a density of 1.3 people per square kilometer. Applied to a territory of 395,000 square kilometers, this density gives a total of 513,500 people. Since Denevan does not distinguish between Colombia and Venezuela, it is difficult to know what proportion of this number he would assign to the former. Nevertheless, if we assume that at least half of the 513,500 people lived in what is now Colombia, the figure of 256,750 people is over five times the estimate advanced by Jaramillo.[66]

Nancy Morey accepts as plausible Denevan's density of 1.3 and in "Ethnohistory of the Colombian and Venezuelan Llanos" draws from the historical materials arguments to support the notion of a dense population. The chroniclers of the sixteenth and seventeenth centuries, she points out, consistently reported large populations living along the major rivers and even in the least hospitable interfluvial zone. In northern Venezuela they sighted substantial villages, and the first Spanish armies, made up of as many as five hundred soldiers, accompanied by thousands of Indian and black slaves, lived off the local inhabitants during their wanderings through the plains—further evidence that the villages they encountered were large and well-supplied. Morey notes that the missionaries described many Indian groups that had formal leadership, trade and economic specialization and inequality in access to basic resources. In accordance with the cultural evolution theory advanced by Baker and Sanders, such societies would require from ten to twelve thousand people for organizational stability.[67] Widespread trading and warfare within the Llanos is yet another indication that the area was occupied to the limits of its potential, given the exploitative techniques used by its inhabitants, and that even the least favorable regions were occupied by representatives of different subsistence types. Calling for further archival and archeological investigations, Morey concludes that "the Llanos was not a marginal area with only small and scattered populations. It is a region of much more importance to South American culture history than has usually been assumed."[68]

The issues raised by Jaramillo, Denevan, and Morey suggest that scholars will continue their debate over the size of the aboriginal population for years to come. After contact, however, it can be demonstrated that the Indians, regardless of their absolute numbers and in spite of heavy attrition due to disease, warfare, and abuse over three centuries, always vastly outnumbered the Spanish and blacks who made their way to the plains. For example, the fairly reliable 1778 census of the Provincia de los Llanos indicates that of a total population of 20,892, 7 percent (1,558) were whites, 19 percent (4,026) were mestizos, 119 (less than 1 percent) were black slaves, and 73 percent (15,189) were Indians. This figure did not include the Indians in the missions of the Llanos of San Juan and San Martín and those outside Spanish control.[69] Throughout the colonial period, the Spanish dominated a small part of the Llanos, but the Indians populated it, served as a labor force, and taught the whites how to survive. Racial miscegenation was a dynamic force, and the key institutions were those directly associated with the Indians—the encomienda and the mission. As a result, the region, perhaps more than any other in Colombia, today still shows "in all aspects the persistence of the shock and acculturized effects of the Spanish conquest on the Indian population."[70]

In sum, the Llanos are a geographically complex region offering much diversity within a combined tropical forest and plains environment. In pre-Columbian times variations in climate, soil fertility, and animal resources produced a number of interdependent and related cultures of disputed density. Farmers and foragers fought and traded with one another and with their neighbors in the Andes, the Guiana highlands, and the Amazon basin. Some of their survival techniques, such as slash-and-burn agriculture and setting fire to the grassland in order to hunt or travel, were ecologically destructive, yet on the eve of discovery, human presence in the Llanos for thousands of years had apparently made little impact on the natural environment.[71] The Indians had adapted to the limits and possibilities imposed by nature.

The arrival of the Europeans disrupted this equilibrium. After some initial enthusiasm, the conquistadors found little to admire about either the land or the people. The heat, rain, and insects were insufferable. The miserable villages were a far cry from the magnificent Andean cities, filled with gold and silver artifacts. The Spanish proved less able than the Indians to adjust to the unique geography. When the dream of El Dorado faded, they abandoned the Llanos for the amenities of the highlands, leaving a few hardy encomenderos, missionaries, and ranchers to establish a far-flung frontier.

2 *Establishing the Frontier, 1531–1650*

A decade before Gonzalo Jiménez de Quesada reached the Sabana of Bogotá by following the Magdalena River and ascending the Andes, Europeans were scouring the Llanos east of the mountains in a tenacious search for El Dorado and a passage by the supposed South Sea to Asia. Jiménez de Quesada's conquest of the populous Chibcha empire, in 1538, was decisive, for it determined that Spanish rule would center in the highlands of the New Kingdom of Granada. The opening of the Audiencia, the division of Indians into encomiendas, and the arrival of settlers established Santa Fe de Bogotá as a key city within the Viceroyalty of Peru. Meanwhile the Llanos, separated from the sabana by the steep slopes of the Eastern Cordillera, became a frontier—a tropical wilderness where Spaniards went to seek their fortunes. With passing years the adventurers searching for El Dorado gave way to more pragmatic captains, encomenderos, and missionaries, who founded towns, grazed cattle, and gathered the Indians around missions. Between 1531 and 1650 varying geographic and demographic conditions within the Llanos shaped the development of Hispanic civilization there and guided the region's relationship with the core settlements in the Andes.

The extensive exploration of the Llanos in the sixteenth century is impressive testimony to European faith in the existence of El Dorado. As Irving Leonard skillfully demonstrated in *Books of the Brave,* the Spanish conquistadors were motivated not only by a trust in their destiny to achieve magnificent deeds through Christian zeal and military valor, but also by the ideal of chivalric quest, as popularized in the contemporary romance *Amadís de Gaula*.[1] The medieval mind that took for granted the authenticity of exotic animals, beings, and kingdoms eagerly credited Indian reports that such creatures and places could be found in the yet unknown portions of South America. Persistent tales of a fabulous golden kingdom located somewhere in the mountains, plains, or jungles of the northern third of South America lured thousands of men to their deaths and spurred the first expeditions to the Llanos.

Early in the sixteenth century, numerous accounts of the House of the Sun, or El Dorado—a land inhabited by Indians possessing great wealth—bombarded the Spanish settlers in Hispaniola. One version drew inspiration from a Chibcha religious ceremony. Every year the Muisca met at Guatavita Lake, twenty miles from Bogotá, to venerate their goddess, Bachué, the mother of the human race (who had risen from the waters with a child in her arms), and to honor a princess condemned to sleep forever in the depths for having failed in her duties as ruler and wife. The worshippers threw gold objects into the lake, but the ritual's climax came when the Zipa, or King of Kings, naked and covered with gold dust, jumped from a raft into the water, washing off the precious substance as he swam.[2] Although this ceremony specifically featured a Gilded Man, the first descriptions of Chibcha El Dorado reaching the Spanish Caribbean intimated only that these Indians of the Andes were very wealthy. When Ambrosio Alfinger, the German governor of Coro, Venezuela, arrived at the Magdalena River, in 1531, to investigate further, the Indians there told him of a rich province called Xerira—probably referring to the Jerida plateau, inhabited by Guane Indians, at the northern limit of Chibcha territory. Alfinger died on a second expedition to find Xerira in 1533, but the legend grew when witnesses of his demise confirmed that he had been at the very gates of this mysterious land.[3]

Excitement over Pizarro's conquest of Peru that same year generated a second account of El Dorado. From the Incas came tales of a land of marvelous riches, situated east of the Andes between Peru and Río de la Plata. Credulous Spaniards identified this land variously as Xerira, the Amazon Kingdom, or "the country where cinnamon grows." The Royal Audiencia in Hispaniola credited the reports enough to authorize an expedition to Venezuela, although its plan was not carried out.[4]

A third version of the legend placed El Dorado distinctly in the Llanos. The Guahibo, the nomadic foragers who traded with Indians throughout the grasslands, occasionally obtained golden ornaments fashioned by the Chibchas in the highlands. They told Spanish explorers that a rich kingdom called Meta could be found at the headwaters of the Meta and Gua-

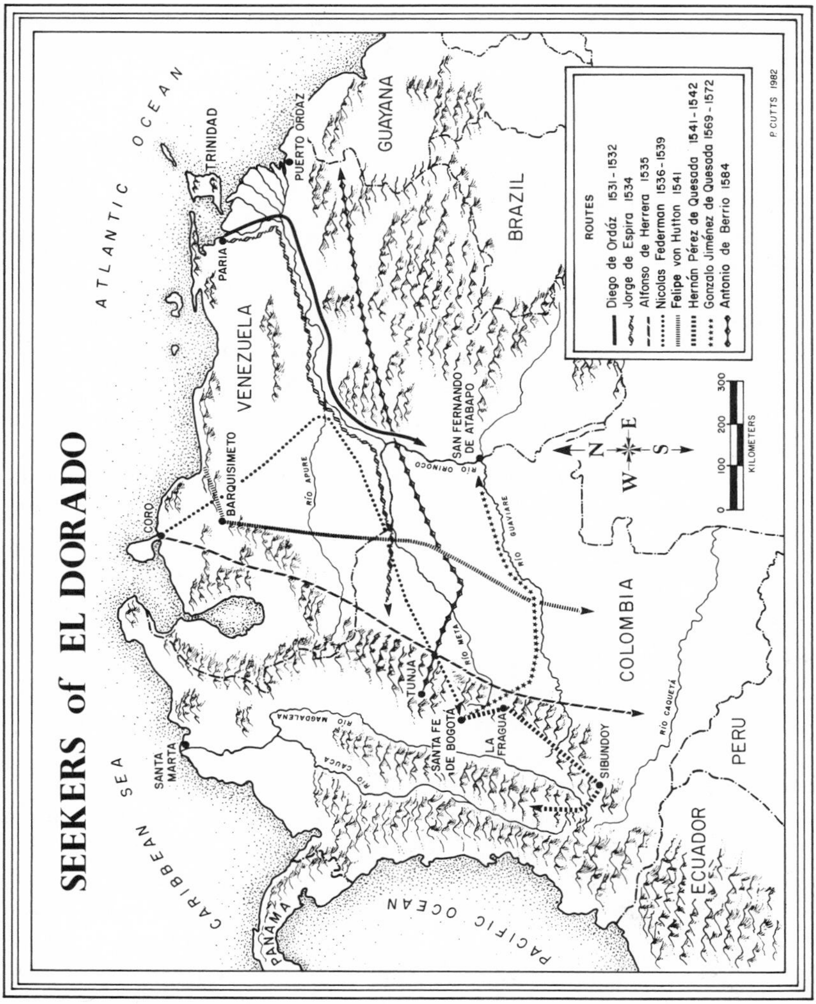
SEEKERS of EL DORADO
ROUTES
Diego de Ordáz 1531-1532
Jorge de Espira 1534
Alfonso de Herrera 1535
Nicolas Federman 1536-1539
Felipe von Hutton 1541
Hernán Pérez de Quesada 1541-1542
Gonzalo Jiménez de Quesada 1569-1572
Antonio de Berrio 1584
ATLANTIC OCEAN
CARIBBEAN SEA
PACIFIC OCEAN
VENEZUELA
COLOMBIA
BRAZIL
GUAYANA
PERU
ECUADOR
PANAMA
TRINIDAD
PARIA
PUERTO ORDAZ
CORO
BARQUISIMETO
SANTA MARTA
TUNJA
SANTA FE DE BOGOTÁ
LA FRAGUA
SIBUNDOY
SAN FERNANDO DE ATABAPO
RÍO ORINOCO
RÍO APURE
RÍO META
RÍO GUAVIARE
RÍO CAQUETÁ
RÍO MAGDALENA
RÍO CAUCA
KILOMETERS
0 100 200 300
N S E W
P. CUTTS 1982

viare rivers. By the 1530s Meta became synonymous with El Dorado, and adventurers searched the Orinoco and Meta rivers in hopes of finding it. As late as 1688, Padre Lucas Fernández de Piedrahita, in *Historia general de las conquistas del Nuevo Reino de Granada,* described the Meta as "the river of Gold, which carries gold as fine as twenty-four carats."[5]

An erroneous conception of the size of South America bolstered the belief in El Dorado. Geographers maintained until the mid-sixteenth century that the continent was a small land mass and very likely a group of islands. This theory supported the conjecture that there was an ocean strait through the supposed islands, which would permit direct travel between Europe and Asia. The early explorers thought that the Pacific lay south of the Caribbean rather than west of it, and that the Andes ran eastward, following the so-called South Sea coastline. Thus the Welser governors carefully explored Lake Maracaibo, in the hopes that it would lead to the strait. When Federman, in 1530, found a flooding tributary of the Orinoco only one hundred leagues from Coro, he hailed it as the South Sea.[6]

The impression that both El Dorado and the South Sea lay just beyond the horizon caused a war of nerves among would-be conquistadors on the Venezuelan coast and later in the Colombian highlands. Captains who recklessly started out for the interior did not hesitate to commit violence or rebellion to circumvent opponents; "the avalanche of people rushing to the imaginary gold country is comparable only to modern gold, oil and rubber rushes."[7]

First to reach the region was Diego de Ordaz, governor of the eastern part of Venezuela known as Paria. A veteran of Cortés's campaign in Mexico, Ordaz followed the Orinoco in 1531–32 beyond the mouth of the Meta River, but was blocked by the rapids at Atures (see map 3). On his return he clashed with Antonio Sedeño, governor of Trinidad, who, also eager to find Meta, overstepped his legal jurisdiction to build a fort in Paria north of the Orinoco Delta. Sedeño imprisoned Ordaz in Cumaná; he later died, possibly poisoned, on a voyage back to Spain.

The crown appointed a new governor of Paria, Jerónimo Ortal, who diligently explored the interior for Meta between 1532 and 1537. Ortal, too, quarrelled with Sedeño, although for a time they attempted to unite their forces. In 1535 he ordered Captain Alonso de Herrera to move inland up the Uyapari. Herrera, who had accompanied Ordaz three years before, explored the Meta River, but was killed by Achaguas near its banks, while waiting out the winter ra ns in Casanare.[8]

Meanwhile the Welsers ın Coro were mounting rival expeditions. In 1528 Charles V ceded to some German merchants the right to settle and develop the islands and mainland of Venezuela lying west of Cape Maracapana and east of the Gobernación of Santa Marta. In 1531 they transferred this grant to the Welser banking house of Augsburg, which governed western Venezuela until 1556. Historians have dealt harshly with the Welser era, calling it the "blackest page of Venezuelan history," but more recently the Colombian scholar Juan Friede has exonerated the Germans, arguing that they behaved little differently from their Spanish counterparts.[9] Unquestionably they were just as eager to find El Dorado; during their tenure, they launched a massive search for it throughout the Llanos.

While Ambrosio Alfinger (Ambrosius Ehinger), the first Welser governor (1529–33), reconnoitered Lake Maracaibo and the Magdalena Valley, his lieutenant, Nicolas Federman (Nikolaus Federmann), pursued the kingdom in the opposite direction. Departing from Coro in 1530, he passed through the present states of Falcón and Lara, following the foothills of the Andes to the Portuguesa River before turning back. After Alfinger's death, in 1533, Federman continued to serve the new governor, Jorge de Espira (Georg Hohermut von Speier) as second-in-command. He remained in Coro on his orders, while Espira took up the search.

In 1534 Espira set off for the hinterland with four hundred men. From Barquisimeto his troops traveled to the Airico de Macaguane (Arauca), where winter flooding forced them to camp for three months. When the waters subsided, they proceeded south through Casanare in a perilous journey plagued by debilitating heat, mosquitoes, disease, and hostile Indians.[10] On fording the Meta River, they came upon a Guayupe village at the foot of the Andes, not far from the site of the present-day town of San Juan de Arama, which Espira called Nuestra Señora de la Asunción. Food was plentiful, and the tired men rested. Espira wanted to explore beyond the Ariari River, but its depth prevented easy crossing. At last, discouraged by floods, sickness, and conflicts with the Indians, he returned to Coro, in 1538, with his mission unaccomplished—the first European to traverse the Llanos completely.[11]

Back in Coro Federman had grown tired of waiting. In 1536 he struck out on his own initiative around Lake Maracaibo, keeping to the east of Espira's route but with the Andes looming on the right to guide him. At Barquisimeto he veered eastward into the plains to avoid colliding with his chief. Zigzagging south, he reached the Orinoco somewhere east of its junction with the Apure, where he incorporated into his band some renegades who had deserted the Ortal expedition the year before. After roaming about the Llanos for a year without uncovering a trace of El Dorado, Federman turned west and crossed the Meta. As Espira had done before him, he rested in Nuestra Señora de la Asunción, renaming it Nuestra Señora de la Fragua, because he ordered a forge built to make tools and to shoe the horses. He wasted the rest of 1538 in futile efforts to find a route through the rugged Cordillera which would lead to the Chibcha highlands. Then, early in 1539, he rallied his exhausted men to challenge again the ice-crested mountains. This time they found a pass through the *páramo* of Sumapaz at the Indian settlement of Pasacorte.[12] The bizarre finale to Federman's odyssey was played out on the Sabana of Bogotá where, after three years of tramping through tropical and mountainous wilderness, the luckless German discovered not only the Chibcha domain but the forces of two Spanish rivals who had arrived before him, Gonzalo Jiménez de Quesada and Sebastián Benalcázar.

Federman's failure to locate either the strait to Asia or El Dorado left the way open for another German expedition. Felipe de Hutten (Philip von Hutton), Coro governor in 1540, had accompanied Jorge de Espira in 1534 and believed that the kingdom lay southeast of the Espira route. Encouraged by the enthusiasm of Pedro de Limpias, Federman's vanguard commander who returned from Bogotá with stories of El Dorado brought from Peru by Benalcázar, Hutten left Coro in August 1541 with 550 men. He took the now familiar itinerary through Barquisimeto, the Llanos of Apure, the Airico de Macaguane, and Casanare to arrive at Nuestra Señora de la Fragua. Here he intended to camp for the winter, but when the Guayupes told him that Hernán Pérez de Quesada had just passed through the town on the same quest, Hutten threw caution to the wind and set out immediately on Pérez's trail, to the south. For the next year he wandered through the jungles of Caquetá, a "journey from nowhere to nowhere," conducted through difficult terrain made impossible by the heavy rains.[13]

When Hutten finally struggled back to La Fragua, the Indians convinced him that El Dorado was to the southeast, in the Vaupés region, and that its capital was a city called Macatoa. With forty of his strongest men, he crossed the Guaviare and found the town, which turned out to be of respectable size but notably lacking in golden houses. The Macatoans, however, insisted that El Dorado was the capital of their neighbors, the Omaguas. They led Hutten into Omagua territory. A climb up a hill overlooking the city in question convinced him that the prize was within his grasp. It was so large that he could not see its farthest end. The streets were straight, the houses well-constructed, and in the central plaza stood a building of great height. Hutten impetuously charged the city, but the Omaguas repulsed the attack, wounding him and many others. Realizing his vulnerability, Hutten resolved to go back to Coro to enlist reinforcements. But bad news awaited him at La Fragua, for the Guayupes reported that a Spanish rebel, Juan de Carvajal, had seized power in Coro. Hutten took precautions but on reaching the coast fell into the hands of Carvajal, who had him beheaded in 1546.[14] Hutten's trek was the last sponsored by the Welsers, who were now convinced that there was no South Sea passage in the interior. Nevertheless, his discovery of the Omagua city reinforced the belief in El Dorado and diverted the future search for it by Spaniards in Venezuela from the Llanos to northwestern Brazil and the headwaters of the Río Negro.

Meanwhile adventurers coming from the highlands of New Granada had been vying with the Germans to be the first to locate the kingdom in the plains. It is ironic that after defeating the Chibchas in 1539 and dredging Guatavita Lake for gold, the Spanish refused to believe they had found the El Dorado they were seeking. The Quesada brothers speculated that their objective lay east of the Chibcha plateau, since they had already explored the country to the west and north, and Benalcázar had come from the south. Overlooking the fact that Federman had spent three fruitless years in just this area, they decided that El Dorado must be in a yet undiscovered mountain range east of the Andes.[15] With unquenchable hope, Hernán Pérez de Quesada in 1541–42, Gonzalo Jiménez de Quesada in 1569–72, and Antonio de Berrio in 1584, 1585, and 1590–92 sought the illusive kingdom in the Llanos.

When Jiménez de Quesada left Santa Fe de Bogotá with Benalcázar and Federman, in 1539, to place their claims over the former Chibcha domain before Charles V in Spain, Hernán Pérez stayed behind as head of the incipient colony. Pérez lost little time in preparing to visit the plains. By 1541 he assembled an expedition of 430 Spaniards on foot and horseback and 8,000 Indians. To insure peace in the highlands during his absence, he summarily executed the Chibcha cacique in Tunja—a senseless crime which did not accomplish the end intended.[16] Of his actions on leaving Tunja, the chroniclers have left conflicting accounts. Some say that he traveled through the land of the Laches and on gaining the Llanos established a town he called Santiago de las Atalayas, to commemorate his mission to *atalayar,* or spy out, El Dorado.[17] Others assert that Pérez explored the province of the Chitareros, looking for the House of the Sun, and returned to Santa Fe before setting off again for the Llanos.[18] J. M. Groot, the great nineteenth-century Colombian historian, favored the second version, suggesting that Pérez got under way again on September 1, 1541, and crossed the Cordillera through the páramo of Fosca. "It is impossible to imagine the labor Pérez needed to pass through those rugged and stony mountains, through woods, swamps and marshes covered by thick fog and penetrated by cold."[19] Scores of Indians and horses died before Pérez reached La Fragua, where he rested for twenty days. Taking Espira's route, he pushed south to the Guaviare. The heat was ghastly and the Indians antagonistic. When all the horses died, Pérez drove his men forward on foot. In Cáqueta, having lost many lives, he at last began to seek a pass through the mountains that would lead back to Santa Fe. Finding it at Sibundoy, he ascended the Cordillera. Over a year after their journey had begun, Pérez and a handful of survivors lurched into Bogotá like walking shadows. Commenting on this pitiful scene, Groot sardonically observes, "Oh, the sensational expedition of Hernán Pérez de Quesada of which the best result was that not everyone perished in an unknown world so that they might return to tell the tale."[20]

Taking up residence in Santa Fe in 1550, Gonzalo Jiménez de Quesada was undismayed by his brother's debacle. Almost immediately he began petitioning Philip II for permission to explore the Llanos. The authorization came in 1568. Appointing him adelantado of New Granada, the king granted Jiménez de Quesada the governorship of four hundred leagues of land in the plains between the Pauto and Caqueta rivers and promised him the coveted title of marquis after he had conquered and settled El Dorado.[21] Despite the advanced age of nearly seventy years, the adelantado had no difficulty in attracting recruits for his campaign. Veterans of the Chibcha war twenty years before jockeyed with younger men for a place in the ranks. In 1569 he departed from the little highland capital with three hundred Spaniards, an unknown number of women, fifteen hundred Indians, herds of cattle, and supplies worth thirteen thousand golden pesos.[22]

Like his brother, Jiménez de Quesada suffered staggering casualities in a six-month journey over the Cordillera. After resting at La Fragua, he led his army south through the waist-high, sharp-edged grass that stretched to the horizon. Mosquitoes, horseflies, and sand flies buzzed ominously, their bites bringing fevers and swellings. In summer the heat was intolerable; during the rainy season it seemed as though flesh would rot from the bones. Still Jiménez de Quesada marched on.[23] At last, near the junction of the Guaviare and Orinoco rivers, where the village of San Fernando de Atabapo stands today, his men refused to continue. After two years of excruciating travel they had found not gold, pearls, great populations, and cultivated fields, but endless plains and dense jungles. Reluctantly Jiménez de Quesada turned back. In 1572 he reappeared in Santa

Fe, accompanied by the sad remnant of his once proud force—twenty-four Spaniards, four Indians, and eighteen half-starved horses.

In his biography, *The Knight of El Dorado,* Germán Arciniegas compares Jiménez de Quesada with the celebrated sixteenth-century literary character Don Quixote. The adelantado's gaunt figure and flowing beard were very like those of the knight of La Mancha. Embarking in his old age on an enterprise more risky than his youthful conquest of the Chibchas was a scheme worthy of Cervantes' demented hero. Arciniegas argues that this madness was that of an age "which turned all values upside down": "He is so much a part of that world that though we see him assailed by hunger, envy, misery, though we watch him cross rivers and mountains like a wraith escaped from an insane asylum, his words really give the impressive sensation of practical wisdom and common sense. Like the helmet made out of a barber's basin, these deluded men sometimes make one laugh and sometimes weep."[24]

The people of Santa Fe did not laugh at the bedraggled Quesada on his return in 1572. Rather they said that it was his misfortune to have looked for the kingdom in the wrong place.[25] Quesada himself still believed that El Dorado existed. At his death in 1579, Antonio de Berrio inherited from him, along with his titles and property, the will to continue the quest.

Berrio launched the last major expedition to the Llanos from the Andean highlands. His first years in Santa Fe were spent in a complicated defense of his governorship of El Dorado against a claim lodged by a Venezuelan adversary, Francisco de Cáceres. Even before the Audiencia had settled the dispute, Berrio left Tunja, in January 1584, with one hundred men, speculating that the kingdom lay near the mouth of the Orinoco River. None had yet explored this area, although Ordaz and Herrera had marched through it. Crossing the Pauto, Berrio pushed eastward across the Llanos between the Meta and Vichada rivers. East of the Orinoco he spied the Sierra Mapicha, in the part of Venezuela that borders on Guyana. Convinced that El Dorado was somewhere in these mountains, he retraced his steps to Tunja, completing the entire trip with only eight fatalities in a record seventeen months.[26]

Berrio made two more attempts. Between 1585 and 1587 he searched the Sierra Mapicha but left off when one of his captains mutinied. In 1590 he began again, this time with broader powers as the officially recognized governor of El Dorado and Guiana. Exploring the Orinoco and Caroní rivers, he founded Santo Tomé de Guayana and San José de Oruña, on Trinidad. From this island he hoped to penetrate farther into Guiana, but in 1595 he was captured by Walter Raleigh and died soon after, leaving the Englishman to carry on the pursuit in northern South America.[27]

It would seem that by the end of the sixteenth century, Europeans had proved conclusively that El Dorado was not located in the Llanos. They had explored the plains from all directions, sailed the treacherous rivers, fought with Indians, and endured nameless terrors and still could not find the mythical kingdom. Pondering over this failure, Juan Rodríguez Fresle wrote in Santa Fe in 1638:

> And although it is true that the captains that conquered Peru and the Gobernaciones of Popayán and Venezuela and this New Kingdom always aspired to the conquest of El Dorado so that the name alone raised their hopes for its conquest, they have not been able to find it although they have paid with many lives and great costs, nor have they found the exact spot where it is after having searched the Llanos, navigated the Orinoco, the Darién, the river of Orellana Marañón and other deep rivers, which although on their banks they found large towns, they have not found the wealth that there is in this New Kingdom in its rich lodes.[28]

From Rodríguez Fresle's time to our own, the conviction that the Llanos contain fabulous wealth has survived. The men who continued to go there in the seventeenth and eighteenth centuries in search of Meta sought their fortunes in the nineteenth century with little more success in cattle ranching or cacao plantations. More recently the lure of petroleum has renewed interest in this region that politicians frequently refer to as the future of Colombia.[29] The content may change, but the myth of El Dorado dies hard. It is a leitmotif of the history of the Llanos.

The seekers of El Dorado were harbingers of Spanish rule. With the founding of towns came the first permanent centers of European influence in the Llanos. Espira, Federman, and, possibly, Hernán Pérez began settlements, but Nuestra Señora de la Asunción, La Fragua, and the original Santiago de las Atalayas did not endure, because their expeditions did not have enough men or supplies to sustain such remote outposts for long. Populating the Llanos was a risky business even in the second half of the sixteenth century. Eventually six Spanish cities took root, to endure through most of the colonial era.

The first successful *fundador* was Juan de Avellaneda, who had accompanied Federman on his 1536–39 peregrination from Coro to Bogotá. In 1555 he left Santa Fe with twenty-five men to look for gold in the land of the Guayupe, south of the Meta River. On crossing the Andes, Avellaneda came upon a village where the cacique was called Mariagua. Living among the Indians was Juan Gutiérrez de Aquillón, a Spaniard who had learned their language and could act as interpreter. The Guayupe, through Aquillón, directed Avellaneda to the banks of the Ariari River, where he discovered a significant amount of alluvial gold. Elated, Avellaneda sent word to Santa Fe. The Royal Audiencia granted him permission to establish a city and encouraged him to continue exploration by dispatching reinforcements and supplies.

In 1556 Avellaneda founded San Juan de los Llanos near the Ariari, naming his city in honor of St. John the Baptist, and adding "de los Llanos" because he believed that he was near the llanos of Venezuela. After a few days it was evident to everyone that the site was too low and subject to flooding. Avellaneda moved San Juan first to the foothills and later to the place where Federman had established La Fragua.[30] To the west rose the rugged Andes, but to the east lay the plains, smooth and flat, with grass taller than a man on horseback. Water and wood was sufficient. Deer, jaguars, and anteaters were abundant. Sweltering beneath the hot sun, the city remained there until the second half of the eighteenth century.[31]

The location of San Juan de los Llanos on the route to El Dorado, the peaceful attitude of the Guayupes, and the proximity of gold fostered a fleeting prosperity. Expeditions that left Santa Fe in the 1560s and 1570s in search of the kingdom regularly stopped there for supplies. Francisco Aguilar, a *vecino* of San Juan who made a modest fortune from Ariari gold, was a major financial backer of Jiménez de Quesada's ruinous expedition in 1569.[32] Avellaneda treated the Indians with care, using gifts and flattery to win their good will. The Guayupes, for their part, were eager to have him live among them, regarding his presence as protection from incursions by rival Spaniards coming from Venezuela. Even when he divided them into repartimientos to work the mines, they did not rebel, and the prospect of extracting gold with Indian labor attracted new people from the highlands.

Shortly after 1556 Avellaneda returned to Santa Fe and received a new commission to make another settlement, deeper within the province. Before he could depart, an order arrived from Spain suspending further discoveries because of the harm being done the Indians. A disappointed Avellaneda returned to San Juan, bringing cattle and men. As soon as the crown lifted its ban on explorations, however, he resolved to seek the rich mines in the Valle de Plata of which the Indians had told him. Collecting seventy eager recruits from Santa Fe, he left San Juan to search an area around the Guaviare River. Not finding the Valle de Plata, he turned back to the Cordillera. In a pleasant-looking valley called San Jerónimo, he founded Nuevo Burgos, but Indian hostility and food shortages forced its abandonment.[33]

Avellaneda went back to San Juan, where he lived out his days as the city sank slowly into obscurity. By the turn of the century fewer expeditions set out for El Dorado. The mines were nearly exhausted, and the Indians diminished. Writing in 1638, Rodríguez Fresle included San Juan in his "Catalogue of Cities" of New Granada, but he noted that only the presence of Avellaneda sustained it.[34]

San Martín was the only other city founded south of the Meta River. Little is known about its origins. Most sources state that Captain Pedro Daza of Tunja began it in 1585, as Medina de las Torres, and that it was subsequently destroyed by Indians. In 1641 it was refounded by Captain Juan de Zarate, as San Martín del Puerto.[35] Little more than a collection of thatched huts, it soon rivaled San Juan, and both cities gave their names to the llanos lying between the Meta and Guaviare rivers. Although its location has been changed several times, San Martín has been in continuous existence until the present day.

More integral to the political and economic growth of the Llanos was Santiago de las Atalayas, founded in 1588 north of the Meta in Casanare—an area claimed by Jiménez de Quesada and his determined adversary, Francisco de Cáceres, governor of La Grita, between San Cristóbal and Mérida, in Venezuela. In 1560 the Audiencia awarded the adelantado an encomienda which included Chita and La Sal—Indian towns on the eastern Andean slopes of the Province of Tunja—as well as Támara, Pisba, and Chita, in the Llanos.[36] Eight years later Philip II appointed him governor of the land between the Pauto and Papamene rivers. The dispute began when Captain Cáceres attempted to reduce *(reducir)* some twelve thousand Indians living along the Cordillera of Guatavita, an area Jiménez de Quesada believed assigned to him. Although the crown sustained Cáceres's actions, Jiménez de Quesada used all legal methods at his disposal to stop the interloper. After the adelantado's death in 1579, Antonio Berrio inherited the quarrel. Fearing that Cáceres would beat him to El Dorado, Berrio dashed off on his first expedition in 1584, with the suit still unsettled. Cáceres, for his part, commissioned Captain Pedro Daza to pacify the Achaguas in the disputed territory. In pursuing this assignment, Daza founded the ill-fated Medina de las Torres in 1585 and Santiago de las Atalayas on September 29, 1588.[37]

Located on the Aguamena River at the foot of the Cordillera southeast of Tunja, Santiago enjoyed a salubrious climate. As the capital of the

Provincia de los Llanos, it administered a vast, largely unknown area which extended to the Orinoco and encompassed both banks of the Meta River. Surrounded by relatively dense Achagua villages, which were quickly assigned to the Spanish in encomiendas, it became the center of a flourishing textile industry where Indians in *obrajes* spun thread and wove cloth from cotton grown in the plains. Rodríguez Fresle included the city in his catalog and Doctor Don Onofre Tomás de Barros y Soto Mayor, who visited it in the 1620s, was favorably impressed. He saw thirty houses, newly whitewashed, special buildings for the *cabildo* and jail, a hospital for poor whites as well as Indians, and a well-built adobe church, with a wooden altar and fine ornaments for the celebration of mass. The vecinos, Barros y Soto Mayor added, were noble and wealthy, paying enough taxes and tithes to maintain the city and its defenses.[38] In 1649 Governor Don Adriano de Vargas, a descendant of Suárez de Vargas, who had marched with Jiménez de Quesada, informed the Audiencia that the city had paid over 1,395 pesos in tithes that year, produced 12,000 varas of linen, sent 2,000 arrobas of fish, 5,000 head of cattle and other foodstuffs to Tunja; and dispatched 6,000 pigs to Cartagena, Saragoza, and other cities of the New Kingdom.[39]

Vargas's report suggests that unlike San Juan de los Llanos, which had already fallen into decline, Santiago in the mid-seventeenth century was fully incorporated into the colonial economy. Moreover, it served as a base for founding other cities in the Llanos of Casanare. In 1644 Vargas established San José de Pore on the Ariporo River and settled nineteen Spaniards with their families in San José de Cravo, at a place called Guanaca, between the Cravo River and a *quebrada* (ravine) known as Taquiramena.[40] Some sources say that Governor Vargas also founded Santa Rosa de Chire, in 1689, others maintain that it was Governor don Pedro Daza who began it, in 1672.[41]

Some years ago Richard Morse pointed out that the short-lived, or ambulatory, town was a predictable feature of colonial Latin America, reflecting the unstable equilibrium of a continent not internally connected by exchange and commerce.[42] Urban instability was characteristic of the Llanos frontier, where the residents frequently moved in search of a healthier site, a better economic base, or to escape Indian attacks.[43] Some cities simply disappeared—among them Nuevo Burgos, Medina de las Torres, Altagracia, San Juan de Hiesma, and Espinosa de las Palmas. The fate of the latter is representative. In 1640 Captain Alonso Pérez de Guzmán received permission from the Audiencia to conquer a large area of the Llanos, to begin a white settlement and to populate a companion town,

Tame, with Jiraras. This grant plunged him into a legal conflict with Don Martín de Mendoza, *corregidor* of the Llanos and an encomendero of Chita, who claimed that the Jiraras in question were supposed to pay tribute to him. Pérez de Guzmán founded Espinosa de las Palmas in the disputed area, but he soon enraged the Indians by selling some of them into slavery. One day when he and thirty soldiers were making an *entrada* (expedition into the wilderness), Jiraras attacked the town, massacring the whites and ambushing the captain and his men on their return. The Audiencia sent Mendoza to subdue the Indians, which he accomplished by hanging fifteen or sixteen of the leaders and pardoning the rest. Mendoza proceeded to repopulate Tame, which was awarded to him in encomienda, but Espinosa de las Palmas remained only a memory.[44]

The survival of San Juan, San Martín, Santiago, Pore, Cravo, and Chire, against all odds, facilitated an ecological revolution in the Llanos—the acclimatization of cattle and horses. In *The Columbian Exchange: Biological and Cultural Consequences of 1492,* Alfred W. Crosby, Jr., suggests that the most characteristically Iberian figure in colonial America was the rancher on horseback surveying his cattle herds. Everywhere the Spanish went in the New World, they brought with them their animals, for they relied on cattle for food and hides and on horses for transportation. The grasslands in northern South America appeared to be ideal for these animals, but the brutally hot climate, unappetizing pasturage, drought and flood cycles, and insect pests held down their numbers for decades. That livestock adjusted at all to the tropical plains is a tribute to the biological resilience of the Andalusian breeds.[45]

In 1541 Alonso Luis de Lugo drove a herd of cattle from Santa Marta to Santa Fe, only to see most of them die during the difficult journey up the Magdalena River and over the Andes. In Venezuela conditions were more propitious. In 1530 Cristóbal Rodríguez imported cattle from Margarita Island and began a *hato* (ranch) in Guárico, at the edge of the Llanos. Soon afterward, settlers led by Juan de Carvajal brought cattle from Coro to the Valley of Alto Tocuyo. Rodríguez, who served with Benalcázar in Santa Fe, knew of the need for animals. He encouraged the Venezuelan ranchers to take their herds to the New Kingdom, where they could demand a good price. For years there were regular cattle drives leaving Tocuyo for Sogamoso and from there on to Tunja and Santa Fe. Some animals may have strayed to the Llanos during these drives, but in small numbers they would have found forage difficult and were easy prey for jaguars and crocodiles. By the end of the century, as cattle became abundant on the sabana, the profits were no longer attractive, and the drives from Venezuela to New Granada ceased.[46]

At about the same time, the Spanish were breaking down Indian defiance and establishing towns on the edge of the Llanos—Barinas in 1575, San Sabastián de los Reyes in 1584, Pedraza la Vieja in 1591, all in Venezuela, and Santiago de las Atalayas in 1588, in New Granada. Residents of these towns could protect the cattle from some dangers, and gradually they began to multiply. The herds grazed freely over the grassland, often abandoned completely by their owners. Soon they were so numerous that they were killed wastefully, to the obtain by-products of grease and hides. By 1650 there were 140,000 steers in the Venezuelan llanos, and Santiago de las Atalayas was regularly sending cattle to the highlands.[47] Twelve years later the Jesuits began Caribabare, the first of several large cattle haciendas which they would found in Casanare.[48]

Natural selection produced in the Colombian llanos two types of creole cattle. North of the Meta River, the Casanareño predominated. A small animal averaging from six hundred to seven hundred pounds, it was jersey-tan in color. It had a long, thin tail with a short, black switch; a thick, prominent dewlap; barrel-shaped body; a long, muscular face; and a coat of short, fine hair—all characteristics of tropical cattle.[49] South of the Meta evolved the San Martinero, slightly larger but less adapted to the Llanos. A darkish red color, it was probably a cross between the Andalusian *retinto* and the Asturian *valle*.[50] Both breeds were hardy, fertile, highly resistant to insects and heat, and tolerant of mineral and nutrient deficiencies. By modern bovine standards they would rank very low, but no modern European breed or cross could live in the Llanos long enough to perpetuate its kind. The Casanareño and the San Martinero made the best of bad situations, subsisting wholly on what nature provided.[51]

The acclimatization of horses was even more difficult, but they too roamed the plains in herds by the mid-seventeenth century. Baron von Humboldt vividly described their painful life, noting that the animals were harassed by gadflies and mosquitoes and attacked at night by enormous bats that fastened on their backs and caused wounds that were soon filled with insects:

> In rainy season, the horses that wander in the savanna and have not time to reach the rising ground of the Llanos, perish by the hundreds. The mares are seen followed by their colts swimming during a part of the day to feed upon the grass, the top of which alone was above the waters. In this state

> they are pursued by the crocodiles and it is by no means uncommon to find the prints of teeth of these carnivorous reptiles on their thighs. The colts are drowned everywhere in large numbers because they are soon tired of swimming and strive to follow the mares in places where these alone can touch the ground.[52]

Yet, Humboldt concluded, "They endure, and when the rivers return to their beds and the savanna is spread over with new grass, the animals seem to enjoy the renewed vegetation of spring."[53]

Raising livestock on unfenced range became the primary occupation of whites and mestizos in the Llanos. The Indians, who added chickens and ducks to their domestic inventory even before Federman's arrival, were less willing to utilize the larger animals. During the seventeenth century, some groups working in encomiendas or living in the missions learned to tend cattle and horses for their white overlords.[54] The Achaguas used horses for herding that they acquired from the missionaries or stole.[55] By the eighteenth century, the Tunebos supplemented their cultivated fields with herds of cattle, and the Guahibo were learning to ride horses and to eat beef.[56] Their raids on cattle belonging to the missions and private ranchers became a major cause of unrest. None of the Indians, however, became true pastoralists, as had the Guajira in the Guajira Peninsula, possibly because of the seasonal fluctuations of flood and drought.[57]

From Tunja and Santiago de las Atalayas, the Spanish extended the frontier in the Llanos by reducing the Indians. The Laches and Tequias, who lived on the slopes of the Eastern Cordillera and paid allegiance to the Chibcha caciques in Cocuy and Tota, put up little resistance. With the surrender of those leaders, they were congregated into towns and divided among encomenderos. The farmers and foragers of the plains succumbed less easily, but by 1650 there were over fourteen hundred tributary Indians in encomiendas and many others enslaved. Exploitation and disease were making inroads into the population, and the Jesuits and Dominicans had founded their first missions, beginning a long contest with secular clergy and settlers for control over the natives.[58]

Throughout the Spanish empire, the encomienda was the institution which smoothed the transition from war to peace. First introduced in Hispaniola, it was a formal grant of Indian crown vassals to a favored Spanish conqueror or colonist. The Indians were required to perform labor service and give tribute to the Spanish encomendero. In return for this royal favor, the Spaniard, who held Indians in trust for the crown, was obliged to render military service in the defense of the colony and had the responsibility of Christianizing his charges. By granting encomiendas, the crown intended both to reward deserving conquerors and settlers and to incorporate the Indians into Christian civilization by placing them under the protection of responsible individuals.

The Quesada brothers began the process of dividing Indians into encomiendas after the conquest of Bogotá, in 1539. Since the Chibchas were organized by *parcialidades,* or *capitanías,* the Quesadas assigned the chief of one of these districts and all his followers to a meritorious Spaniard. The latter relied on the chief to collect tribute and to make his people do the work assigned to them. When the Indians lived in widely scattered hamlets, the Spaniards were obliged to congregate them. They also had to pay the salary of a priest or *doctrinero,* who was to live among the Indians and Christianize them.

The award of encomiendas was not equitable and provoked spirited rivalry. The promulgation of the New Laws, in 1544 in Santa Fe, marked the first effort on the part of the crown to regulate abuses within the system there. After the installation of the Royal Audiencia, in 1549, encomiendas continued to change hands frequently. Those Spaniards who regarded themselves among the nobility of the New Kingdom by virtue of owning an encomienda vigorously defended their privileges, so that the award and regulation of Indian vassals was one of the predominant issues in the early years of the colony.

The first encomendero in the Llanos was Pedro Rodríguez de Salamanca. In April 1544 the governor of Santa Fe, Lope Montalvo de Lugo, granted to this former companion of Federman "two hundred houses in the Llanos between the river that leaves from Guacica and the Carán River with all the caciques and captains within and the Indians subjected to them."[59] The two oldest Indian towns in Casanare, Pauto and Támara, were also founded in this year. In 1551 Rodríguez de Salamanca added to his holdings the repartimiento of Indians at Chita, Chiscas, and the towns of La Sal and Notavia.[60]

By 1563 Gonzalo Jiménez de Quesada had become the principal encomendero of the towns on the Eastern Cordillera of the Province of Tunja and in the Llanos. Three years earlier Philip II had rewarded him for his services by ordering that he be given a grant of one or two repartimientos worth three thousand pesos a year. The Audiencia implemented this order by awarding him, along with other repartimientos, the economienda previously held by Rodríguez Salamanca and vacated at his death.[61] In 1568 it assigned to Jiménez de Quesada an additional encomienda formerly owned by Alonso Martín Cobo, which included four hundred houses of

Tipa, Caquetios, and Moscas Indians living in the foothills and grasslands. The adelantado formally took possession of these Indians on February 22, 1568, in Tunja, where, before the *juez de comisión,* he met with Alonso, a Christian Achagua who represented the other chiefs and Indians in the grant.[62] A *visita* conducted by the *licenciado* Juan López de Cepeda, in 1571, revealed that the encomienda included 1,703 tributary Indians in fourteen separate locations. The grant was one of the longest to endure in the New Kingdom, yielding revenue for Jiménez de Quesada's heirs until the second half of the eighteenth century.[63]

After 1551 royal officials regularly inspected encomiendas in the provinces of Santa Fe and Tunja. Their surveys often included grants in the Llanos of Casanare but not those in the Llanos of San Juan and San Martín, which topography and bad weather made inaccessible to the judges starting out from Santa Fe.[64] These reports, many of which have been published, provide raw data for a demographic analysis of population in the Llanos, but difficulties lie in determining which grants administered from Tunja can be properly considered as belonging in Casanare and in identifying the Llanos communities, which frequently disappeared, were moved, or changed their names. The data presented in table 1 were selected from visitas made in 1603 and 1653 to indicate the growth and/or decline of encomiendas in three districts—the partido of the city of Tunja, Tasas de los Llanos, and the provincia of Santiago de las Atalayas. The inspectors counted Indian tributaries, that is, able-bodied males between seventeen and fifty-four years of age. From these figures it is possible to estimate the entire Indian population of a given area by calculating the ratio of other individuals to the tributaries. Friede and Colmenares have suggested coefficients ranging from 1.4 to 4.8 for Tunja Province, but neither has hazarded a coefficient for the Llanos.[65]

In 1603 there were 2,113 tributaries, divided into seven private encomiendas and two royal grants. Fernando Berrio y Ocuña had the largest holding, with 326 Indians located in the Partido de Tunja and 1,126 in Tasas de los Llanos for a total of 1,452. Smaller encomiendas of 34 to 110 tributaries were held by four individuals, and two royal grants of 70 and 40 Indians completed the Tasas de los Llanos. There were two encomenderos in the Provincia of Santiago de las Atalayas—Governor Diego Suárez de Vargas, who had 154 tributaries in scattered hamlets, and Pedro Daza, with 44 living in Cusiana and Chámeza.

By 1653 the tributaries held in these same districts declined 33 percent, to 1,422 in thirteen private encomiendas. The Berrio grant had dwindled to 833 (282 in the Partido de Tunja and 551 in Tasas de los Llanos), a decrease of 51 percent. The remaining encomiendas under Tasas de los Llanos, totaling 320 tributaries, showed a decline of 30 percent. In the Provincia de Santiago, however, tributaries increased by 30 percent, to 286 divided into eight private encomiendas, reflecting the incorporation of Indians previously outside Spanish control.

Germán Colmenares has shown that the 61,000 tributaries in Tunja Province in 1551 declined to 16,348 in 1602 and to 8,610 in 1635–36—a decrease of 86 percent between 1551 and 1635–36 and of 48 percent between 1602 and 1635–36.[66] The shock of conquest, overwork, and the employment of Indians in the mines in Pamplona had exacted a terrible toll, but the greatest killer was epidemic disease. In 1558 an outbreak of smallpox wiped out more than 15,000 Indians in Tunja, and there were other epidemics in 1568–69, 1587, and 1633.[67] These same factors decimated the Indians in the Llanos, although the impact of epidemics is yet to be documented, and the decline took place at a slower rate because of geographic isolation.[68]

There is no question that enslavement and wanton violence accompanied the reduction of Indians in the Llanos of Casanare and San Juan and San Martín. In 1649 Governor Vargas of Santiago de las Atalayas reported that he personally entered the province of Anayare with thirty-seven soldiers armed at his expense. He reduced the Achaguas of several hamlets to Christianity and sent to the mines of Pamplona fifteen strong Indian men and ten women with two Guahibo babies who had resisted his advance.[69] Indians, who at first were inclined to receive the Spanish peacefully, sometimes retaliated when they were abused. For example, in 1591 Captain Pedro Daza, founder of Santiago, seized an Indian girl, intending to make her a slave in his household. When the chief defended her, Daza struck him. The Indians were so angered by this act that they surprised Daza alone one night and clubbed him to death. Then they fell upon Santiago and burned it to ashes.[70]

More often the Indians were helpless victims. Of many instances of Spanish cruelty recorded by the Jesuit Juan Rivero, perhaps the most notorious is Captain Alonso Jiménez's entrada in 1606, against four thousand Achaguas living along the Meta River. The Indians welcomed Jiménez and his soldiers on their arrival. Jiménez told them to build a church where they might learn the Christian doctrine. When the church was completed, the Indians gathered inside, whereupon Jiménez sealed the doors and ordered his soldiers to attack the defenseless people. After they killed many, they placed the rest in chains and sent them in boats upriver to the mines, where they all perished.[71] Some years later Captain Lázaro

Table 1. Indian Tributaries and Encomenderos in the Llanos of Casanare, 1603 and 1653

1603[a]	1653[b]	
Location	Indian Tributaries	Encomendero
Partido de la Ciudad de Tunja		
Chita	219	Fernando Berrio y Ocuña
La Sal	51	Fernando Berrio y Ocuña
Chiscas	56	Fernando Berrio y Ocuña
	326	
Tasas de Los Llanos		
Támara	678	Fernando Berrio y Ocuña
Pauto	219	Fernando Berrio y Ocuña
Aricaporo & Prto. de Casanare	——	
Pisba, Borama, Pancote y Chauquera	229	Fernando Berrio y Ocuña
Ochica	45	Antonio Rodríguez Cazalla
Labranzagrande	70	Royal
Cravo	40	Royal
Coasa	96	Antonio de Esquivel
Morcote &	110	Antonio de Esquivel
Paya	60	Pedro Niño
Susbaque & Tunebas	34	Juan de la Fuente
	1,581	
Provincia de Santiago de las Atalayas		
Cabita &	11	Diego Suárez de Vargas
Cupiagua	47	Diego Suárez de Vargas
Caibacoa y Gobero	76	Diego Suárez de Vargas
Cusiana & Chámeza	44	Pedro Daza
Yayuros	——	
Caraguata	——	
Osamena	18	Diego Suárez de Vargas
Vijua &	——	
Ogatagaje	——	
Tia	——	
	206	
Total	2,113	

[a]"Tasas de la Provincia de Tunja del Nuevo Reino de Granada, por Luis Enríquez, Santa Fe, 10 de julio de 1603," in Julian Bautista Ruíz Rivera, *Fuentes para la demografía histórica de Nueva Granada* (Sevilla, 1972):73–108.

[b]"Encomiendas, encomenderos e indígenas tributarios del Nuevo Reino de Granada en la primera mitad del siglo XVII," *ACHSC* 1 (1964):410–530.

Table 1 (continued)

	1653[b]
Indian Tributaries	Encomendero
181	Martín Mendoza y Berrio
58	Martín Mendoza y Berrio
43	Martín Mendoza y Berrio
282	
341	Martín Mendoza y Berrio
53	Martín Mendoza y Berrio
76	Martín Mendoza y Berrio
81	Martín Mendoza y Berrio
73	Juan de Borja
44	Juan de Borja
30	Juan de Borja
36	Miguel de Fonseca
116	Pedro Niño de Zambrano
21	Diego de Paredes Calderón
1,153	
38	Ana de Odroñez y Valdelomar
19	Ana de Ordoñez y Valdelomar
50	Adrien de Vargas
51	Pedro Daza
38	Gregorio de Rojas
15	Antonio de Tapia
7	Fernando Suárez de Vargas
22	Diego Patiño de Argumedo
26	Diego Patiño de Argumedo
3	Alonso Sánchez Chamorro
269	
1,422	

Cruz crossed the Meta and seized many Achaguas. While they were camped for the night, one of the captives tried to club Cruz to death with a musket. The soldiers seized the would-be assassin, slaying him and others as well. In another case cited by Rivero, an unnamed Spanish slave hunter captured a great number of Achaguas and marched them to the Pauto River. The exhausted Indians, wishing something to eat and drink, cried out "Mata! Mata!" which in their language meant "Wait!" The alarmed Spanish, imagining that the Indians were urging one another to kill, immediately massacred them all.[72] The archival records reveal other cases as well. In 1619 Francisco de Santiago, a vecino of Santiago de las Atalayas, prosecuted Cristóbal Marín and his accomplices for killing Indians and committing other crimes against them, and in 1659 Antonio, captain of the Indians of Camajagua, asked for official help against the persecutions of Captain Pedro Collado, vecino of San Juan de los Llanos.[73]

Open, unabashed traffic in slaves was endemic and more lucrative than herding cattle. From their base in Santiago, the Spanish raided Indians living in Airico and Barraguan, two plains regions south of the Meta and east of the Llanos of San Juan and San Martín. Maestre de Campo Antonio de Tapia returned from one of these entradas with more than 320 Achagua and Caquetio slaves, and in 1657 Captain Juan López Picón brought 140 slaves from the Airico.[74] In 1659 the Indians around San Martín forcefully complained against being transported to Santiago de las Atalayas, where they were enslaved and their children sold.[75] The Spanish sold their hapless prisoners to local settlers, who employed them in the obrajes or at menial tasks. Guahibos and Caribs cooperated in the traffic, raiding the Achaguas and Sálivas for captives they traded to the Spanish for material goods. Slaves from the Llanos were also transported to Brazil and Dutch Guiana, where plantation workers were much in demand.[76]

Throughout the plains the institution of Indian slavery was widespread and furthered mestizaje. The Achaguas had kept slaves even before European contact, but in the seventeenth century they and the Sálivas became the chief victims of slaving operations. By 1664 these once powerful peoples were fleeing to the Jesuits because of starvation. Every dry season they had to hide in the forest without making cooking fires, to escape capture. When they came out again at the beginning of the rainy season, they found their gardens ravaged by the Guahibo.[77] The Spanish enslaved men and boys, but took women as maids and concubines. It was not uncommon for a white man to have as many as five or six wives, who lived within a single household. He would choose, from among his many half-Indian offspring, the most intelligent and energetic male to legitimize. As years passed a mestizo group began to emerge.[78] In 1733 Rivero wrote that there was no white or mestizo in the Llanos who did not have an Achagua slave, and that the more slaves a man owned, the richer he considered himself.[79]

Encomienda Indians had a better chance of preserving their culture since their overlords were expected to group them into towns. The presence of royal officials and priests facilitated this process. In 1586 Miguel Fonte, *juez poblador* by commission of the Audiencia, founded the towns of Paya and Morcote for Indians in Pedro Niño's encomienda. At each site Fonte ordered the Indians to build their houses and to construct an adobe church.[80] In 1602 the *visitador* who inspected the encomiendas near Labranzagrande reported that Captain Cravo was living in the Llanos with seventy to eighty-nine Indians who did not pay any tribute or have the advantage of receiving the Christian doctrine. The visitador condemned the scattered living arrangements on the grounds that the Indians were easy prey for the Guahibos.[81] In the same year, a visitador investigating the encomienda of Captain Juan de la Fuente Calderón ordered him to move eighty tributaries with their families to a new site on the mesa of Subaque. Fuente Calderón was to lay out the town with a plaza and clean, straight streets, and to build a church twenty-four varas long and eight varas wide.[82] Inspection of Adrian Vargas's encomienda in Caibacoa and Gobero, in 1636, brought an order that Vargas return these Indians to the town of Vijua, where the church was located. In secret testimony the *cura doctrinero* declared that he had served Vargas and his father for thirty years and that the Indians had originally been in Vijua, but that Don Francisco Vargas had moved them sometime before to their present place.[83] With so much resistance from Spanish and Indians, congregated communities grew slowly in Casanare. When the archbishop of Santa Fe conducted his pastoral visit there in 1621, he reported that there were only three towns deserving of the name—Chita, Pisba, and Paya.[84]

To Christianize the Indians, the encomendero paid the salaries of a parish priest or doctrinero for each town. It is believed that Jiménez de Quesada first hired a Dominican for the post in Chita. The adelantado actually lived in this cold mountain town for several years and signed a contract for building the church in 1577, two year before his death.[85] After 1586 Augustinians monopolized the *curatos* in Casanare working among the Tunebos and Jiraras of Labranzagrande, Ochica, Suame, Cohasá and Sabanalarga. By the early seventeenth century they were also installed in Pisba, Paya, Chita, and La Salina. Little is known about their evangelization effort, except that in 1620 some towns were secularized.[86] The Jesuits, when they first arrived in 1625, were dismayed by the low level of Christian understanding exhibited by the Indians.

The economic value of encomiendas lay in the crops produced by the tributaries, their artisan skills and manual labor. On *resguardos,* or reserved land, they planted corn, yuca, and cotton, delivering part of the crop in June and December to pay their *demoras* and other taxes. The Indians harvested many arrobas of fish from the rivers. They collected honey, nuts, and beeswax from the forest. They made indigo dye and wove *fique,* the all-purpose sacking of the Llanos.[87]

The most profitable of these activities was raising cotton and processing it into thread and blankets. The Quesada-Berrio encomienda was one of the wealthiest in the province of Tunja because it encompassed all the operations necessary to produce cotton cloth. Indians around Támara gathered as much as 160 *cargas* (1 carga equals about 40 pounds) of cotton a year, which was delivered to Indian towns in the Cordillera. In 1571 6,825 arrobas were sent to caciques in Chita alone. In that town the Indians paid tribute in blankets. Each *parcialidad* (clan) had to deliver to the encomendero the number of blankets fixed in the *tasa.* When the population dwindled, members of the community remained responsible for the original number of blankets, forcing them to employ women and children in their manufacture. An added source of income was the salt well, located near La Sal. In summer the Indians transported nearly 100 cargas of salt, which they dried in the sun.[88] By the second half of the eighteenth century, the Quesada-Berrio encomienda still produced one thousand pesos of annual revenue, and in 1754 the royal hacienda had accumulated 32,246 varas of *lienzo* (cotton cloth), valued at ten thousand pesos from this grant.[89]

Despite this apparent wealth, the heirs of Jiménez de Quesada shared the fate of other Tunja encomenderos, all of whom were heavily in debt by the early seventeenth century. When Martín de Mendoza y Berrio inherited the grant in 1626, its income was already mortgaged for six years to doña Ana de las Alas, widow of Governor Sancho de Alquia. At the end of that time, Mendoza y Berrio had to pay half the product of the encomienda to his mother, María de la Hoz y Berrio, five hundred *ducados* (gold coin worth about seven pesetas by the end of the sixteenth century) to his sister, María de Oruña, and a life-time pension of two hundred *ducados* to another sister living in a convent. In 1631 he surrendered the administration of the grant to one of his three creditors. The new manager collected the tribute. He allotted one-third of it to Berrio for food and applied the rest to pay off his debts. For seven years this arrangement seemed to work, even showing a profit after the manager had paid the salaries of the doctrinero and *mayordomo,* the titles, sales tax, the pensions, and the creditors. In 1638 Mendoza y Berrio was in difficulty again because he did not honor the agreement and tried to take over an obraje among the Chiscas. After this action the Audiencia expressly prohibited him from interfering, in order to protect the interest of his creditors. Mendoza y Berrio's financial plight, Colmenares argues, was typical of Tunja encomenderos, whose incomes were heavily encumbered by pensions or fixed rents. A report from President Martín de Saavedra y Guzmán (1637–44) suggests that by 1644, the encomenderos, far from being a wealthy elite, were an impoverished, rural, and illiterate aristocracy, struggling vainly for the perpetuation of a privilege or to obtain an income from the Royal Treasury.[90]

Royal regulation of the encomiendas did not eliminate routine abuse of the tributaries. The encomenderos scorned the protective civil and ecclesiastical dispositions to collect excessive tribute, overwork the Indians, fail to assign them resguardos, deny them the services of the church and permit them to be victimized by unscrupulous merchants. The fines which those encomenderos found guilty were required to pay, were not sufficiently steep to bring about a change in their behavior.[91] In this exploitative situation, incidents of cruelty abounded. Rivero writes of an encomendero "no less known for the nobility of his blood than for his impetuous disposition," who ordered some Achaguas to fish in order to entertain some nuns who were visiting him and to repay them for sweets and preserves which they had brought. When the Indians failed to obey his order, the encomendero regarded their refusal as a stain on his honor, which could be erased only by the shedding of blood. He executed twenty Achaguas on the sands of the Duya River. This incident, Rivero charges, was typical of many outrages the encomenderos inflicted on the Indians. Working conditions were uniformly barbarous, especially in the obrajes. There men, women and children were kept spinning and weaving all day as if they were in jail, "more oppressed and subjugated than if they were slaves having to survive fatigue, fear of punishment and the cruelty of their masters."[92]

In 1621 Don Hernando Arias de Ugarte, archbishop of Santa Fe, traveled to Chita and other towns in Casanare to investigate the condition of the Indians under Spanish rule. He learned that there were 3,114 Christianized Indians living in the recently secularized *doctrinas,* 763 in the administrative center of Chita, 527 in Morcote, 373 in Pisba, 147 in Pauto, and 1,304 in Támara. Only 100 Indians made confessions to the archbishop. Many were so ignorant of Christian dogma that they fled on being shown an image of the crucified Christ. Of the four priests assigned to the doctrinas, two—the *bachiller* Cristóbal de Velasco in Támara and Padre Andrés Pérez Nieto in Morcote—were reasonably conscientious. The *presbitero* Gonzalo Martín de Saldaña, serving in Chita, was an old man who, because of a broken leg, as he himself admitted, "was not good for anything else except to remain in his house commending himself to God," while Padre Felipe Zambrano made excuses to keep from taking up his curato in Pauto.[93] Archbishop Ugarte was deeply concerned by what he had seen. He decided to invite the general of the Jesuits, who resided in Santa Fe, to take charge of these towns, initiating missionary activity in Casanare and precipitating a bitter struggle between the regular and secular clergy.

Jesuits had been active in the New Kingdom for twenty years. The first members of the Company of Jesus arrived in 1590. In 1598 they founded the Colegio de San Bartolomé where they studied, along with the customary courses in arts, grammar, and theology, the Chibcha language and prepared prayers and catechisms in that tongue.[94] Jesuits were already ministering to the Indians on the sabana when their general accepted the archbishop's invitation to work in Casanare. With the concurrence of Juan de Borja, who served as president of the New Kingdom from 1606 to 1628, Ugarte signed the *auto* on October 1, 1624, delegating to the Jesuits coadjudicatorship of Chita and the doctrinas of Támara, Pauto, and Morcote.

On January 25, 1625 Padres Jerónimo de Tolosa, José Dadey, and Diego de Acuña arrived in Chita, where they were joined later by Domingo de Molina and José de Tobalina. Establishing their headquarters in that town and Morcote, they traveled to the other doctrinas to make new converts and rebaptize those who had not understood what they had first received. The Jesuits encouraged the Indians to leave their scattered homes in the serranías and to resettle in towns. They performed new marriages and revalidated old ones. In a short time, each had learned from three to seven Indian dialects, and Padre Dadey had edited a grammar, dictionary, and catechism in the language spoken by the Indians of Paya. Their effective actions won over to Spanish rule many formerly warlike Indians.

Despite this progress, or perhaps because of it, the Jesuits enflamed the resentment of the secular clergy. P. Gonzalo Martín was unwilling to accept P. Jerónimo de Tolosa as coadjutor of Chita. He led the former curas doctrineros in protesting the infringement of his prerogatives. Martín's steady stream of complaints fell on sympathetic ears when Don Julian de Cortázar replaced Ugarte as archbishop, in 1628. No friend of the

Jesuits, Cortázar wrote to the king on January 10, 1628, asking him to reinstate the seculars in Chita, Támara, Pauto, and Morcote. Cortázar defended the earlier work of these curas. He reminded the king that the crown had a special responsibility toward sons and grandsons of the conquistadors, who without these positions would have no source of income. Finally he urged the withdrawal of the Jesuits, on the grounds that they could not be disciplined in the ordinary way because they were outside the jurisdiction of the prelates.[95]

Cortázar, having already made up his mind about the case, did not wait for the king to reply. As soon as he learned that Padre Martín was physically able to carry on his duties, he declared an end to the coadjudicatorship in Chita, on May 25, 1628, and asked P. Tolosa to leave. Cortázar's order stirred a protest from the local Indian leaders, who believed that if the Jesuits withdrew, the Spanish would molest them and force them to pay illegal tribute. Neither this reaction nor the unexpected death of P. Martín, on June 18, stopped the archbishop, who declared the Chita curato vacant and accepted more than twenty applications from other secular clergy eager for the appointment. Nevertheless, by the time he named the cura of Gámeza, Alonso Martín Cortés, *cura ad interim,* Padre Tolosa had already taken unilateral control of Chita and refused, on July 9, 1628, to surrender it to Cortázar's appointee.

The lines of the conflict were drawn. The Jesuits, backed by the Indians and some Spanish in Chita, would not abandon the doctrina. The secular clergy, supported by the archbishop, demanded their ouster. Cortázar attempted to resolve the impasse by collecting testimony from Spanish and Indians about the relative merits of the competing groups of religious. The witnesses brought to light no negligence on the part of either. They praised the seculars for setting a good example and teaching the doctrine, but they also lauded the zeal of the Jesuits. No evidence emerged to prove that the Jesuits were conducting illegal commerce with the Indians, a charge frequently made against them. The mayor of Tame stated that the missionaries had accepted wax and thread from the Indians, but that they had given them knives, shirts, and blankets in exchange. Moreover, the Jesuits prohibited whites from living among the Indians in the Llanos and thus protected them from being cheated. Another witness volunteered that the Jesuits had purchased some Achaguas in order to begin towns, but he went on to affirm that they had forbidden the enslavement of Indians. Recognizing that this testimony was not especially reliable, since the witnesses were carefully selected, the historian Juan Manuel Pacheco remarks that neither encomenderos nor merchants accused the Jesuits of wrongdoing and that the tone of the statements was favorable toward their activities.[96]

The missionaries defended themselves in a letter to the Royal Audiencia, dated September 6, 1628. Rather than taking advantage of the Indians, they explained, they had shared their poverty. The people of the Llanos had no gold or silver. They used shirts, blankets, and knives brought from the New Kingdom as currency. Some Indians sold black wax, honey, balls of cotton thread, fruit, chickens, and, in rare instances, cotton blankets. The Spanish exploited these activities. They forced the Indians to work for them, treating them worse than slaves and kidnapping their children. The Jesuits affirmed that when they purchased supplies from the Indians, they paid the price demanded by the seller, because they themselves lived more frugally than the natives, the Indians offered to help them in return for receiving the benefits of Christianity. Vowing that they would never enslave Indians, since such a move worked against the ends of religion, the Jesuits laid their case before the *oidores* (appeal judges, members of the audiencia).

Meanwhile, Padre Alonso Martín arrived in Chita, on July 9, to take up his duties as cura ad interim, but Tolosa would not surrender to him the keys to the church. Archbishop Cortázar commanded the faithful of Chita to receive P. Martín or face excommunication, and he sent the *visitador general* of the archdiocese to oversee the transfer. The confrontation came on July 31. Before the Indians assembled in the plaza, the visitador ordered Tolosa to hand over the keys. When the Jesuit refused, he called for a blacksmith to force the door open. The Indians became alarmed, crying and shouting that they did not want Tolosa to leave them. Men who had accompanied the visitador assaulted them, and after a struggle they placed four Indians, including the *alcalde* (town magistrate), in jail. On being informed of this affair, the Audiencia called for a moratorium until it could complete an investigation. Archbishop Cortázar was so angry that he wrote to a colleague that "he had ready twenty mules, to go in person to throw the Company out of there and to see if there was any one who could keep him from being cura of that town which was said to have 8,000 pesos in income."[97] While Cortázar excommunicated Tolosa and prohibited him from celebrating mass in the church, the Indian leaders of Chita went to Santa Fe to present petitions on behalf of the Jesuits.

The dispute might have dragged on indefinitely had not Jesuit leaders in Santa Fe decided that incurring the ill will of the archbishop was too great a price to pay for controlling the doctrinas. On August 17, 1628, the rector of the Colegio of Santa Fe, in the name of the provincial, presented their resignation to the Audiencia. Cortázar immediately named Doctor Pedro Guillén de Arce as *párroco* (parish priest) of Chita. For the time being, the matter was closed.

The missionaries grieved to abandon the work they had begun with such optimism. Even after they left the Llanos, authorities received testimony extolling their efforts. In 1632 the Audiencia reported that encomenderos and Indians alike mourned the loss of the Jesuits and asked for their reinstatement. On their return thirty years later, the Jesuits discovered that the memory of the early missionaries was still vivid and positive.[98]

While the first Jesuits were working in Casanare, the Dominicans were opening a mission field in the Llanos of San Juan and San Martín. In 1620 the Order of Preachers founded the Convent of Santo Eccehomo, in Tunja Province, and from that year on they regarded the Indians on the eastern slopes of the Cordillera as suitable subjects for proselytism.[99] The history of their mission at Medina was not free of conflict, but the relative success of the Dominicans there as compared with the Jesuits reflected the greater geographic, economic, and political isolation of the Llanos of San Juan and San Martín and their lack of importance within the New Kingdom.

In 1620 Fr. Alonso Ronquillo left Santo Eccehomo and traveled over "mountains horrifying because of their huge trees, rough paths, precipices, dangerous rapids and deep canyons formed by rivers which could be crossed only by hanging on to hemp ropes," to reach the territory of the Chíos, Mambitas, and Suraguas, in the foothills along the Llanos of San Juan and San Martín.[100] Ronquillo baptized and reduced three hundred families. He then asked his provincial, Fr. Leandro de Garfías, to request that a cura doctrinero be appointed to the new town to insure that the Indians would not return to their old way of life. Garfías dispatched another Dominican, Fr. Juan Martínez Melo, to inspect Ronquillo's progress. On receiving a favorable report, he informed President Borja, who, with the concurrence of Archbishop Ugarte, assigned Ronquillo to the post. Ronquillo built a church in the town, which he called Medina, and continued his ministry with great energy, baptizing more than two thousand Indians.[101]

Ronquillo's activities aroused no jealous reponse from secular clergy, but the encomenderos of the region were anxious to get control of the mission. At his death, in 1642, President Borja assigned Medina to the encomienda of Mariscal Don Francisco Vanegas, of the Order of Calatrava. Vanegas's heirs decided to move the Indians to a site called Guadua, where their labor would be more useful. The Dominican Order protested this transfer, and General Don Diego de Egües, who governed the New Kingdom between 1662 and 1664 and who did much to foster the missions, supported their stand. He ordered the Indians returned to Medina, where they continued to live under the protection of Fr. Nicolas Benevite. On recounting this history, Alonso de Zamora, the Dominican chronicler, lamented that all too often Indians reduced by missionaries fell into the hands of encomenderos who mistreated them and permitted them to return to paganism.[102] In this case, however, strong official support insured that Ronquillo's work was not in vain.

Between 1531 and 1650, the regions that made up the New Kingdom of Granada were frontiers of one kind or another in relation to Santa Fe, as Hispanic rule spread throughout the colony. In the Llanos unique conditions south and north of the Meta River shaped the economic and political ties that developed between these regions and the highlands. Official interest in the Llanos of San Juan and San Martín was at first very high. As long as the Spanish believed that El Dorado lay to the east, the wretched climate and difficult topography did not stop them from exploring in every direction. Avellaneda's discovery of gold near San Juan triggered a quick rush of settlers to that city. Yet once the incentive of easy wealth faded, the Spanish were no longer willing to tolerate the difficult life afforded by the plains. The barrier posed by the nearly insurmountable Eastern Cordillera limited contact between San Juan and Santa Fe and the dynamic quality of the frontier south of the Meta quickly faded. Rodríguez Fresle's description of San Juan in 1638 is that of a dying city.

The Llanos of Casanare, on the other hand, remained more accessible to influences coming from west and east. North of the Meta, the presence of large groups of sedentary Indians which could be divided into encomiendas reinforced the El Dorado dream. White settlers came down to the plains from Tunja, stimulated by the rivalry between Jiménez de Quesada and Francisco de Cáceres. By 1620 Santiago de las Atalayas, the provincial capital, was a vital, prosperous city. The regular shipment of cotton, textiles, foodstuffs, and livestock to Tunja and other cities in the New Kingdom indicates that the western portion of Casanare was integrated into the colonial economy.

Events in the Provincia de los Llanos commanded the attention of the archbishop and Audiencia, as the controversy over the Jesuits in Chita and environs in the 1620s demonstrates. Of perpetual concern for Santa Fe authorities was the vulnerability of Casanare to enemy invasion from the east. By the mid-sixteenth century, the Dutch, English, and Portuguese had enclaves on the Atlantic coast—in Guiana, the Orinoco Delta, and the Amazon. In theory, at least, any of these powers could mount an expedition on the Orinoco, sail west along the Meta or Casanare, and penetrate the heartland of the New Kingdom before an army could be transported over the Andes to prevent the attack. While the reality of such a threat seems remote today, given the distances involved and lack of knowledge about the territory, in the sixteenth century the possibility was very real. In 1561 when the renegade Basque conquistador, Lope de Aguirre, cut a bloody swath through Venezuela, sacking Burburata, Tocuyo, Mérida, Trujillo, and Valencia, the inhabitants of the New Kingdom were terrified that he would extend his onslaught to the west. The Audiencia hurried to appoint adelantado Jiménez de Quesada to organize a defense, when news was at last received that Aguirre was dead, shot by one of his own men in Barquisimeto.[103]

The rumored revolt of don Diego de Torres, Cacique of Turmequé, in Tunja Province, revived the old fear. According to Rodríguez Fresle, Torres, a mestizo, was a man of wealth and a fine horseman—qualities that had won him many friends and a following among the Indians. In 1581 the unscrupulous fiscal of the Audiencia, Miguel de Orozco, accused Visitador Juan Bautista Monzón and Torres of plotting to lead an Indian uprising. Reports quickly circulated that a horde of Caribs from the Llanos, reinforced by mulattos, mestizos, and blacks would aid the rebels. Then came whisperings of a league with the English and an army already advancing from Guiana up the Casanare River. The colony was in ferment, and Tunja officials guarded every pass along the road by which the enemy might come. When continued tranquility proved the threat imaginary, the fiscal imprisoned Monzón and Torres on trumped-up charges, but the cacique escaped and fled to Spain. The crisis ended in 1582, with the arrival of a new visitador, who freed Monzón and suspended Orozco.[104]

Officials remained aware of the vulnerability of Spanish defenses in the east. The need to shore up the frontier as well as the desire to Hispanicize the Indians prompted the government to initiate a missionary thrust, a policy which brought competing religious orders to the Llanos after 1640 and fostered what some historians have called Casanare's Golden Age.

3 *The Missionary Thrust, 1650–1767*

Between 1650 and 1761 Spanish settlement in the Llanos languished. In contrast to the rapidly multiplying herds of cattle and horses, few Europeans ventured out to a region that offered so much hardship and so little reward. Santa Rosa de Chire, founded in 1672 or 1689, was the only new city. Like the older towns, it was little more than an isolated outpost in the grassy wilderness.

Nevertheless, the frontier expanded east, propelled by what Herbert E. Bolton has called "one of the most conspicuous features of Spain's frontiering genius"—the mission.[1] By 1767 Augustinians, Jesuits, Recoletos, and Franciscans had converted thousands of Indians in the Llanos of Casanare and San Juan and San Martín. The process was a violent one, for the Indians did not readily surrender their freedom. The missionaries battled encomenderos and slavers, Guahibos and Caribs, while their reductions served as the bulwark of Spanish defense against Dutch and Portuguese incursions. Over time the neophytes, through agriculture, crafts, textiles, and cattle raising, became the backbone of the regional economy, transforming Casanare into a productive province within the Viceroyalty of New Granada.[2] While historians have tended to exaggerate these achievements, a review of the development of the missions during this era reveals a remarkable ability, especially on the part of the Jesuits, to incorporate the Indians within Spanish rule—an ability which by the arrival of the Royal Boundary Commission, in 1756, was subject to increasing attack.

In 1761, the year Don José Solís Folch de Cardón turned over the viceregal post in Santa Fe to Pedro Messía de la Cerda and retired to a Franciscan monastery, Padre Basilio Vicente de Oviedo, the creole cura of Mogotes (Santander) completed the eleventh volume in his magnum opus, *Pensamientos y noticias escogidas para utilidad de curas.* Among the manuscripts, all of which remained unpublished despite persistent efforts to gain royal support, was a work entitled *Cualidades y riquezas del Nuevo Reino de Granada,* in which Oviedo, in order to provide a guide for his fellow priests, described all three hundred parishes in the Archbishopric of Santa Fe and ranked them in five categories according to such criteria as distance from the capital, climate, character of the population, and ecclesiastical income. Since its publication in 1930, by the Academia Colombiana de Historia, *Cualidades y riquezas* has become an indispensable source for colonial historians. Oviedo's candid assessments paint a vivid description of the Spanish towns and missions in the Llanos in the mid-eighteenth century.

The Provincia de los Llanos, then encompassing the Llanos of Casanare and the Airico of Macaguane (Arauca), boasted three Spanish cities. Santiago de las Atalayas (the capital), San José de Pore, and Santa Rosa de Chire. Santa Bárbara de Cravo, founded by the governor, don Adriano de Vargas, in 1649 as San José de Cravo, had sunk to the status of pueblo, although one hundred vecinos continued to live there. Oviedo rated Santiago in the third order of parishes (the first order was the highest) or roughly equivalent to Suba, Usaquén, or Fusugasugá in the highlands. In addition to the residence of the governor, Santiago had its own cabildo, two small *pueblos agregados*—Aguamena and Cusiana—and jurisdiction over Surimena, Casimena, Cravo, Sabanalarga, Chámeza, Labranzagrande, Pisba, and Paya. A population of four hundred vecinos contributed an annual ecclesiastical income of one thousand pesos.

Also rated in the third order, but overshadowing the capital in size and importance, was San José de Pore, with five hundred vecinos who paid their curate twelve hundred pesos a year. Pore had a cabildo, and within its jurisdiction were Manare, Macuco, Ten Támara, Pital, and Morcote, four of which were significant textile centers. The city's wealth derived from ranching and from its location on the trail from the Llanos of Casanare to Labranzagrande and Sogamoso. Vaqueros stopped for supplies on their cattle drives to the highlands, and the local mestizos and Indians tanned hides into leather "as good as those of Florida."[3]

Santa Rosa de Chire was less auspicious. Several days' journey northeast of Santiago, it was the last white settlement before Barinas Province, in Venezuela. Within its district were the Jesuit missions of Betoyes, Macaguane, Tame, Patute, Puerto de Casanare and Hacienda Caribabare, but its church was a humble structure, thatched with palms and poorly ornamented. One hundred vecinos afforded a meager ecclesiastical living of four hundred pesos a year. Chire's poverty, combined with its hot, unhealthy climate, placed it within Oviedo's fifth and least desirable order of parishes.

In similar straits were San Juan and San Martín, lying to the south of Santiago and separated from it by the Meta and Upía Rivers. By 1761 San Juan faced certain extinction. Once a center of crown government, it now survived as a base for Franciscan missionaries. With forty vecinos and jurisdiction over one small pueblo agregado, Tamane, the parish had little to offer an ambitious priest. Many years before, the gold along the banks of the Ariari had been exhausted. Now the people eked out a wretched existence farming, herding cattle, or gathering wild cacao from the forests. San Martín had an equally miserable-looking church, but was responsible for three towns—Apiay, Medina, and Tumbia. Its sixty vecinos produced an ecclesiastical income of four hundred pesos a year.

Bad climate and geographic isolation were the principal liabilities of San Juan and San Martín. While some individuals managed to live a long life, such as the cura maestro Piñeros, who, as Oviedo pointed out, served San Martín for eighty-eight years, retaining his reason to the end (although he was "very dried up with little flesh and seldom left the town except to go to San Juan"), nearly everyone suffered from chills and fever caused by the heat and insects.[4] Communication with other parts of the realm was uncertain. To reach Santa Fe travelers had to ford deep rivers and cross the mountains on a trail so rough that the journey by horse or mule was feasible only during the dry-season months of January and February. An anonymous explorer of the Ariari River in the 1760s wrote that "the condition of the country and that of the inhabitants in the Christian towns is unhappy, poor and with no hope for better ideas: all flee from future wealth preferring present misery, and even to equip the ordinary pack trains from San Martín to San Juan, there is no one who has enough animals, pack saddles and harnesses. They all pool together to outfit a single animal, and none of these are mules."[5]

Oviedo shared the explorer's grim appraisal, relegating San Juan and San Martín to his fifth category, the equivalent of exile, yet he did not find the Llanos uniformly disagreeable. He conceded that the higher altitude of the territory around Santiago and Pore alleviated the tropical climate. The forests contained many kinds of woods, oils, and medicinal products. Where the land was fertile, Christians as well as gentile Indians raised yuca, plátanos, and corn. They hunted jaguars and tapirs. Adept on horseback, they lassoed deer and wild cattle, from which they stripped the hides.[6]

The abundant cattle herds noted by Oviedo were a significant economic development of this period. By 1767 there were ranches in the higher elevations of the Llanos of Casanare and Arauca, within a zone of one hundred miles along the Andes between the Pauto and Arauca rivers and growing in density northward into Venezuela. The largest herds were managed by the Jesuits, but in Casanare private enterprise also played a role. Salt for the animals was obtained in Chámeza and Medina. Mules were raised around Labranzagrande. *Cofradías* (lay brotherhoods supporting ecclesiastical functions) based on cattle hatos existed in Pore, Santiago, Puerto de Casanare, and Manare. Famous throughout the eighteenth century were the cattle drives from the Casanare River to Labranzagrande, the site of major cattle fairs. There were large herds south of the Meta, but ranching there was limited by lack of a market. It was from Casanare via Pore, Támara, and Labranzagrande that most Llanos cattle reached the highlands.[7]

The encomienda as an institution had lost none of its force by the beginning of the eighteenth century. A visita conducted through most of the New Kingdom in 1690 by Francisco de Vergara Azcarate revealed that in the Llanos of Casanare there were 419 Indians in royal encomiendas, 855 in private encomiendas in the Corregimiento de Chita, and 595 in private encomiendas in the Corregimiento de los Llanos (see table 2). Three new towns—Tame, Macaguane, and Iximena—had recently been brought into the system, and the total of 1,819 tributaries, an increase of 397 (28 percent) over the 1,422 held in 1653, reflected the system's expansion over formerly independent tribes.[8]

While not without interest, Spanish cities, cattle raising, and the encomiendas took a back seat to the dramatic expansion of the missions during this era. By 1650, throughout the Spanish Empire, the mission was replacing the encomienda-doctrina as the principal method of winning Indians to Christianity on the frontier. A direct outgrowth of the doctrina, the mission had the same objective but employed different methods. Where before the encomendero had to finance the work of Hispanicizing the Indians, now the major responsibility for the exploration of new land, reducing natives to towns, and building churches and roads fell to the regular clergy.[9] In the Llanos five religious orders were given an opportunity to establish a hold on Indians too wily to be conquered by Spanish soldiers and too poor to compensate such an effort. The results of over one hundred years of their labors richly justified the crown's confidence.

Table 2. Indian Tributaries in Royal and Private Encomiendas in the Llanos of Casanare, 1690

Royal Encomiendas		Private Encomiendas, Corregimiento de Chita		Private Encomiendas, Corregimiento de los Llanos	
Tributaries	Towns	Tributaries	Towns	Tributaries	Towns
48	Cravo	218	Morcote	17	Chámeza
29	Labranzagrande	71	Boavita	19	Cusiana
103	San Salvador	37	Paya	15	Ochica
	de Casanare	189	Chita	28	Achagus de Avila
57	*Macaguane	44	Chiscas & Tunebas	195	Támara
138	*Tame	77	La Sal	72	Guaseco
44	*Iximena	63	Comí	111	Pauto
419		93	Guacamaya	81	Pisba
		63	Panquera	31	Unao
		855		11	Vigua
				15	Cupiaga & Cavita
				595	

Total
Tributaries 1,819

Source: "Informe de Francisco de Vergara Azcarate sobre estipendios de indios encomendados y por encomendar, Santa Fe, 27 mayo 1690," in Julián Bautista Ruís Rivera, *Fuentes,* 109–57.

*Newly converted towns originally placed under the crown. The Junta General de Tribunales later ordered that the corregidor de los Llanos should collect their tribute and give it to the Jesuits. For that reason Vergara Azcarate listed them also under Corregimiento de los Llanos.

The first attempts by Jesuits and Dominicans to start missions in the 1620s provoked stout resistance from secular clergy and Spanish settlers, but the orders did not relinquish their goal. Forty years later the state gave them sufficient backing to counter these obstacles. The decision to promote missions in the Llanos came during the presidency of don Diego de Egües (1662–64), who regarded the Indians as "the most neglected and backward of his subjects."[10] In 1662 Egües organized the Junta de Propaganda Fide. Composed of the archbishop, the *provisor* (cleric exercising a bishop's ordinary judicial authority) the *vicario general* (an ecclesiastical judge whose authority extended throughout the archdiocese), the prelates of each religious order, and the senior oidor of the Audiencia, this group met weekly to discuss the work of the Church in the New Kingdom. On July 12, 1662, the junta, aiming to encourage the conversion of the Indians, divided the Llanos into five large territories and assigned responsibility for each one to a different religious order. On July 18 Egües reinforced this action by prohibiting the governor from himself making or permitting others to make entradas with soldiers.[11] He put all Christianized Indians under royal protection and ordered pictures of the king's coat of arms placed in their villages to prevent the settlers from enslaving them.[12] The crown expected the regulars to finance the work out of their own funds, but it did award each mission, on its founding, 1,000 pesos to pay for bells, vestments, tools and other expenses and pledged to pay annual stipends, or *sínodos,* of 350 to 450 pesos a year to missionaries in the field.[13]

The July 12 agreement gave to each religious order the sections in the Llanos in which it had already demonstrated interest. The assignments south of the Meta River were vague, because of a lack of accurate geographic knowledge. The Dominicans received the mission among the Chíos and Mambitas, in Medina, begun by Fr. Ronquillo. Secular clergy were to continue in the cities of San Juan and San Martín. The territory east of them, or "the part of the Llanos visited by P. Bernardo de Lira in 1655," went to the Franciscans.[14] The agreement confirmed the Augustinians in the doctrinas of Chita, Támara and surrounding towns in Casanare, all of which they had been serving for many years, in some cases since 1585. It also permitted them to enter the Llanos of San Juan and San Martín from their doctrina in Fómeque.[15] The junta ordered the Recoletos (a branch of the Augustinians that appeared in New Granada in 1604, sometimes called Candelarios) to found missions between the Upía and Cusiana rivers. Finally, it awarded to the Jesuits the plains from the Pauto River to San Cristóbal and Barinas, excepting the towns designated as

Augustinian, and all the Llanos of Caracas, following an imaginary line from the Pauto River to the jungles south of the Meta.[16] Despite its imprecision, this arrangement proved workable, for it remained in effect with only minor alterations until the expulsion of the Jesuits in 1767.

Between 1662 and 1767, the five orders carried out their commitments with varying success and enthusiasm. The Augustinians had the easiest task in Casanare, since their doctrinas were the wealthiest in the province. They were already serving the Tunebos and Jiraras in Chita, Támara, Paya, Pisba, La Salina, Guativa, Guaseco, Morcote, Labranzagrande, and Chámeza prior to the 1662 agreement, which simply confirmed their presence. They founded only one new mission on the eastern slope of the Cordillera, Sácama, in 1678, although in 1736 they moved Guaseco to a better site and renamed it Ten.[17] The textile industry continued to flourish. By 1770 the Augustinians controlled approximately 6,458 Indians in ten towns, which in their stability and size resembled secularized Indian parishes more than frontier missions (see table 3 and map 4).

From their doctrina in Cáqueza, the Augustinians pushed into virgin territory in the Llanos of San Juan and San Martín, but failed to sustain a mission. In 1663 the first prior and vicario provincial, P. Pedro Lavado, accompanied by P. Juan Bautista Rondón, reduced fifteen hundred Indians in San Agustín de Jarica and Santo Tomás, not far from San Martín. New personnel arrived in the following years. In 1686, due to the deaths of Rondón and Lavado and crippling raids by encomenderos, only one town remained, with thirty houses. Reorganization took place in 1688, but there is no indication that either San Agustín de Jarica or Santo Tomás existed in the eighteenth century.[18] Likewise the Dominicans, who were active on the Andean fringes of the Llanos, failed to start any permanent reductions east of Medina.[19]

The orders exclusively involved with proselytizing Indians in the plains were the Franciscans, south of the Meta, and the Recoletos and Jesuits, in Casanare. Unlike the Jesuits, neither Franciscans nor Recoletos produced a historian to record their exploits. Since many key documents have been lost or destroyed, their role in the Llanos has been largely ignored.[20] Yet the Franciscans developed a vital mission field in the Llanos of San Juan and San Martín, and the Recoletos managed to found three more or less permanent reductions in Casanare.

In 1656 the Franciscans Bernardo de Lira and Juan Troyano reached the Saes living in an area called Buchipa, in the Llanos of San Juan and San Martín. A year later they founded San Miguel de Ariari. In 1662 the Junta de Propaganda Fide validated their claim to this territory.[21] Unhealthy

Table 3. Missions in the Llanos circa 1760

Region	Religious Order	Mission	Indian Population
Casanare	Augustinians	Chita	200
		Támara	2,079
		Ten	484
		Pital	60
		Labranzagrande	140
		Chámeza	171
		Paya	544
		Pisba	590
		Morcote	2,165
		La Salina	25
			6,458[a]
Casanare	Recoletos	Sabana Alta	50
		Iximena	200
		San Pedro de Upía	50
			300[b]
Casanare	Jesuits	Güicán	?
		Pauto (Manare)	600
		San Salvador del Puerto	350
		Tame	1,800
		Patute	70
		Macaguane	1,000
		Betoyes	1,600
			5,420[c]
Meta River	Jesuits	Surimena	400
		Macuco	800
		Casimena	700
		Jiramena	300
			2,200
	Total Jesuits		7,620[c]
Llanos of San Juan	Dominicans	Medina	100[d]
Llanos of San Juan	Franciscans	Yamane	60
		Curanabe	60
		El Anime	60
		Vijagual	60
		Tamane	60
			360[e]
Total		31 missions	14,838

[a]From the census taken in 1778 of the Provincia de los Llanos by José Caicedo, by royal order of Nov. 10, 1776.

[b]Ganuza, *Monografía de las misiones vivas,* 1:224.

[c]Alvarado, *Informe reservado,* 124.

[d]Estimate.

[e]Arcila Robledo, *Las misiones franciscanas,* 246.

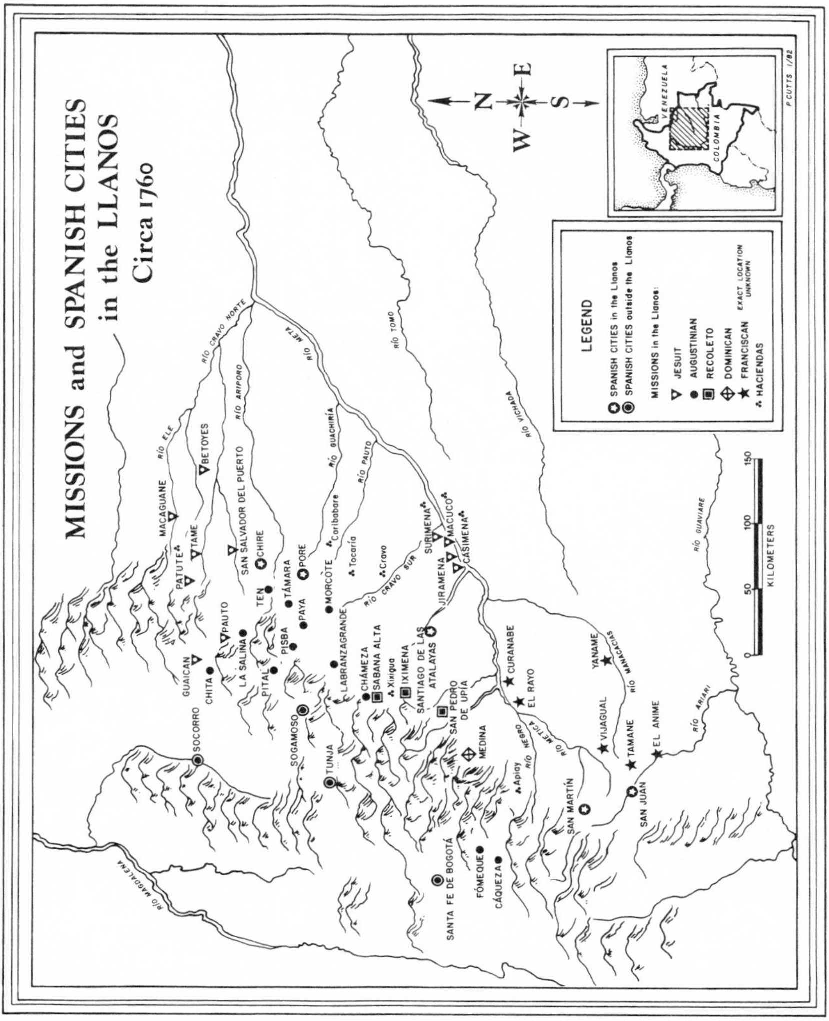

MISSIONS and SPANISH CITIES in the LLANOS
Circa 1760
LEGEND
SPANISH CITIES in the Llanos
SPANISH CITIES outside the Llanos
MISSIONS in the Llanos:
JESUIT
AUGUSTINIAN
RECOLETO
DOMINICAN
FRANCISCAN
HACIENDAS
EXACT LOCATION UNKNOWN
VENEZUELA
COLOMBIA
N
E
S
W
KILOMETERS
0
50
100
150
P CUTTS 1/82
RÍO MAGDALENA
RÍO CRAVO NORTE
RÍO ELE
RÍO ARIPORO
RÍO META
RÍO TOMO
RÍO GUACHIRÍA
RÍO PAUTO
RÍO CRAVO SUR
RÍO VICHADA
RÍO GUAVIARE
RÍO ARIARI
RÍO NEGRO
RÍO METICA
RÍO MANACACÍAS
SOCORRO
GUAICAN
CHITA
MACAGUANE
PATUTE
TAME
BETOYES
PAUTO
LA SALINA
SAN SALVADOR DEL PUERTO
CHIRE
TEN
PITAL
PISBA
TÁMARA
PAYA
PORE
MORCOTE
Caribabare
Tocaría
Cravo
SOGAMOSO
TUNJA
LABRANZAGRANDE
CHÁMEZA
SABANA ALTA
Xixigua
IXIMENA
SANTIAGO DE LAS ATALAYAS
JIRAMENA
SURIMENA
MACUCO
CASIMENA
SAN PEDRO DE UPÍA
MEDINA
CURANABE
EL RAYO
Apiay
SANTA FE DE BOGOTÁ
FÓMEQUE
CÁQUEZA
SAN MARTÍN
VIJAGUAL
TAMANE
YANAME
EL ANIME
SAN JUAN

climate, opposition from civil authorities in San Juan, and raids by white settlers retarded expansion. The reductions remained small and mobile. Their populations fluctuated month to month and day to day as neophytes left the community to return to the forest. It was not unusual for an entire town to move to a new site that either the priest or the Indians believed to be more promising. These conditions make it difficult to locate the missions accurately and to estimate how many people they contained. In 1702 the Franciscans reported that they had explored the Sierra de la Macarena, founded Santo Eccehomo de Curanabe and San Antonio del Marayal, and noted that Indians still cultivated plots at El Anime and Cumaral, two former missions now deserted.[22] In 1737 Captain Agustín Solórzano estimated that about sixty natives were living in each of five reductions of Yamane, Curanabe, El Anime, Vijagual, and El Rayo.[23] By 1760 the Franciscans had taken charge of San Juan and founded Tamane, giving them a total of about 360 Indians in six missions.

The Recoletos concentrated on the territory between the Upía and Cusiana rivers. Among the first four missionaries to the Llanos was Fr. Cristóbal Alarcón, a vecino of Santiago de las Atalayas, who joined the order after the death of his wife. In 1663 they persuaded some Achaguas to settle in Sabana Alta (sometimes called Upamena), on the banks of the Cusiana. In 1664 they brought 260 Achaguas across the Meta and congregated them at Concepción de Iximena, located by the *caño* (stream) of Dumagua.[24] Despite raids by encomenderos, disease, and lack of food, the two missions thrived, supported by a cattle hacienda, Xixigua, which the Recoletos founded on land donated by Juan de Alarcón along the Tua River. In the eighteenth century they began San Pedro de Upía, in the mountains by the river of the same name, but lack of finances retarded further growth. In 1733 the Recoletos tried to hand over their missions to seculars, but priests could not be found and they had to continue administering Iximena and Upía. They did quit the Hacienda Xixigua, although Indians who lived in Sabana Alta continued tending cattle on the estate.[25]

Dwarfing the achievements of the Franciscans and Recoletos were those of the Jesuits, who made plans on a grander scale. The Jesuit Province in New Granada, with its Colegio Máximo in Santa Fe, had jurisdiction over Venezuela and the island of Santo Domingo (Hispaniola). It supported educational institutions throughout the New Kingdom (Tunja, Cartagena, Pamplona, Antioquia, Mompos, and Honda), as well as in Mérida and Santo Domingo, but its missions were concentrated east of the Andes.[26] The goal of the province was to found reductions not only in Casanare and along the Meta River, but also in Guayana, in order to control traffic on the Orinoco River and to open up direct contact with the Atlantic and Europe. Royal officials subsidized this effort to some extent, both financially and militarily, recognizing the political and commercial advantages of a direct water route east. But the main economic support came from a system of Jesuit-owned and operated haciendas. As a result, and despite some setbacks, the Jesuits created by 1760 an extensive and prosperous mission system in the Llanos, bettered only by their more famous reductions in Paraguay.[27]

The Jesuits began their second offensive in Casanare at the prompting of two Indians from Tame, who arrived in Santa Fe, early in 1659, to ask that they return. In April the fathers Bartolomé Pérez and Francisco Alvarez reconnoitered the field and, being well received, recommended that missions be resumed. To facilitate the undertaking, the provincial exchanged the Jesuit doctrina of Tópaga, near Sogamoso, for the town of Pauto (present-day Manare), more conveniently situated at the gateway to the Llanos.[28] There, in 1661, P. Antonio de Monteverde, vicario and superior of the missions, installed his office, while other Jesuits ministered to the Jiraras in Tame, the Achaguas in San Salvador de Casanare, and the Tunebos in Patute. Three other reductions begun in Macaguane, San Ignacio, and San Joaquín de Atanare failed, ravaged by smallpox and hostile Guahibos, although Macaguane was refounded in 1676.

To support the Jesuits, President Egües authorized the governor in Santiago de las Atalayas to turn over to them three cattle estancias lying between Pauto and San Salvador, in a section of the plains where Indian attacks had discouraged Spanish settlers. The Jesuits consolidated the estates to form Hacienda Caribabare. In 1678 they transferred cattle from this herd to another hacienda, Tocaría. By the end of the century, they had acquired three more estates—Cravo, Patute, and Apiay, the last located south of the Meta, in the Llanos of San Juan and San Martín.[29] In addition, the crown paid annual *sínodos* to the missionaries by 1680 and awarded them the income from the royal encomiendas in Macaguane, Tame, and Iximena.[30]

Jesuit penetration into Guayana did not bring the success won in Casanare. The presence of great numbers of unconverted Indians and the possibilities of uninhibited travel along the Casanare and Orinoco rivers were powerful incentives for such a move. Once missions were established, the Jesuits planned to defend the rivers and use them, rather than the Magdalena, to introduce tools, supplies, food, and personnel to the Llanos. They sent expeditions to Guayana in 1664 and 1668, but heavy assaults by Caribs and Guahibos destroyed the reductions and added many names to the list of Jesuit martyrs. Assignment of *escoltas,* or military squadrons in the pay of the king, to the missions in 1681 could not stem the tide. In 1695, admitting temporary defeat, the Jesuits withdrew.[31]

The years between 1695 and 1715 mark a hiatus in activity. The Jesuits resigned themselves to making entradas into the Llanos of Casanare and consolidating captured Indians within their existing missions. In 1711 the provincial tried to free up the missionaries by requesting that these reductions be handed over to seculars, but in 1715 the Protector of the Indians in Santa Fe denied his petition.[32] By that time reinforcements had arrived from Europe and had completed training in Santa Fe for work on the frontier. The assignment of Joseph Gumilla to Tame, Casanare, in 1715 began a third offensive that planted missions on the Meta between the Cusiana and Cravo Sur rivers and along the banks of the Middle Orinoco.

Joseph Gumilla, perhaps the best-known Jesuit to work in the Llanos, was born in Cárcer, Spain, in 1686. He left Seville for America in 1705 with forty-three other Jesuits and spent ten years in Santa Fe, studying at the Colegio de San Bartolomé.[33] Arriving in Tame, he spent a year mastering the Betoy language and writing a grammar and dictionary in that tongue. Then he reduced a group of these Indians at San Ignacio de los Betoyes, on the eastern bank of the Casanare about three leagues from San Salvador. Betoyes was the last Jesuit mission begun in northern Casanare, which in 1767 had seven reductions with a population of 5,420.[34]

Gumilla was serving as superior in Casanare (1723–30) when the Jesuits turned their attention to the Achaguas and Sálivas, along the Meta. In 1723 P. José Cabarte founded San Francisco Regis de Guanapalo, which was later moved to another site and called Surimena. In 1727 Juan Rivero, historian and linguist, began Nuestra Señora de la Concepción, also moved several times and after 1756 called Jiramena.[35] In 1732 P. Manuel Roman baptized the Sáliva in San Miguel de Macuco, and in 1746 Juan Espinosa added Casimena peopled by Guahibos.[36] To supply meat to the new converts, hatos were begun at Macuco, Surimena, and Casimena, with cattle acquired from Casanare. These herds grew rapidly and, as table 4 shows, by 1760 rivaled those belonging to the older haciendas, with the exception of Caribabare. The population of the four missions stabilized at 2,200 in that same year.[37]

Gumilla's main objective was to gain control of the Orinoco. In 1731 he went to Guayana and Trinidad, to enlist the backing of royal officials. In 1732 he founded Concepción de los Guaiquires, San José de los Mapoyes, Santa Teresa de Tabage, and Nuestra Señora de los Angeles. The Caribs continued to defy this new thrust along the great river, but with

Table 4. Jesuit Haciendas in the Llanos, 1767

Region	Hacienda	Cattle	Mules	Stallions	Mares
Casanare	Caribabare	10,606	26	1,384	——
	Tocaría	——	——	——	——
	Cravo	5,946	11	369	——
	Patute	921	——	42	——
	Apiay	1,693	22	360	——
Meta River	Surimena	4,000	——	200	200
	Macuco	6,900	——	150	142
	Casimena	4,000	——	85	800
	Total	44,066	59	2,550	1,142

Source: Figures for haciendas in Casanare are found in Colmenares, *Las haciendas de los jesuítas,* 127. Colmenares does not include totals for Tocaría. Figures for the Meta haciendas are from Delgado, *Excursiones en Casanare,* 164.

the aid of escoltas the Jesuits organized their neophytes into permanent militias that included cavalry. Supported by homemade cannon and artillery, these groups staved off hostile Indians and incursions of Dutch pirates, who regularly sailed the Orinoco looking for slaves and trade in tropical products.[38]

Opposition raised by other religious orders active in Guayana proved more difficult to reconcile. In 1734 an agreement was signed by which the Capuchins accepted the territory from the mouth of the Orinoco to Angostura, the Observants took the region from Angostura to the Cuchivero River, and the Jesuits took the territory farther west. This accord did not end the dispute. In 1738 Gumilla left for Spain, where, in order to generate support for the Jesuit position, he pubished *El Orinoco ilustrado: historia natural, civil y geográfico de este gran río.*[39] He returned to Santa Fe in 1743 and died in the mission territory seventeen years later.[40]

Resigning themselves to the middle Orinoco, the Jesuits capitalized on the friendly reception shown them by the Sáliva. By 1767 they had founded six permanent reductions with 2,320 Indians, sustained by several haciendas producing sugar, cattle, and tropical products.[41] Organized as a unit separate from the missions in Casanare and Meta, with their own superior, the Orinoco reductions lay geographically outside the Llanos of New Granada and will not be considered further in this discussion. Nevertheless, it is important to note that the Jesuits had achieved their goal of opening the Orinoco for travel and trade—a factor that enhanced the economic viability of the missions farther to the west.[42]

Between 1662 and 1767, the Franciscans in the Llanos of San Juan and San Martín, and the Augustinians, Recoletos and Jesuits in Casanare had incorporated 14,838 Indians into thirty-one missions (table 3). The Franciscan and Recoleto towns were not prepossessing but the ten Augustinian textile-producing towns on the Andean slopes, with 6,458 Indians, nearly balanced the eleven Jesuit reductions in the foothills and plains, with 7,620. In addition the Jesuits administered eight cattle haciendas with a combined herd of 44,066 cattle, 59 mules, 2,550 stallions and 1,142 mares (table 4). The establishment of this mission frontier had not been achieved without a price. Throughout the Llanos, the conversion of the Indians, however peacefully intentioned, both engendered and encountered violence. Even before European contact, warfare between sedentary peoples and nomads had been endemic—a situation exacerbated by the arrival of the Spanish and their continual raids for encomienda workers and slaves. The missionaries discovered that once they had broken down the natural resistance of the Indians, they had to protect their wards from attack by white settlers, Guahibos, and Caribs.

Ideally the missionaries aspired to convert the Indians by convincing them through peaceful persuasion of the spiritual benefits of Christianity. In practice, as Joseph Gumilla pointed out in *El Orinoco ilustrado,* material incentives were more effective than spiritual ones; for, as St. Paul wrote, "the human animal who is still in the rough will not perceive spiritual things although he may talk and explain about them."[43] Gumilla argued that in the Llanos, where the Indians could easily withdraw to inaccessible forests overnight, the missionaries had to demonstrate that life in a Christian village was preferable to their old ways. Among techniques which Gumilla endorsed, drawn from his years of experience in Casanare and Guayana, were preaching in the Indian language; using Christian natives to act as go-betweens; presenting gifts of hatchets, machetes, beads, knives, and fishhooks; and enticing the Indians to settle down by offering them good land, tools, and medical care. Thus, he concluded, "with benefits, softness and practical shows of love, are won those earthly wills."[44]

The acquisition of European goods and protection from their enemies prompted many Indian groups to accept missionary authority temporarily, but they returned to their old life when these needs were satisfied. In 1737 a vexed Franciscan noted that as soon as hatchets, machetes, and tools were exhausted, the Indians left the reductions. "The priest may flatter them with love and affection, but all is reduced to a gift."[45] In 1661 the Jesuit Juan Fernández Pedroche assembled as many as one hundred Tunebos in a town, only to find that they would disappear overnight.[46] A year later the Jirara and Airico Indians in Tame and Macaguane agreed to accept the Jesuits if they would defend them from the encomenderos and guarantee that they would not have to pay tribute. Once Father Antonio Monteverde had organized Tame, his work was threatened variously by an angry Jirara cacique named Castaño, a Tunebo medicine man, and a mestizo named Hernando Ortiz, "a man of bad customs and twisted ways." When, in 1683, the Audiencia ordered the Tame Indians to pay tribute, they rebelled. At the appearance of the corregidor, they fled to the wilderness and successfully repulsed with arrows two Spanish expeditions that came in pursuit. The fugitives were plotting to burn Tame to the ground, when some deaths in their ranks filled them with fear. In the end they submitted once again to the priest, now P. Felipe Gómez. Similarly, in 1696, incited by their shaman, the Indians of Macaguane burned the house of the missionaries.[47]

The antagonism of the encomenderos and the local royal authorities toward the missionaries generated widespread violence. When the Jesuits returned to Casanare, in 1661, they learned that doña Serafina de Orozco was asserting her rights as encomendero over all the Achaguas, reduced or not. The governor of Santiago de las Atalayas, Pedro Ordoñez y Vargas (1656–72), threatened to raid the missions to seize slaves, although he eventually gave up his plan.[48] Finally, Estéban Sánchez Chamorro, nephew of another governor and vecino of San José de Cravo, nourished a consuming hatred after the Jesuits had prevented him from taking slaves and had obtained an order from the President of the New Kingdom forcing him to return to her husband an Achagua woman he had seized. Sánchez Chamorro caused so much trouble that Egües ordered him to leave Casanare, but after Egües's death he returned and continued to molest the reductions.[49]

In the Augustinian portion of Casanare, some Achaguas fled an encomienda held by Captain Agustín García Rato in the 1660s and hid in the jungle. Promising that they would not have to return to García, a missionary convinced them to join the reduction at Iximena, where they lived peacefully for ten years. Then, in 1767, García claimed the Indians as his own, an appeal upheld by authorities in Santiago de las Atalayas and later by the Audiencia. Reluctantly the Augustinians handed over the Indians. In 1687 they reported that slave hunters had nearly destroyed their missions in Casanare.[50]

The situation was no better in the Llanos of San Juan and San Martín. In 1675 Franciscan Felipe Lozano wrote his provincial that the vecinos of San Juan treated the Indians so badly that they had almost been exterminated. "Around here no one pays attention to the royal guidelines because they have only monetary penalties, and they laugh at them because there is no one to enforce them."[51] The arrival of a new Governor determined to place in encomiendas all the Indians who were *vacos* (yet unclaimed) strengthened the hand of the vecinos. When the neophytes of Anime burned the church and fled, the governor ordered the misssionaries to help organize an entrada to seize the fugitives and divide them among the settlers. The Franciscans were appalled by the governor's demand and asked the Audiencia for permission to leave the region as long as he remained. In November 1675 the Audiencia denied their request, but did fine the governor and order him to aid the Franciscans in their work.[52]

The Guahibos were a constant menace. Rivero wrote that, having no villages of fields of their own, they wandered like "the gypsies in Spain," taking what they wanted from the other tribes.[53] The missionaries could not intimidate these great hunters and archers, who raided the Achaguas and Sálivas to capture slaves. In 1668, for example, Guahibos led by a cacique named Bacacore besieged for a month the Jesuit mission of San Joaquín de Atanare, located on a tributary of the Orinoco. Even after Bacacore was defeated, his followers did not give up. Their repeated attacks forced the missionaries to leave the site and to incorporate the Indians of San Joaquín de Atanare with those at San Salvador del Puerto.[54] Throughout the Llanos, Spanish and Indians alike regarded the Guahibo as the most dangerous tribe, and Rivero credited them with substantially reducing the Achagua population by 1720.

Often the Guahibo attacks were instigated by the infamous Caribs, peoples of a language group that included a number of different tribes living in the Guiana highlands and on the Atlantic coast and islands. Before European contact, the Caribs had mixed raiding with trading to obtain agricultural products. They seldom risked direct confrontation with other groups. Considering themselves a superior people, they preferred to establish alliances through marriage and became aggressors when these alliances broke down. In the seventeenth century, the Dutch, English, and French began to supply the Caribs with guns and material goods in exchange for slaves.

An increase of Jesuit activity on the Orinoco River further heightened their aggressive inclinations. Realizing that the missionaries were determined to stop the slave trade, the Caribs declared all out war on the reductions, abetted by their European customers, who furnished weapons to combat the guards posted in missions and sometimes even traveled with them, dressed as Indians.[55] Their offensive halted the first effort of the Jesuits to expand in the Orinoco. In 1692 P. Manual Pérez informed his provincial that there would be no missions until the Caribs could be contained, for they, "insolent for having committed so many hostilities without being punished, have made themselves owners of all the Orinoco and all the Indians obey them."[56]

To curb the Carib menace, the crown assigned the first detachment of soldiers to the Llanos in 1681 to protect the Jesuits and reduce Indians in Guiana. In 1693 it increased the original six-man force to twenty-five, whose salaries were paid by the corregidor of the Partido de los Llanos.[57] In 1717 the king issued a cedula directing the president of the Audiencia of Santa Fe to augment the salaries of men serving in the escoltas to equal the wages of the soldiers in Cartagena and Santa Marta. In 1753 he boosted the force to forty-eight, including a captain and a sergeant. Each soldier earned 132 pesos annually and the captain 995 pesos, but payment was frequently delayed. Based in the Orinoco missions, this handful of men was supposed to repel Indian attacks, deter reduced Indians from escaping, and also guard the missions in Casanare and Meta.[58]

The Franciscans were the only other order which seems to have been assigned an escolta. In 1750 the comisario Clemente Forero asked the viceroy to increase the detachment so that every mission would have at least two soldiers.[59] Despite the fact that the soldiers were often the most desperate characters, inclined to desert or to mistreat the natives, the missionaries regarded them as an asset and constantly asked for more.

It is easy enough to understand that men as determined as the missionaries, operating in a lawless environment, resorted to violence themselves when peaceful overtures were rebuffed. Such charges were continually made, but were difficult to prove. In 1692 the governor of the Llanos, Eralo José del Enciso, accused the Jesuits of being lazy, of being concerned with getting wealthy, and of enslaving the Indians. The Audiencia sent three different visitadors to investigate, but in the end they exonerated the missionaries.[60] Enrique Alvarado, who lived with the Jesuits in their Guayana missions for several years, alleged that despite all their talk of making entradas with love and persuasion, they routinely reduced the Indians with arms and soldiers. When the Indians tried to escape, they forcefully detained them.[61] Humboldt also reported that the Jesuits, from their missions at Carichana and Atures on the Orinoco, raided independent Indians, sacking and burning their villages and distributing the prisoners among the most distant missions to impede their escape. The practice of abducting Indian children and placing them in the missions seems to have been especially common.[62]

If the missionaries in the Llanos were somewhat successful in limiting the Spanish predations on the Indians, they unwittingly contributed to the disruption of native culture in other ways. Mission Indians were more frequently exposed to disease; in the seventeenth century the reduced neophytes suffered at least ten epidemics. Other villages were displaced by forced moves into reductions or by flight from mission activity. The priests restricted the freedom of their wards to hunt and fish, exposing them to malnutrition. A low birthrate was prevalent throughout the missions, as Indian women showed a reluctance to have children. The missionaries were aware of a general and serious population decline through the seventeenth and eighteenth centuries, but were powerless to modify the factors that contributed to it. By the time of the Wars of Independence, the Indian groups that survived were profoundly altered as a result of direct contact with settlers and missionaries.[63]

The priest, on securing the consent of some Indians to be baptized, turned to the task of organizing a town. Usually he selected a site near a river which afforded fertile land and made communication with other settlements possible. If the original choice proved to be undesirable, he moved the town to a better place without much ceremony, and high mobility was characteristic of all the reductions. The first house built by the Indians was for the missionary, who used it as a residence and church. As the community grew, the Indians would construct a proper church out of *bahareque* (walls of sticks interwoven with reeds and covered with mud) and palms, or just palms. The decoration of the church with the ornaments, statues, pictures, and bells required by the Catholic faith was a matter of pride and was achieved over a period of years.[64]

The Jesuit missions followed a classic design. Around the central plaza stood the church, government house, public granaries, and the priest's house. Streets laid at right angles stretched out from the plaza. The Indians built their houses, sometimes large enough for several families, out of local materials. The men wore linen breeches and cotton shirts made like a poncho, with a hole in the center for the head. Women dressed in a kind of shift that hung from their shoulders, leaving the arms uncovered and reaching the middle of the leg.[65] In the Franciscan reductions, the

Indians lived near their fields during the week and returned to the town on weekends to fulfill their religious obligations. They wore garments similar in design to those in Casanare but fashioned out of palm cloth.[66]

To instruct the Indians in the faith, missionaries drew upon methods developed in the doctrinas. They studied the Indian languages and prepared dictionaries and grammars so that they could teach the Indians the catechism in their own tongue as well as the Latin phrases of the mass. After explaining the essential doctrines for salvation, they baptized the Indians on the supposition that their rudimentary understanding would be perfected over the course of years by enforced attendance at doctrinal classes and participation in church ceremonies.[67]

Music played an important role in the rituals, and music schools were common in the towns. The Indians learned solfeggio in order to sing in choirs and mastered such diverse instruments as harp, violin, trumpet, flute and bassoon. They belonged to cofradías, sodalities of men and women, which celebrated special holidays with great fervor. In his sermons the priest would exhort the Indians to take the sacraments often. He took pride in their growth in the faith. Rivero reported that the Achaguas of San Salvador, Pauto, Tame, and Macaguane attended mass daily. Many confessed each week. "But what is still more admirable is to see the solemnity with which they celebrate their fiestas and give praise to the true God with the skill of their song and of musical instruments, hearing in our towns, group music with voices converted into choirs like those of angels to praise God."[68]

To prepare their wards to be vassals of the king of Spain, the missionaries selected Indians to occupy the political posts found in the Spanish towns. Each reduction had native captains, lieutenants, and sergeants, distinguishable by their insignia of office, and *fiscales,* who acted as policemen.[69] They assisted the priest in keeping order, by noting absences at church services and acts of idleness or drunkenness. Rivero wrote that on Saturday afternoons the neophytes assembled in two lines outside the house of the priest. Before they entered the church to say the rosary, the *fiscal* would read out the faults committed during the week and administer punishment, which might be whipping, internment, or confinement in the stocks. Rivero asserted that the Indian officials were "so vigilant and severe without pardoning anyone, that they might be a model of many ancient republics."[70]

The Indians were eager learners. The missionaries taught them to read and write. In San Salvador del Puerto the Achaguas composed several books in their own language, including two treatises on aspects of the

Christian faith, and they enjoyed plays written in Achagua.[71] In craft shops they learned how to manage cables, saws, forges, and looms. Gumilla wrote that an effective way to start a new town was to get a blacksmith to assemble a forge, because the Indians wanted to learn this skill in order to make the tools that they prized.[72] Indians of the plains were fascinated by the opportunity to learn how to weave cotton thread to make cloth. Some became expert in carpentry, sculpture, smelting, and tailoring, the nature of the crafts depending on the location of the mission. Most highly skilled were the spinners and weavers in Támara and Morcote, who produced textiles as fine as the printed cotton cloth *(ruán)* of Castile and Quito.[73]

Agriculture was basic to the missions. Each reduction had a common field, the *campo de Díos,* which the Indians worked to meet community needs and to provide for widows, children, and the disabled. The harvest was stored in the public granary and the surplus sold to surrounding communities, in order to purchase tools, seeds, clothes, and other items not made at the mission. A smaller field, called the *campo del hombre,* was divided into lots and worked by individuals without the right to sell the harvest, although the harvest belonged to them. Horses and plows were public property. All the neophytes received an equal quantity of goods. The communal holding of wealth broke down their aversion to work.[74] This arrangement functioned well for the Jesuits, who buttressed it with efficiently run haciendas. It was less successful for the Franciscans in the Llanos of San Juan and San Martín who, unlike the other communities, repudiated any form of endowment and invested in the missions only what they earned or what was given to them.[75] In 1769 the Franciscan comisario reported that in the reductions around San Juan, "the Indians and missionaries alike have nothing more to eat than *casabe* [manioc bread] and plátano and many times they do not have meat."[76]

Royal orders exempted the Indians from paying tribute for the first ten years they lived in the reductions. In practice this privilege was sometimes extended much longer. By 1761 Betoyes, Patute, Macuco, Surimena, and Casimena were still exempt, while neophytes in San Salvador, Tame, and Macaguane had paid tribute since 1685 in *quiripa* or in kind.[77] All mission Indians paid a variety of ecclesiastial taxes called *estipendios, primicias, obvenciones,* and *limosnas* to support their priests and cofradías, using products raised in subsistence plots—maize, yuca, and plátanos. In the forest areas they collected pineapples, cacao, sassafras, coffee, and vanilla. In more temperate zones they cultivated vegetables and made pottery and baskets. At Medina and La Sal, where there were salt wells along the river, the Indians collected wood and boiled water to extract the vital substance. Oviedo wrote that they paid their primicias with money they received from selling the salt, since they had no cultivated fields from which to draw their income.[78]

While the Franciscan missions failed to develop beyond this subsistence level, the towns run by the Augustinians prospered from the production of cotton textiles. The climate of Támara, Ten, Morcote, Labranzagrande, Pisba, and Paya favored the cultivation of cotton. Docile, humble, and hardworking Indians planted and harvested the fiber, which they spun into thread to pay their cofradías and to finance their fiestas. In Morcote they made white and striped cotton blankets, handkerchiefs, banners, and many other special textiles. Specialities of Támara were blue-and-white-striped cotton bedspreads and handkerchiefs "as fine as any of those coming from Quito and much sought after by people of distinction."[79] The high quality of their cloth made Morcote and Támara the most prosperous towns on the mission frontier.

Historians sometimes attribute textile manufacturing to the Jesuit reductions, but cotton was important only in Manare, where the Indians also made earthen and china jars and other pottery.[80] The wealth of the Jesuit missions derived primarily from the five haciendas in Casanare and three subordinate hatos on the Meta River. An official known as the *procurador* administered all these estates within a single unit. They were devoted to cattle and horses, although at Caribabare and Tocaría sugarcane was cultivated and processed.

The procurador, who resided at the *procuraría* at the Hacienda Caribabare, differed from the superior of the Casanare-Meta missions, in that he was responsible for material rather than spiritual needs.[81] He exercised complete autonomy over financial matters and worked to find markets for the hacienda products, a task which kept him in contact with both local merchants and those of more distant regions. On the individual haciendas, brother coadjutors supervised daily operations. They were assisted by mayordomos and *caporales,* who trained and directed the workers. Indians from the reductions served as mayordomos, vaqueros, and peons, in exchange for food and clothing.[82]

Black slaves, employed in large numbers on Jesuit haciendas in other parts of New Granada, were not used much in the Llanos. The order did transfer slaves from their Hacienda Lengupa, near Tunja, to operate the sugar mills at Caribabare and Tocaría and to make *aguardiente* (sugar cane liquor) and *panela* (raw brown sugar). On these estates blacks served as caporales and household servants, but the task of tending cattle—seasonal and physically undemanding—offered too many opportunities for escape. The Jesuits found it more economical and less dangerous to hire Indians and mestizos instead. At Caribabare the entire black work force numbered seventeen males, eight females, and thirty children, and there were no slaves at all at Apiay, Patute, and Cravo.[83]

The procurador supplied all the missionaries with food and clothing. At the warehouse at Caribabare, he stored the hides, tallow, animal byproducts, sugar, and aguardiente produced on the estates. To obtain other provisions, he traded with a wide variety of sources. He exchanged meat and sugar with Morcote, Chita, and Támara for cotton thread and cloth. He sent horses and mules to Barinas, until the increasing herds there eliminated the demand. During the reign of Viceroy Sebastián de Eslava (1739–49) the Jesuits shipped cattle to Santa Fe, although rival economic interests in the highlands eventually ended this practice. Tools, crude iron, and other items originally introduced from Martinque were transported through Guiana and along the Orinoco River. An inventory of the contents of the warehouse in 1767 listed bolts of cloth from Barcelona, León, and Rouen, French lace, and goods from Brittany, as well as blankets and linen made in Socorro, Vélez, and Morcote.[84]

The importance of the haciendas to the reductions and the regional economy should not be underestimated. Income from the estates paid the missionaries' expenses—the costs of entradas, gifts to attract the Indians, clothing, messenger service, visitas. From the hacienda herds, cattle and horses could be separated to begin hatos for new missions.[85] The warehouse served as a general store for all the individuals of the Llanos, who went there for provisions. Alvarado wrote, "I saw *vecinos* of Santiago de las Atalayas and others from the Llanos do business with the missionaries and procuradors since the country is so agreeable, the cattle have multiplied and they are happy to sell."[86]

How much profit the haciendas returned to the Jesuits is more difficult to assess. In *Las haciendas de los jesuítas en el Nuevo Reino de Granada,* Germán Colmenares investigated the management of over eighty estates devoted to cacao, sugar, and cattle operated by the Jesuits in New Granada and Quito. Among the twenty-two cattle ranches he analyzed, Caribabare, with its herd of 10,606, ranked second in size only to the gigantic Hacienda Doyma, in the Magdalena Valley, with 14,229 head. Cravo's herd of 5,964 gave it fifth place.[87] In a comparison of the net income of fifty haciendas of all types between 1765 and 1767, Colmenares found that Caribabare showed the greatest profit, earning 8,898 pesos over a nineteen-month period as compared with Doyma's profit of 912 pesos over seventeen months.[88] The Colombian historian concluded that as a whole the haciendas in New Granada were worth only a fraction of the Jesuit estates in Peru and Mexico. Nevertheless, the sum of their wealth was more than any private fortune in the viceroyalty, and the scale of their operations in the Llanos outdistanced any of the private ranches run by Spaniards.[89]

By mid-eighteenth century the mission frontier had stabilized throughout the Llanos. The religious communities had incorporated the Indians into Spanish rule, protected them from the encomenderos, and formed a line of defense against the Caribs, French, and Dutch. In the Llanos of San Juan and San Martín, the Franciscans had sustained their presence over one hundred years by accommodating the nomadic ways of the Indians and sharing with them their hand-to-mouth existence. Little is known about the Recoleto missions in Casanare. The Augustinians were preparing to turn over all their textile-producing towns except Támara to secular priests. In the plains and along the Meta River lay the Jesuit reductions and haciendas, an empire of sorts which historians have extolled as a kind of primitive utopia, where the missionaries with their heads and hearts created a "small Llanero democracy" about which modern socialists can only dream.[90]

But trouble was already brewing. For years, since the presidency of Egües, royal policy had favored the mission over white settlements as the best way to populate, defend, and develop the eastern frontier. The crown's financial, military, and moral support of the religious communities, however token, was more than that for private citizens. Resentment smoldered among the vecinos of Pore, Santiago de las Atalayas, and Chire, who believed that the Jesuits were making a fortune by abusing their privileges. Their complaints fell upon deaf ears, until the arrival of the Royal Boundary Commission, in 1756, during the reign of Viceroy Don José Solís Folch de Cardón (1753-61), brought to New Granada an articulate, outspoken critic of Jesuit operations, Eugenio de Alvarado. His petitions to Solís on behalf of the commission did little immediate harm to the Jesuits but prompted the viceroy to take a new interest in state development of communications and defense in the Llanos.

On January 13, 1750, Spain and Portugal signed the Treaty of Madrid, a secret pact designed to supersede the Treaty of Tordesillas of 1494 by redrawing the boundary between their South American empires. The agreement created one mixed commission to survey disputed territory in the Río de la Plata and another to work north of latitude 16°, in the Marañón and Orinoco wilderness. Ferdinand VI's minister of state, José de Carvajal, appointed José de Iturriaga to head the Spanish northern commission and Colonel Eugenio de Alvarado, José de Solano, and Antonio de Urrutia to act as his subalterns.[91]

In 1754 the commissioners arrived in Cumaná, Venezuela. Making their way through Guiana up the Raudal River, a tributary of the Atures, they lived with the Jesuits in the Orinoco missions for two years, without making contact with their Portuguese counterparts on the Río Negro. By December 1756 they had consumed their supplies and were at the point of death when Iturriaga decided to inform Viceroy Solís of their plight. He sent José de Solano with petitions to Santa Fe asking not only for food and financial aid, but also for authority to take control of the escolta attached to the Orinoco missions, since altercations between the Jesuits and the commissioners had already occurred.

Solano struck out for the capital in February 1757. His journey took him up the Meta River to Apiay, where at the Jesuit hacienda he secured pack animals to complete his trip over the Cordillera. When Solano reached Santa Fe, in April, the viceroy received him with enthusiasm. He contributed 130,000 pesos from the royal treasury to support the work of the commission, but refused to grant to Iturriaga control of the escolta assigned to the Jesuits.[92]

Solano returned to the Orinoco in December 1757. During the next two years, the commissioners founded three settlements—San Fernando de Atabapo, at the confluence of the Guaviare and Orinoco rivers, Ciudad Real, and Real Corona, to defend the river against the Dutch and Caribs. They tried to cultivate quinine, cacao, and cinnamon and wrangled endlessly with the Jesuits, but they made little headway in surveying the border. In April 1759 Iturriaga dispatched Eugenio de Alvarado to Santa Fe to request further assistance from Solís. Distinguished from Solano by his political acumen and entrepreneurial initiative, Alvarado was also more open in his hatred of the Jesuits. During his several months' stay in the capital, he barraged Solís with petitions calling for increased support to the commission, reduction of the Jesuit role as defenders of the eastern border, and colonization of the Llanos of San Juan and San Martín.[93]

To cover the immediate needs of the commissioners, Alvarado asked the viceroy for an annual subsidy of 10,000 pesos. He also urged him to improve the supply lines from Santa Fe to the Orinoco. Alvarado believed that the cities of San Martín and San Juan should be the principal staging areas for shipping supplies to the Orinoco and Guiana. He asked Solís to appoint José Morales, the expedition's cosmographer, governor of San

Martín, in order that he might supervise construction of boats to carry flour, meat, and other food down the Ariari and Guayabero rivers, a request which Solís quickly granted. Alvarado arranged to buy for the commission all the cattle that might be brought to San Martín each January, and while in Santa Fe he contracted with a merchant, don Juan de Espada, to purvey the flour required by the commissioners.[94]

Dependable communication to the Llanos entailed improving the road between the capital and San Martín. On July 1, 1759, Alvarado implored the viceroy to sponsor this project, explaining that the present trail followed the edge of a sheer precipice from Cáqueza to the Llanos. The road was risky in both wet and dry seasons, obstructed by waterfalls and requiring travelers to cross and recross the Río Negro—"the dragon in the road to Apiay." As an engineer, Alvarado offered his services to open up an older trail "which for being forgotten is new" that left Cáqueza to descend the Cordillera between Oriente and Mediodía, emerging between Apiay and San Martín, at a place called Sabanagrande. Besides being less dangerous, this route would cut three days of travel time. As a clinching argument, Alvarado promised Solís that the work would quickly repay the royal treasury by reducing shipping costs and enabling twice as many of the cattle presently sent to Santa Fe from the Llanos to survive their exhausting trip.[95] To demonstrate the practicality of his plan, Alvarado, even before Solís could approve it, engaged José Nieto, a vecino of Cáqueza, to hire manual laborers. He reported that on September 4, pack-animal owners in Cáqueza had met and pledged to offer regular service on the new trail, when it was finished, between December and March, at a cost of eight pesos per mule, one of which they would contribute to a fund for road maintenance.[96]

Alvarado took no pains to hide his dislike of the Jesuits. In 1767 he would write, at the request of the conde de Aranda, a damning report calling for their expulsion.[97] In 1759 he accused them of deliberately obstructing the work of the commission by opposing navigation of the Ariari and by numerous other actions. He urged Solís to diminish Jesuit power and shore up the eastern frontier by removing the fifteen-man escolta and its captain, Don Juan Bonalde, from the Orinoco missions, where they were largely inactive, and relocating them in San Fernando de Atabapo, where they could protect the towns founded in the Upper Orinoco by the commission. Garrisons already stationed in the Lower Orinoco would complement Bonalde's troops in their new location, while troops could be sent from Caracas to the Middle Orinoco, and from Maracaibo to the Upper Orinoco and the Llanos. As another defensive move,

Alvarado proposed that Solís create a sixty-man militia based in San Martín, which would protect the Franciscans and white settlers from the Indians.[98] A letter from Governor José Morales supported this plan, stating that while the Indians were adept at using firearms, the vecinos of San Juan and San Martín had only knives for weapons and lived so scattered about with their cattle and fields that even a small Indian force could overpower them.[99]

To circumvent the Jesuits further, Alvarado put forward a scheme originating with Iturriaga, which called for colonization of the plains and the Orinoco. In a letter dated November 20, 1759, Alvarado suggested to Solís that he order the corregidors of Tunja, Sogamoso, and Santiago de las Atalayas to arrest all vagabonds and neer-do-wells and, with due precautions to keep them from fleeing, transport them in groups to San Martín, where they could be located in colonies.[100] Since strong, healthy pioneers were needed, Alvarado stipulated that the men should be from eighteen to thirty-five years old and the women from fifteen to thirty, and that they should not be criminals nor have been imprisoned for atrocious crimes. Solís's response to Alvarado is not known, but he did not act on the suggestion. Nevertheless, the plan was the first to call for Spanish immigration to the Llanos since the time of Jiménez de Quesada.

The work of the royal boundary commissioners, who had direct and secret orders from King Ferdinand VI, was one of the major issues during Solís's reign. From the beginning the viceroy had generously supported their activities, and throughout 1759 he gave careful consideration to Alvarado's petitions. In his *Relación de mando* he reported that he had paid the commissioners ten thousand pesos each June and thirty thousand each October.[101] He appointed José Morales governor of San Martín and gave Alvarado permission to build the road from Cáqueza to that city, disbursing money from the royal hacienda. He further ordered cattle drivers using the road to pay a tax of one real per head into a special fund for repairing damage done by floods and rain. Completed in 1760, the new road was undoubtedly an improvement over the old one, but it does not seem to have greatly increased trade or communication between the Llanos and the highlands.[102]

Solís moved with caution on those requests which masked Alvarado's campaign against the Jesuits. In a letter to the colonel of January 6, 1760, he pointed out that repeated royal cedulas had conceded escoltas to the missions and that he could not countermand them without consulting with the king.[103] On the other hand, he did bolster defense of the east by ordering soldiers sent from Maracaibo to Barinas, from Caracas to the Orinoco, and from Cumaná to the missions, and in his *Relación* he warned that it might be necessary to discharge soldiers in the escoltas "because they do not perform well, are most costly and inconvenient for other reasons."[104] Solís sent the governor of the Llanos in Santiago the much needed weapons to repel Indian attacks, even though that action depleted the supply remaining in the Sala de Armas in Santa Fe. He gave Alvarado sixty-six guns and permission to organize a militia company in San Martín.[105] Finally he ordered the oidor don Antonio Berástegui to make a visita de tierra in the Llanos of San Juan and San Martín, the first to be carried out there in more than a century.[106] These policies, which demonstrated that Solís was aware of the potential economic and strategic importance of the Llanos as well as his unwillingness to be dragged into the quarrel between the commissioners and the Jesuits, reveal him to be, in the words of his biographer Demetrio Ramos, a "prudent man and good governor."[107]

The royal boundary commissioners might have stimulated further interest in the Llanos had not the death of Ferdinand VI, on August 10, 1759, brought in its wake a cedula suspending their activities. In 1760 the Treaty of Madrid was annulled, and the crown ordered the commissioners to return to Spain.[108] After six years they had made slight progress in redrawing the border with Brazil, and besides exploring various parts of Guayana, the Orinoco, and the Amazon and founding some ephemeral towns, they left behind little of permanence besides a voluminous archive of reports and communications.[109] For a few more years, the missionaries would dominate the eastern frontier unmolested, but the criticisms articulated by the commissioners against the Jesuits did not go unheard in Madrid. In 1767 the expulsion of the order throughout the Spanish Empire heralded a major reorganization of missions in the Llanos and opened a turbulent era of consolidation and change.

4 *Crisis in Casanare, 1767 and 1781*
The Expulsion of the Jesuits and the Comunero Revolt

In the second half of the eighteenth century, the Bourbon Enlightenment spawned readjustments in the Spanish Empire which had important consequences for the Provincia de los Llanos. The questioning spirit exhibited by the royal boundary commissioners was characteristic of the reign of Charles III (1759–88), whose far-reaching reforms simultaneously revitalized imperial rule and sparked the discontent that would lead to its demise. In particular the decision to expel the Jesuits, in 1767, disrupted the missions in Casanare and along the Meta. Fourteen years later, Bourbon financial policies had even greater repercussions. Creoles and Indians in the Provincia de los Llanos joined inhabitants of other regions of New Granada in a violent protest known as the Comunero Revolt against the imposition of new taxes. Archbishop-Viceroy Caballero y Góngora's able leadership eventually banked the flame of discontent, but creole frustration continued. These two crises had little impact on the geographically isolated Llanos of San Juan and San Martín, but the inhabitants of Casanare, linked since the days of Jiménez de Quesada with the fortunes of Tunja, were both passive and active participants in the events that heralded the twilight of Spanish rule.

As we have seen in the previous chapter, by the 1760s the Jesuits had outstripped four other religious orders active in the Llanos to control approximately 7,620 Indians in eleven missions in Casanare and on the Meta River. They managed eight haciendas with forty-five thousand head of cattle and nearly four thousand horses, where they also raised sugarcane, bananas, fruit, coffee, and rice. Along the Orinoco in Guiana they operated a separate system of reductions and haciendas, with 2,200 neophytes. They promoted trade with Santa Fe and Guayana via the Meta and Orinoco rivers. The Procuraría at Hacienda Caribabare served as the commercial hub of the economy of the Provincia de los Llanos.

Given the extent of this empire, it is not surprising that the Jesuits' success vexed the local officials and settlers. The most eloquent exposé of the order's activities in the Llanos, however, the *Informe reservado,* was written in 1767 by an outsider, the energetic Colonel Eugenio de Alvarado. As second-in-command of the Royal Boundary Commission, Alvarado lived with the Jesuits in their Guayana missions between 1754 and 1760. The fathers provided the commissioners with supplies as well as housing, but from the beginning, Alvarado was convinced that they deliberately blocked the work of surveying the border with Brazil. When asked by Charles III's minister, the conde de Aranda, to inform the crown about the conduct of the Jesuits on the La Plata, Marañón, and Orinoco rivers and to state whether their religion and service to the king justified their stay, he responded with alacrity.

Composed of nine chapters, the *Informe reservado* combines a history of the Jesuits in Casanare and the Orinoco with a critical analysis of the internal organization of their missions and haciendas. Alvarado's numerous objections to the order fell into four general categories. First he argued that the Jesuits exploited the Indians instead of civilizing them. Despite what they wrote in their books about peaceful persuasion, the fathers themselves made armed entradas into the wilderness to capture neophytes. They ruled these wards as if they were sheep and made them work like slaves. On the cattle hatos they compensated their Indian peons in kind rather than paying them wages.[1] The great accomplishments of the Jesuits were more legend than fact, fueled by their own duplicity. In the Llanos they had not begun a new town since 1749. Instead, they moved existing reductions to new locations and changed their names to give the impression that many more existed than those actually established.[2]

Second Alvarado claimed that the Jesuits victimized the Spanish colonists. They took away Indians that rightfully belonged to the encomenderos. They prevented them from living in the Spanish towns and shielded them from the authority of the corregidors. The order's use of Indian peons on the ranches took away jobs from the whites, and in the vicinity of the haciendas, the Spanish obeyed the Jesuits rather than the king's officials.[3]

Third the colonel asserted that the Jesuits were disloyal to the King and constituted a state within a state. The fathers were not subject to the rule of the bishops, their principal allegiance was to the pope. They controlled the escoltas which obeyed only their orders, and their commerce was prejudicial to the viceroyalty.[4] Finally Alvarado charged that the Jesuits intentionally opposed the boundary commissioners by urging Indians to flee from them and by obstructing their use of the Meta River. He concluded that God's providence had reserved the question of the border with Brazil to be the "touchstone by which the King could learn that it is not convenient for His service or for the Catholic religion that the Jesuit fathers remain there." They should be expelled from the Llanos of Casanare because "they have not been useful to God, to the King in the Reyno de Santa Fe, its Llanos and the banks of the Meta and Orinoco Rivers."[5]

To what extent Alvarado spoke for the inhabitants of the Llanos is not known, but his report struck the right note in Madrid, where the conde de Aranda and the conde de Compomanes were collecting similar data from all parts of the empire. The swelling opposition to the order in Bourbon Europe was a result of Enlightenment philosophy, renewed religious nationalism, and resistance to papal authority.[6] Jesuit refusal to surrender the Guaraní missions to the Portuguese provoked the War of the Seven Reductions in 1754–56. Their conduct in that conflict and allegations of their involvement in an unsuccessful attempt to assassinate King Joseph, in 1758, emboldened the marquis de Pombal to expel them from Portugal and Brazil in 1759. In Spain the immediate provocation was the widely held belief that the Jesuits had instituted popular riots in Madrid, in 1766, against the minister of finance, the marquis de Esquilache. Campomanes and Aranda recommended expulsion on the grounds of conspiracy against the government, and Charles III signed the decree on February 27, 1767. In the following months officials expedited the order throughout the empire. By the end of the year, some twenty-five hundred Jesuits had been forced out of America in a dramatic and devastating move by the crown to reassert royal authority over the Church.[7]

The arrival of Charles III's decree in Santa Fe, on July 7, 1767, presented Viceroy Pedro Messía de la Cerda with the gravest crisis of his administration (1761–72). In addition to their missions in the Llanos and Guayana, the Jesuits ran haciendas throughout New Granada. They administered the prestigious Universidad Javeriana and the Colegio de San Bartolomé in the capital and twelve other colleges that enrolled over five thousand students.[8] Education of the creole elite was almost entirely in their hands. A practicing Catholic and friend of the Jesuits, the viceroy was well aware of their extraordinary influence in the colonial economy and culture. Nevertheless, with the collaboration of the fiscal protector of the Audiencia, Francisco Moreno y Escandón, he executed the order, sending secret instructions to officials in each of the cities where the Jesuits resided.

On August 1 specially appointed judges in Santa Fe notified the Jesuits that they were under arrest and confiscated all their possessions—a process repeated in the next few days in Tunja, Honda, Pamplona, Popayán, Cartagena, Mompos, and Santiago de las Atalayas. The Jesuits left by groups from the different cities, some going first to Mompos on the Magdalena and then to Cartagena and others directly to Maracaibo, where they boarded ships for their final destination, the Papal States. The government reassigned their missions to other religious orders and placed all confiscated property, or temporalities, including churches, colleges, houses, religious objects, mines, and haciendas under the jurisdiction of the Junta de Temporalidades—a committee composed of the viceroy, the archbishop, the *oidor decano,* and the fiscal. By the end of November, 262 priests, coadjutors, and novices had been expelled, extinguishing the work of the order in New Granada, Venezuela, Panama and Santo Domingo.[9]

In his *Historia eclesiástica y civil,* José Manuel Groot vividly describes the expulsion of the missionaries from the Provincia de los Llanos. The governor, don Francisco Domínguez de Tejada, served as *juez ejecutor* (official with the power to seize property). He complied with the order with an enthusiasm equal to that of Moreno y Escandón. He traveled through the Llanos accompanied by notaries, paid for out of his own pocket. He personally took the inventories of the haciendas, filling twenty-two notebooks of judicial procedures because he did not have a scribe. He gathered together all the Jesuits in Casanare and Meta at Tocaría and engaged mules to take them to Maracaibo, where they would join the nine fathers evicted from the Orinoco. "After all of this, he went to Santa Fe to present his expense account, which totalled more than 1,500 pesos, which he handed over to the King, manifesting that he was well paid and satisfied with having served His Majesty."[10]

The crown divided the ex-Jesuit missions among three other religious orders. The Dominicans received San Salvador del Puerto, Tame, Patute, Macaguane and Betoyes. The Franciscans took Santiago de Manare (formerly known as Pauto), Concepción de Nuestra Señora de Guanaca (Güicán), and Jiramena. The other Meta missions—Surimena, Macuco, and Casimena, went to the Recoletos. Hatos specifically attached to the reductions, such as those of Surimena, Macuco, Casimena, Manare, and Jiramena, were awarded to the order which received the missions. The Dominicans ran Cravo, Tocaría, and Caribabare for a few months, with disastrous consequences. By 1769 these estates joined Patute and Apiay under the aegis of the Junta de Temporalidades.

The junta was eager to sell these estates, but there were few buyers with enough capital, even after a decree of November 8, 1769, permitted the division of the properties and others, in 1772, extended the terms of payment, allowing the estates to be sold through long-term mortgages called *censos*.[11] Despite these concessions, most purchasers were unable to pay off their mortgages. When they defaulted, the junta repossessed the estates and auctioned them off once again. Apiay, sold to Nicolás Bernal in 1767 for 4,200 pesos, was later transferred to Juan José de Rojas, for the same amount, and in 1781 sold for a third time to Antonio Romero, for 6,342 pesos.[12] Tocaría, purchased in 1771 by Felix Luís Bermúdez, a vecino of Tunja, for 35,025 pesos, was resold in 1775 to José Joaquín Lasso de la Vega, for 15,500 pesos.[13] Don Pedro de Castro y Lemus bought Cravo for 18,295 pesos, but defaulted on payment in 1778. The Junta de Temporalidades eventually sold it again, in 1788, to Agustín Justo de Medina, for 24,461 pesos.[14] Juan Gómez Cabeza de Vaca purchased the largest of the estates, Caribabare, in 1775 for 18,050 pesos. When he went bankrupt, in 1790, the junta had him arrested. It assessed the value of Caribabare at 20,806 pesos, but in 1794 accepted Don Juan Felipe Carvajal's offer of 15,500 pesos.[15] In 1800 Francisco Larrarte and Domingo Benites together bought the hacienda from Carvajal for 21,500 pesos.[16] Regardless of ownership, however, the crown continued to assign income from the estates to support the missions. Thus the Dominicans annually received one hundred pesos for each of their reductions, and when the Capuchins arrived, in 1789, to work in Cuiloto (present-day Arauca), it was this revenue that helped to pay their expenses.[17]

In the Llanos as well as in the rest of New Granada, the expulsion of the Jesuits took place swiftly and without popular outcry. Historians have found this lack of protest remarkable, especially when they note that the enforcement of the decree in New Spain and La Plata provoked strong demonstrations of public support on behalf of the Jesuits. Part of the explanation lies in Messía de la Cerda's adroit handling of the situation. The viceroy followed the instructions from the conde de Aranda to the letter. He impressed his subordinates with the seriousness of the decree and the necessity for immediate action. The speed, efficiency, and secrecy by which the Jesuits were ousted prevented their supporters from coming to their defense. The Jesuits themselves did not attempt to rouse popular indignation. They submitted loyally to the will of the king. Charles Fleener, whose unpublished dissertation "The Expulsion of the Jesuits from the

Viceroyalty of New Granada, 1767" remains the best summary of the event and its ramifications, adds that in New Granada, as opposed to New Spain and La Plata, there was no accumulation of keenly felt grievances outstanding in 1767, which might have been used by opponents of the expulsion to galvanize popular resistance. Such conditions did not materialize until fourteen years later, in the outbreak of the Comunero Revolt.[18]

Despite its peaceful implementation, Colombian scholars over the years have tended to regard Charles III's decree as "unjust, impolitic, arbitrary and prejudicial to the extreme," a measure which precipitated a decline in education, agriculture, and culture in New Granada.[19] In their *Historia de Colombia,* Henao and Arrubla maintain that "the gravest and most irreparable harm was the ruin of the missions established by those zealous apostles of Christ who left founded and flourishing many towns and villages in the regions of the Meta and the Orinoco."[20] The thesis that the missions in Casanare collapsed after 1767 was first suggested in 1849 by José Antonio Plaza, in *Memorias para la historia de Nueva Granada.* It has been reiterated by the Jesuit apologists J. J. Borda and Hipólito Jerez, by the historians J. M. Groot and Indalecio Liévano Aguirre, and by *pensadores* such as Eduardo Carranza.[21] These authors assert that the Jesuits had converted the Llanos into a "vast emporium of wealth," which their eviction destroyed. The religious orders that took over their missions in 1767 were unable to sustain them because of internal corruption and ineptitude. As a result the cattle herds declined and the Indians ran off to the forest. By the end of the eighteenth century, only wilderness remained where tens of villages had once stood. Civilization in the Llanos, they conclude, suffered a mortal blow from which it has never recovered.

The appeal of this thesis is understandable. It draws support from evidence presented by the viceroys in their *Relaciones del mando* and by nineteenth century historians, especially Groot, whose *Historia eclesiástica y civil* continues to be a key source for this period. It reflects admiration for the proven talents of the Jesuits and offers a plausible explanation for the decline of Casanare in the post-independence years. Nevertheless, in the light of this more comprehensive study of the Llanos before and after 1767, it can no longer go unchallenged. It has already been shown that Jesuit activity in the plains, significant as it was, amounted to something less than "tens of villages" and a "vast emporium of wealth." Likewise, when the record of the religious orders who took over the missions is evaluated against the changing political, economic, and social conditions of the late eighteenth century, it will be seen that while some failed to overcome internal and external obstacles, other communities sustained and even expanded their missions until the outbreak of the Wars of Independence. Before turning to this important question, it will be helpful to look at the second crisis in the highlands that had ramifications for the Llanos, the Comunero Revolt of 1781.

If Charles III's American subjects acquiesced in the expulsion of the Jesuits, Bourbon financial policy was another matter. As the crown attempted to squeeze greater profits from the colonies by adopting so-called free trade and raising taxes, they became less and less willing to pay. Violent opposition was manifest in almost every part of the empire, but particularly in Peru and New Granada, where the appointment of visitadores generales to reform the treasuries and increase revenues intensified the fiscal pressures. In Peru the outburst took the form of an Indian revolt, led by Túpac Amaru, in 1780–81.[22] In New Granada the Comunero Revolt rocked the heartland and spilled out into Casanare.

The principal cause of the crisis was the ruthless procedures initiated by the regent visitador, General Juan Francisco Gutiérrez de Piñeres, whom the crown sent to Santa Fe, in 1779, to raise money for the recently declared war against England. In the absence of the viceroy, Manuel Antonio Flórez (1776–82), who had stationed himself in Cartagena to supervise the defense of that important city, Gutiérrez de Piñeres increased the *alcabala,* or sales tax, to 6 percent. He boosted levies on salt, tobacco, and playing cards (all unpopular government monopolies), and imposed new taxes on cotton cloth. This severe program, which threatened to inflate the prices of foodstuffs and consumer goods and the cost of industry, was made doubly offensive by the harsh methods favored by the tax collectors.[23]

On March 16, 1781, rebellion flared in Socorro, where the regent's policies combined with the recent institution of free trade to threaten what had been a flourishing textile industry. Refusing to pay the new taxes, about six thousand insurgents attacked the government warehouses in the town, drove out the Spanish authorities, and elected their own officers. The initial movement was popular and predominantly creole. The leader was Juan Francisco Berbeo; his subalterns were small traders, farmers, and municipal officials. As the revolt spread to Tunja, Antioquia, Neiva, Pamplona, and Casanare, a number of Indians, encouraged by the example of Túpac Amaru and enraged by the mestizo encroachment on their resguardos, added their support.

By June 2 twenty thousand badly armed but angry people were assembling in the village of Zipaquirá, a day's distance from Santa Fe, clamoring for the suppression of the tobacco monopoly and the abolition of many taxes and the office of visitador general.[24] Thoroughly alarmed, Gutiérrez de Piñeres reactivated the Junta Superior de Tribunales, a standing committee of the Royal Audiencia and the leading representatives of the fiscal administration, to arrange an agreement with the Socorranos before the latter forcefully imposed a settlement by invading the capital. When the chief negotiator for the junta, Archbishop Antonio Caballero y Góngora, arrived in Zipaquirá, he received from Berbeo the *Capitulaciones*—a statement of thirty-five demands calling for administrative reforms, more opportunities for creoles, and better treatment for the Indians.[25] Not wanting the conflict to escalate and being defenseless against the ragged army, on June 6 Caballero y Góngora signed the document, which was approved by the Audiencia on the following day. With victory at hand, Berbeo ordered his followers to disperse and surrendered, along with many of his associates, to the authorities.

His triumph proved fleeting. When news of the treaty reached Cartagena, Viceroy Flórez categorically disavowed it, and on July 6 sent five hundred soldiers to Santa Fe to restore order. Led by the hot-tempered mestizo José Antonio Galán, those Comuneros who had not yet given up continued the struggle until Galán was captured in Onzaga, Santander, on October 13. With order restored, Viceroy Flórez reimposed the hated taxes, and tried and executed Galán, along with three associates, on February 1, 1782. Shortly thereafter he resigned his post to accept a promotion to viceroy of New Spain. By July 1782 the crown had appointed Caballero y Góngora as his successor. One of the first acts of the archbishop-viceroy was to issue, on August 7, a general pardon to all those involved in the revolt.[26] Peace returned but on the terms of the royal authorities, not those of the Comuneros.

Scholars have paid considerable attention to the Comunero Revolt, which stands as the most serious armed protest to occur in New Granada before 1810. While some argue that the Comuneros were reformists, who sought the lowering of taxes without challenging Spain's right to rule, others see them as precursors to political independence; still others argue that the insurrection was a would-be social revolution from below, betrayed by those above. In his prize-winning study *The People and the King,* the late John Phelan took a different tack by asserting that in the long run, the Comuneros did not fail, for once the authorities had reestablished the principle of royal control, they set about making significant concessions to the sources of discontent that prompted the protest.[27]

For Phelan the real nature of this complicated crisis was political and constitutional—a clash between the forces of imperial centralization and colonial decentralization. He demonstrates that the *Capitulaciones* reflected the aspirations of four social groups—nobles, plebeians, Indians, and blacks. He also points out that the insurrection took on a different character in the many regions it affected. In the Llanos creole vecinos attempted to gain their own ends by inciting the Indians, long abused by corregidors and clergy, to rise against their tormentors.[28]

On May 19, nearly two months after the first riots in Socorro, the vecinos of Pore, Santiago de las Atalayas, and Santa Rosa de Chire abolished the new taxes, the Indian tribute, and the sales tax. In Pore they deposed the cabildo and the tax administrators, forcing the sales-tax collector to return money he had recently collected. In Santiago they ousted the cabildo and the governor, don José Caicedo y Flórez Ladrón de Guevara, who, warned in advance of the coming rebellion, prudently withdrew to his house in Morcote.

Don Francisco Javier de Mendoza, a native of Miraflores and owner of an hato on the banks of the Guachiría River, took command in Pore, assuming the titles of captain general and governor of the province. He received a commission as captain of the Común from the supreme Council of War in Socorro. Of his creole colleagues, the records preserve only the names of Eugenio and Gregorio Bohórquez, co-captains of Chire. Gathering the Indians of Pore, Támara, Ten, Manare, and other towns, Mendoza freed them from paying tribute. Identifying himself as the *apoderado,* or lieutenant, of the Inca, he made them swear allegiance to the king of America, Túpac Amaru, unaware that he had been executed in Cuzco on May 15, and to obey the orders of the Comunero captains of Socorro. In each town the Indians chose captains and officials of the Común, appointing women in those places where the men were away herding cattle.[29]

The proclamation in Pore and other nearby towns of a letter dated May 23 and signed by the Común of Cocuy further inflamed the Indians. Cocuy was a highland village north and east of Sogamoso, and the letter, addressed to the captains and lieutenants of Támara, Ten, and Manare, stated that Túpac Amaru had been crowned king and that he was going to do away with all taxes. "Thus, we advise you that if the governor attempts to impose the taxes do not let him do it. If he tries to punish you, rise up against him. If they do not lift the taxes, we are going to Santa Fe de Bogotá to make war on the Santafereños. If you have not done what we told you to do by the time we return, we will make war against you."[30]

Indians from Támara read this letter in each town. They explained to the villagers that they did not have to attend mass or catechismal classes unless they wished to, because the priests could not longer oblige them to do anything. José Tapia, the vicar general of the province of Santiago, witnessed this event in Morcote. In an emotional account of the rebellion, which he wrote on July 10 to Salvador Plata in Socorro, he stated that the Támaras had told him that the order was not from Cocuy but had been drafted in Pore.[31] This, too, was the opinion of Governor Caicedo, who seeing that Mendoza intended to incite the Indians against him, quickly gathered his papers and fled Morcote for Socotá, leaving his less portable belongings with Tapia for safekeeping.[32]

On May 26 twenty Indians from Támara, Ten, and Manare, armed with bows and arrows, appeared in Morcote and attacked the governor's abandoned house. They destroyed everything they could find and then tried to enter the church to seize some banners. When the vicar general dissuaded them from that objective, they ordered him to surrender all property of the governor which remained in his possession. They threatened to cut him into pieces, to burn his house, and to carry him in ropes to Pore if he did not obey. Faced with these unappealing alternatives, Tapia agreed to hand over the goods. He asked them on whose orders they were acting, and "all unanimously confessed that it was don Javier de Mendoza."[33]

Determined to apprehend Caicedo, the force, now swollen to fifteen hundred men, set out on the road to Pisba and Paya. Overtaking Francisco de Lara, who was escorting part of the governor's property on muleback, they threw him off his mount, tied him up, and dragged him on to the jail in Pisba, where they attacked the house of the priest. Continuing to Paya, they taunted the cura of that village and confiscated the property of the *estanquero* (retailer of monopoly goods) and *asentista* (contractor) of Labranzagrande, both of whom had taken refuge in Paya earlier, to escape an angry mob. The Indians then returned to Pisba, where they bound and flogged the local *teniente* (deputy) and his brother. Only the arrival of the priest, dressed in his vestments and carrying the sacraments, deterred them from hanging the two. Weary at last, they retraced their steps to Morcote. Reclaiming the Governor's property from Tapia, they took it away, along with some mules and a servant.

For six weeks the Indians continued to harass the priests and whites. In his letter Tapia reported that curas throughout the province found themselves the objects of ridicule. In Manare Indians heaped indignities on the priest; in Ten they kept the priest a prisoner in his house for a week. The villagers of Morcote had remained faithful, but elsewhere Indians refused to attend religious services, and at least four died without receiving the sacraments. They routinely persecuted whites and threatened them with exile. In Pore they demanded that Juan Martín and Felipe Rueda, two brothers who served as sales-tax collectors, pay back all the money they had collected. The Ruedas fled, and one, half-crazed, was living in Chire, while the other was a fugitive somewhere else in the country. Tapia concluded that "finally this province seems like the confusion of hell. Everyone gives orders, everyone contradicts everyone else. One sees and hears nothing but crimes, proof of which is the childishness that has led them to name women captains which they employ to mistreat white women."[34]

The vicar general left no doubt that Javier de Mendoza was responsible for these acts. At each crossroad the captain general had installed an armed patrol, paid for by money pilfered from the cofradías and the royal treasury. The Indians themselves had told him that Mendoza had urged them to do what they wanted in all the towns, assuring them that if the priests fled in fright, the so-called new king had written him that he would provide for them.[35] Governor Caicedo seconded this allegation in a letter to Socorro, dated June 21. Caicedo asked the War Council to force Mendoza to restore his servants and property because he had taken them wrongfully and was using the excuse of the Comunero rebellion to cloak a personal vendetta.[36]

Mendoza responded that the Indians were acting on their own. To back up this assertion, he produced a letter from the Indians of Támara listing their grievances against the governor, but the council was not convinced and on July 17 ordered him to surrender the goods.[37] Royal officials likewise regarded the creole as guilty. Viceroy Flórez wrote to the minister of the Indies that Mendoza, aided by some corregidors, had seized the tax monies and had persuaded the Indians to stop paying tribute and to attack the priests and the governor. In its July 31 report to Charles III, the Junta Superior de Tribunales stated that Mendoza had caused the uproar in the Llanos by deposing the royal officials, forcing the governor to flee and freeing the Indians from paying tribute and from instruction in Christian dogma.[38]

The authorities were anxious to subdue Mendoza and restore royal control. The signing of the *Capitulaciones* in Zipaquirá, which brought a lull in the hostilities in the interior, was not honored in Casanare. By June 23 José Antonio Galán had again sounded the call to arms by attacking the town of Honda and later Ibagué, Ambalema, Villa de la Purificación, and Tocaima. On that same day the Junta Superior de Tribunales decided to appoint commissioners to go to Pore in order to enjoin Mendoza to cease his hostilities and to cooperate in the reestablishment of peace. The commissioners were to carry secret instructions to capture or kill Mendoza if he continued to resist. On July 14, the same day that it named

Juan Antonio Fernández Recamán to capture Galán, the junta designated José Antonio Chaparro, a resident of Sogamoso, to implement its earlier order offering a reward of five hundred *patacones* to be paid punctually for the capture of Mendoza, dead or alive.[39]

While it is not clear whether Chaparro attempted to carry out this assignment, it is certain that the authorities had already rejected as fruitless any plan to send regular troops to Casanare, because of the distance, impassable roads, and lack of manpower. They favored instead some kind of privately organized effort. When Archbishop Caballero y Góngora arrived in Socorro on July 16, accompanied by six Capuchin missionaries, he appointed José Antonio Villalonga to head such an expedition, assisted by Francisco José Becerra and Fernando Rodríguez. The prelate gave to Villalonga a letter of introduction to the priests and officials remaining in the Llanos, requesting their support.[40] In addition, he carried a letter addressed to Mendoza from the Comunero leaders in Socorro—Salvador Plata, Ramón Ramírez, Antonio José Monsalve, and Francisco Rosillo—ordering him to receive Villalonga, to restore the deposed cabildos and governor, and to assist in the pacification of the province.[41] According to Villalonga's report to the king, written three years later, the marqués de San Jorge Miguel Lozano de Peralta, a controversial figure already implicated in the Comunero cause, financed the expedition with money taken from his personal fortune and from his earnings as administrator of an encomienda in the Llanos.[42]

Villalonga assembled his expedition in Zipaquirá and left for Sogamoso in early August, following the route through Ubaté. At Socotá he conferred with José Caicedo, who informed him of the lamentable situation in Casanare—of the general commotion and of the seizure of royal funds and his property by Indian rebels and rioting vecinos.[43] Caicedo had learned through reliable sources that Mendoza, after receiving the order from Socorro, had resolved to resist to the end. Calling the Indians together, he told them that they might return the property if they wished, but that he would not order them to do it, and that he was ready to defy the captains of Socorro should they try to enforce their request. The Indians angrily responded that they "did not want to deliver anything, that they wanted war, and they would take away from those of Socorro the desire to be writing letters."[44] Caicedo estimated that three thousand Indians and many creoles would support Mendoza. Some of the latter would leave him as soon as they saw the army from the interior, but he had at least eleven *chapetones* (Spaniards) who were reliable and to whom he had entrusted sixty guns, the only usable firearms that existed in Casanare.

Caicedo assured Villalonga that Mendoza was absolutely determined to continue as the supreme legislator of the province. Royal officials who believed that he was still obeying orders from Socorro were deceiving themselves.[45]

Duly informed, Villalonga led his force across the Cordillera at the Páramo of Pisba, taking some urban militia along as auxiliaries. After a difficult journey over the extended and arduous road, he reached Pore, where he notified the cabildo and those of Chire and Santiago of his arrival. He called upon them to obey his orders and to help in the pacification. Some rebels continued to fight, but many vecinos and clergy with their Indians joined his cause. By the end of September, Villalonga had restored order in Támara, Ten, Manare, Paya, Cravo, Pisba, Labranzagrande, and other places that had been afflicted. The stolen funds of the haciendas of Tocaría and Cravo were returned, as well as the money taken from the royal treasury. No members of the expedition were lost, but three rebels were killed; Javier de Mendoza was among the twenty prisoners taken.[46]

Villalonga returned to Santa Fe to report to the Audiencia. His full statement, written on June 28, 1784, gave the glory of the victory to the marqués de San Jorge, for "responding to our request, and reinforcing our desire that we might be granted this commission, giving the rule and council in order that we might succeed, and finally having given us the necessary pesos on his own account, to help with the expenses that faced us in this matter."[47] Villalonga's testimony was one of many pieces of evidence which the marqués brought forward in 1784 to exonerate himself from charges of openly and secretly aiding the Comuneros.

The written accounts of the revolt in Casanare show that there were two factions—the creole vecinos, led by Javier Mendoza, and the Indians, whose armed strength peaked at perhaps three thousand men. While Vicar General Tapia implied that the entire province was in turmoil, a reconstruction of the settlement pattern gives a more accurate idea of the extent of the conflict. On October 14, 1778, Governor Caicedo completed the census of the Provincia de los Llanos, in response to an edict issued by Viceroy Guirior (1772–76), on November 10, 1776 (table 5). The *padrón* (census) shows three Spanish cities, together with the towns and missions in each jurisdiction. Of the total population of 20,892, 7 percent (including 23 clergy and 1,535 vecinos) were whites, 73 percent (15,189) were Indians, 19 percent (4,026) were mestizos, and 116 (less than one percent) were black slaves.[48] Map 5 shows the location of these settlements, based on information from colonial and modern maps and accounts by missionaries. The revolt began in Pore and then spread to Santiago and Chire. Nunchía,

Table 5. Population of the Provincia de los Llanos, 1778

Town	Clergy: Sec.	Reg.	Whites	Ind.	Mest.	Slaves	Total
*Cuidad de Santiago	1	1	492	55	286	37	837
Iximena	—	1	670	174	484	6	1,335
Chámesa	—	1	92	171	114	—	378
Casimena	—	1	6	380	3	—	390
Surimena	—	1	11	908	17	1	938
*Cuidad de Pore	2	—	129	42	804	40	1,017
Nunchía (parroq.)	1	—	16	33	606	23	679
Macuco	—	1	2	619	8	—	630
Guanapalo	—	1	—	637	—	—	638
*Morcote	1	—	2	2,165	35	1	2,204
*Támara	1	—	3	2,079	57	1	2,141
*Paya	1	—	1	544	60	—	606
*Pisba	—	1	—	590	8	—	599
*Labranzagrande	1	—	8	140	587	—	736
*Cravo	1	—	10	692	380	10	1,093
*Ciudad de Chire	—	—	57	—	298	—	355
*Ten	1	—	—	484	62	—	547
*Manare	—	1	—	625	9	—	635
Tame	—	—	17	1,739	89	—	1,845
Macaguane	—	1	—	1,635	4	—	1,640
Betoyes	—	1	19	1,276	—	—	1,296
Patute	—	—	—	66	65	—	131
Puerto	—	1	—	114	—	—	115
Aguariva	—	1	—	21	50	—	72
Total	10	13	1,535	15,189	4,026	119	20,892

Source: Adapted from the census taken in 1778 of the Provincia de los Llanos by José Caideco, by royal order of Nov. 10, 1776.
*Towns joining the revolt.

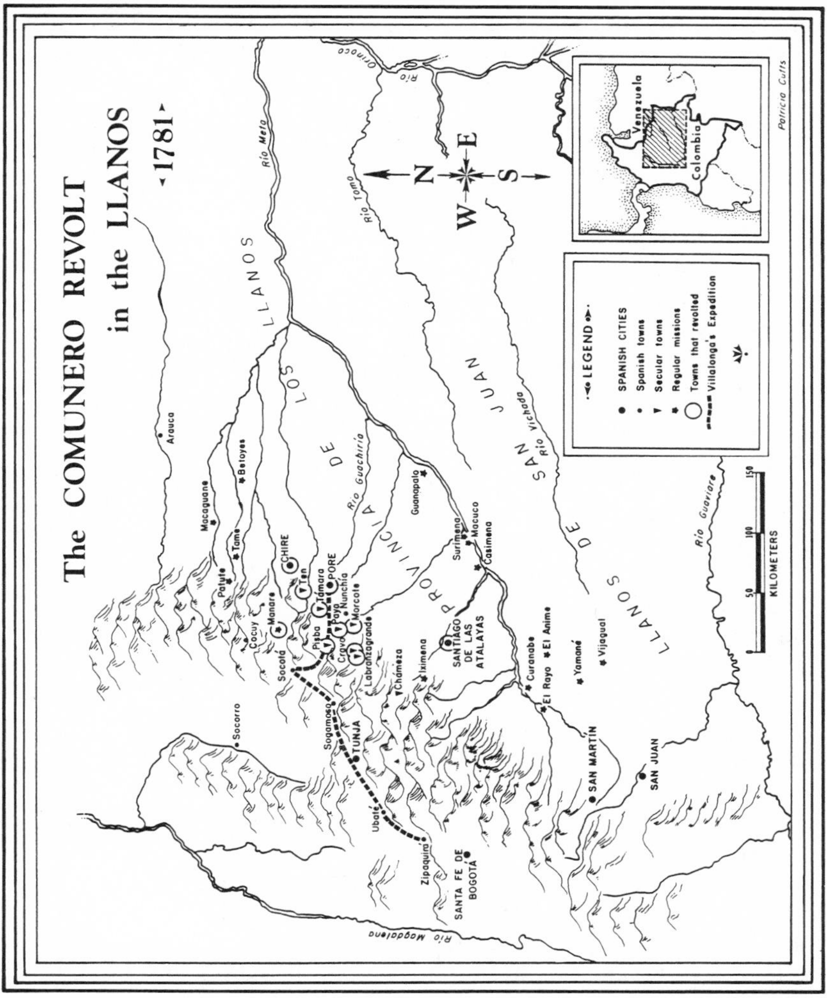

The COMUNERO REVOLT in the LLANOS
·1781·
LEGEND
SPANISH CITIES
Spanish towns
Secular towns
Regular missions
Towns that revolted
Villalonga's Expedition
KILOMETERS
0
50
100
150
N
E
S
W
Venezuela
Colombia
Patricia Cults
LLANOS DE LOS
PROVINCIA
SAN JUAN
LLANOS DE SAN JUAN
Río Meta
Río Orinoco
Río Tomo
Río Vichada
Río Guaviare
Río Guachiria
Río Magdalena
Arauca
Macaguane
Betoyes
Tame
Patute
Cocuy
Manare
Socotá
Socorro
CHIRE
Ten
Támara
PORE
Pisba
Paya
Nunchía
Morcote
Labranzagrande
Chámeza
Iximena
Guanapalo
Surimena
Macuco
Casimena
SANTIAGO DE LAS ATALAYAS
Curanabe
El Rayo
El Animé
Yamané
Vijagual
Sogamoso
TUNJA
Ubaté
Zipaquirá
SANTA FE DE BOGOTÁ
SAN MARTÍN
SAN JUAN

a mestizo parish founded only eleven years previously, did not join it, nor did Iximena, which registered the largest white population. The insurrection moved rapidly to Morcote, Támara, Paya, Pisba, Labranzagrande, and Cravo, all in Pore's jurisdiction, and Ten and Manare in the district of Chire. With the exception of Santiago, these towns were all in the same area, in or near the Andean foothills to the west and north of Pore. The rebellious towns account for 10,805 people, or about one-half the population in the province. The settlements north of Santiago, in the Llanos of San Juan and San Martín, along the Meta River, and in the Airico de Macaguane (Arauca) were undisturbed.

In *The People and the King,* John Phelan notes that Indian behavior was more radical in Casanare than in the interior. In Santa Fe, Tunja, Vélez, and Sogamoso, natives demanded the return of their resguardos and salt mines, but they did not repudiate Hispanic culture, nor reject the Church and its ministers. Phelan argues that this violence in Casanare was the result of the failure of the Jesuits and their successors to Christianize the Indians. "After the expulsion of the Society of Jesus, the Dominicans, the Franciscans and the Augustinians took their place. The natives were only imperfectly Christianized by the Jesuits, and their successors were patently ineffective. The neophytes showed acute hostility to their spiritual mentors. The irate Indians attacked churches and forced the clergy to flee."[49]

The difficulty with this interpretation is that only one of the towns that joined the revolt, Manare, was an ex-Jesuit mission operated in 1781 by Franciscans.[50] Since the early sixteenth century, Augustinians had been in charge of Ten, Támara, Morcote, Paya, Pisba, and Labranzagrande. The Junta de Propaganda Fide confirmed their rule in 1662. In his history of the Augustinian missions in Colombia, José Pérez Gómez avers that they continued to administer these towns "until they were secularized in the second half of the eighteenth century."[51] The census of 1778 distinguished types of clergy and indicated that seculars were serving in Ten, Támara, Morcote, Paya, and Cravo, while there were regulars in Manare and Pisba. No unrest occurred in the ex-Jesuit missions of Tame, Macaguane, Betoyes, Patute, or Puerto (controlled in 1781 by Dominicans), nor in Macuco, Surimena, and Casimena (the ex-Jesuit missions awarded to the Recoletos).[52] The brunt of the revolt, then, came from Indians living in towns subject to Hispanic rule for a century and a half, and it fell on secular rather than regular clergy.

A better explanation for the ferocity partially lies in the involvement of the rebel towns in the Tunja-based textile industry. Soon after the conquest, Tunja emerged as the principal center for textile production and distribution throughout New Granada. With a dense population of Indians suited to encomienda labor, the rapid adaptation of sheep to the highland valleys assuring a supply of wool, and the accessibility to cotton grown in the lower altitudes of Casanare, Tunja's primacy was unassailable. The Indians held in encomienda in the Provincia de los Llanos and in the towns run by the Augustinians were actively involved in seeding cotton, harvesting the fiber, and weaving thread and cloth, which they used to pay their tribute and other taxes. As we have already seen, as late as 1754 the remnants of the enormous Quesada-Berrio encomienda had accumulated in the treasury of the Royal Hacienda 32,246 varas of cotton cloth worth ten thousand pesos, and Father Oviedo, in 1761, commended the fine textile products produced by the natives of Támara, Ten, Morcote, Manare, Labranzagrande, Pisba, and Paya.[53]

By Oviedo's time, however, Socorro had surpassed Tunja as a producer in textiles; only in the Llanos did the industry retain its old importance.[54] At an altitude of four thousand feet above sea level, Socorro's fertile valleys and warm climate supported a variety of crops, including sugarcane and cotton as well as livestock. Its location on the highway between Vélez to the south and Pamplona to the north made it a natural trade and commercial center for a large hinterland. A high population growth rate fostered the development of economic activities. In contrast the sharply declining Indian population around Tunja had drastically reduced the prosperity of that once splendid city.[55] The unchanged organization and techniques of its textile production were no match for the newer methods adopted in Socorro. By 1750 locally made cloth, which used to be called *de Tunja,* was now designated *de Socorro.*

Royal officials recognized the significance of cotton in Casanare and wished to promote its production, especially in the wake of the economic shock caused by the expulsion of the Jesuits, in 1767. In his extensive report to Messía de la Cerda on the condition of the viceroyalty, in 1772, Fiscal Moreno y Escandón cited the general poverty of the Llanos, where Spanish cities scarcely deserved the name. The only commerce in the region was the manufacture of cloth, which formed part of a limited trade with the interior.[56] Viceroy Guirior, in his *Relación del mando* of 1776, recommended to his successor, Manuel Antonio Flórez, that he should encourage the cultivation of cotton in the district of Socorro and in the Provincia de los Llanos, where the Indians "live by the cloth which they make and merit being imitated." Guirior urged the corregidors to take measures which would increase the output of ruanas (ponchos), shirts, and other textiles "since experience shows that if the vecinos cannot obtain local textiles, they will buy those of foreigners."[57]

In his zeal to reorganize, rationalize, and increase the tax income of New Grenada, Visitador General Gutiérrez de Piñeres ignored this good advice. His *Instrucción general para el más exacto y arreglado manejo de las Reales Rentas de Alcabalas y Armada de Barlovento,* issued October 12, 1780, extended the sales tax to many items previously exempt, including cotton and thread. This decision was as harmful to the Indians in Casanare as to the Socorranos, because raising cotton, spinning thread, and weaving textiles sustained many households in both regions. The tax on thread was especially objectionable, since the poor used it in place of money in their purchases and other transactions.[58] Combined with the prohibition against the cultivation of tobacco, this reform placed the poor in an impossible position. The widespread distress it generated is reflected in the ninth clause of the *Capitulaciones,* which called for the limitation of the sales tax to 2 percent on certain items and the complete exemption of cotton "for being a product that fittingly only the poor seed and gather and we ask that it be established as a general rule."[59]

By April 1781 Gutiérrez de Piñeres realized that the posting of sales tax on cotton was a serious blunder. To mitigate popular unrest, he rescinded the tax on the sale, purchase, or exchange of cotton and cotton thread in Muzo, Vélez, Tunja, Leiva, San Gil, El Socorro, and the Provincia de los Llanos, because in those districts it was the principal industry of the poor and was used regularly as a measure of exchange.[60] With the revolt in Socorro well under way, the Comunero captains chose to ignore this decree, if news of it actually reached them. It was likewise too late to repair the damage in Casanare, where the Indians, besides resenting the special taxes, were seething over José Caicedo's routine abuse of tribute collection.[61]

In a letter addressed to Javier de Mendoza, on July 16, 1781, the people of Támara alleged that after serving as governor for five years, Caicedo owed money to Indian weavers in Manare, Ten, Támara, Morcote, Paya, and Pisba. More specifically, abandoning the practice of previous governors, he had forced them all to go to Morcote to sell their cloth, rather than purchasing it in their native towns. They frequently had to make several trips to Morcote before he would pay them. Even then, if the cloth was found to be slightly underweight, he would not pay for it, or would pay only a fraction of its value. Finally the governor had taken mules from them unjustly, and when their mules died of snakebites, he held them responsible. For these reasons, the Támaras said, they would fight rather than return the property seized from Caicedo, which they intended to divide up among his creditors.[62]

Caicedo did not directly respond to these charges, but he did tell Salvador Plata that his confiscated goods included both cloth that he had collected for the Christmas tercio, or tribute, of 1780 and that which he had purchased privately. According to his calculations, it was the townspeople who owed him money. He asked Plata to order them to pay him quickly and to surrender his servants, mules, and property. Once he had received this merchandise, he promised to move all his private business out of the province, for he had no desire to return and no trustworthy agent there to look after his interests.[63]

It seems likely that the duties on cotton and Caicedo's sharp business methods provoked the Indians to attack the tax collectors of various towns and to chase the governor away to Socotá. Since they used cotton thread and cloth to pay religious fees, and since the clergy, like the governor, habitually took more than was their due, the same motivation may have led them to turn on the priests in Paya, Ten, and Manare. The documents suggest that Javier de Mendoza openly encouraged them in these excesses. His attitude reflected a growing antagonism toward the clergy that was spreading throughout colonial society.

In the past historians have paid scant attention to the anticlerical aspects of the Comunero Revolt, but John Phelan, in his analysis of the *Capitulaciones,* discovered that 12.5 percent of these demands, or six separate clauses, concerned alleged abuses of the clergy. The seventh clause, for example, accused the corregidors and parish priests of working together to exploit the Indians, since a portion of the tribute tax collected by the corregidors provided the stipend for those priests administering Indian parishes. It also censored ecclesiastical notaries, whose services were necessary for baptisms, weddings, and funerals, for grossly overcharging their clients. Five other clauses developed the argument that the clergy were charging illegal and excessive fees. Taken together, they imply that there was dissatisfaction with the heavy fees that all groups had to pay in order to maintain the ecclesiastical establishment and that not only were the Indians oppressed by these exactions, but the creoles and mestizos were also.[64] To these kinds of complaints in Casanare must be added a deep-seated creole hostility toward missionaries, who from the early seventeenth century (with government support) had sought to monopolize the Indians, while the vecinos had to rely on their own resources to wrest a meager living from the inhospitable plains.

From the first arrival of the Jesuits in the Llanos, in 1620s, settlers and officials had resented their presence. The encomenderos saw themselves stripped of potential laborers. When they accused the clergy of hunting the Indians down as slaves and failing in their jobs as spiritual mentors, their charges elicited little sympathy. Even when the crown authorized an investigation, it would usually exonerate the missionaries. The creole ranchers looked with envy on the large haciendas, so efficiently run by the Jesuits, who were aided by special concessions from the state. Germán Arciniegas points out that because of the dominant role of the missionaries, the post of corregidor in the Llanos remained very weak. He cites a contemporary document in which a corregidor complained that he could not take charge of his district because the priests had absolute control over the towns. "The fathers, aware that their house is a convent, do not accept the jurisdiction of the corregidor over it; there they stop everyone and hide contraband, as they did with Captain Don Joseph Patiño, for whom they hid more than five thousand pesos of foreign goods which they sold publicly in Santa Fe." In this situation, the official added, the Indians obeyed only the priests and regarded the corregidor as a "judge of straw."[65]

If the creoles silently rejoiced at the ouster of the Jesuits, they profited little from the reform. The crown simultaneously reassigned the missions to other religious orders. The Junta de Temporalidades sold the haciendas in Casanare, after a brief period of Dominican rule, at public auction. Inevitably the highest bidders were wealthy creoles from Tunja or Santa Fe, such as Felix Luís Bermúdez, who purchased Tocaría in 1771. The crown continued to assign income from these estates to support the missions. It is significant that one of Mendoza's first moves after deposing Caicedo was to seize the Tocaría and Cravo haciendas in the jurisdiction of Pore and to stop sales of cattle until receiving further orders from Socorro.[66] In August 1781 he ordered the administrator of Cravo, Joseph Miguel Cadenas, imprisoned and appointed another man, named Aranda, to keep the accounts.[67] While the Indians still under regular rule were geographically isolated from Pore, Mendoza could and did incite the natives in nearby towns to rise against the secular priests.

It seems likely that in the Comunero crisis ranchers such as Mendoza and the Bohórquez brothers saw a chance not only to abolish taxes, which fell on cattle as well as on cotton, but also to deal a blow against an old enemy, the clergy. The commitment of the creoles was steadfast enough to require that Villalonga's pacification be sent to the Llanos. As late as September, vecinos from Santiago de las Atalayas joined Galán's band in Mogotes, hoping that he would lead a new expedition on Santa Fe.[68] Galán himself considered fleeing to the Llanos and hiding until he might receive a pardon, but he failed to act on that option before being captured in Onzaga, on October 13.[69]

Mendoza, in addition, had two personal grievances against Governor Caicedo. First he charged that Caicedo was the regent's *sarcillo,* using a local term for lackey, because he had imposed and enforced the new tax regulations. Second the governor had arbitrarily expanded the number of aldermen in the Pore cabildo from five to ten, "in order to increase taxes and suck from the people their money when in such a poor district, five aldermen were sufficient."[70] Caicedo, who belonged to a prominent clan of creole officeholders in Santa Fe, vigorously refuted both allegations. In a letter to Salvador Plata, he stated that he was only fulfilling his obligation as governor of the province in obeying the orders of the regent. "It is public knowledge that I did not establish in said province any tax beyond those which I found established and other than the Regent imposed, and it is known that as Governor, I did not have the power to do it."[71] Moreover, he continued, it was completely within his authority as governor to expand the membership in the cabildo. Keenly aware of the misery and misfortune of Pore, he had taken this step as a way to encourage individuals to improve their position by holding offices from which they could obtain personal honor and give luster to their city. Mendoza, he charged, objected not to the measure itself, but to his lack of appointment to one of the newly created posts. "Justice will show," Caicedo concluded, "how Mendoza proceeded against me . . . using the excuse of the Común which with justice can be defended, to revenge unjustly his passions and his private resentments and whose public actions only go against the just aspirations of the Común."[72]

Two hundred years later, the figure of Javier de Mendoza remains an enigma. While Cárdenas Acosta argues that in the conduct of the revolt Mendoza did not commit any outrage or punishable act and that his behavior was adjusted to the standards of a gentleman, the royal authorities considered him guilty as charged.[73] The documents show that it was he who organized the revolt, represented himself as an official of Túpac Amaru, freed the Indians from paying tribute, and exhorted them to attack the clergy and the governor. When ordered by Salvador Plata to restore Caicedo's property, Mendoza replied that the Indians were out of control and that he could not muster sufficient force to take away from them what they did not want to give, yet as late as September, he was counting on their support to repel Villalonga's army.[74] Mendoza did not betray the Indians. He resisted until he was captured by a superior force, yet he has not shared José Antonio Galán's mantle as a social revolutionary or precursor of independence. It is not clear whether his obscurity is due to the ambiguity of his motives or from the limitation of his activities to an isolated province that historians have consistently regarded as unimportant in the development of colonial New Granada.

Between 1767 and 1781 reforms initiated in Madrid and implemented by royal authorities in Santa Fe disrupted the equilibrium of frontier society in Casanare, which had evolved over two centuries of Spanish rule. The expulsion of the Jesuits produced no local protest but heralded a reorganization and reaffirmation of the mission system, to be discussed in the next chapter. By 1781 Gutiérrez de Pineres's ill-advised financial reforms sparked a violent revolt in nearly half the towns in the Provincia de los Llanos. The unusual excesses perpetuated by the Indians were not due to their insufficient Hispanicization, as Phelan has postulated, but were the consequence of several other factors—their involvement in the declining Tunja-based textile industry, the attempt by the regent to squeeze more income from the textile workers, the unpopular policies adopted by Governor Caicedo, and the complicity of the creoles led by Javier de Mendoza, who, resenting the privileged status of the priests, did nothing to protect them and in fact encouraged the Indians to take their revenge.[75]

The aftermath of the revolt brought little change for either group. On October 20, 1781, Viceroy Flórez issued a general pardon, reduced the price of tobacco and aguardiente, rolled back the alcabala sales tax to the traditional 2 percent in the highlands and 4 percent in the maritime provinces, and abolished the Armada de Barlovento sales tax. Still exempt from tax were cotton and cotton thread.[76] The archbishop reiterated these reforms in his general pardon of August 7, 1782, but beyond continuing support of the missionaries in Casanare, neither he nor his successors initiated any new scheme for economic development there. Tied to the declining fortunes of Tunja, the cotton industry did not revive, and cattle raising, largely a spontaneous development, would become the principal economic activity on the eve of independence.

The events of 1781 did have one unanticipated consequence for Spanish rule in the Llanos. Fearing reprisals for their involvement in the insurrection in spite of the general pardon, many inhabitants of the interior sought refuge in the isolated missions of Casanare. Both Baron von Humboldt and José Cortés Madariaga, who visited the towns along the Meta River in 1802 and 1811, respectively, noted that especially in the ex-Jesuit mission of Macuco, large numbers of *Socorranos refugiados* had settled.[77] It was these fellow Socorranos that José María Rosillo and Vicente Cadena hoped to unite in their abortive attempt in 1809 to declare war against Spain from Casanare.[78] A decade later some of these displaced Comuneros would give their lives in Bolívar's heroic march to Boyacá.

5 *The Missions Renewed, 1767–1810*

Bourbon Policy and the Llanos

The expulsion of the Jesuits and the financial measures imposed by Gutiérrez de Piñeres were reforms applied throughout New Granada that had important consequences for the Llanos. Other Bourbon innovations had little impact. For example, Allan J. Kuethe has shown that in the Caribbean provinces of Riohacha and Darién, the viceroys after 1773 abandoned the traditional mission-oriented operations to depend increasingly on the military as their primary instrument for expanding and enforcing royal authority. "Whereas in the times past the missionary had been the government's chief agent in frontier expansion, now in a time of an increased militarization of government policy, the soldier emerged in the foreground, the winning of souls, previously an important consideration along with extending government control, became almost an afterthought, eclipsed by the desire for a rapid and effective occupation."[1]

No such change took place in the Llanos. While historians have postulated that the missions collapsed there after the expulsion of the Jesuits, a review of the efforts of the Dominicans, Capuchins, Franciscans, and Recoletos who replaced them reveals that despite many obstacles and major setbacks, the missions recovered from the 1767 crisis and flourished until 1810 with renewed vigor. The viceroys scrutinized carefully the activities of the religious orders, but they continued to rely on them to Hispanicize the eastern frontier. In contrast Bourbon schemes to stimulate commerce never materialized, and their dependence on badly trained, badly paid escolta soldiers, rather than on regular militia units, left the

Llanos vulnerable to Spain's foreign enemies and to creole radicals, impatient to bring about New Granada's independence.

In the last half of the eighteenth century, the Dominicans, Capuchins, Franciscans, and Recoletos had to overcome four liabilities in order to sustain viable missions among the Indians of the Llanos. First, while the Bourbon viceroys after 1767 reconfirmed the regular clergy as the focal point of the Spanish presence in Casanare and near San Juan and San Martín, they were suspicious of them on principle and receptive to complaints about their faltering vocation and discipline. In 1772 Fiscal Moreno y Escandón informed Messía de la Cerda that all the missions in the Llanos were at least one hundred years old, and that they had declined so measurably that they could not meet royal expectations nor justify the funds spent in their support.[2] Francisco Silvestre Sánchez, former governor of Antioquia, wrote in his 1789 *Descripción del Reino de Santa Fe de Bogotá* that the reductions in Casanare had not advanced after the Jesuits departed, because the remaining religious orders lacked the means to convert the Indians.[3] In 1796 Viceroy José de Ezpeleta (1789-97) concluded that the missions were declining because the clergy refused to learn the native languages, practiced ineffective methods in the reductions, and were unable to attract competent postulants.[4]

These negative assessments reflect a second liability, the changing political and social climate in Europe and America, which subjected the traditionally revered religious vocation to searching skepticism. Setting the tone was Charles III's far-reaching reform of religious orders in Spain. His government intervened directly to strengthen discipline, to reduce the number of monks, and to regulate the administration of charity and the payment of priests. As more economic and social opportunities became available, fewer young people chose to join the beleaguered communities. In 1797 the religious made up 1.6 percent of the Spanish population, while in 1768 they had totalled 2.5 percent. Although the orders engaged in teaching and charity remained fairly popular, the meditative communities fell into a state of general decadence.[5] In New Granada it was not unusual for the Dominicans, Capuchins, or Recoletos to cite lack of personnel as a reason for refusing to take on a new mission field. Representative was P. Fr. Domingo Barragón, the Dominican provincial in Santa Fe, who explained to his superior in 1801 that Viceroy Mendinueta had issued repeated orders that he send more priests to the doctrinas, but that without trained men, the only way he could comply with these directives would be to send young brothers who had not completed their studies.[6]

The internal structure of the religious orders was a third problem. In berating them for their deficiencies, the viceroys would sometimes exhort them to adopt the practices of the extinguished Jesuits. Like the other orders, the Jesuits took vows of poverty, chastity, and obedience. What made them different was that they were not founded for a specific purpose, nor were they tied to a particular monastery or type of work. As a result flexibility and mobility were their chief characteristics. The order adopted high standards of recruitment, training, and organization. Its centralized, international structure enabled the assignment of missionary posts according to a fixed plan. The discipline practiced by other communities became, among the Jesuits, near military obedience to the pope. By the eighteenth century, skillful procuradors and rectors had built up the wealth of the order with its large estates, houses, and easy access to credit, creating a corporate affluence that seemed to contradict the vow of poverty pronounced by the members.[7]

These features, which explain the success of the Jesuits as well as the king's decision to expel them, could not be copied by the other orders. Their recruitment and instruction were less rigorous. The brothers were trained within the cloister and sent indiscriminately to all types of ministries. Everything depended upon an individual's character and mind. It was difficult to obtain any unity of action. Superiors could not necessarily order men into the missions against their wills, and a brother who accepted a post might be a zealous proselytizer but totally lacking in the practical skills needed to run the reduction.[8]

Finally, by the late eighteenth century, conditions in the Llanos were changing. Anthropological evidence suggests that the Indians were increasingly antagonistic toward the missionaries. The continued abuse by white settlers, who thought nothing of enslaving or killing natives, forced previously peaceful tribes to adopt a warlike stance.[9] The Guahibos, in particular, attacked on one side by Caribs seeking slaves to sell to the Dutch and by the Spanish on the other, were ferocious in their self-defense. In 1785 the governor of the Llanos, Francisco Domínguez, informed the Audiencia that white atrocities had provoked bloody reprisals from the Guahibos and had created a tense situation in Casanare. He urged that missionaries be sent to mediate between the settlers and the Indians.[10] The missionaries, for their part, demanded that the government assign them soldiers for protection. The viceroys grudgingly acceded to these requests, but the escoltas were insufficient. By the beginning of the nineteenth century, a state of perpetual war existed in eastern Casanare. In 1803 Viceroy Mendinueta recognized that one or two soldiers could not keep the neophytes from fleeing nor protect the missions from gentile attacks. He recommended that the government arm each settler, so that every "*vecino* will be a soldier and an assistant in the reduction of Indians"—a policy fortunately never put into effect, for it is hard to imagine an action more likely to increase the tension.[11]

Castigated by authorities in Europe and America, beset by internal weaknesses, and frustrated by the rising Indian hostility, many missionaries were unequal to the task. With the exception of Támara, the Augustinians surrendered their towns to secular priests by the 1780s.[12] Of the orders still active, the Dominicans and Capuchins suffered the worst trials. It is their shortcomings which historians most often recount to demonstrate the demise of the missions in the Llanos after 1767.

Six Dominicans arrived on October 4, 1767, to take over the ex-Jesuit towns of San Salvador del Puerto, Tame, Patute, Macaguane, and Betoyes and the haciendas of Caribabare, Tocaría, and Cravo. The order administered fourteen reductions in Barinas, Piedras, Apure, and Guanare, in Venezuela, but its previous experience in the plains of New Granada was limited to Medina, in the foothills northwest of San Juan.[13] In less than two years, the Dominicans surrendered control of the haciendas to the Junta de Temporalidades. Soon after, beset by insufficient funding and the deaths of many missionaries, they withdrew from the reductions, which the crown promptly secularized.[14]

In 1784, at the request of the governor of the Provincia de los Llanos, Joaquín Fernández, the Dominicans returned to the five missions and continued to operate them despite many problems until the Wars of Independence. Heavy Guahibo attacks brought demands in 1785 for military protection.[15] The order could not find suitable replacements for missionaries who died at their posts. Some towns went for months without a priest. Discipline was lax, and while most Dominicans were honorable, a few used their position for personal gain or to mistreat the Indians.

Lack of finances crippled the effort, especially after the Junta de Temporalidades confiscated Tocaría, Cravo, and Caribabare. On the one hand, the Dominicans freely admitted that their brief attempt to run the estates had been disastrous. In 1784 they refused to return to Casanare if it involved taking them over again. On the other hand, the missions could not be self-supporting without the food and income produced by the haciendas. The crown annually awarded each reduction one hundred pesos from the profits of Tocaría, Cravo, and Caribabare, but this sum was considerably less than the amount extracted from the estates by the Jesuits. It was not enough to pay for the food, clothing, and tools that the Indians demanded for fishing, hunting, and cultivating. The Dominicans reported that the neophytes deserted when they did not receive the material goods they had come to expect.[16] By the time of Mendinueta, this burden had been partially eased by allowing each mission to maintain a small hato to produce its own supplies.[17]

In 1789 Governor Manuel Villavicencio submitted a sober report on the state of the reductions. Of the four Dominicans still active, he wrote, only Fray Domingo Obregón governed Betoyes in a manner reminiscent of the Jesuits. Advancing age limited the dedication of Fray Francisco Cortázar, pastor of Patute. Fray Joaquín Aramburo, in Puerto de Casanare, had an irascible disposition. He abused the Achaguas and profited personally from the hato owned by the community. The provincial, on learning of his scandalous behavior, had requested him to leave. In Tame the priest was so severe that the Indians ran away. Villavicencio completed his unflattering assessment of Dominican achievements after twenty-two years in Casanare by noting that the fifth town, Macaguane, had been without a missionary for six months.[18]

Even less successful were the Capuchins, who were relative newcomers to New Granada. Begun as a reform movement of the Franciscans, in 1525, the Order of Friars Minor Capuchin broke away in 1619 and reached its maximum strength in the mid-eighteenth century. First active as missionaries in Santa Marta and Barinas, the Capuchins did not found a monastery in Santa Fe until 1777. Since their rule did not permit the profession of creoles, all Capuchins in New Granada were Spaniards who, after ten years of service, might return to the motherhouse, in Valencia. Their staunch regalism endeared them to Bourbon officials. During the Comunero Revolt, they served as chief advisors to Archbishop Caballero y Góngora.

In 1789 the Capuchins accepted a mission field in Cuiloto, Arauca. Only four years before, Don Gregorio Lemus, a creole from Barinas, had settled in this region drained by the Cravo, Ele, and Lipa rivers and had founded a hato. Soon afterward, some Guahibos came to him, proposing to settle in towns under his direction if he would get them a priest. Lemus informed the regidor (town councillor) of Pore, who in turn notified the governor of the Llanos. Acceding to the latter's recommendation, the Junta de Tribunales in Santa Fe named Lemus corregidor of Cuiloto, with jurisdiction over four reductions formed by 830 Indians, and granted to each town an annual subsidy from Caribabare, Cravo, and Tocaría. Viceroy Gil y Lemus (January 8 to July 31, 1789) planned to assign the new parish to the Dominicans, but when they did not respond to his invitation, he asked the Capuchins instead, explaining that their zeal and application to apostolic tasks ideally suited them for the job.[20]

The Capuchins got off to an excellent start. Within a year they were ministering to 1,035 Indians in five reductions and negotiating with five other more distant settlements disposed to accept their rule.[21] Then in May 1791 the order abruptly renounced the reductions, alleging insufficient personnel to man them.[22] Archbishop Baltazar Martínez de Compañón had already remonstrated with the Capuchins for lapses in discipline in Darién and Santa Fe. He suggested that they send to Cuiloto brothers who had recently arrived from Spain, but the order responded that the new arrivals could not be forced to go to the Llanos because of agreements they had signed before leaving Spain. P. Antonio Cervera, one of the original Cuiloto missionaries, broke the impasse by volunteering to return there as superior, and to find five other brothers and laymen to accompany him. Viceroy Ezpeleta rewarded his resolution by subsidizing the endeavor with 1,957 pesos.[23]

But adversity followed the Capuchins upon their return, in 1793. Guahibos assaulted the reductions. Gregorio Lemus died, and the Indians, "who loved him dearly," asked that his brother, Cayetano, replace him as corregidor. When Don Cayetano also died, in 1796, they began to desert the towns. By this time two missionaries had completed ten years of service and petitioned leave to return to Spain. Another, against all regulations, had established a private cattle herd next to the hato he was administering for the missions. Antonio Cervera reported these developments with deep consternation. Bowed down by his seventy-four years, he asked to return to Santa Fe in order to die in the monastery. The viceroy and archbishop, their earlier investigation of Capuchin conduct in Socorro and Santa Marta completed, had just issued the order a warning that never, for any cause, might the monks dispense with the dictates of their rule. In this mood they decided to release Cervera from his assignment in Cuiloto and to award the parish to the Recoletos, bringing to an unhappy end Capuchin activities in the Llanos.[24]

José Manuel Groot's narrative of these events, bolstered by documents reprinted in the appendix of his *Historia eclesiástica y civil,* has long provided the basis for the thesis that the missions collapsed after the expulsion of the Jesuits, in 1767. Neither the Dominicans nor the Capuchins have produced a historian to offer a rebuttal or to defend their work in Casanare and Cuiloto. Nevertheless it is important to remember that the Capuchins were proselytizing in a region that had never been in Jesuit hands, and that although they were withdrawn in disgrace, they left a base in Cuiloto upon which the Recoletos could build. More significantly, despite all difficulties, the population of the five ex-Jesuit missions run by the Dominicans actually grew. According to Enrique Alvarado there were 4,200 Indians in these towns in 1767.[25] In 1793 the Dominican provincial calculated the population at 5,316, in 1803 Viceroy Mendinueta reported it at 5,425.[26] A growth of 26 percent over thirty-five years argues forcefully that the missions were not decaying.

The Franciscans, unlike the Capuchins and the Dominicans, had toiled in the Llanos of San Juan and San Martín for over a century. In 1767 they acquired Güicán and Manare, with its hato in Casanare, and Jiramena, with its hato on the Meta River. In 1790 the provincial, R. P. Juan José Alvarez, reported that the Tunebos of Güicán were prospering, and in Manare there were "many Indians all baptized," who grew yuca, maize, and cotton. In addition Fr. Juan Antonio Nieto had founded a new settlement at El Pantano, with ninety Lunas and Tunebas.[27] Jiramena fared less well. In 1783 its population had fallen to 123, down 14 from the 137 of 1767. Padre Alvarez, who visited there in 1790, found the climate hot and unhealthy. Subsequently Jiramena was moved to another site and renamed, perhaps more appropriately, Nuestra Señora de los Dolores de Pajure. In 1806 its population consisted of 140 Amarizana Indians.[28]

Letters written by Franciscans during this era show that geographic isolation, material poverty, and rejection by the Indians who lived near San Juan and San Martín were affecting morale. On February 11, 1769, Fr. Francisco García Gálvez bewailed the "rough roads, thundering rivers and horrible heat" that complicated his journey to San Martín to take up duties as superior. He found the place a "desert." "The people are separated from one another entire days by road, so that the city is so solitary that there is not a Christian to set eyes upon." Intending to go on to San Juan, García Gálvez learned that the trip would require two days of travel. The rivers were very dangerous, and he would have to hire pack animals and find provisions. He confessed that "I remain very discouraged in health and everything else."[29]

His second letter to the provincial, written March 12, 1769, was no less pessimistic. Travel between the missions was almost impossible. More than twenty ravines and three flooding rivers isolated Yamane from San Martín. All the settlements were so poor that the Indians and missionaries lived on casabe and plátanos. García Gálvez's secretary, Fr. Cristóbal del Real, had asked to be relieved of his duties because the natives "were the most horrible riffraff" he had seen, and at times he wanted to kill them.[30] At about the same time another friar, José Prieto, wrote that "I have to supply the Indians of our town with meat and the other things that are given them, and if one does not give them what they want, they do not want to attend anything and go back to the wilderness which is what happens in all the towns every day, so that already I do not have the patience to endure so much hunger and so much work."[31]

Equally demoralizing was the open hostility which the local officials showed toward the missionaries. In 1801 Eugenio Rondón *(alcalde ordinario* of San Martín), Luís Labrea (former cura of Medina), and Juan Andrés formally charged Padre Fray Joaquín Zubieta, comisario of the Franciscan missions, with deliberately relocating towns in order to collect more stipends from the government. On June 18 Zubieta replied that these charges were inspired by vengeance rather than religious zeal, since he had been active in an investigation against Labrea and Rondón for mistreating the people of Medina. The missions at Maricuare, El Rayo, Iraca, and Pachaquiaro had been moved, he explained, not in order to defraud the government, but rather to find a healthier location, to improve inter-settlement communication, and to protect the Indians from abuse by the vecinos of San Martín and San Juan. Moreover relocation was consistent with the nomadic habits of the natives. In his twenty-one years of experience, Zubieta had seen many towns moved at the initiative of the Indians. Relocation was not only legal, but vital to the survival of the missions.[32]

To clarify the controversy, Viceroy Amar y Borbón asked the provincial, Fray Vicente Olarte, to investigate personally the reductions in the Llanos of San Juan and San Martín. Olarte's report, dated October 29, 1806, shows a total of 1,542 Guahibos and Achaguas living in seven towns, distributed as follows: San Miguel de Tua (formerly Macurrubá), 328; Santa Cruz de Marayal (formerly Pachaquiaro), 280; San Antonio de Cabuyaro (formerly Iracá), 166; Nuestra Señora de los Dolores de Pajure (formerly Jiramena), 140; Nuestra Señora del Campo del Arrojo (formerly El Rayo), 212; Concepción de Arama, 268; and Maricuare (formerly Macatía), 148. The headquarters of the missions were in San Miguel de Tua. Here the thatched church, with two average-size bells, was poor but decent. The Indians took good care of their homes and fields, producing enough food to sustain the community. Olarte wrote that Tua's population of 328 included 69 unbaptized Guahibos, who had recently appeared out of the wilderness. In all the towns Indians were serving as captains, lieutenants, fiscals, and alcaldes. They received Christian instruction and celebrated the rites of the Church. Olarte strongly supported Zubieta's decision to move the communities. In their new location, on the Humadea River, they enjoyed a much better climate. The river facilitated transportation and communication. From this location it would be easier to foster trade with Sogamoso, Miraflores, Gachetá, and Tunja than from the former, more isolated position near the cities of San Juan and San Martín.[33]

Despite his generally positive evaluation, Olarte identified many problems that still plagued the missionaries. To assist them he recommended that the crown increase their stipends, since the two hundred pesos which each priest currently received barely covered his travel expenses to reach his post. If additional money could not be found, Olarte suggested that twenty thousand cattle be taken from the herds in Casanare and divided among the Franciscan reductions. The crown should supply each mission with four or five firearms, because long experience had proved that without guns it was not possible "to reduce the savages nor to keep the domesticated ones." Finally he seconded a proposal made by Viceroy Mendinueta that a bishop of the Provincia de los Llanos be appointed, with responsibilities similar to the newly created episcopal post among the Mainas Indians in Quito Province.[34]

Olarte's report was persuasive. On January 20, 1807, the fiscal in Santa Fe exonerated the Franciscans from all charges of misconduct. He recommended that the crown pay their stipends and award them control of the hato of Jiramena, originally begun by the Jesuits. Eighteen months later, on September 20, 1808, the Audiencia ruled that seven thousand cattle be dispatched to the Franciscan missions from the ex-Jesuit hatos now run by Recoletos. No action was taken on providing firearms or on creating a new bishopric.[35]

By all accounts the Recoletos after 1767 were the most successful missionaries of the Llanos. Before the expulsion they had administered three reductions in Casanare—Sabana Alta (Upamena), founded in 1662, Iximena, founded in 1664, and San Pedro de Upía, founded in the early eighteenth century. From the Jesuits the Recoletos received Surimena, Macuco, and Casimena, with their haciendas—all on the banks of the Meta between the Cusiana and Cravo Sur rivers. Striking out from this base they founded five new towns and an equal number of haciendas, stretching eastward along the Meta. By 1796 their progress was so encouraging that Viceroy Ezpeleta assigned them the Cuiloto missions, begun by the Capuchins, and the king granted them permission to found a college in Morcote to train and aid their missionaries.

The fate of the original Recoleto reductions at this time is obscure. In his 1761 compendium of parishes, Oviedo listed only Sabana Alta, describing it as a "very small town of few Indians with a small, thatched church too poor for any adornment."[36] Caicedo's *Padrón* of 1778 listed neither Sabana Alta nor San Pedro de Upía, but did include Iximena, with a substantial population of 1,335. Of that number, however, only 174 were classified as Indians, while 670 whites and 484 mestizos made up the balance. It appears that Iximena was no longer a mission in the strict sense of the word, although it was still served by Recoletos. A report by the corregidor del Meta, in 1805, registered Sabana Alta, Iximena, and Chámeza as tribute-paying towns.[37] San Pedro seems to have joined the ranks of the countless settlements that quietly disappeared.

Beginning in 1773 the Recoletos expanded eastward along the Meta. P. Miguel de los Dolores, assisted by two converted Indian captains from Macuco, founded San Agustín de Guanapalo with 200 Guahibos. In 1782 he settled another 400 Guahibos in San Pablo de Guacacía. In 1793 he began a third town, San José de Caviuna, and P. Pablo de la Madre de Dios founded San Nicolas de Buenavista. In 1794 P. Pablo Sánchez began Santa Rosalia de Cabapune. The last reduction, San Guillermo de Arimena (Barrancón), was founded in 1805 by P. Pablo Sánchez. In 1796 Viceroy Ezpeleta reported that the Meta mission had 4,309 Indians.[38] By 1810 the Recoletos ruled 8,070 Indians in nine reductions on the banks of the great river.[39]

Underwriting this drive was a proven ability to manage the ex-Jesuit estates and a policy of creating hatos for each new mission. In 1767, when they received the haciendas of Surimena, Macuco and Casimena, the combined herd stood at 14,900 cattle, 430 stallions, and 1,142 mares. Continuing the Jesuit practice, the Recoletos appointed a missionary to serve as chief administrator, while an experienced Indian or mestizo acted as mayordomo. Assisted by a lieutenant and a council of twelve old men, the mayordomo directed the peons in the work of the ranch. He kept the accounts and worked with the local corregidor to coordinate the buying and selling of cattle. No strangers were admitted to the estates. The crown gave each missionary nineteen guns and a keg of gunpowder to ward off hostile Indians. "With this truly patriarchal regime and the peace which the hatos enjoyed," wrote Daniel Delgado, "they prospered in an astonishing manner."[40] The profits were so substantial that in 1789 the Recoletos renounced financial support from the crown and won permission to transfer herds from the older estates to begin hatos for the new missions.[41] Eight years later Guanapalo, Guacacía, Caviuna, Buenavista, and Santa Rosalia each had its own ranch; by 1810 the nine Recoleto estates had a combined herd of 104,400 cattle, 2,981 stallions, and 6,044 mares.[42]

Like the other orders, the Recoletos could not avoid antagonizing local officials. A formidable enemy was José Planes, who was appointed corregidor of the Partido del Meta in 1805. Planes believed that the Recoletos were remiss in their dealings with the Indians, and his first action on taking possession of the partido was to inspect the missions, four of which were north of the Meta and five to the south. In a memorial addressed to Viceroy Amar y Borbón, Planes painted a gloomy picture. He considered Arimena the best of the reductions because of its excellent location, healthy climate, and hardworking natives. "This town alone maintains all the other missions with its *casabe,* yuca, plátano, and better farmland than the others and much fish," he wrote, before qualifying that it had no priest and that people were dying without benefit of the holy sacraments.[43]

The other missions presented a variety of problems. Casimena was nearly deserted, because its inhabitants had moved to the Franciscan town of Macurrubá. The Indian officials in Surimena had asked him to remove their priest, threatening to set fire to the village and flee if he did not do what they wanted. In Macuco, where Planes resided, the Indians were peaceful but unhappy, because their priest was old and did not say mass. In Caviuna there were likewise many complaints about the priest. Communication between towns was interrupted by marauding Guahibos, who ambushed travelers with poisoned arrows. High water prevented the corregidor from reaching Buenavista, and presumably he could not get to Guanapalo, Santa Rosalia, or Guacacía, since he had nothing at all to say about them.

In general Planes blamed the prefect for Recoleto shortcomings, charging that his advanced age prevented him from supervising the missions with the energy that was required. He recommended that he be replaced, and that the viceroy divide the Partido del Meta into two districts, appointing one corregidor for the towns north of the Meta and another for those to the south, supplying both with soldiers to keep the peace. Finally he requested that part of his annual salary of five hundred pesos be paid out of the profits of the mission hatos.[44]

The governor of the Llanos, Remigio María Bobadilla, when asked by the fiscal and protector of the Indians to comment on Planes's memorial, confirmed his pessimistic description of the missions. Like Planes, Bobadilla believed that a new prefect should be appointed who could command the Indians' respect, since the incumbent was very old and had not even founded a school where they could learn Spanish and "erase their savage ideas."[45] He spoke against dividing the partido, arguing that an active, competent corregidor should have no difficulty in supervising all the towns. Bobadilla admitted that defense was a constant worry. While soldiers were not necessary, he suggested that the corregidor train the white settlers to use the thirty-two guns at his disposal.[46]

In his response to the charges made by Planes and Bobadilla, the Recoleto superior in Santa Fe, Fray Clemente de San Javier, conceded that the missions had deteriorated. The men responsible for this decline were Carlos Daza and José Planes, who had succeeded one another in the post of corregidor during the last seven years. Unlike their predecessor, Estanislao Zambrano, who had exercised skill and vigilance to insure the progress of the missions, both Daza and Planes, were men of bad character, dedicated to their own personal interests, and they encouraged the whites to enslave the Indians. The scheme to apply five hundred pesos to the corregidor's salary from the hatos was the best way to go about destroying them. Fray Clemente defended the prefect, who had faithfully fulfilled his duties for nineteen years, founding one new town, converting and educating many Indians, promoting the growth of the hatos, and observing the divine services of the Church.[47] His testimony carried the day. The fiscal quashed the investigation, although eventually the Recoletos did replace the elderly prefect with a younger man, the "zealous and competent P. Fr. Pedro Cuervo."[48]

Taking into account climatic obstacles, Indian attacks, and the opposition of local authorities, the Recoleto missions on the Meta stand as a considerable achievement. The official census of 1810 showed nine towns with 8,070 Indians. In 1811 José Cortés Madariaga visited all the missions on his journey from Santa Fe to Caracas via the Meta River, he estimated their population at 3,801, a figure considerably lower than the official one. Nevertheless, with the exception of Arimena, which had neither priest nor church, the Venezuelan plenipotentiary found the reductions healthy and functioning. He was particularly impressed by the Sálivas of Macuco, who demonstrated a talent for music. Padre Cuervo told him that he had preserved the native orchestra, composed of violins, cello, recorder, guitars, and triangle, which the Jesuits had begun. He added that "Each month Macuco pays its musicians to stimulate the youth to apply themselves to vocal and instrumental music, and with this measure it has succeeded in improving the chapel, solemnizing the religious functions with the sumptuous dignity of the God to whom they are dedicated."[49] In Macuco, at least, the Jesuit skill at Hispanicizing the Indians had not been completely lost.

In the last days of his reign, Viceroy Ezpeleta, with the approval of the archbishop, awarded the Cuiloto missions to the Recoletos. The order immediately designated four priests and a lay brother to serve the former

Capuchin towns, but lack of funds delayed their departure from Santa Fe. The provincial informed the viceroy, on December 17, 1796, that if the missionaries used their sínodos to pay their travel expenses, they would not have enough money to organize the reductions in a region notorious for lacking almost everything. The fiscal recognized the justice of this argument and granted, on January 17, 1797, an additional sixty pesos to each missionary making the trip to Cuiloto. The Recoletos departed soon thereafter. By June they had installed themselves in Soledad de Cravo, San José de Ele, San Joaquín de Lipa, and San Javier de Cuiloto, all in the jurisdiction of the city of Chire.[50]

Misfortune still dogged the Cuiloto missions. On January 4, 1798, the Recoletos reported that the Indians were leaving the settlements because there was no escolta to restrain them. The four whites who lived in the neighborhood did not have firearms, and all the towns were defenseless against the Guahibos. Without tools to give to the neophytes, the priests could not sustain the communities. They warned that "If some help is not sent, the missions will be finished here."[51]

The situation had not improved by 1800. The prefect, P. Miguel Blanco, wrote to Archbishop Fr. Fernando del Portillo that without soldiers, the missionaries could not keep the Indians in the towns. Their stipends were insufficient to cover their own needs, let alone those of their wards. Blanco had used his own salary to buy clothes for the Guahibos in Cravo and to pay for rebuilding the house of the cura and the church, which the natives constructed. Indicating that his figures were approximate because the Indians lived in scattered hamlets and some were away fishing, Blanco set the population of the towns at 642, distributed as follows. Soledad de Cravo, 141; San Javier de Cuiloto, 141; San José de Ele, 180; and San Joaquín de Lipa, 180.[52]

According to a report from the interim corregidor of Cuiloto, by July 3, 1802, the Indians had no tools to cultivate the land and hunted for their food with bows and arrows. Pedro José Garavito wrote that "they live naked because they have nothing to cover themselves with, and this same need obliges them to leave their towns to rob and commit other excesses that they would not do if their situation were better."[53] Lack of priests remained a difficulty. Only Cuiloto had a permanent missionary. The Recoletos left the rest after two or three months, for trivial reasons: "What is needed for these missions are some religious men of mature reflection—exact, judicious and of a competent age, since the ones who have come recently do not accommodate to the country, become bored, and for other reasons do not fulfill their jobs, leaving these towns abandoned and their inhabitants exposed to the hardships already mentioned."[54] To rectify this "disorder without equal," Garavito recommended the appointment of a new prefect, when Padre Frey Miguel Blanco had served in this capacity, he had required the Indians to attend classes in Christian doctrine.

The missions continued to languish. On November 12, 1807, the corregidor noted that only 117 persons lived in all the villages combined, and that figure included 34 white families. Cravo had fifteen houses; Cuiloto, forty-four; Ele, twenty-three; and Lipa was deserted. The flooding of the Ele, Lipa, and Cravo rivers limited communication, and to the east numerous nomadic Indians, "ferocious and treacherous, had no other occupation than to rob." Weary of reporting the same familiar problems, the corregidor ended his letter by saying, "We see these things every day but there never arrives here any favorable thing."[55]

A Recoleto plan to build a college in Morcote promised some relief, but the project never fully materialized. In 1794 Fr. Justo de Santa Teresa, comisario of the Meta missions, first proposed the establishment of a convent near Cuiloto in order to enable missionaries to reach the reductions more quickly, to provide them with a place for rest and recreation, and to serve as a school for young brothers. Charles IV authorized the plan on August 31, 1799, and agreed to permit the order in Spain to send twenty-five to thirty additional men to New Granada. To subsidize the college, designed to accommodate sixteen priests and four laymen, Archbishop Portillo assigned to it the tithes produced by the parish of Morcote and those of Labranzagrande, Pore, and Santiago, if they were needed. On April 21, 1800, the Recoletos in Santa Fe elected a prior for Morcote and chose eight priests to accompany him. They planned to send another eight men to the college when the thirty recruits arrived from Spain.

By 1803 Recoletos were serving the parishes of Morcote and Labranzagrande, which earlier had become vacant, but the construction of the college did not go forward. In 1806 Manuel de Villavicencio, former governor of the Llanos, died and left instructions in his will that a house which he owned in Morcote be sold at a reduced price to the Recoletos, to serve as their college. His wishes were carried out, but again work was delayed, this time by a lawsuit brought against the order by the new governor, Remigio Bobadilla. The thirty missionaries did not come from Spain, and while a report dated June 22, 1810, verified that there was a small Recoleto convent in Morcote, the dreamed-of colegio never functioned in a way that might have reinforced the missions.[56] The failure of this endeavor was undoubtedly one more factor that prompted Viceroy Mendinueta to propose that a bishopric be created in the Llanos to unify the work of the various religious communities, promote the reduction of the Indians, and facilitate settlement of the wilderness by white colonists from other provinces.[57]

It is evident from this brief review of the work of the Dominicans, Capuchins, Franciscans, and Recoletos that the renewal of the missions in the Llanos after 1767, promoted by all the viceroys from Guirior to Amar y Borbón, was not an unqualified success. Lack of money, insufficient personnel, disputes with local officials, and Indian attacks paralyzed the Capuchins and limited to some degree the other orders. Yet it is also evident that the missions did not collapse with the expulsion of the Jesuits, as historians since the time of José Antonio Plaza and José Manuel Groot have maintained. Table 6 presents a summary of the population of the missions in the Llanos around the year 1800. A comparison of these admittedly approximate figures with those listed for the missions in 1767, given in table 4, shows that there were 15,679 Indians in thirty-one missions in 1800, a gain of 5 percent over the total of 14,838 Indians in the same number of missions in 1767. Comparison of the location of the reductions shown in map 4 and map 6 reveals that by 1800 the missionaries had pushed into Arauca and along the Meta River. The Franciscans made substantial gains, but the Recoletos were the true heirs of the Jesuits. Their success on the Meta, in striking contrast to their dismal efforts in Cuiloto, suggests that careful management of the cattle hatos was a critical factor. An inventory in 1767 showed that the Jesuits had a combined herd of 44,066 cattle, 59 mules, 2,550 stallions, and 1,142 mares, in eight haciendas. By 1810, under Recoleto administration, the herd had increased to 104,400 cattle, 2,981 stallions, and 6,044 mares, in eight haciendas. Neither civilization nor the economy of the Llanos collapsed with the expulsion of the Jesuits. The missions survived the crisis of 1767 to become casualties of the War of Independence.

Beyond reviving the missions, the Bourbons were unable to stimulate economic development of the Llanos. Cotton, textiles, and cattle retained local importance but had little export value, since the population centers in the highlands could get these products more cheaply from other regions. The reduction of Indians along the Meta accentuated the potential advantages of direct trade with Guiana and Spain via the Orinoco River, but determined merchants of Cartagena blocked all schemes, even those put forward by the viceroy, to promote an eastern commercial route that might compete with the Magdalena River trade.

Since the seventeenth century, Europeans who sailed the Orinoco and Meta had insisted that some day this river system would rival the Magda-

Table 6. Missions in the Llanos, circa 1800

Region	Religious Order	Mission	Indian Population
Casanare	Dominicans	San Salvador del Puerto	——
		Tame	——
		Patute	——
		Macaguane	——
		Betoyes	——
			5,425[a]
Casanare	Recoletos	Iximena	?
		Sabana Alta	?
		San Pedro de Upía	?
			?
Cuiloto (Arauca)	Recoletos	Cravo	141
		Cuiloto	141
		Ele	180
		Lipa	180
			642
Meta River	Recoletos	Macuco	1,800
		Surimena	2,068
		Casimena	1,032
		Guanapalo	766
		Guacacia	631
		Caviuna	458
		Buenavista	450
		Cabapune	460
		Arimena	405
			8,070
	Total Recoletos		8,712[b]
Casanare	Franciscans	Güicán	?
		Manare	?
		El Pantano	?
			?
Llanos of San Juan	Franciscans	Tua	328
		Marayal	280
		Cabuyaro	166
		Pajure	140
		Campo del Arrojo	212
		Concepción de Arama	268
		Maricuare	148
			1,542
Total		31 missions	15,679

[a]Posada y Ibáñez, *Relaciones del mando,* 2:441.
[b]Ganuza, *Monografía de las misiones vivas,* 2:99.
[c]Arcila Robledo, *Las misiones franciscans,* 259–61.

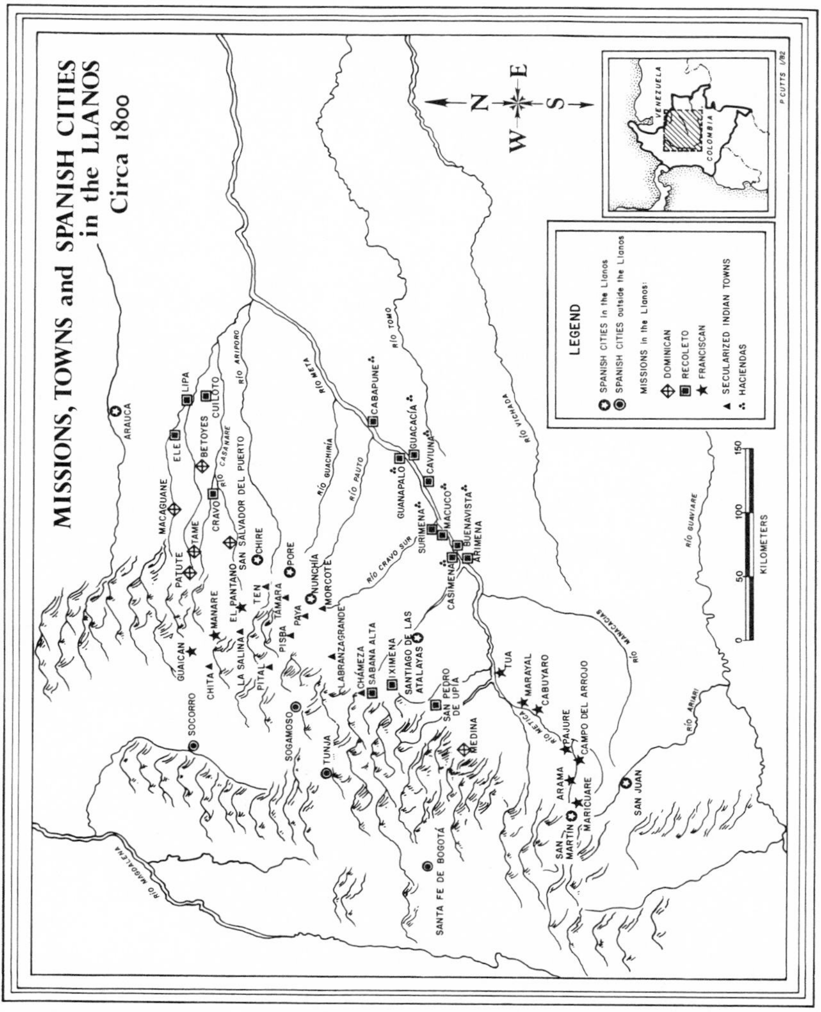
MISSIONS, TOWNS and SPANISH CITIES
in the LLANOS
Circa 1800
LEGEND
SPANISH CITIES in the Llanos
SPANISH CITIES outside the Llanos
MISSIONS in the Llanos:
DOMINICAN
RECOLETO
FRANCISCAN
SECULARIZED INDIAN TOWNS
HACIENDAS
KILOMETERS
0
50
100
150
N
E
S
W
VENEZUELA
COLOMBIA
P CUTTS 1/82
ARAUCA
MACAGUANE
ELE
LIPA
BETOYES
CUILOTO
TAME
PATUTE
CRAVO
SAN SALVADOR DEL PUERTO
CHIRE
PORE
NUNCHÍA
MORCOTE
SOCORRO
GUAICAN
CHITA
MANARE
LA SALINA
EL PANTANO
TEN
TÁMARA
PAYA
PISBA
PITAL
LABRANZAGRANDE
SOGAMOSO
TUNJA
CHÁMEZA
SABANA ALTA
IXIMENA
SANTIAGO DE LAS ATALAYAS
SAN PEDRO DE UPÍA
MEDINA
CABAPUNE
GUACACÍA
GUANAPALO
CAVIUNA
SURIMENA
MACUCO
BUENAVISTA
CASIMENA
ARIMENA
TUA
MARAYAL
CABUYARO
PAJURE
CAMPO DEL ARROJO
ARAMA
MARICUARE
SAN MARTÍN
SAN JUAN
SANTA FE DE BOGOTÁ
RÍO MAGDALENA
RÍO CASANARE
RÍO ARIPORO
RÍO META
RÍO TOMO
RÍO GUACHIRÍA
RÍO PAUTO
RÍO CRAVO SUR
RÍO VICHADA
RÍO GUAVIARE
RÍO MANACACÍAS
RÍO ARIARI
RÍO METICA

lena in commercial importance.[58] By the eighteenth century, the Jesuits were making good use of the river highway to ship textiles, hides, tropical products, salt, and flour between their missions in Casanare and Guayana as well as to Santa Fe, Trinidad, and Spain. Competing with the legal trade was a steady traffic in contraband, as residents of the Llanos conspired with inhabitants of Curaçao and French and Dutch Guiana to smuggle forbidden goods into the viceroyalty.[59] In the 1750s the magnitude of commerce was substantial enough to convince Border Commissioner Alvarado to recommend that the crown make every effort to legalize it.[60] Citing the high prices of flour, rice, seeds, salted meat, tobacco, cotton, hides, and indigo shipped from Cartagena to Spain, Silvestre Sánchez, in his 1789 *Descripción del Reino de Santa Fe de Bogotá,* argued that such goods might be sent more cheaply along the Meta and Orinoco, since the port of Nueva Guayana was closer to Spain than was Cartagena and less exposed to foreign attack.[61]

Viceroy Caballero y Góngora agreed with Silvestre Sánchez. Among other schemes put forward by this aggressive, imaginative administrator during his seven-year reign was a plan to develop the neglected commerce of Guiana and Trinidad by building three roads to link these regions with New Granada and the Orinoco-Meta waterway. The first would be built from Cúcuta to the Apure River, enabling cacao planters to ship their harvest directly to Guiana rather than to Maracaibo. The second would connect Chita, in the Eastern Cordillera, with San Salvador, on the Casanare River, by cutting across the ravine of Sácama and continuing through Sabanalarga. The third would extend from Sogamoso to San Miguel de Macuco, on the Meta River. Caballero y Góngora pointed out that the completion of these roads would stimulate the export to Guiana of sugar, beans, and anise, as well as flour, the key item in demand there. At the time, the Caracas Company employed a factor at San Salvador to purchase flour, but he seldom managed to collect more than half of the eight thousand cargas needed in Guiana. The new roads would alleviate this situation, and they would contribute more than one hundred thousand pesos to the income of the province, much of which would be earned by the boatmen, muleteers, and laborers involved in the expanded trade.[62]

Caballero y Góngora's plan would undoubtedly have stimulated the economy of Casanare as well, but it was never implemented. François DePons and Baron von Humboldt, two perceptive Europeans who traveled along the Orinoco at the turn of the century, blamed the lack of commerce on the obstructionist tactics of the merchants of Cartagena and Santa Marta. After extolling the advantages of navigation on the Meta, "which nature seems to have destined to form vast commercial relations between the whole eastern part of the Kingdom of Santa Fe and Spanish Guiana," DePons wrote that the merchants of Cartagena had persuaded the crown to prohibit all trade on the river except flour and cotton, which could only be exchanged in Guiana for money. In 1804 the merchants of Guiana protested this discriminatory policy, but to no avail. Trade remained limited to hammocks, blankets, coarse articles of cotton, and flour in insufficient quantities. The effect of these restrictions was to destroy the initiative of the llanos cultivator, who found it easier to recline in his hammock and make do with his daily privations "than to fatigue himself to produce commodities, knowing that the time and expense required to transport them to Cartagena would absorb all their worth and sometimes more."[63] Baron von Humboldt agreed that official shackles on trade along the Meta induced by the Cartagena merchants had prevented the development of a commerce that "will one day be of great political importance to the inhabitants of Guayana and Venezuela." He lamented "the strange policy which teaches mother countries to leave those regions uncultivated where nature has deposited all the germs of fertility."[64]

If opening the isolated Llanos to trade to the east was an idea too utopian to merit serious consideration, even the maintenance of the rough trails that provided precarious communication with the highlands was beyond the means of the crown. In 1805 the cabildo of Santiago de las Atalayas asked authorities in Santa Fe to repair the road known as Pie de Gallo, which connected the city with the main road from Pore to Labranzagrande, used by ranchers to drive their cattle to Tunja and from there to Vélez, Socorro, and San Gil. The condition of the trail, which passed over the páramo of Toquillo, was horrendous. Many animals fell to their deaths trying to cross the rocky cliffs and ravines. The royal fiscal, on investigating the situation, agreed that repairs were called for, but ruled that the ranchers themselves should bear the cost. On October 7, 1805, he ordered the governor of the Llanos to begin repairs without any subsidy from the royal hacienda.[65]

The crown was equally unwilling to expand its military presence in the Llanos beyond the escoltas assigned to the missions and haciendas. Royal reluctance to station regular militia on the eastern frontier, as had been done in Darién and Riohacha, sprang from a conviction that the Llanos and the Orinoco jungles, in their tropical immensity, formed an impenetrable natural barrier against foreign invasion.[66] Even after the British seizure of Trinidad in 1797 disrupted this complacency, a militia was never organized, despite the urging of Viceroy Mendinueta. His successor, Amar y Borbón, reaped the consequences when Rosillo, Cadena, and Salgar raised the banner for independence in Casanare in 1810.

Throughout the colonial era, the only soldiers in the Llanos belonged to the escoltas and aided the missionaries by making entradas, keeping the neophytes from fleeing, and protecting the towns from attack. Because of the escalating warfare between whites and Indians, by the late eighteenth century missionaries, townspeople, reduced Indians, and ranchers were besieging Santa Fe with requests to create new escoltas or to reinforce the old ones. Even when these requests were granted, the sources suggest that the soldiers, badly paid and ill disciplined, were too scarce to be of much assistance.

On April 14, 1782, Pablo Serano, corregidor of the missions of Meta, described the sorry state of the escolta assigned to his district. First begun over one hundred years before, the squadron consisted of a captain and six soldiers, one of whom was too old to fight. They were armed with five ancient rifles, three blunderbusses, and seven pairs of leg irons, but had no gunpowder, shot, or balls. The law entitled the captain to a salary of 1,000 pesos and each soldier to 130 pesos per year. In the 1770s, when Francisco Domínguez de Tejada was governor, they had actually received only 50 pesos annually, and that solely because Domínguez had ordered them paid from the profits of the haciendas of Cravo and Tocaría. After José Caicedo became governor, in 1776, they were not paid at all. For years the soldiers had been supporting themselves and their horses on the little that Serano himself could scrape together to give them. Now they were threatening to leave their posts if they did not receive their wages. Serano begged the regent, Gutiérrez de Piñeres, to pay the men and sent two soldiers to deliver his letter, so that they might make a personal plea. Evidently this strategy was unsuccessful. Subsequent letters written by Serano, on June 19 and September 2, indicate that no action had been taken.[67]

In 1763 the cabildo and cura of San Juan de los Llanos wrote to the Audiencia that their town was so beset by belligerent Indians that the inhabitants were moving away. The escolta, made up of vecinos from San Martín and San Juan, was a large one. Twenty soldiers and their officers were based in San Martín, and forty in San Juan, which as the capital and more exposed to the Indians, required a larger force. Unfortunately several soldiers and officers, including the captain, had left San Juan and were living in San Martín. The force remaining was too small to defend the city, and Indians had already killed a lieutenant. Each day the situation worsened. The cura, Fr. Antonio Vicente Gómez, asked the Audiencia to forbid military personnel from leaving San Juan, but the hoped-for decree was not forthcoming.[68]

In 1772 the Franciscans won permission to have an escolta of eight to ten men. A royal cedula of 1775 reiterated the order, assigning a corporal and several soldiers to the reductions around San Martín. When the Franciscans discovered on the Guayabero River a new group of Indians, which they wished to convert, they requested four more soldiers from Viceroy Guirior. Three arrived in time to participate in the founding of Arama, Macatía, and Maricuare. Caballero y Góngora granted two additional soldiers to reduce the Indians living near Apiay. By 1789 there were fourteen soldiers but only enough money to pay ten, and even that amount was not delivered. Lacking money for wages, the Franciscan comisario was forced to dismiss the men by 1806.[69]

Perhaps the most critical situation was that in Cuiloto, where the Guahibos were extremely aggressive and the soldiers notoriously unreliable. In 1805 Guahibo attacks forced the Recoletos to abandon Lipa, Ele, and Cravo. Egged on by the non-Christians, some formerly reduced Indians ambushed a cattle driver by the side of the road. Governor Bobadilla reported that the escolta of ten men could not cope with the crimes being committed, and that at present there was no official to punish the guilty, since he had just dismissed the corregidor for selling aguardiente in Cuiloto and illegally keeping an hato of four thousand cattle.[70] On November 12, 1806, and again on February 22, 1807, Fr. Agustín Villate complained to the fiscal that the soldiers were "insubordinate, scandalous, without honor and filled with vices." They needed a commander who could discipline them, but their corporal was of equally bad character. Villate suggested that the two hundred pesos budgeted to pay a lay brother in the missions be added to the corporal's salary to make the position more attractive to a responsible individual.[71]

Beginning with Messía de la Cerda, the viceroys had long questioned the value of using escoltas to convert Indians. Caballero y Góngora wrote, in his *Relación de mando,* that he did not doubt the sincerity of the missionaries, but experience showed that the neophytes would not stay in the towns unless they could give them the clothes, machetes, knives, and other items which they demanded. Exasperated, the missionaries asked for soldiers to restrain the Indians by force, and the crown paid for these escoltas because they seemed to be the only way to keep the Indians in the missions:

> Such is the conduct which the Indians observe and such the progress of their reduction to civil and religious life perpetually charged by the laws and royal cedulas, but I dare to say that while other means analogous to nature are not attempted, there will not be enough assistance, escoltas or gifts to take this business of such interest to the State and to Religion out of this destructive lethargy. . . . So we see that multiplying the escoltas at notable expense to the Royal Exchequer has only obtained that they [the Indians] enter society and religion through force and fear.[72]

Caballero y Góngora suggested that the state should replace the escoltas with techniques more compatible with the inclinations of human nature, but it was not until 1803 that Viceroy Mendinueta came up with a specific plan for the Llanos. Like his predecessor, Mendinueta believed that one or two soldiers were insufficient to keep the reduced Indians from fleeing or to protect them from attacks. His three-step proposal included creating a bishopric, founding colleges to train the missionaries, and promoting white colonization. With reference to the last point, he argued that the abundant, fertile land in the Llanos was bound to attract settlers, each of whom could become a soldier and assist in the conversion through the "softness of example and the attraction of affection." The Indians would observe Spanish customs as they communicated and traded with the whites and would recognize the advantages of being under an established order. Much progress would result, proving this peaceful method preferable to the violence inherent in the use of escoltas.[73]

Mendinueta's unusual concern about conditions in the Llanos reflected his awareness that the Orinoco-Meta river system formed a highway for potential enemy invasion. Such a possibility had existed since the sixteenth century and had been a factor in royal support of Jesuit efforts to found missions in Guayana and along the Orinoco. After quelling the Comunero Revolt, Caballero y Góngora in 1782 commissioned don Antonio de la Torre, an infantry captain in the royal army, to reconnoiter the territory from Sogamoso to Macuco along the Meta, and from there to Guayana, returning by way of the Casanare River, in order "to determine points that should be fortified to prevent a possible enemy invasion and to study where it would be convenient to establish towns for the defense and civilization of those places."[74] La Torre carried out his assignment, producing a map of the region in question in 1783, but no extra defense measures were taken until after Trinidad fell to the British, in February 1797.

When Mendinueta became viceroy on January 3, 1797, he faced escalating tension inside and outside New Granada. The creoles of Santa Fe were increasingly willing to ridicule Spanish officials. Only two years before, the Audiencia had sentenced Antonio Nariño to perpetual exile from America for publishing a translation of the French *Declaration of the Rights of Man*. Nariño's escape from custody in Cádiz, in April 1796, and his subsequent plotting with the English, proved especially unsettling after Spain joined France in war with England. Mendinueta feared that the British, from their newly won base in Trinidad, might try to penetrate the heartland of New Granada by following the Orinoco River into the Provincia de los Llanos. When, in July 1797, he learned that Nariño had reentered the viceroyalty, he concluded that the wily creole was preparing a popular uprising in support of just such a British invasion.[75]

To meet the emergency, Mendinueta placed the provincial and military authorities on special alert. He ordered two hundred veteran troops from Cartagena to Santa Fe and asked the governors of Havana and Puerto Rico for military assistance. He sent Remigio María Bobadilla, an officer from the Auxiliary Battalion, to replace the incumbent governor of the Llanos, José Sobrino, who besides being a civilian was a brother of one of Nariño's colleagues. Mendinueta empowered Bobadilla to take all necessary precautions in the province, which by its location near the Orinoco could become a passageway for an enemy thrust into the interior. The meager number of troops at his disposal, however, did not permit him to detail soldiers to Casanare.[76]

Nariño's surrender to the archbishop of Santa Fe abruptly ended the crisis, but his subsequent confession justified Mendinueta's alarm. His plan had called for a small naval squadron from Trinidad to feign an attack on Cartagena, in order to draw in Spanish troops from other garrisoned areas. Meanwhile the British were to begin a genuine invasion up the Orinoco and the Meta, joining forces with creole revolutionaries in the Andean highlands. Nariño expected the fighting to begin in Palogordo, a small town outside Santa Fe. From this center he intended to take possession of the narrows and bridge crossings of the mountain trails, which would give him control of all villages within half a day's ride. He then planned to send messages to cabildos, priests, and militiamen, urging them to join the insurrection. Nariño believed that the beleaguered Spanish would surrender as rapidly as they had to the Comuneros in 1781, but his scheme depended on massive popular support. As he traveled in disguise from Cartagena to Santa Fe, in June 1797, he realized that this support would not be forthcoming. Fearing betrayal and defeat, Nariño surrendered on July 19, the same day Mendinueta wrote to Manuel Godoy in Spain, detailing the preparations he had taken to thwart the invasion.[77]

Once the danger had passed, Bobadilla stayed on as governor of Casanare. The crown reconstituted the province as a *gobierno político y militar,* insuring that the chief executive, appointed by the king rather than by the viceroy, would be a military officer. Mendinueta ordered that enlistment be taken for a militia and suggested to his successor, Amar y Borbón, that he station in Casanare a three- to four-hundred man unit, either mounted or infantry, which could be financed by taxes levied on houses, haciendas, and ranches in the province. As long as Spain controlled Guiana, such measures were precautionary, but should Guayana fall to the enemy, the Province de los Llanos would be a frontier worthy of attention. The Orinoco approach was difficult but not impossible. If the enemy, through extraordinary effort, could reach the Llanos, they could easily penetrate the heartland of New Granada. "Fear of such grave consequences obliges us not to scorn the danger completely."[78]

Had subsequent officials taken Mendinueta's wise counsel to heart, it is conceivable that Santander and Bolívar would not have been able to rout the Spanish at Boyacá by mounting an expedition from the Llanos. As it was, any determination to fortify the eastern wilderness subsided with the evaporation of the British threat. A regular milita unit was never created. In 1810, when José María Rosillo, Vincente Cadena, and Carlos Salgar incited the people of Casanare to revolt, they were captured by a hastily assembled force made up of the escolta stationed in Ariporo and civilians led by the alcaldes of Chire and La Mesa. As Caballero y Góngora had done thirty years before, Amar y Borbón completed the pacification by dispatching from Santa Fe an expeditionary force to occupy the province.

Napoleon's invasion of Spain, in 1808, ended the hope of this aged and nearly deaf viceroy for a peaceful and honorable retirement. Reaction in New Granada was typical. With apparent unanimity, peninsulars and creoles declared their loyalty to Ferdinand VII and to the Seville Junta, which claimed to exercise power on his behalf. Amar y Borbón prepared for a possible French invasion, but the greatest danger lay within. In August 1809 he faced a violent uprising in Quito. The rebels, though still loyal to Ferdinand VII, refused to acknowledge the Seville Junta. They abolished the Audiencia in Quito and set up their own government. In Santa Fe, on September 5, the viceroy convoked an assembly of officials, ecclesiastics, and important citizens for consultation. The creoles favored a conciliatory policy toward the insurgents. Instead Amar y Borbón sent a punitive expedition, which crushed the revolt. He summoned reinforcements from Cartagena and imprisoned potential troublemakers, including Antonio Nariño, who, after being released from jail in 1803, was living quietly on his hacienda. These actions hardened the will of the radical elements to resist. On November 20, 1809, the Santa Fe cabildo signed the *Memorial de agravios,* written by Camilo Torres, which demanded equality with Spaniards for creoles—an inflammatory document which the viceroy suppressed.[79]

Manifestations of discontent were not limited to the capital. Patriots in Socorro schemed to acquire arms for a rebellion by sabotaging the expedition sent to Quito. When their hastily prepared plan aborted, the conspirators went into hiding. Three of them—José María Rosillo, Carlos Salgar, and Vicente Cadena—refused to give up the idea. They believed that they could get the necessary weapons by raiding the arsenals in the Meta missions.[80] In the Llanos there were no regular troops to oppose them, and the many Socorranos who had sought refuge there after the Comunero Revolt would help them. Once they had seized the arms, they could return to Socorro and begin the revolution.[81]

On January 11, 1810, the three youths embarked on their desperate adventure by reading before an astonished crowd in the town of San Pedro, near Socorro, a proclamation accusing Amar y Borbón of planning to hand New Granada over to the French. Addressed to Ferdinand VII, the statement called upon all "noble Americans" to arm themselves in defense of their beloved country, religion and king. Rosillo, Salgar, and Cadena then made their way over rough mountain trails to the Meta missions, accompanied by Pedro Pablo Ramos, from Barinas, and Eduardo Salamanca, a deserter from the Cartagena garrison.

Rosillo and his companions stopped at Cabuyaro, San Miguel de Macurrubá, Casimena, and Arimena. The startled Recoletos welcomed them. At each reduction the rebels acquired weapons and attracted followers. They soon reached Macuco, where they intended to imprison the corregidor, José Planes. On learning that he was in Guanapalo, they went directly to that town and captured him. Fr. José Antonio Jaramillo, cura of Guanapalo, gave them supplies, horses, a blunderbuss, and a small cannon. With their prisoner in tow, they made a triumphal return to Macuco, shouting vivas to country, religion, and king. Rosillo forced Planes to read a proclamation, which he and Salgar had written, similar to that pronounced in San Pedro, but dated February 10, 1810. The prefect of the missions, Fr. Pedro Cuervo de la Trinidad, who lived in Macuco, lodged the rebel leaders in his house, found horses and money for them, and permitted them to take along some Indians who were skilled bowmen.

The rebels went on to Pore, stopping first briefly at Trinidad, where they received more weapons and food. Their force now consisted of thirty-five armed men, three small cannons, ammunition, and extra arms. Rosillo planned to arrest Governor Bobadilla and to confiscate the weapons stored in the provincial capital. He attacked Pore at dawn on February 15. The astonished inhabitants offered no resistance. When Rosillo discovered that Bobadilla was away in Támara, he ordered his house occupied and all weapons seized. The local cabildo members, recovering their wits after their initial shock, threw the rebels off guard by inviting Rosillo and Salgar to meet with them to explain their actions. Salgar accepted. He attended the meeting, but sensing a trap as the discussion began, escaped, aided by his companions, waiting outside. The rebels left Pore the same afternoon, marching on to Nunchía where they were met by the alcalde, don Pedro Pinzón, a former Comunero. Soon they set off for Morcote, intending to return to Socorro with all possible speed.

But Rosillo, Salgar, and Cadena had underestimated the antagonism which their actions had kindled in Pore. As soon as they left the town, the authorities uncovered arms which the rebels had failed to find. They organized a militia of twenty-five men, including the escolta of Ariporo and the alcaldes of La Mesa and Chire, commanded by Don Javier Quintero, alcalde de la Santa Hermandad. On February 18 this makeshift force surprised the rebels at their campsite near Morcote, killing one, wounding two or three, recovering all the firearms, and taking ten prisoners, among whom was Vicente Cadena. The rest fled, but Rosillo was apprehended a few days later, at the Hacienda of Tocaría, and jailed in Pore. Carlos Salgar managed to reach Tunja before he was taken. From there he was transported to Santa Fe, remaining imprisoned until he was freed, on July 20.[82]

Meanwhile news of the disturbance in the Llanos had reached the capital. The viceroy and the Audiencia immediately sent a detachment of veteran soldiers, commanded by Lieutenant Colonel Juan Sámano, to restore order, but on learning that Pore authorities had captured the rebels, they recalled Sámano. A reduced troop of twenty-five infantry and five horsemen continued, on led by Subteniente Francisco Sarga. The Audiencia, with the concurrence of Amar y Borbón, ordered Sarga to discuss the situation with Governor Bobadilla and to make his own investigation. Within three days Sarga was to hand over the ringleaders for execution, dispatching their heads and the cases drawn up against them to Santa Fe. To assist in the prosecution, don Pedro Nieto, lawyer and alcalde provincial of Tunja, was to go to Pore "without reply or excuse."

When Bobadilla received a copy of these instructions, dated February 27, he was appalled by their arbitrary nature. On March 8 he wrote to Amar y Borbón, enclosing Rosillo's deposition and requesting permission to send the prisoners to Santa Fe, where they might expect a fair trial. The viceroy was adamant. On March 24 he demanded that Bobadilla comply with the earlier order. On April 28 Dr. Nieto reported to the governor that José María Rosillo and Vicente Cadena should be declared public enemies of the state and the country and condemned to die by hanging for the crime of sedition. Bobadilla drew up the death sentence and set the execution for April 30. Since Pore had no gallows, he decided that the soldiers commanded by Sarga should shoot the condemned men. At 1:00 P.M. on the appointed day, a firing squad carried out the sentence. In accordance with his instructions, Bobadilla had the heads of the dead men cut off and sent to Santa Fe the same afternoon.[83]

The brave but foolhardy actions of Rosillo, Salgar, and Cadena have earned for them a place of honor among the precursors and martyrs of Independence. Seen within the context of Spanish policy toward the Llanos, their unsuccessful revolt exposed the inadequacy of the defense strategy adopted by the Bourbons. With no permanent troops in Casanare, the province invited invasion from both east and west, yet the viceroys could not believe that the remote plains were truly in danger. They preferred to rely upon missionaries to secure the frontier by subduing the Indians and upon tiny escoltas to protect the missionaries. In 1810 the soldiers proved their loyalty, but the clergy appear to have welcomed the rebels with open arms. On July 13 a *real acuerdo* (a tribunal including the viceroy, oidores, and fiscultes) censored Fr. Pedro Cuervo of Macuco, Fr. Hipólito Pino of Casimena, and Fr. José Antonio Jaramillo of Guanapalo for giving Rosillo arms, money, food, and horses, yet the Recoleto provincial did not remove these missionaries from their posts as instructed, perhaps because he had no one to replace them.[84]

The inhabitants of the Llanos showed scant enthusiasm for the unfortunate rebels. It is true that Salgar, Rosillo, and Cadena attracted some recruits, their band included several Indians and at least one black, a slave to whom they promised freedom in Cabuyaro.[85] On the other hand, neither the proclamation read in Macuco nor the taking of Pore proved to be a spark that could ignite the creoles' latent discontent with Spanish rule. It is likely that isolated as they were from the momentous events occurring in Europe, Quito, and Santa Fe, the Casanareños were more surprised than anything else by the appearance of these wild-eyed radicals from the interior—all of whom were *guates,* or outsiders. Finding their own safety threatened, the leaders in Pore organized a counterforce and easily defeated the intruders.

The viceroy's barbaric execution of the rebels was entirely another matter. It was bad enough that two youths, both New Granadans in the flower of their manhood, had been judged, sentenced, and killed by unqualified officials without being permitted to make a defense, to have a lawyer, or to justify their behavior, but to parade their bloodied, putrified heads before the frightened eyes of the multitude in Santa Fe was, as Francisco José de Caldas angrily wrote, an outrage that moved every heart. "Young, old, man, woman, all had indignation written on their faces! . . . It is incredible the degree of blindness these Ministers had reached!"[86] The residents of Pore who witnessed the callous executions must have felt the same cold fury. Amar y Borbón's brutal actions, far more than the rhetoric of Rosillo and Salgar, hardened the resolve of those patriots who, within a few months, would lead Casanare down the road to independence.

6 *Ranches, Towns and Mestizaje*
Continuity and Change in the Late Eighteenth Century

Ranches and towns complemented the missions as the key Hispanic institutions in the Llanos. Although the expulsion of the Jesuits disrupted cattle raising in Casanare, after 1767 the haciendas of Apiay, Tocaría, Cravo, and Caribabare still had substantial herds, while ubiquitous smaller hatos supported reductions, parish churches, and private families. Two new Spanish towns appeared as the old ones declined, but the most dramatic development was miscegenation. By 1810 mestizos dominated or formed a highly visible minority in many settlements, and it is possible to distinguish elements of an emerging regional subculture which would come to be known as *llanero*.

Cattle represented the principal source of wealth throughout the Llanos except in the cotton- and textile-producing towns around Pore. The animals were by now thoroughly acclimated, they required little care or investment. A herd of fifty could be expected to increase to four hundred within five years. Along with the mission hatos, many secularized Indian towns had their own herds. Cattle financed cofradías in Pore, Santiago de las Atalayas, Chire, Puerto de Casanare, and Manare. Privately owned hatos, including the ex-Jesuit estates of Cravo, Tocaría, Apiay, and Caribabare, supplied meat to the surrounding communities and annually dispatched six thousand live animals to the highlands over the Cáqueza, Lenjugá, Pie de Gallo, Labranzagrande, Socotá, and Chía roads. In Pore, artisans tanned hides into fine leathers. Mules were raised in Labranzagrande. Salt could be obtained in Chámeza.[1] In 1786 Governor Joaquín

Fernández recommended that a tax on cattle herds or exports would be the best way to generate funds to support the missions.[2]

The eighteenth-century ranch was not prepossessing. The term *hato* originally meant *herd,* and reflected the seminomadic type of animal husbandry that first appeared in the Llanos. Later the word was transferred to the ranch buildings and meant "the place where the herd is."[3] Constructed of *palo y paja* (sticks interwoven with reeds) or bahareque, these buildings commonly included a house for the mayordomo, or administrator, and a bunkhouse *(caney,* or *ramada)* for the peons. There were one or two permanent corrals, a smaller *corraleja* (for tame cattle), and a plátano or yuca garden, with perhaps a few chickens. When the estate of don José Barragón, ex-administrator of Tocaría, was embargoed in 1791, his assets included a house in Pore and an hato at a place called Curama. On the hato was a small house of palo y paja with two wooden doors and a window, furnished with a single table and two branding irons. There was a separate building, also of palo y paja, which served as a kitchen. Barragón had eighty-two tame cattle *(reses mansas de cría),* two hundred more of the same quality that had not been rounded up, and forty horses. Since his clothes, household goods, and other possessions were in the house in Pore, it is clear that he went to the hato only when work required his presence.[4]

Most of the archival material concerning ranching before 1810 relates to the ex-Jesuit haciendas in Casanare administered by the Junta de Temporalidades. The collected documents of this branch of the colonial government fill twenty-nine volumes and encompass all papers concerning sales, working operations, inventories, and budgets of the properties seized from the order. These sources indicate that Apiay, Cravo, Tocaría, and Caribabare were vast estates. In 1767 Tocaría, for example, consisted of four hatos—El Derecho, San Javier, Garcita, and Aripa y Las Cachas, as well as an administrator's house and a chapel.[5] A 1781 inventory showed that Apiay had 1,682 cattle, 370 horses, 22 mules, 11 oxen, and 2 burros, distributed on three hatos—Apiay, Cumaral, and Patire. Together these subunits equalled more than 11,498 hectares (28,410 acres), valued at 6,342 pesos 6 reals.[6]

When Juan Felipe Carvajal bought Caribabare in 1794 for 15,500 pesos, the estate had 1,031 horses and 5,821 cattle on six hatos extending along both sides of the Casanare River (see table 7). Each hato had one to five buildings made of bahareque or palo y paja, some plantings of plátano, one or more corrals, and (with the exception of Cordero) a corraleja. There were chickens at La Yegüera and Tunapuna and several yokes of oxen at San Nicholas and La Raya. San Antonio and Tunapuna were devoted

Table 7. Hacienda Caribabare: Hatos, Buildings, Corrals, and Livestock, 1793

Hato	Buildings			Corrals		Horses			Cattle		
	Admin.	Peons	Kitchen	Corral	Corraleja	Stallions	Mares	Total	Tame	Wild	Total
La Yegüera	1	2	—	2	1	89	79	168	—	2,370	2,370
Cordero	1	—	—	1	—	1	25	26	116	—	116
San Nicholas	—	1	1	2	1	79	223	302	170	2,083	2,253
La Raya	2	1	1	3	1	130	169	299	82	1,000	1,082
San Antonio	2	1	1	2	1	32	87	119	—	—	—
Tunapuna	1	3	1	2	1	32	85	117	—	—	—
Total	7	8	4	12	5	363	668	1,031	378	5,453	5,821

Source: ANH, Temporalidades, vol. 5, fols. 12–32.

exclusively to horses. Cattle on the other hatos were worth from twelve reals to twenty pesos a head, depending on their relative tameness.[7]

The 5,821 cattle inventoried on Caribabare in 1793 represented a decline of more than 45 percent from the 10,606 there in 1767. The horses made a better showing, with 1,031 in 1793 as compared to 1,384 twenty-six years earlier. Elimination of sugarcane was another significant change. The Jesuits had planted five large cane fields, employing a gang of black slaves to cut the crop and operate the *trapiche* (grinding mill). They sold aguardiente and panela to towns throughout the Llanos. After 1767 the administrators of Caribabare halted this activity because the government had imposed a monopoly on the production and sale of aguardiente and because panela could be made everywhere. They reassigned the slaves to tending cattle. In 1773 Governor Francisco Domínguez reported that the blacks, living in total idleness, were rebellious and claimed that they would obey only their former masters, the Jesuits. He pointed out that the slaves were unsuited to ranch work because they were lazy; it cost more to provide them food and clothing than to pay free wage laborers. His recommendation that the slaves be sold found favor with royal officials. On April 27, 1773, fifty-three adults and children were taken to Santa Fe for auction. On July 3 Francisco Joseph Torrijos purchased the entire group to work at his gold mine in Ibagué.[8] After that time Tocaría was the only ex-Jesuit hacienda in the Llanos that still had black slaves.[9]

Directed by administrators and mayordomos, tributary Indians, whites, and mestizos were the workers of Cravo, Tocaría, Apiay, and Caribabare. They were employed as peones (day laborers) or *concertados* (contract laborers) at a fixed salary. The peons received a wage of one real, paid for each day actually worked. Since they were only hired when the estate operations demanded extra hands, their employment was sporadic. For example, to help with the *vaquerías* (roundups) held in July, September, November, and April of 1788–89, the administrator of Tocaría hired seventeen *peones realeros,* who worked between four and ten weeks and earned salaries ranging from three to eight pesos.[10]

A concertado was a tributary Indian, white, or mestizo who signed a contract to work for six months or a year for a prearranged salary at a designated task such as mayordomo, caporal, or vaquero. Between September 1, 1767, and May 31, 1770, the work force at Tocaría consisted of twenty-eight concertados vaqueros, who were non-Indian, and seventeen indios tributarios concertados. Non-Indian concertados earned from two to seventy-two pesos for that time period, plus a ration of bread and meat for each day worked. The indios tributarios received much less—from two and a half to thirty-three pesos for the same amount of time and a daily food ration, but as additional compensation, the hacienda administrator paid their tribute obligations.

Cravo, Caribabare, and Tocaría employed many tributary Indians who lived in the towns of Cravo, Paya, Manare, Tame, Morcote, and Támara, but, as Hermes Tovar Pinzón has pointed out, with passing years there was a marked preference to hire free laborers as concertados. This trend, common to estates throughout New Granada, reflected the decline of the Indians, a greater abundance of mestizos, and the desire on the part of the ranchers to be free of the religious and social obligations involved in the hiring of Indians. For example, if a tributary Indian fled from the estate, the administrator was still required to pay his tribute tax. To avoid such entanglements, he preferred to pay higher wages to free individuals. This development was slower in the Llanos than in other regions, for Indians continued to make up a majority of the population. Nevertheless there is evidence that miscegenation was creating a large, floating group of non-Indian salaried laborers who worked only part of the year and lived at the poverty level.[12]

It is often argued that after the expulsion of the Jesuits, the haciendas in Casanare decayed rapidly. The dwindling cattle herds at Caribabare support this assertion, and there is no doubt that the new owners, most of whom were absentees, lacked the business acumen, management experience, and institutional support enjoyed by the Jesuits. Three other problems also plagued them—unscrupulous administrators, cattle rustling, and Indian attacks.

In 1780, when Governor Caicedo proposed to investigate his account books, the administrator of Cravo, don Alonso de Vargas, fled to the Llanos of San Juan and San Martín. Three years later the owner, Pedro de Castro y Lemus, who had been jailed for bankruptcy, accused Vargas of defrauding the estate, taking too much money for himself, and failing to present yearly reports of profits, losses, and operating expenses. Vargas, he charged, had permitted the hacienda to deteriorate by selling off the herd, mishandling the Indian laborers, and allowing cattle to stray to other hatos. In short, Castro y Lemus held Vargas responsible for his financial ruin and regarded the administrator's flight as an open admission of his guilt.[13]

In 1791 the Junta de Temporalidades accused don José Barragón, administrator of Tocaría for six years, of irregularities in his accounts and ordered him taken into custody at his home in Pore. Authorities embargoed Barragón's property and remanded him to Santa Fe for trial, where he was duly convicted.[14] A similar fate awaited Francisco Javier de Quiñones, administrator of Caribabare from 1786 to 1791. Quiñones's mistake was to ask the governor of the Llanos in 1790 to assign him one hundred Indians from Tame, Macaguane, and Betoyes and twenty-five whites to defend Caribabare from the Guahibos. An investigation into the cause of the Indian attacks brought to light charges of negligence. Witnesses swore that Quiñones remained at his house in Chire instead of supervising the hacienda. It was public knowledge that he was often drunk and that he had sent his wife away to live with her parents, so that he could freely indulge in his vices. Juan Manuel de Navas, a vecino of Chire, stated that Quiñones habitually killed four steers each month for his own consumption, instead of the two to which he was legally entitled. He failed to record cattle sales in the account books and wasted money by building large houses on all the hatos, "even those which are only used when they make *vaquerías* and afterwards are abandoned."[15] The fiscal in Santa Fe found Quiñones's conduct inexcusable. He ordered him removed from his post and tried in 1793, the same year that Juan Cabeza de Vaca was forced to sell Caribabare.[16]

Widespread rustling was a menace faced by all owners of cattle whether they were parish priests, Indians, missionaries, or ranchers. There are many cases of men tried for stealing cattle in the Llanos in the late eighteenth century. For example, in 1791 don Jacobo Fernández de Zeijas y Torrijos, cura of Pore, brought charges against Felipe Suescún, his sons, and Roque Bello for stealing cattle that had belonged to the church since 1784—thefts so serious that "the mayordomo and other experienced men *(hombres prácticos)* assure me that within a few days the herd will be extinguished."[17] More subtle but just as damaging were the tactics adopted by Juan Agustín Umaña and Juan José Zapata. In 1805 the Indians of Arimena, Casimena, and Surimena complained that these men had established hatos close to the herds belonging to the missions of Surimena and Casimena. When they rounded up cattle, they took animals belonging to the Indians, "most of which are without brands or marks because here there are many strays; they do not brand cattle because they are too wild and secondly because the mayordomo and the peons cannot find all the cattle in these plains which are impassable *(intransitables)* and sometimes, they cannot round up the cattle."[18] The Cura of Arimena testified that the herd attached to his town had declined by seven thousand head between 1803 and 1808, due to constant pilferage by Umaña and Zapata.[19] In some cases the accused were punished. In 1808 Pore officials charged Enrique Pérez with taking cattle without the consent of the owners, selling the animals, and keeping the profits. He was found guilty and sentenced to serve four years in the presidio at Cartagena.[20]

Guahibo raids aginst white and Indian settlements and hatos reached warlike proportions in northeastern Casanare and Arauca. One of the most extensive conflicts was sparked by Juan Francisco Parrales, an escaped black slave from Venezuela, originally hired by Governor Feliciano de Otero in 1797 to reduce the Guahibos engaged in attacking Caribabare. Parrales settled three hundred Indians at Cachama, the deserted hato within the boundaries of the hacienda. When he did not receive tools, clothes, and food promised by Otero to support the new community, he permitted the Indians to seize animals belonging to the estate. Francisco Carvajal, owner of Caribabare, protested that Parrales was teaching the Indians to ride horses and steal cattle. His Guahibos had attacked the Indians in San Salvador del Puerto and destroyed their crops. They had even entered Chire and stolen the horses which the vecinos had tied in front of their houses. Carvajal asked the governor, who by now was Remigio María Bobadilla, to retaliate by organizing an escolta, but Bobadilla refused to act.[21]

The Guahibos, who never stayed very long in one place, burned Cachamba in 1799 and scattered. Some moved to San Salvador de Casanare, where whites and Indians alike found their thievery intolerable. In 1800 Parrales collected seven hundred of them once again and settled at a place called Sumi. Soon the new owners of Caribabare, Domingo Benites and Juan Francisco Larrarte, were complaining that the Guahibos were systematically plundering their herds. Then, in November 1801, a mysterious fire destroyed Sumi. Witnesses came forward to testify that Benites and Larrarte had paid Parrales to burn down the town. On the strength of this evidence, the fiscal del crimen ordered Governor Bobadilla to arrest the two men and embargo their property. Benites and Larrarte claimed in their defense that the "Negro Parrales" had acted on his own to induce the "barbarians" to burn Sumi and to commit other excesses.[22] The case dragged on for years. While the fate of the owners of Caribabare is unclear, the crown did authorize Governor Bobadilla to create an escolta to restore order.[23]

Despite mismanagement, rustling, and Indian attacks, the value of the haciendas increased. Apiay, which sold in 1767 for 4,200 pesos, was purchased in 1782 by Arturo Romero for 6,342 pesos 2 reals.[24] The widow of Pedro de Castro y Lemus, who had bought Cravo in 1779 for 18,295 pesos, sold it in 1792 to Agustín Justo de Medina for 24,461 pesos.[25] Juan Felipe Carvajal acquired Caribabare in 1794 for 15,500 pesos and sold it six years later to Francisco Larrarte and Domingo Benites for 21,500 pesos.[26] In 1803 Domingo Benites reported that after three years of careful supervision, cattle on Hato San Nicholas had tripled, from 5,000 to 15,000 head, and his horses had nearly quadrupled, from 440 to 1,600.[27]

Throughout the colonial era, the crown encouraged the founding of cities as an essential part of the conquest and settlement. The Spanish immigrants were urban oriented, and especially on the frontier, regarded towns as centers of order and direction for civilized life, in contrast to the presumed disorder presented by the Indian cultures.[28] The usual process was for a group of families to cluster together in a hamlet, or *casería,* which eventually became a vice-parish subordinate to the nearest parish. Legally, defined a parish was a community destined exclusively for the residence of Spaniards, with a church, a jail, and civil magistrates. Before the archbishop would authorize the creation of a new parish, the population had to be large enough to support three cofradías, which in turn had to generate sufficient income to pay the priest a minimum annual stipend of from 150 to 200 pesos and to furnish the church with the essential ornaments of ritual.[29] A distinct hierarchy existed between cities, towns, villas, and parishes. Struggles between urban centers seeking to enhance their political or administrative prestige lay at the root of many conflicts in colonial New Granada.[30]

In 1789 Caballero y Góngora noted that the population of Antioquia had grown by 20 percent during the previous decade and estimated that the population of the entire viceroyalty was increasing at a rate of 1.5 percent per year.[31] In the Llanos demographic growth was much slower. Three years before, Governor Fernández had urged the archbishop-viceroy to publish a decree in the Province of Socorro to induce families there to relocate in the plains. He felt that it was vital to establish parroquias and villas at strategic points between Indian reductions. The Spanish presence would keep the Indians from deserting and help stave off the Guahibos. Fernández proposed that a new town should be located on the Meta River across from Macuco and another near Guanapalo. Both sites had a good climate and fertile land.[32] Despite increasing numbers of people in other regions of the viceroyalty and the need for settlers in the Llanos, however, few immigrants came. Those who did gravitated to the older cities. Between 1767 and 1810 only two new parishes were created in Casanare and none in the Llanos of San Juan and San Martín.

The first town developed on land well suited to agriculture and cattle, bounded by the Tocaría and Pauto rivers and halfway between Pore and Morcote. In the sixteenth century the parroquia of Tocaría had been located there, but after burning down twice, it was suppressed. By 1770 more than one hundred people were again living at the site, and since they were expected to attend mass in Morcote, a journey made difficult by impassable roads during the rainy season, they petitioned the archbishop to recognize them as a separate parish.

The Cura of Morcote, don Juan Laureano de Rosas y Torres, and Governor Francisco Domínguez de Tejada supported their request. Rosas y Torres testified that hazardous roads prevented many settlers from fulfilling their religious obligations. Those who reached Morcote had no place to stay, especially during Holy Week and other festivals. They lodged with Indians, getting their hosts drunk on aguardiente and taking advantage of them. "It is clear to me," the cura added, "that in some towns already, many Indians are mestizos and this can be from no other cause than mixing with whites in those places." The creation of a new *parroquia* would stop this practice, for "whites should not live among the Indians and their resguardos."[33] Governor Domínguez de Tejada reiterated these arguments and suggested that the new church could be equipped with the sacred ornaments taken from the confiscated Jesuit chapel at Caribabare. The case was a strong one. On November 27, 1770, the archepiscopal office approved the new parish of San Carlos de Nunchía.[34]

Given the geographical barrier presented by the Eastern Cordillera on the western side of the Llanos, a more likely route of immigration lay from Venezuela, on the east. Since the sixteenth century a trickle of fugitive slaves and creoles from Barinas and Caracas had made their way along the tributaries of the Orinoco to take up residence in Casanare and the Llanos of San Juan and San Martín. Already acclimated to the tropics, they had a distinct advantage over would-be settlers from the Andes. Thus it comes as no surprise that Venezuelans founded the second town, near the missions of Cuiloto, calling it the Villa of Santa Bárbara de Arauca.

On December 4, 1780, two men from Barinas, Juan Isidro Daboin, a secular priest, and Antonio Useche, a laborer, crossed the Arauca River and came upon some partially christianized Guahibos. Receiving a cordial reception, the men decided to stay, and Daboin assumed reponsibility for the spiritual direction of the natives. He went to Morcote where Governor Caicedo granted him permission to bring in more settlers with their slaves and cattle from Barinas, Cuiloto, and Betoyes and authorized him to distribute land for grazing and crops. By 1784 one hundred whites and blacks had built palm-thatched huts in the town and had begun hatos in the surrounding plains. Santa Bárbara flourished because its location on the Arauca River facilitated trade with Venezuela. By 1793 it had earned the status of vice-parroquia of Chire, which meant that the priest in Chire served its chapel on a regular basis. More importantly the designation meant that Santa Bárbara was to be reserved for Spaniards and would not become another Indian town.[35]

The appearance of only two new towns on the vast Llanos frontier during a period of forty years suggests that the white population increased very slowly, a conclusion born out by the marked decline of the older cities. In 1773 Governor Francisco Manuel de Quiros reported that Santiago de las Atalayas, Pore, and Chire were all reduced to great poverty. So few individuals qualified for public office lived in Chire that he had suppressed the cabildo, leaving municipal government in the hands of a single *alcalde pedaneo* (parish judge). The vecinos resented this action. Egged on by their cura, Lorenzo Justiano Joseph Ferrena, they had illegally elected two alcaldes ordinarios and a procurador general (legal representative) "in grave harm to themselves for they have to pay for the cost of these titles in the midst of their poverty, and it is harmful to the public good because the people are inept and incapable to serve as judges."[36] Quiros asked the Audiencia to suppress this illegitimate cabildo and to permit the cabildo of Pore to nominate the alcalde pedaneo authorized for Chire.

In the same letter Quiros complained that Padre Ferrena, for his own particular ends, was attempting to relocate Chire, a city which had already been moved five times. Having built a chapel at a site called Manaure, a half day's ride away, the priest was compelling the vecinos to transfer their homes to the new locale. Ferrena, who had already petitioned the crown to sanction the move, insisted that the climate at the old spot was so bad that everyone suffered from chills and fever and that nearly all the houses and the church were in ruins. By contrast Manaure, on the Río Carona, was peaceful and dry, with a good breeze. It had pure water, an abundance of wood, and a complete chapel.[37] Ferrena maintained that the vecinos supported the move, but Governor Quiros's opposition carried greater weight. The archbishop ordered the headstrong priest to resume his duties at the old church.[38]

Like the residents of Chire, the vecinos of Santiago de las Atalayas were also searching for a better location. Situated on the Aguamena River, at the base of a mountain which cut off fresh winds, their city was unusually humid. They suffered continually from disease. In 1770 Governor Domínguez affirmed that if a new locale were not found, Santiago would be completely ruined. In 1776 the residents considered and rejected a site called Busumena. Then, after a fire burned down part of the church and several buildings on December 7, 1777, the cura, José María Arteaga, with the backing of the cabildo and several vecinos, decided to rebuild at Chitamena, on the other side of the Cusiana River. Construction went forward and by August 1778 a church, cabildo building, and more than one hundred houses stood at the new site. Testifying that Chitamena was healthy and possessed all the necessary requirements to assure prosperity, the cabildo asked Viceroy Flórez to make the move official.[39]

Flórez hesitated. Representatives of three hundred people who had remained at the original site disputed the cabildo's petition. They claimed that they were too poor to relocate in Chitamena. Their spokesman, Juan María Pérez, accused Padre Artega, the alcaldes, and a French *chapetón* (foreigner), called Juan Bautista Bustón, of engineering the move to further their personal interests and to enable the rich people to be closer to their hatos. In the meantime the poor of Santiago were deprived of the services of their priest. To reach Chitamena they had to cross the raging waters of the Cusiana, a passage so dangerous that one woman had seen her newly baptized child swept out of her arms as she forded the river. The people who had stayed in Santiago were so angry that they were considering appealing to the vecinos of Pore to supply them with men and arms to force the Chitamena group to return. Juan María Pérez wrote many letters presenting this case and concluded them all by begging the viceroy to order the church and the cabildo house rebuilt on the original site.[40]

The feud between the two settlements continued for years. On November 14, 1781, the archbishop ordered Artega either to assign an assistant clergyman to the old church in Santiago or to place a boat on the river to insure the safety of the children and sick who came across, but the priest did not comply.[41] In 1788 Manuel Villavicencio took office as governor. Investigating all aspects of the dispute, he concluded that the old city offered little possibility for further development. The new site had an excellent climate and a location that would foster commerce, agriculture, and manufacturing throughout the province. The people living there were honorable and decent and their number was growing. Despite Villavicencio's endorsement of Chitamena, the viceroy refused to sanction the move so long as a significant number of people remained in Santiago. On February 23, 1789, he suspended approval until the time when all those involved could agree on a course of action.[42]

Such consensus was impossible. By 1796 the vecinos of Santiago were taking a new tack by suing the residents in Barroblanco (Iximena) to try to force them to move to Santiago.[43] Continuous litigation was another sign of the decay of the ancient capital, which disappeared from maps of Casanare during the Wars of Independence.

Meanwhile, to the south, San Juan de los Llanos, the first city founded in the plains, was struggling for its survival. In 1763 its cabildo reported that because of Indian attacks so many vecinos had died or moved to San Martín that there were not enough left to fill the municipal offices. A militia formed by citizens of both cities was insubordinate. Some of the soldiers and their officers, including the captain, who were supposed to live in San Juan, had decamped to San Martín, leaving the former town defenseless.[44] A letter from the cura affirmed that the Indian raids grew worse every day. Those people who remained in San Juan were in debt to the royal hacienda and unhappy because they had so few neighbors. The cura urged that a decree be issued forbidding the military to leave the city and that other steps be taken to encourage whites to emigrate to San Juan.[45]

As usual nothing happened to resolve the situation, and the rivalry smoldered. In 1785 when Fermín García Parado, alcalde of San Juan, wanted to lead an entrada against a settlement *(palenque)* of free blacks that he regarded as a menace, the captain of the escolta in San Martín refused to cooperate, on the grounds that Juan Félix Buitrago, a member of the palenque, was an honorable soldier under his command. As the Franciscans also supported Buitrago, testifying that he had assisted them in reducing Indians, García Parado took matters into his own hands. He captured Buitrago and confiscated his property, in 1787. Buitrago later sued to recover his possessions, which included thirty-three cattle, three horses, a saddle, a change of clothing, two books, a writing table, and a shotgun, but the documents do not indicate how the case was resolved.[46] The incident is important for the light it throws on the only palenque known to have existed in the Llanos, and it also shows the tension between the white inhabitants of the two cities.

In the end San Juan seems to have destroyed itself. In 1794 the mysterious death of the priest in El Rayo, an Indian town, and a severe quarrel between civil and religious authorities prompted the royal fiscal to send the corregidor of Cáqueza, Manuel Ruíz Gámez, to investigate. Ruíz Gámez arrived in San Juan on November 18, after a perilous journey over mountains without any roads and across rivers swollen by winter rains. He collected evidence from everyone involved, some of whom had taken refuge in San Martín. He concluded that both the alcalde, Francisco Lucena, and his son-in-law, who served as procurador, were corrupt and that there was no one in San Juan honest and capable enough to hold public office.[47]

On January 7 the fiscal ordered the imprisonment of Lucena and his henchmen and the confiscation of their property. This last scandal demoralized the remaining vecinos who, seeking greater security for their families, joined the exodus to San Martín. Like Santiago, San Juan disappeared from maps by 1810. All that remains of it today is a church bell with the inscription of the convent of San Juan and the date, 1619, it can be seen in the modern town of San Juan de Arama.[48]

Of the six Spanish cities founded in the sixteenth and early seventeenth centuries, only San José de Pore was economically and politically viable by the end of the eighteenth century. This vitality sprang from its location on the main cattle trail and its involvement in the production of hides and meat. It is also significant that, according to the census of 1778, mestizos made up 79 percent of Pore's population. Miscegenation was taking place in the Llanos at a slower pace than in other parts of New Granada, but it was a fundamental process that produced a distinctive regional subculture.

Jaime Jaramillo Uribe has described mestizaje as the most dynamic factor in New Granada society in the eighteenth century.[49] Using Francisco Silvestre's figures, based on the census of 1778, for those provinces which became the Republic of New Granada, he has shown that 47.85 percent of 738,523 inhabitants, or 353,435, were classified as mestizo, while the 189,279 whites made up 25.62 percent, 143,810 Indians made up 19.47, percent and 51,999 slaves made up 7.04 percent of the total.[50] Governor Caicedo's census of the Provincia de los Llanos in 1778 reveals that Indians there still accounted for 73 percent of the population—a proportion that would have been even higher if the natives living in the plains and forests beyond Spanish control had been included (see table 8). Nevertheless, mestizos at 19 percent were the next largest group and easily outdistanced the whites at 7 percent and the black slaves at less than 1 percent.

Table 9 ranks the cities and towns according to the percentage of whites, mestizos, and Indians in their populations. Although more whites lived in Iximena, only in Santiago did they form over half the population. In Chire and Pore, cities officially reserved for Spaniards, whites made up 16 and 12 percent, respectively, while mestizos made up 84 and 79 percent of the population. Mestizos also dominated Nunchía (89 percent), Labranzagrande (79 percent), and Aguariva (60 percent). They made up 40 percent of Patute and more than 30 percent of Iximena, Cravo, and Santiago. Indians continued to be concentrated in the missions. They constituted at least 97 percent of the inhabitants of eleven towns, yet in all but three of these legally segregated communities there were mestizo

Table 8. Population of the Provincia de los Llanos by racial groups, 1778

Town	Whites* No.	%	Indians No.	%	Mestizos No.	%	Slaves No.	%	Total
Ciudad de Santiago	494	56	55	6	286	33	37	4	872
Iximena	671	50	174	13	484	36	6	.4	1,335
Chámesa	93	24	171	45	114	30	—	—	378
Casimena	7	2	380	97	3	.7	—	—	390
Surimena	12	1	908	97	17	2	1	.1	938
Ciudad de Pore	131	12	42	4	804	79	40	3	1,017
Nunchía (parroq.)	17	2	33	5	606	89	23	3	679
Macuco	3	.3	619	98	8	1	—	—	630
Guanapalo	1	.2	637	99	—	—	—	—	638
Morcote	3	.1	2,165	98	35	1.5	1	**	2,204
Támara	4	.2	2,079	97	57	2	1	**	2,141
Paya	2	.3	544	90	60	9	—	—	606
Pisba	1	.2	590	98	8	1	—	—	599
Labranzagrande	9	1	140	19	587	80	—	—	736
Cravo	11	1	692	63	380	35	10	1	1,093
Cuidad de Chire	57	16	—	—	298	84	—	—	355
Ten	1	.2	484	88	62	11	—	—	547
Manare	1	.1	625	98	9	1	—	—	635
Tame	17	1	1,739	94	89	4	—	—	1,845
Macaguane	1	**	1,635	99	4	.2	—	—	1,640
Betoyes	20	1	1,276	98	—	—	—	—	1,296
Patute	—	—	66	50	65	50	—	—	131
Puerto	1	1	114	99	—	—	—	—	115
Aguariva	1	1	21	29	50	69	—	—	72
Total	1,115	7.5	15,189	72.7	4,026	19.27	119	.6	20,892

Source: Adopted from the census taken in 1778 of the Provincia de los Llanos by José Caicedo, by royal order of Nov. 10, 1776.
*Includes secular and regular clergy.
**Negligible percent.

Table 9. Cities and Towns in the Provincia de los Llanos, Ranked by Racial Groups, 1778

Whites (%)			
Santiago	56	*1% or less:* Casimena, Surimena, Macuco, Guanapalo, Morcote, Támara, Paya, Pisba, Labranzagrande, Cravo, Ten, Manare, Tame, Macaguane, Betoyes, Patute, Puerto, Aguariva	
Iximena	50		
Chámesa	24		
Chire	16		
Pore	12		
Nunchía	2		
Mestizos (%)			
Nunchía	89	Ten	11
Chire	84	Paya	9
Pore	79	Tame	4
Labranzagrande	79	Surimena	2
Aguariva	69	Támara	2
Patute	49		
Iximena	36		
Cravo	35	*1% or less:* Casimena, Macuco, Guanapalo, Pisba, Manare, Macaguane, Betoyes, Puerto	
Santiago	33		
Chámesa	30		
Indians (%)			
Guanapalo	99	Paya	90
Macaguane	99	Ten	88
Puerto	99	Cravo	63
Betoyes	98	Patute	53
Manare	98	Chámeza	45
Macuco	98	Aguariva	29
Morcote	98	Labranzagrande	19
Pisba	98	Iximena	13
Támara	97	Santiago	6
Casimena	97	Nunchía	5
Surimena	97	Pore	4
Tame	94	Chire	0

Source: Adapted from the census taken in 1778 of the Provincia de los Llanos by José Caicedo, by royal order of Nov. 10, 1776.

agregados, bearing out the fear voiced by the cura of Morcote in 1770, that mestizaje, however undesirable, was rapidly taking place.

Historians have written little about mestizos in the eighteenth century. The term *mestizo* was applied indiscriminately to individuals of a variety of racial backgrounds. Often it was synonymous with *vagabond* or *criminal.* Colmenares observes that while many data are available on Indians, whites, and slaves, information about mixed-bloods, poor whites, and artisans is inferior in quality and very dispersed.[51] Similarly little attention has been paid to a related issue, the colonial roots of the regional mestizo subcultures such as the *antioqueños, costeños, pastusos,* and *boyacenses,* which after the Wars of Independence flourished vigorously at the expense of the growth of Colombian nationalism. As a result the origins of the Llaneros, certainly one of the most picturesque regional types of the nineteenth century, has never been carefully investigated, the studies that do exist confuse their evolution with that of their more famous counterparts to the east, in Venezuela.[52]

The Venezuelan llanos share the geographical characteristics of those of New Granada, but are more accessible from the northern highlands and Caribbean coast because the Coastal Range is less rugged than the Eastern Cordillera of Colombia. In the late eighteenth century Bourbon policy fostered a spectacular growth of ranching south of Caracas Province. Legalization of the export of hides and live animals to the Antilles reinforced the already steady demand for salted meat, leather, and hides in the central highland valleys and the coast. Creoles began to acquire ranches in Guárico, Apure, Cojedes, and Barinas.[53] The historian Frederico Brito Figueroa has estimated that by 1810 ranching covered an area of 150 leagues between El Pau, to the east, and Mérida, to the west. Under the control of absentee owners were 1,200,000 cattle, 180,000 horses, and 90,000 mules, along with innumerable sheep and lambs.[54] For the entire Venezuelan llanos, the figure of 4,500,000 cattle in 1812 is commonly cited.[55]

A burgeoning population paralleled this economic boom. The Venezuelan llanos attracted peninsulars and foreign planters fleeing social and political upheaval in the Antilles, as well as thousands of fugitive slaves. By 1789 it was estimated that there was a floating population of over 24,000 partially Hispanicized Indians and black runaways who lived as outlaws, attacking towns and stealing cattle. Creole landowners made repeated but unsuccessful attempts to control these vagrants by requiring them to live in fixed towns and by setting harsh penalties for people engaged in rustling and smuggling.[56]

It was these black and zambo (mixed black and Indian) peons, who worked as legitimate vaqueros or lived completely outside the law, that were first identified as Llaneros. In the original French edition of his classic work, *Voyage aux régions équinoxiales du nouveau continent fait en 1799, 1800, 1801, 1802, 1803 et 1804* (Paris, 1815), Baron von Humboldt wrote that "the Llaneros, or inhabitants of the plains, send their products, especially corn, hides, and animals to the port of Cumaná. . . . We saw arriving without cease the mules led by the Indians or the mulattoes."[57] In later editions, Humboldt enlarged on this portrait by describing a ranch that he visited on his way to Calabozo. The hato, he wrote, consisted of a solitary house surrounded by smaller huts covered with palms and skins. Men naked to the waist and armed with lances tended the cattle, oxen, horses, and mules that wandered over the unfenced plains. "These mulattoes, who are known by the name of *peones llaneros,* are partly freedmen and partly slaves. There does not exist a race more constantly exposed to the devouring heat of the tropical sun. Their food is meat dried in the air, and a little salted, and of this even their horses sometimes eat. Always in the saddle, they fancy they cannot make the slightest excursion on foot."[58] When the creoles in Caracas declared independence, in 1811, it was these peones llaneros who, fearing the repressive policies of the patriots more than those of the royalists, followed the lead of José Tomas Boves to bring down the Second Republic, in 1814.

In contrast to Venezuela, New Granada had no economic boom to spur the expansion of ranching in the Llanos, if a large floating population of vagabonds existed, it was not threatening either to the hacendados or to royal authorities. More striking still was the small number of blacks—whether slave, free, or fugitive. Where in Venezuela Africans dominated the population of the Llanos by the eighteenth century, in the Provincia de los Llanos, the census of 1778 counted only 119 slaves in all of Casanare, although blacks and mulattoes undoubtedly made up some of those listed as mestizo ("libres y varios colores").

In his essay on the cultural evolution of the Colombian llanero, Manuel Zapata Olivella argues that the African presence has been "discrete" but not absent.[59] Slaves accompanied the conquistadors to the plains. Pedro de Aguado recorded that Juan de Avellaneda, founder of San Juan de los Llanos, in 1556, employed blacks as well as Indians to wash gold from the Ariari River. On his expedition to the so-called Valle de Plata, he sent seven blacks, "his slaves which he had brought with him," as advance scouts to cross the Guaviari River and return with news of the Indians.[60] Settlers from the Eastern Cordillera brought blacks with them as personal slaves, a mark of distinction in the remote cities.[61] Other Africans entered from Venezuela, traveling from Coro to Quito along the roads of San Martín, Neiva, Mocoa, and Pasto. The area around Cúcuta, the natural gateway to Arauca, became a meeting place for slaves, missionaries, and those dedicated to commerce between the Magdalena and the Llanos.[62] Blacks worked as boatmen on the rivers and occasionally in the tasks of herding cattle. The Jesuits imported groups of slaves to run the sugar mills. They also served as foremen and domestic servants on the haciendas of Caribabare and Tocaría.

Their numbers remained small for several reasons. Few black women came. The men intermingled with Indian women to produce zambos.[63] The lack of mining centers made slave labor unnecessary, and Indians were abundant for the work that was required. After the expulsion of the Jesuits, the governor of the Llanos shipped the fifty-three slaves remaining on Tocaría to Santa Fe to be sold, in 1773, because he regarded their presence as a liability rather than an asset. Due to the remoteness of Cartagena, Antioquia, Valle de Cauca, and the Pacific coast—the principal slave regions in New Granada—few escapees sought refuge in the Llanos. The only palenque mentioned by eighteenth-century sources was that already cited, outside the cities of San Juan and San Martín. In 1785 it consisted of Xavier Buitrago, his six sons, and some other relatives. The origins of the Buitragos are not known, but one member of the community, Juan de la Cruz Granadillo, admitted (before he was executed for having allegedly murdered an alcalde of San Juan) that he was an escaped slave from Coro.[64] Although the authorities in San Juan regarded the palenque as a threat, the escolta and the Franciscans in San Martín came to its defense. Witnesses on behalf of Juan Félix Buitrago described him as an honest citizen and soldier, who had aided in the reduction of Indians for ten years.[65]

The case of Juan Francisco Parrales also appears to be somewhat exceptional. Parrales was the escaped slave from Calabozo who became a leader of the Guahibos along the Arauca River, teaching them to ride horses and to steal cattle from the surrounding hatos. Parrales lived with the Indians in the forest and took two Guahibo sisters as concubines. The whites were afraid of him, yet he enjoyed quasi-official status, being commissioned by Governors Sobrino and Bobadilla to reduce the Indians and teach them to live as Spaniards. If one can speculate on these two isolated instances, it would seem that the Buitragos and Parrales are representative of black and Venezuelan influence within the basically mestizo cultural matrix in the llanos of New Granada—an influence most pronounced in Arauca and on the eastern perimeter, and one that would increase dramatically during and after the Wars of Independence.

A more valid colonial prototype for the Colombian llanero lies in the Indian and mestizo peons and *concertados*. Employed on the haciendas and hatos, these vaqueros adapted cattle-raising techniques that had originated in medieval Iberia to the tropical conditions of the plains. Eighteenth-century descriptions of their dress, diet, housing, and working conditions reveal elements of a subculture that writers in the nineteenth and twentieth centuries would celebrate in song, story, and the popular press.

The itemized account books of the ex-Jesuit haciendas show that the peons and concertados wore trousers and shirts made from locally produced cloth, hemp sandals, sombreros, and ruanas. Their diet was meat and *casabe* bread, augmented by plátano, maize, cacao, salt, panela, and aguardiente.[66] Some vaqueros lived with their families, but most were single men, housed in the caneys or ramadas.

The bahareque ranch buildings thatched with straw were simple and sparsely furnished. According to an inventory of Hato La Yegüera, taken in 1793, the administrator's house consisted of a *sala, aposenta,* pantry, and another room. It had four wooden doors with iron rings and one with a lock. There was a balustered window in the sala. Two wooden tables, four cowskin chairs, "all broken," three chests, and a metal washstand made up the furniture. For tableware there were three pewter plates, a broken stone platter, and three bottles. There were three curved machetes, "very worn without handles," two axes, two saws, an old hoe, and a broken shovel. Two branding irons, three lances, two *tijeras de trasquillar,* and two *cuchillos carneros,* proclaimed the principal work of the ranch. Finally there was an arsenal of five shotguns *(escopetas)*, three of which were broken, and an unworkable blunderbuss *(trabuco)*. In the neighboring caney, occupied by the peons, were two large water jars, fourteen plates, twenty-one small bowls, four saddles, a pair of stirrups, a bridle, two pack saddles, and two branding irons.[67]

Work on the hatos was seasonal. Peons and concertados often left a job after two or three months. Rounding up and branding wild cattle were the main tasks; the busiest days were when cattle were driven to another hacienda or to a town to be sold. A fascinating description of a drive, or *saca,* is included among the documents of the Royal Boundary Commission of 1754–59. Colonel Eugenio de Alvarado, while headquartered at San Martín, in June 1759, decided to purchase three thousand cattle from ranchers in the Provincia de los Llanos to supply his expedition. His agent in Santiago de las Atalayas reported that cattle sold for two pesos a head at hatos in Casanare, three pesos a head at Hacienda Tocaría, and four pesos a head in the cities of Pore, Chire, and Santiago. To transfer one hundred cattle, Alvarado would have to hire four peons on horseback and a *puntero*—a peon to lead the herd. He would need a muleteer, two pack mules to carry meat and bread, and either a mayordomo or a soldier to take charge of the drive. Horses for the vaqueros could be purchased at fifteen pesos each. The mayordomo required nine horses, one to ride and eight replacement mounts. It would also be necessary to purchase a large branding iron, to mark cattle which got tired along the way and would have to be left. The seller of the cattle would supply the vaqueros with their morning and afternoon rations of casabe, meat, and *cacao de panela* (chocolate drink), but Alvarado would have to pay their wages. For the trip from Casanare to Apiay via Chire, Pore, and Santiago, the peons would expect to earn eighteen pesos each, but they would accept less if paid in goods from Spain or made locally.[68]

Such documents as those cited above provide tantalizing glimpses into the lives of the cowboys of eighteenth-century New Granada. Of their women, however, almost nothing is known. Most of them were undoubtedly Indians, contributing to the Americanization of Iberian customs. They cultivated the yuca, maize, cacao, and tobacco that supplemented the European beef and the African plátano. They wove cotton into shirts and ruanas and fashioned hemp into sandals that replaced the European boots. From the Indians the vaqueros learned how to build houses and boats out of materials found in the Llanos. They learned to sleep in hammocks, use lances, hunt deer and jaguars, and sail the treacherous rivers. Like the Indians they adopted a nomadic way of life.[69]

Racial miscegenation and the amalgamation of Spanish, Indian, and to a lesser extent, African customs produced in the Llanos a distinctive group of horse-riding, cattle keeping people. During the War of Independence, these Llaneros played a key role in the patriot victory over the Spanish. The earliest published description of them by a Colombian, written eight years after the Battle of Boyacá, identifies characteristics that take on mythic qualities in later accounts. In *Historia de la revolución de Colombia,* first published in 1827, José Manuel Restrepo wrote:[70]

> In the years preceding the Revolution, the character of the inhabitants of the eastern plains of Venezuela and New Granada, composed of negros and mulattoes, of Indians and whites, was marked with a particular tincture. Accustomed from their first infancy to fighting with jaguars and ferocious bulls, living on horseback, mounting fearlessly the most

indomitable stallions, armed with a lance, they feared nothing and their favorite occupation was to watch over and manage the numerous herds on the Llanos; thus, they swam the deepest rivers, without worrying about the alligators or the other voracious fish, placing one hand on their horse who swam at their side. These qualities made the Llanero an appropriate man for war, and in the War of Independence we have seen realized the presentiments of some celebrated travelers. The fearless Llaneros were prodigiously brave, and with lance and horse, executed the most brilliant actions that are mentioned in the pages of the *Historia Colombiana*.

The Llanos of Casanare, 1856. This watercolor and the others dated 1856 were painted by Manuel María Paz, who went to the Llanos of Casanare in that year as a member of a commission led by the Italian cartographer Agustín Codazzi. These paintings are the oldest and most authentic pictures of the Llanos. They are reproduced in *Album de la Comisión Cartogràfica* (Bogotá, 1953) edited by Julio Londoño.

The Venezuelan Llanos, 1868. This anonymous etching shows a river in the Llanos with a *garcero* or nesting place for herons in the foreground. It was published as an illustration for Ramón Páez, *Travels and Adventures in South and Central America* (New York, 1868).

The Llanos of San Martín, 1878. The French artist Edouard Riou made this etching to illustrate Edouard Andre's account of his travels in Colombia, Ecuador, and Peru. It was published in the French periodical *Tour de Monde* in 1878. The Riou illustrations are reproduced in Eduardo Acevedo Latorre, *Geografía Pintoresca de Colombia* (Bogotá, 1968).

A Pasture in the Llanos: The Garrapateros (birds that eat ticks) from a drawing by Edouard Riou (1833–1900).

Guahibo Indians, 1856

Sálivo women preparing *casabe,* 1856

Indians and whites encamped on the Meta River, 1856

Branding cattle in Casanare, 1856

A Venezuelan roundup, 1868 (Páez, *Travels and Adventures*)

Roundup in the Llanos of San Martín, 1878 (Riou, *Tour de Monde)*

Left: Gonzalo Jiménez de Quesada, Adelantado of New Granada and an early explorer of the Llanos. Etching by Rodríguez originally published in the illustrated periodical *Pape/Periódico Ilustrado* (Bogotá).

Right: Fray Ignacio Mariño, Dominican missionary and patriot leader in Casanare. The original oil painting is in the Museo Nacional in Bogotá. This photo is a copy of a reproduction in Roberto María Tisnes J., *Fray Ignacio Mariño, O.P.* (Bogotá, 1963).

Simón Bolívar, Supreme Chief of the Republic and Captain General of the Armies of Venezuela and New Granada. Engraving by M. N. Bate from an original drawing published in 1819. The original is in the Museo Nacional, Bogotá. This photo is a copy of a reproduction in Enrique Uribe White, *Iconografía del Libertador* (Bogotá, 1967).

Llaneros capturing a Spanish gunboat, 1818. One of the most famous exploits of José Antonio Páez was the capture of a Spanish gunboat by his Llanero cavalry in 1818. Páez recounts the incident in his *Autobiografía* (Caracas, 1973): 127–36. This etching is in Páez, *Travels and Adventures*.

Crossing the Páramo of Pisba. Oil painting of the ordeal of the Liberation Army by Francisco A. Cano. The original is in the Quinta de Bolívar, Bogotá. This photo is a copy of a reproduction in Tisnes, *Fray Ignacio Mariño, O.P.*

The Battle of Boyacá. Picture by José María Espinosa. Originally published in *Revista Bolívar* (Bogotá, no. 33). This photo is a copy of a reproduction in Uribe White, *Iconografía del Libertador.*

7 *The Wars of Independence, 1810–1821*

On July 20, 1810, revolutionaries in Santa Fe convened a *cabildo abierto* (open town meeting), deposed Viceroy Amar y Borbón, and created a Supreme Junta to run the government. Two months later a Provisional Junta in Pore overthrew the local royal authorities, plunging the Llanos into an eleven-year struggle for independence from Spanish rule.

War shattered the geographic isolation of the plains, which for centuries had limited Spanish presence to a few hundred encomenderos, ranchers, missionaries, and officials. During the First Republic (July 20, 1810, to May 26, 1816), Casanare became an extension of the battlefields of highland New Granada and Venezuela. Throughout the Spanish Reconquest (May 26, 1816 to August 7, 1819) patriots from both regions fled to the vast tropical grasslands. While elsewhere in the viceroyalty the republican cause lay dying, they generated a new offensive (August 25, 1818, to June 24, 1821). Led by Simón Bolívar and Francisco de Paula Santander, displaced creoles, British volunteers, and llaneros embarked on the Liberation Campaign, which broke Spanish control of New Granada at the Battle of Boyacá (August 7, 1819). Bolstered by José Antonio Páez and his Army of Apure, they went on to free Venezuela at the Battle of Carabobo (June 24, 1821).

The Llanos witnessed some of the greatest feats in the wars for independence. A review of the three phases of the fighting reveals that they supplied immeasurable cattle and horses, providential refuge, and "the human element stronger than all other forces" to realize liberty from Spain. As Fabio Lozano y Lozano has written, "In the Llanos—for us the immense Province of Casanare—the flag of Independence was never lowered, not a day, not an hour, not a minute. . . . The Province of Casanare was, throughout the War of Independence, a sure sanctuary for the emancipatory idea, a true seedbed for the armies of the Republic."[1]

The First Republic (July 20, 1810, to May 26, 1816)

The creoles who seized power in Santa Fe on July 20 met little resistance from the Spanish army. They deported the former imperial officials in a process that was relatively peaceful. It was when they sought to proclaim their ascendancy over the entire colony that bitter ideological struggles split nearly every district, town, and family. Santa Fe and the surrounding region of Cundinamarca became a centralist base. There the patriots formed a republic, in March 1811. They elected as president Jorge Tadeo Lozano, whom Antonio Nariño replaced the following September. Other regions constituted a rival government, the Federation of New Granada Provinces, with its capital at Tunja and its own president, Camilo Torres. Some cities, like Cartagena, declared their independence from both these governments as well as from Spain. These federalist tendencies grew out of predictable economic and regional rivalries, but the result was anarchy.[2]

Vicious civil warfare marked the era of the First Republic, aptly nicknamed the *patria boba* (foolish fatherland). Even Simón Bolívar, who (hoping to use New Granada as a base to recover Venezuela) managed to unite Santa Fe and Tunja, in December 1814, was unable to bludgeon Cartagena into submission. The Spanish had only to wait for the factions to destroy one another. In July 1815 General Pablo Morillo began the reconquest, landing at Santa Marta, on the Caribbean. Vanquishing Cartagena, Antioquia, and Popayán, four separate armies fought their way into the interior. By May 1816 the First Republic collapsed, and the Spanish again dominated the highlands.

These events produced repercussions in the Provincia de los Llanos. On September 13, 1810, creoles seized power in Pore, clearing out the royalists and setting up a Provisional Junta. As in the rest of the country, public opinion divided into centralist and federalist camps. In February 1811 the junta sent fifty guns, two mortars, and two thousand pesos to the Congress of New Granada then meeting in Santa Fe, but after the establishment of the federation, in Tunja, it supported Camilo Torres. In 1812 Colonel Juan José Molina, a socorrano serving as governor, organized the military resources of the province. He sent a representative to the Congress of the United Provinces, held October 4, 1812, in Villa de Leiva.

A contingent of soldiers from Casanare served in the army that Antonio Baraya led to defeat against Nariño in Santa Fe on January 9, 1813.

Mesmerized by power clashes in the highlands, the Congress of the United Provinces showed little concern over the royalist threat in the Llanos. In 1813 Governor Molina begged for assistance in containing the guerrilla bands that were invading Arauca from Venezuela. At first the delegates agreed to help and assigned to Molina the remnants of the Third and Fifth Battalions, commanded by General Joaquín Ricaurte. Before these troops could set out, Simón Bolívar arrived, fresh from his victory at Ocaña. The congress embraced his plan to invade Venezuela, awarding him the rank of brigadier and supplying money and arms for what became known as the Admirable Campaign (May–August 1813). Molina bowed to majority will. He ceded to Bolívar the Ricaurte Battalion and later sent him five thousand pesos, collected in Casanare.[3]

Thus the creole leaders during the era of the First Republic left Casanare to fend for itself. From the beginning they thought of the Llanos primarily as a place for retreat in the event of a Spanish victory. Even as a refuge the continual flooding, disease, and disagreeable climate deterred all but the most hardy. José Manuel Restrepo observed that when the republic's collapse was imminent, in May 1816, the patriot army might have saved itself by withdrawing immediately to the Llanos. President José Fernández Madrid actually gave the order, but with the exception of Serviez and Santander, the officers refused to comply. They retreated instead to Popayán, where Morillo's army defeated them. "Our first patriots," lamented Restrepo, "preferred to fall into the hands of the Spanish rather than to go to the Llanuras of the Oriente."[4]

Between 1810 and 1816, the violent social revolution engulfing Venezuela was the dominant force shaping developments in Casanare. On April 19, 1810, creoles drove the Spanish authorities out of Caracas. A year later they established the First Republic on July 5, 1811. The determination of the *mantuanos* (estate-owning creoles) to monopolize all power quickly alienated the *pardo* (mixed-blood), slave, and llanero masses, who saw they had little to gain from the new state.[5] As Spanish troops, led by Domingo de Monteverde, invaded Coro, royalist sympathizers in the interior had little difficulty in organizing mission Indians, llaneros, and small farmers to oppose those towns in rebellion.

The fall of the First Republic, on July 30, 1812, left the country hopelessly in conflict. Undaunted by the swift counterattack and supported by New Granada, Bolívar launched the Admirable Campaign with a call for "war to the death." Retaking Caracas, he proclaimed the Second Republic and ruled as dictator from August 1813 to September 1814, but his control over most of the country was never complete. Royalists remained entrenched in Maracaibo, Guayana, Coro, Puerto Cabello, and the Llanos. By 1815 constant civil strife had claimed the lives of 150,000 people.[6]

In contrast to the Casanareños, who never wavered in their commitment to independence, the Venezuelan plainsmen fought first for the king. Since the mid-eighteenth century, a huge floating population of escaped slaves, Indians, and social outcasts of all kinds had inhabited the llanos of Barinas, Apure, Cojedes, and Guárico. At times they worked on ranches. At times they robbed the surrounding settlements. Despite the efforts of the crown to control them, they lived beyond the reach of the law. The leaders of the First Republic sought to rectify this situation by passing the "Ordenanzas of the Llanos of 1811"—a series of decrees which would have required these people to register with local authorities, to carry an identity card, and to belong to a ranch on pain of imprisonment or death.[7] The llaneros doggedly opposed this undisguised attempt to reduce them to serfdom. It was easy for Sebastián de la Calzada, Antonio Puig, José Yáñez, and José Tomás Boves to play upon their fears and to organize them into cavalry bands. In the name of Ferdinand VII, they swept down on republican strongholds, sacking, pillaging, and plundering, in a savage reply to Bolívar's war to the death. Fed by social and racial hatreds, the withering of economic opportunities, lack of money, and an inadequate food supply, the struggle generated its own momentum with little regard for the orders of Juan Manuel de Cagigal, who in February 1814 replaced Monteverde as the Spanish commander in chief.[8] On June 15, 1814, Boves and his mounted hordes routed the combined forces of Simón Bolívar and Santiago Mariño to bring down the Second Republic.

Of the provinces of New Granada, Casanare was the most exposed to the warfare ripping through Barinas and Apure. First José Yáñez, affectionately nicknamed Nana by his followers, and then Colonel Sebastián Calzada and the Fifth Spanish Division, threatened to invade Arauca. Unable to get help from the highlands, Governor Molina raised locally an army of six hundred men, who with guns, carbines, lances, machetes, and *chozos* (pikes of palm wood) defended the border for fifteen months.[9] The commanders were Francisco Olmedilla, in 1814, and Joaquín Ricaurte, in 1815, assisted by Fray Ignacio Mariño, Ramón Nonato Pérez, and José Antonio Páez.

Francisco Olmedilla already had a reputation for bravery when he became military governor of Casanare in 1814. Born in Pore in 1780, he joined the revolution at its outset. In July 1813 he followed Bolívar in his invasion of Venezuela. When he was sent to Barinas, Olmedilla destroyed several royalist bands. Later he fought in Arauca, on December 5, 1813.[10]

Olmedilla's principal challenge as military governor was to stop Calzada's advance from Apure and Barinas. He raised a new army, to which the congress of New Granada contributed two hundred veterans. In July he incorporated Joaquín Ricaurte and the soldiers who had retreated from Venezuela after Boves' defeat of Bolívar. In October a young Venezuelan captain, frustrated by patriot reversals in Apure, presented himself in Pore, Olmedilla placed José Antonio Páez in charge of a cavalry squadron in Betoyes. He now commanded one thousand men, scattered along a line extending from Betoyes to Chire.

On January 31, 1815, Olmedilla attacked the Spanish army, led by Pacheco Briceño at Guasdualito. He defeated eight hundred cavalry and infantry, taking three hundred prisoners, whom he summarily executed. Inexplicably, soon afterwards he became disgusted with the patriot government and was convinced that the revolutionary cause was doomed. At Cuiloto Olmedilla handed over the army to his lieutenant, the brutal, incompetent Fernando Figueredo, and removed himself to Pore.[11] From there he set off for the jungles of Vichada, planning to build a settlement beyond the range of patriot or Spanish retribution.

Outraged by his behavior, the new governor of Casanare, Andrés Solano, quickly dispatched José Antonio Páez to apprehend the deserter. Páez caught up with his former commander in the Llanos of San Juan and San Martín and convinced him to surrender peacefully. He brought Olmedilla back to Pore, where he was imprisoned for seven months until vigorous efforts by highly placed friends, including the future archbishop of Caracas, Ramón Ignacio Méndez, won for him a pardon from the government.[12]

Joaquín Ricaurte, who succeeded Olmedilla as military chief in Casanare in February 1815, also proved unequal to the task. A native of Santa Fe, Ricaurte had signed the Act of Independence on July 21, 1810. He was Baraya's second-in-command during the ill-fated attack on the capital. He served under Bolívar in the Admirable Campaign and gravitated to Casanare in July 1814.[13] As commander in chief his goal was to keep Colonel Calzada, who was regrouping at Guasdualito, from crossing Casanare to attack highland New Granada. While the rainy season prevented Calzada from making his move, Ricaurte mustered 1,300 cavalry and infantry troops and stationed detachments to guard the crossing points at the Lipa, Ele, and Casanare rivers.

The armies met on October 31, 1815, on an open plain near Chire, a site chosen by Ricaurte and well suited to his cavalry. Miguel Guerrero, Ramón Nonato Pérez, and José Antonio Páez led a charge that put Calzada's infantry to flight. Their triumph, however, was illusory because Ricaurte, having positioned himself a league away from the action, failed to order a second assault. As his cavalry fruitlessly pursued some of the fugitives, the bulk of the Spanish troops regrouped on a wooded hill that horsemen could not penetrate. Calzada's army was intact, although he had lost 350 men killed or taken prisoner and 800 horses and mules. He continued his drive up the Andes along the Chita road, arriving in Cocuy in early November. His defeat of General Urdaneta at the Battle of Bálaga, on November 25, was a mortal blow to the First Republic. In Boyacá he joined forces with Miguel de la Torre, coming from Ocaña, and together the two armies triumphantly entered Santa Fe, in May 1816.[14]

The loss at Bálaga shook the government. Seeking to distract Calzada and to deprive him of auxiliaries from Venezuela, it ordered Ricaurte to occupy Guasdualito. Ill and dispirited, Ricaurte passed along this assignment to Commander Miguel Guerrero, who crossed the Arauca River and smashed the Spanish at Mata de Miel, on December 14. Key to Guerrero's victory and others won at Palmarito (February 2, 1816) and again at Mata de Miel (February 16, 1816) was the electrifying leadership of his lieutenant, José Antonio Páez.

Suspicious and cunning, built like an ox, Páez was an unrivalled guerrillero, expert in cavalry tactics and fighting in tropical conditions.[15] Born in Barinas Province in 1790, from his youth he had worked on hatos, learning the skills of the llaneros. After he joined the patriots, in 1813, his loyalty never wavered; he emigrated to Casanare with the expressed plan of gathering forces to recapture Apure from the Spanish.[16]

Páez's courage and ability contrasted sharply with the incompetence of Olmedilla and Ricaurte. Amid the anarchy, isolation, and demoralization in Casanare in early 1816, the llaneros found in this brash officer and "complete llanero" a man they would follow.[17] While the patriot army in Casanare degenerated into lawless bands harassing civilians, Páez, ensconced in Guasdualito, on the Venezuelan side of the Apure, grew in popularity. When Ricaurte resigned because of ill health, the government of New Granada named Miguel Valdés to succeed him, but the de facto commander of the Army of the Oriente was José Antonio Páez.

Between 1810 and 1816 guerrillas in Casanare were only partially successful in stopping the Spanish from sweeping into New Granada from the east. The fighting took the same pattern of sacking, pillage, and plunder that had become the norm in Venezuela. With the fall of the First

Republic, in May 1816, the plainsmen were joined by a few hundred soldiers and thousands of civilians fleeing from the imperial armies in the highlands. Threatened now on all sides, the patriots in Casanare and Páez in Apure kept the flame of independence alive during the Spanish Reconquest.

The Spanish Reconquest (May 26, 1816, to August 7, 1819)

In April 1816 President Camilo Torres recognized that the collapse of the New Granadan Republic was imminent. He placed General Manuel Serviez and Colonel Francisco de Paula Santander in command of the army and turned over the government to José Fernández Madrid, who would have the unenviable task of negotiating with General Morillo. Serviez proposed to withdraw the entire army to the Llanos, joining forces with Miguel Valdés and the Army of the Oriente. The other officers rejected his plan, so that on May 4, he and Santander began the retreat with only 56 infantry and 150 cavalry.

Serviez and Santander reached Pore on June 23, with two Spanish divisions led by General La Torre and Colonel Villavicencio in hot pursuit. On June 29, at Guachiría, they clashed with Villavicencio's men and forced them to retire up the Cordillera. By July 1 they arrived at Chire, where they met Rafael Urdaneta, who had been in Casanare since his defeat at Bálaga. Nine days later La Torre occupied Pore.[18] He publicly executed several rebels, including Francisco Olmedilla, whom the Spanish had captured at his refuge in Santa Rosalia, south of the Meta.[19] Leaving some men to hold the provincial capital, La Torre struck out for Venezuela, stopping long enough to burn Chire to the ground on the way. The principal cities of the Llanos were again in Spanish hands.

Reconquest brought unrelieved suffering to the restored viceroyalty. Tired of the fractricidal struggles between centralists and federalists, many had welcomed the return of peninsular rule. Their initial sympathy turned to hatred when Morillo imposed a reign of terror.[20] The Spanish general was determined to punish the creoles for rebelling and to make New Granada a supply base for his army in Venezuela. One of his first acts in Santa Fe was to create three tribunals: the War Council, to judge compromised patriots, the Council of Purification, to judge those who were less compromised, and the Council of Confiscation *(Junta de Secuestro),* for the seizure of goods. Hauled before these courts, some patriots were "purified" by paying massive fines. Others suffered banishment, forced labor, military conscription, or imprisonment. Five hundred were executed in a calculated campaign against the upper class.[21] Officials commandeered peasants for projected public works, such as the construction of thirteen roads, two of which led toward the Llanos. The workers had to supply their own daily ration of food and to leave their homes and families for months. According to José Manuel Restrepo, "The roads came to be true prisons in which the Spanish forced a large number of the inhabitants of New Granada to work as punishment for their love of Independence, Liberty, and Equality."[22]

In September 1817 Morillo appointed Juan Sámano military governor, with orders to continue these harsh policies. The pacification of Venezuela was not yet complete. The agricultural regions of the Eastern Cordillera, the industry of Socorro, and the mines of Antioquia had to contribute to the reconquest. In January 1817 he returned to Caracas and stationed his army along the Andes. Meanwhile Bolívar held Guayana, Mariño had freed Cumaná, General Rojas was keeping the republican cause alive in Maturín, and in the Llanos was Páez, the "Lion of Apure."[23]

While Morillo tightened the Spanish clamp on the Andes, the resistance movement in Casanare dissolved into chaos. Just out of La Torre's reach lay two republican columns—the first made up of recent arrivals from the highlands, led by Serviez and Santander, the second composed of casanareños, led by Urdaneta and Juan Nepomuceno Moreno. There were several smaller guerrilla bands, the most important located in Arauca, under Ramón Nonato Pérez. East of the Arauca River, in Trinidad de Arichuna, was an army of Venezuelans, commanded by Colonel Miguel Valdés and Páez. Finally there was a steadily growing mass of displaced civilians.[24]

United in their hatred of the Spanish, the ill-assorted armies were rent by the ambitious rivalries of their leaders and the deep antipathy that had sprung up between New Granadans and Venezuelans. When Urdaneta first came to Casanare, he held a commission from President Fernández Madrid to take command of the Army of the Oriente. Valdés refused to relinquish this post. Urdaneta then assumed the title of dictator of Casanare and chief of the army, but Valdés sent a squadron from Guasdualito to depose him. By the time Santander and Serviez reached Chire, Colonel Moreno was self-appointed governor of Casanare, Urdaneta was in charge of defending the province, and Valdés continued to call himself commander of the Army of the Oriente.[25]

These leaders agreed to meet to resolve their differences, at Villa de Arauca on July 16, 1816. Attending the council were Serviez, Santander, representing Urdaneta, Domingo Mesa y Burgos, representing Moreno,

Valdés, Páez, and several others. They proclaimed a republic, electing Fernando Serrano, former governor of Pamplona, as president, and Santander as commander in chief of the army. Believing himself unacceptable to the Venezuelans, Santander declined the honor, but his colleagues pressed him into accepting. The council resolved to move the army and civilian refugees to Guasdualito for greater safety because La Torre was advancing steadily from the west. All the patriot leaders joined the exodus except Ramón Nonato Pérez who, spurning an invitation proffered by Santander, remained in Cuiloto with two hundred llaneros and a large group of civilians.

Once the patriots crossed the Arauca River, it was evident that Páez alone could hold the loyalty of the troops, many of whom were Venezuelans. On September 16 soldiers at Trinidad de Arichuna mutinied and declared him civil and military chief and commander general of the army. Páez acceded to their demands. He immediately canceled the civil government created on July 16 and ruled as dictator. Santander, Urdaneta, and Serviez declared their loyalty, and he rewarded each with the command of a division.[26] In December Pérez joined Páez in Yagual, forced out of Arauca at last by La Torre's arrival with eighteen hundred men. Páez justified his consolidation of power by leading the army to victory at Yagual (October 8, 1815), Achaguas (October 13, 1815), Nutrias (November 12, 1815), and Mucuritas (January 28, 1817), where one thousand patriots stopped four thousand soldiers led by La Torre and Calzada, inflicting the first genuine reversal suffered by Morillo's army since landing in America.[27]

Páez directed these operations with an audacity, astuteness, and personal valor that became legendary. A plainsman himself, he capitalized on the unique attributes of his unorthodox cavalry, which he described in his *Autobiografía*. The llaneros were hatless and barefoot. Those who had clothes wore them; those who did not mounted naked on their horses, hoping to acquire clothing from the enemy. The best riders carried a broad lance; the rest carried chozos. Their saddles were simply saddletrees of wood *(fustes)* secured with tanned leather straps.[28] Their rations were dried meat, which they moistened before eating.

Marches began at daybreak. At 11.00 A.M. they rested, bathed the horses, looked for grass, ate a frugal lunch, slept, smoked, and talked. From 3.00 P.M. until sundown they continued on their way; in spite of the climate, it was possible to cover from fifty to sixty miles a day. At night they made camp without showing a light to the enemy. Páez undertook these marches to elude a more powerful force or to make a surprise attack. If the first charge was not successful, he disbanded into small units and pulled back to reform behind the line of fire. When the battle was won, the llaneros drove before them all the captured horses loaded with booty.[29]

Discipline consisted of obeying blindly the order of the chief in charge at the moment. Beyond that injunction Páez permitted his men to engage in the most horrendous crimes. They routinely took horses and cattle where they found them without any account and as common property. Páez later explained that "In the lower Apure, the only men to be found were execrable types; they formed bands to plunder the countryside, rob houses and commit crimes. . . . A Llanero chief has to cajole his soldiers with hard cash, otherwise, they will ruin by their depredations the regions through which they pass."[30]

The New Granadans from the highlands felt deeply the privations of this mode of fighting. The llaneros were inured to living on meat alone and did not notice the lack of other food. They were impervious to the cruel rainy season. Swimmers by habit, they stopped for no river, and no risk intimidated them. The emigrants, on the other hand, were a heterogeneous group of officers, priests, lawyers, gentlemen, women, children, and servants, who were accustomed to an entirely different way of life.[31] Now all were forced to live together, military and civilian, men, women, old people, and children—all ate meat roasted without salt and all went barefoot.[32]

Near Yagual, at a site inaccessible to the Spaniards, Páez made camp for nearly ten thousand emigrants, who were an encumbrance in battle. His first care was to provide them with food and shelter. Then he set the women spinning. As wild cotton was found in abundance, they were not idle. Little by little they adapted to the solitary place and their lives became more tolerable.[33]

The nonllanero officers served valiantly at Yagual, Achaguas, and Nutrias, but the incompatibility of the creole-European ways with those of the llaneros led most of them to leave the division. Bandits murdered Serviez, Miguel Valdés, and Luis Girardot before they had a chance to make this decision. One by one, Urdaneta, Antonio Obando, José María Cordoba, José María Vergara, and José Concha obtained their passports and journeyed down the Orinoco in search of other armies more congenial in style and direction. Santander left at the beginning of 1817 for Guayana, where he joined Bolívar and Manuel Piar.[34]

The battle of Mucuritas gave Páez control of the Llanos between the Arauca and Apure rivers. From his base at Yagual, he sent Captain Juan

Galea to revive resistance in Casanare, in February 1817. During the remainder of the year, he raided Spanish positions in Barinas. By December Bolívar, reestablished at Angostura, realized that if he could bring Páez under his command, he would dominate a vast area from the Orinoco to the Andes. Marching with three thousand troops over three hundred miles to Apure, he met the llanero chief for the first time near San Juan de Payara, on January 30, 1818. During this dramatic encounter between two extraordinary men, Páez recognized Bolívar's sovereignty. Soon after they launched a joint offensive that brought victory at Calabozo (February 12) and defeat at Sémen (March 16) and Cojedes (May 2). Again Bolívar withdrew to the lower Orinoco.[35]

Meanwhile the patriots in Casanare were regrouping. In the latter part of 1816, Spanish detachments commanded by Colonel Bayer held Pore and Chire, but not the countryside. Guerrilla bands freely roamed the grasslands. Fray Ignacio Mariño, the Dominican who armed the Indians of his former parish, Tame, Macaguane and Betoyes, Francisco Rodríguez, and Ramón Nonato Pérez became formidable opponents. They ambushed the Spanish whenever they left the safety of the towns. Bayer's soldiers pursued the guerrillas. Occasionally they took prisoners, but they could not annihilate the movement.[36] Morillo's stern warnings to the inhabitants of the Llanos to accept his rule or be exterminated only inflamed their will to resist.[37]

Páez's decision to send Juan Galea back to Casanare after the Battle of Mucuritas was the spark that ignited these smoldering coals of defiance. On his way to Arauca, Galea incorporated Juan José Reyes, Fernando Vargas, Domingo Montoya, and others in his retinue. In early March they came upon a column of Spanish cavalry that Antonio Pla was taking to Guasdualito, by order of Colonel Bayer. Catching the royalists off guard, Galea easily defeated them. Receiving only confused reports of the skirmish, Bayer left Pore with ten soldiers, intending to rendezvous with Pla. A little beyond the Casanare River, he fell into the hands of Galea's men, who killed him. On March 27 Galea seized Chire from the astonished Spanish. Then, dressed in enemy uniforms, his soldiers pressed on and took Pore. With rare good luck, he had destroyed the expeditionary army and liberated Casanare, all within a month. On receiving this joyous news, Páez sent Ramón Nonato Pérez and Juan Nepomuceno Moreno back to Casanare, to serve as military chief and governor, respectively, while Galea continued his march up the Andean foothills, harassing the Spanish in Labranzagrande and the Salina de Chita.[38]

In Santa Fe Governor Juan Sámano reacted swiftly to reports of the patriot triumphs. He ordered the Second Battalion of Numancia, stationed up to then in Santa Fe, to Labranzagrande and Morcote and the First Battalion of the King to Sogamoso, Chita, and Salina, to guard all the roads that led to the highlands from the Llanos. Then Lieutenant Colonel Carlos Tolrá marched to Pore with six hundred infantry, but finding that he could not venture into the plains without horses, he pulled back to Morcote. Finally Captain Carlos María Ortega, with three companies of the Battalion Tambo, occupied the town of Fundación de Upía, in the Llanos of San Juan and San Martín. Samano wrote of these measures to Morillo in Venezuela, adding that he intended to dispatch a large army to the Llanos once the rainy season had ended. On August 1 Morillo responded that the proposed offensive had little chance of succeeding, since experience had shown that men and horses acclimated to the highlands could not adapt to the tropical plains or to the style of fighting there. He urged Sámano to concentrate his defense at the mountain passes, in order to contain the guerrillas within the Llanos.[39]

Galea's victories heartened scores of underground revolutionaries in Santa Fe, who were stubbornly working to undercut the Spanish regime. Popular rumors abounded that almost any day a patriot army would sweep over the Andes and liberate the capital. Sámano's deployment of troops from Santa Fe, Socorro, and Tunja lent credence to this hope. By August 1817 two separate conspiracies were under way to prepare for the anticipated invasion.

The first group of plotters sought to facilitate the desertion of patriots impressed by Morillo and Sámano into royalist regiments. The most famous member of this ring was Policarpa Salvarrieta, a young seamstress who worked for wealthy patrons in Santa Fe. Deeply committed to independence, she helped deserters get to Casanare, and from time to time smuggled arms, supplies, and information to Ramón Nonato Pérez. One of the deserters she aided was Antonio Arredondo who, fleeing from the Battalion of Numancia, managed to reach Pérez in September 1817 and take command of the patriot Battalion Constantes.[40] Once Sámano got wind of the conspiracy, on August 23, others were not so fortunate. In the early days of September, the Spanish captured nine deserters on their way to the Llanos. Among them was Alejo Sabaraín, Policarpa's fiancé. The men were found to be carrying letters from the seamstress to Pérez and other incriminating documents. Now thoroughly compromised, Policarpa was imprisoned with the others. All were speedily tried and condemned to death. Refusing to plead for clemency, Policarpa was shot with eight male companions on November 14, 1817, the first woman to be executed in Santa Fe.[41] Popular awareness of her heroic defiance made her death a rallying point for the patriot cause.[42]

The second conspiracy was likewise unsuccessful. Begun by Ambrosio and Vicente Almeyda, it was intended to generate mutiny within the Spanish army as soon as word was received that the llaneros were advancing up the Cordillera. The execution of Policarpa and her associates jeopardized the Almeydas. Fearing to delay any longer, they began the rebellion on their own in the Valle of Tenza, on the eastern side of the Cordillera, near a trail leading to the Llanos.[43] With a hastily gathered force of 250 peasants, the Almeydas took Chocontá, in early November. They advanced to Suesca and Nemocón, but were defeated by Carlos Tolrá, on November 21. The little army quickly disintegrated. The Spanish captured some of the participants and executed them on February 21, 1818, but both Almeydas escaped to the Llanos.[44]

In December 1817 Sámano succeeded Francisco Montalvo as viceroy of New Granada. He had stifled the patriots in Santa Fe, but those in Casanare were beyond his grasp. In February 1818 Pérez seized the Spanish garrisons at Fundación de Upía and San Martín, expelling the last of the royalists from the plains. Sámano tried to recoup by sending Colonel Tolrá, with five hundred infantry, to San Martín, but they got no farther than Medina. Finding the town deserted and fearing to push ahead into the plains without horses or food, Tolrá returned to the capital.[45] As Morillo had predicted, the llaneros were invulnerable in their own land.

Unfortunately the patriots faced problems other than the Spanish threat. Mutual jealousies, petty rivalries, and nascent nationalism were taking a toll. Above all the leaders in Casanare resented Páez's overlordship, and for his part, the Venezuelan commander bitterly regretted his selection of Pérez and Moreno to serve as the principal provincial officers. In mid 1817 he charged Pérez with insubordination and appointed Commandante Miguel Antonio Vásquez to take over as military chief of Casanare. Vásquez was to arrest his predecessor and deliver him to the Achagua headquarters, in order that he might explain his behavior in person.

Pérez refused to step down. He defied Páez by appealing to a higher authority, Simón Bolívar. In December 1817 a delegation from Casanare made up of Fray Ignacio Mariño, Antonio Arredondo, and Agustín Rodríguez appeared at Bolívar's camp in Angostura, carrying documents supporting Pérez and denouncing Páez. Some of these were statements taken from residents of San Ignacio de Betoyes, in October 1817. Fernando Monrraz, Nicholás León, Mateo León, and Santiago Rodríguez all swore that Pérez had given every possible assistance and protection to the emigrant community in that town. Francisco Javier Pérez, Domingo Antonio de Vargas, Colonel Juan José Molina, Lieutenant Colonel Manuel Ortega, and the interim governor, Andrés Solano, praised his efforts in defending the Llanos against the Spanish.[46]

Mariño, Arredondo, and Rodríguez also presented a petition to Bolívar which boldly began: "The undersigned, commissioned by the Comandante General of the troops of Casanare in New Granada near the Government of Venezuela, have the honor to inform you that the Province of Casanare has been happily liberated by the effort and cooperation of its people. . . ."[47] This achievement, it continued, was due to Ramón Nonato Pérez and not to José Antonio Páez, who as commander of the Army of Apure only tried to drain Casanare of its vital resources. Therefore Casanare would not obey Páez; it would submit solely to Bolívar. Mariño, Arredondo, and Rodríguez urged Bolívar to confirm Pérez and Moreno as comandante general and governor and to aid in the defense of Casanare until the people of the province might begin a campaign against the Spanish in highland New Granada.[48]

Bolívar's immediate response is not known. It is clear that however sympathetic he was to the desire of Casanare for self-determination, he was not ready to encroach upon Páez's jurisdiction. The issue was unresolved when he arrived in Calabozo, Apure. Bolívar wrote to Pérez on February 22, 1818. He conceded that Casanare had the right to be politically independent of Barinas, but stated that for military reasons it must continue to submit to the leader of the Army of Apure. He ordered Pérez to deliver the government to Vásquez and the army to Juan Galea and to present himself in person "to clarify his position and receive justice."[49] Pérez obeyed. He reported to Bolívar in San Fernando, in May 1818. On July 14 he was found guilty of insubordination and sentenced to serve without a command.

True to character Pérez ignored the sentence. By October he had assumed leadership of two hundred followers in Guasdualito. At this time Arredondo had two hundred men in Betoyes, Juan Nepomuceno Moreno claimed to be governor, Juan Galea called himself comandante general, and there were at least fifteen warring lesser caudillos. Bolívar tried to restore order by sending Colonel Justo Briceño, a Venezuelan, to take over as jefe militar. Traveling from Betoyes to Manare, Briceño came upon Arredondo and his men; he demanded their allegiance. Arredondo refused to recognize his authority or that of Paez. Briceño appealed directly to Arredondo's men, but only forty soldiers and a single officer, all Venezuelans, joined him. The New Granadans would not accept him. In open defiance, Arredondo led the remaining four hundred to Zapatosa, where he joined the Almeyda brothers.[50] Páez sent Commander Pedro Fortoul and later Colonel Miguel Guerrero to placate Arredondo, but the latter rejected their mediation. As Cayo Leonidas Peñuela rightfully concludes, "The Llanura, then was in complete anarchy."[51]

Hardening resentment of Venezuelan rule lay at the root of this disorder. Regional antagonism solidified in the early years of the war. Because of the notorious savagery of the struggle in Venezuela, the New Granadans regarded their neighbors as cruel, licentious brutes.[52] The Venezuelans, for their part, scorned the New Granadans as barbarians, too inept and cowardly to win battles. Morillo used every opportunity to exacerbate this prejudice by extolling the bravery of Venezuelans and denigrating the men of New Granada. Aggravating the situation in Casanare was the dictatorial style of Páez's leadership.

Writing to Paez on June 22, 1818, Santander eloquently articulated the sentiments of the New Granadans who, grateful as they were for Venezuelan support, resisted absorption into that nation. Casanare, he wrote, had never been a part of Venezuela. It had belonged to a confederation that had its own laws, institutions, and officials. Without the consent of all the people who created them, these laws could not be abolished except by perpetuating the same kind of tyranny exercised by the Spanish. Why then did Páez send only Venezuelans to govern Casanare? One did not throw out the Spaniards only to impose a new yoke. "Casanare is dependent on you, and would that you might bring her complete happiness. Galea commands, Vásquez governs; would that Casanare might be happy under their orders." Pleading for more sensitivity Santander asked. "Do you want to have your name passed to posterity with more honor? Would you want to exchange the illustrious title of liberator for that of oppressor of your brothers? Will you not do your part to make the New Granadans happy who today are oppressed?"[53]

Páez did not reply immediately, but after Bolívar appointed Santander as commander in chief of Casanare, in August 1818, he realized that separation of the two regions was inevitable. Writing to Santander on October 30, 1818, he confessed that he was thankful to be relieved of a province whose people were so perverse that not even Colonel Guerrero had been able to calm them. "Perhaps it is because he is Venezuelan. This cursed rivalry, or rather this distinction of names irritates me, and God grant that it does not bring us to civil war if we do not destroy it. . . . At last you are going to your Casanare, but who knows how you will succeed. . . .

In this miserable province without resources, men, or anything, I wish you good luck, for you will need all your ability to succeed with these people."[54]

During the reconquest, while the Spanish reoccupied the highlands of New Granada and Venezuela, José Antonio Páez expanded his llanero army and seized Casanare and Apure for the patriots. Despite the need for solidarity, bad feelings between New Granadans and Venezuelans intensified. By 1818 it was evident that the Casanareños had rejected Páez and would submit only to Bolívar. The latter, having reestablished a beachhead in Angostura the year before, saw Morillo block his offensive from Apure in the first half of 1818. The conflict in Venezuela had reached a stalemate. In New Granada, however, the enemy was vulnerable. Royalist control between Cartagena and Quito rested on the questionable loyalty of ten thousand soldiers, many of whom were Americans whose identification with the imperialist cause was waning.[55] Bolívar's decision to switch the theater of war to New Granada bristled with risks but promised rich rewards. In August 1818 he sent Santander to Casanare to mobilize a new army—the first step in a patriot offensive that would culminate in irrevocable victories at Boyacá and Carabobo.

The Patriot Offensive (August 25, 1818, to June 21, 1821)

Bolívar promoted Santander to brigadier general on August 12, 1818. Thirteen days later he named him chief of the Liberating Army of New Granada. Santander's instructions were to unite, organize, and expand the troops in Casanare and to establish communications with headquarters. Free to act on his own initiative, he was to harass the enemy whenever possible and to invade Spanish territory without hesitation if an opportunity presented itself.[56]

Bolívar's choice could not have been more fortunate. The fractious caudillos in Casanare demanded a compatriot to command them. Santander, with a reputation for bravery and leadership, was eager for the assignment. Fellow officers greeted his appointment with enthusiasm. Manuel Cedeño and Antonio Sucre sent him their congratulations.[57] Even Bolívar's aide-de-camp, Daniel Florencio O'Leary, who came to hate Santander with a cold passion, wrote in his *Memorias.* "Young, enthusiastic and ambitious, he was of all the New Granadans that were found in the general headquarters the most qualified for the post to which Bolívar appointed him."[58]

Santander left Angostura on August 27 and sailed up the Orinoco with four subordinates—Colonel Jacinto Lara, a Venezuelan, and Antonio

Obando, Vicente González, and Joaquín Paris, all New Granadans. The boats carried twelve hundred guns, ammunition, and a small armory. On October 25 some llaneros, on orders from General Páez halted, the party at the mouth of the Meta River, pending confirmation from Bolívar. Receiving Bolívar's assurance that Santander was to command in Casanare, Páez permitted them to continue.[59] On November 1, 1818, he issued a proclamation renouncing control over Casanare and urging the inhabitants to support Santander.[60]

Santander anchored at Guanapalo on November 27. He immediately summoned the governor, Juan Nepomuceno Moreno. Moreno greeted him warmly, but painted a somber picture of the disorder within the province. Arredondo was still hiding out in Zapatosa. The cavalry had disintegrated into tiny bands. Their caudillos were in complete disagreement and refused to obey one another. The soldiers were nearly naked. Because the royalists held the salt mines at Chita, Sácama, and Muneque, their diet was reduced to meat without salt. The province had no income or material resources, and five thousand Spanish were threatening to invade at any moment.[61] Santander was undaunted. In five months he unified the officers, organized a civil government, shored up the economy, and formed an army.

Santander achieved unity by tactfully building on the goodwill generated by his arrival. He recognized that Moreno wielded considerable influence and confirmed him as governor. At the same time, by relying on Manuel Baños to handle routine administration as lieutenant governor, he could grant Moreno's wish to remain with his cavalry. Although Bolívar had recommended that Pérez be made head of cavalry, Santander arranged for him to stay with his men in Guasdualito, choosing instead Commander Pedro Fortoul.[62] He wrote a conciliatory note to Arredondo, who replied fervently, on November 28. "You should not doubt for a moment my obedience; my person, the arms, the officers—all are at your disposition since our desires are none other than to fight under the orders of a Jefe of your education, experience and wisdom."[63] Reflecting on the growing solidarity, Santander observed that "All submitted to me, obeyed me, and worked actively with me in the formation of a beautiful division to which New Granadans owe so much for their liberty in the campaign of 1819."[64]

Santander favored union with Venezuela but not assimilation. Since Páez had canceled the republic founded on July 16, 1816, no formal civil government had existed. With his officers behind him, he moved to reestablish the sovereignty of New Granada. Santander convoked in Pore an assembly of prominent citizens. On December 18, 1818, this body issued a declaration asserting that since Casanare was the only province of the union remaining free, it would represent the entire federation until the rest of the territory won independence. The declaration authorized Casanare to assume the political and military functions of the extinguished republic. It renewed the diplomatic credentials of New Granadan diplomats abroad, a measure vital to the representatives in Venezuela. It recognized Bolívar as commander in chief of the armies of New Granada, but not as jefe civil y militar of Venezuela. By this device Santander revived the old Republic of New Granada and gave Casanare its own officials, organization, and army. The five delegates he sent to the Congress of Angostura, in February 1819, represented Casanare as an entity independent of Venezuela.[65]

Santander revamped the political and economic administration of the province. Installing his headquarters at La Laguna, outside Pore, he divided the territory into departments and each department into cantons. In theory each canton was ruled by a juez mayor, who was to have exclusive control of civil and political affairs, and a comandante, who was concerned with military matters. In practice the comandantes dominated. Writing to Governor Moreno, on December 8, Santander explained that only the comandantes could recruit men, cattle, and food, and that the jueces mayores had to obey them, because "otherwise, decrees directed for the good of the republic may not be carried out."[66]

On January 14, 1819, Santander informed Bolívar that the public treasury had been revitalized and that he hoped to raise enough revenue to equip a military hospital. To generate income he decreed stern but just collections of tithes, the alcabala, and taxes on tobacco and aguardiente.[67] He confiscated the gold and silver holy objects that remained in the churches, ordering them melted down and stamped into pesos at a mint constructed for that purpose. This makeshift currency circulated only within Casanare. It paid the most pressing expenses and made possible the construction of hospitals at Trinidad, Manare, and Tame.[68]

By 1818 rampant pillaging of cattle for six years had depleted the once abundant herds. Santander had no choice but to continue vaquerías if he was to feed his army. Commerce within the province was limited to trade between four towns whose residents herded cattle and planted only the crops necessary for their own subsistence.[69] Nevertheless he tried to encourage agriculture by ordering army recruiters to exempt family men who cultivated fields and by releasing soldiers from their duties to attend to agricultural tasks.[70]

Of all Santander's objectives, mobilizing an army was the most crucial. According to Colonel Moreno, in November 1818 there were only 800 badly armed riders scattered in small groups in the plains north and south of the Meta River and 130 armed infantry in La Laguna. No more than one thousand horses remained in the province. The enemy held fortified posts in Medina, Miraflores, Paya, Chita, and Puebloviejo.[71]

Santander established his supply base in Santa Rosalia, on the south bank of the Meta. If the Spanish attacked, he resolved to retreat into the Llanos of San Juan and San Martín, where cattle were still numerous and where it would be possible to maintain communication with Guayana and Apure by means of the river. He decreed a general enlistment, drafting all able-bodied men, for those who did not know how to ride could serve in the infantry. Most of the new recruits were Indians, pressed unwillingly into service. For example, on December 20, Santander ordered Colonel Jacinto Lara to conscript three to four hundred Indians in Tame. Lara was to call the men together and to tell them that they had two months to learn how to fight. He was to teach and discipline them day and night. To gain their compliance, he was to promise them that they could return to their homes after they had fought at La Salina.[72]

The desertion of reluctant recruits was a nagging problem. Santander warned Comandante Manuel Ortega to be vigilant in preventing the escape of Indians from Tame and Macaguane.[73] He told Fray Ignacio Delgadillo to persuade the Betoyes Indians to comply by assuring them that they could serve in the cavalry, not in the infantry.[74] In spite of such difficulties, by February 1819 he had created a division of twenty-one hundred men—two infantry battalions with five hundred places each and one thousand cavalry organized in squadrons. Although Santander lamented being unable to supply them with uniforms, the troops were disciplined and adequately fed.[75] On March 17 he proudly proclaimed, from La Laguna: "An army formidable by its number, formidable for its bravery, more formidable for its discipline, forms the hopes of all the New Granadans. . . . Discord has disappeared and in its place rule order, organization and tranquility. . . . The soldier, the laborer, the cleric, all have cooperated with great interest in the creation of troops, their organization, their subsistence and the reestablishment of order and public tranquility."[76] This announcement came none too soon. In April Santander faced his first major test—the long-dreaded invasion by Colonel Barreiro.

In August 1818 at about the same time Santander set out from Angostura for Casanare, José María Barreiro arrived in Santa Fe to take command of the Third Spanish Division, the post vacated by Sámano when he became viceroy the previous December. Barreiro reorganized the army and concentrated on defending the mountain passes that led to the Llanos. His troops clashed occasionally with the patriots on the Andean slopes, but did not advance into the plains proper.

Rebels who fell into Spanish hands could expect no quarter. Sámano scorned the republicans in Casanare. By his express order, squadron commanders were to destroy all ranches and buildings in rebel territory. On November 30, 1818, Barreiro warmly praised the commander of the Miraflores column, who had captured defenseless peasant men and women, burning their sugarcane mills and cropland on the Upía River. In the future, he added, "When our troops occupy enemy territory, do not leave any man in it that might be able to bear arms."[77]

In April 1819 Barreiro began a full-scale invasion of Casanare. He had 1,256 infantry and 542 cavalry at Morcote and another 500 troops at Sácama. By April 5 the army had advanced to the confluence of the Tocaría and Labranzagrande rivers. They reached Pore on April 19, only to find the city deserted. Barreiro decided to march on to La Laguna. He divided his force, in order to approach Santander's headquarters by several routes, but the patriots had withdrawn to Barranca del Palmar, near the Meta River.

The Spanish fought brief engagements with rebels but did not come upon the main body of troops. Once the rainy season began, the climate took its toll. The men saw herds of cattle but did not know how to catch them for food. Their highland horses would not eat the coarse, unpalatable grass. Indians serving as guides deserted, as did an alarming number of soldiers. Forced to countermarch to Pore, Barreiro beat a hasty retreat up the Cordillera, with Santander in pursuit. The patriots took Morcote and Paya. One detachment surprised the outpost at Salina de Chita and another seized the garrison that guarded the Miraflores road.[78]

It was a demoralizing setback for the Spanish. Barreiro lost between two and three hundred men and nearly all his horses. During the fifteen-day foray, he received no aid from any of the inhabitants of the Llanos. He glimpsed the discipline of Santander's army and realized that his soldiers could not survive on the open plains. On April 15, 1819, he wrote to Morillo: "The Llano is desolate and I do not believe that we can obtain its pacification, my opinion is that it is entirely lost. All its inhabitants are our decided enemies."[79]

For Santander the campaign could not have been more successful. His officers had urged him to attack, but remembering the example of Páez in Apure, he calmed the hotheads and insisted on retreat. As a result the very immensity of the plains vanquished the royalists, while the patriots emerged unscathed. Bolívar now had proof that the New Granadans could overcome the Spanish.[80]

In Venezuela during the early months of 1819, Bolívar and Páez faced a determined push by General Morillo, who crossed the Apure River at San Fernando on January 24. Bolívar had just returned from Angostura and established camp at San Juan de Payara. Counting the divisions led by Páez, Anzoátegui, and Cedeño, he had thirty-four hundred infantry and one thousand cavalry at his disposal. Bolívar was planning to attack the Spanish near Calabozo, when he received word that more British recruits had arrived at Angostura. Turning over command to Páez, now promoted to major general, he embarked for Angostura to greet the new arrivals and to install the first Congress of the Republic of Colombia, which he had convoked the previous September.

On February 15 Bolívar addressed twenty-six delegates representing the provinces of Caracas, Barcelona, Cumaná, Barinas, Guayana, and Margarita (the five representatives from Casanare had not yet arrived). Setting forth specific recommendations for a constitution to replace the first Venezuelan charter of 1811, his speech was a brilliant tour de force. The wildly cheering delegates elected him president and absolute military chief. It was a glorious moment that secured Bolívar's personal popularity, silenced his enemies, and presented the republic to the world as an independent state.[81] Leaving the governmental details to the congress and the administration of the republic to Vice-President Francisco Antonio Zea, Bolívar retraced his journey along the Orinoco and rejoined Páez on March 11.[82]

Morillo had already penetrated the Llanos. On March 9 he occupied Achaguas. Páez waited for him to leave the shelter of the town and then attacked, on April 2, at a place called Las Queseras del Medio. While Bolívar looked on, 150 llaneros swooped down on a much larger Spanish force, slaying all those who showed the least resistance and forcing Morillo to pull back to Achaguas. Las Queseras del Medio was an important victory for Páez. A grateful Bolívar issued a general proclamation to "los bravos de Apure" and awarded to each of those who had not fallen the Cross of the Liberators, an order he had instituted. Yet the stalemate between the two armies remained unbroken.[83] Morillo dominated the plains to the left of the Arauca River, while Bolívar and Páez controlled those to the right.

In early May Colonel Jacinto Lara burst into Bolívar's headquarters in Rincón Hondo, bringing news of Barreiro's defeat. Bolívar at once grasped the advantage to be gained from a successful invasion of New Granada. As he had written to Páez sometime earlier, "We will force Morillo either to evacuate Venezuela in order to defend New Granada, or alternatively allow the latter to be entirely lost."[84] At a council of war on May 23, he explained his plan to his officers. The bulk of the army would march to Casanare to unite with Santander's division. Together they would cross the Llanos and scale the Andes, taking the most difficult, and therefore unguarded, route to Chita. While Páez diverted attention by leading his cavalry from Apure to Cúcuta, Bolívar and Santander would surprise the Spanish, dealing a mortal blow at Tunja. Finally Bolívar vowed that once New Granada was free, he would liberate Venezuela, Quito, Peru, and Upper Peru.[85]

The army left Mantecal on May 21 at the height of the rainy season (see map 7). Bolívar had thirteen hundred infantry in four battalions—Rifles, Barcelona, Bravos de Páez, and Legión Británica—and eight hundred cavalry in four squadrons. Many women marched with the men. Known as *juanas,* they served as nurses and camp followers and bore arms when necessary.[86] The army passed through Guasdualito and crossed the Arauca River on June 5. It took seven days to cover the 180 kilometers to Tame. Drenched by constant rain, the men waded through water up to the waist, carrying their guns on their shoulders and sleeping at night on their horses in the water. Only a few had ragged jackets. The rest were without clothing and wore only the guayuco or loincloth made of leaves and bark.[87]

On June 11 the soldiers straggled into Santander's camp in Tame. The New Granadan llaneros welcomed them with food and shelter. Bolívar ordered a three-day rest and used it to rearrange his troops. With Santander's twelve hundred infantry and six hundred riders, he now had over four thousand men within striking range of Santa Fe. He reserved command for himself, leaving Carlos Soublette as chief of staff. Santander's Vanguard Division would lead the way, while the division headed by José Antonio Anzoátegui brought up the rear. Remaining behind in Tame was Colonel José Concha, with orders to distract the Spanish by feigning an attack on Medina.[88]

On June 17 they set out once again, following the flooded road to Pore. Crossing the swollen Casanare, Ariporo, and Nunchía rivers was especially treacherous. Bolívar's boats were insufficient, so he had others made of cowhides sewn together. In these the guns and powder and those soldiers who could not swim were ferried across. Swarms of mosquitoes

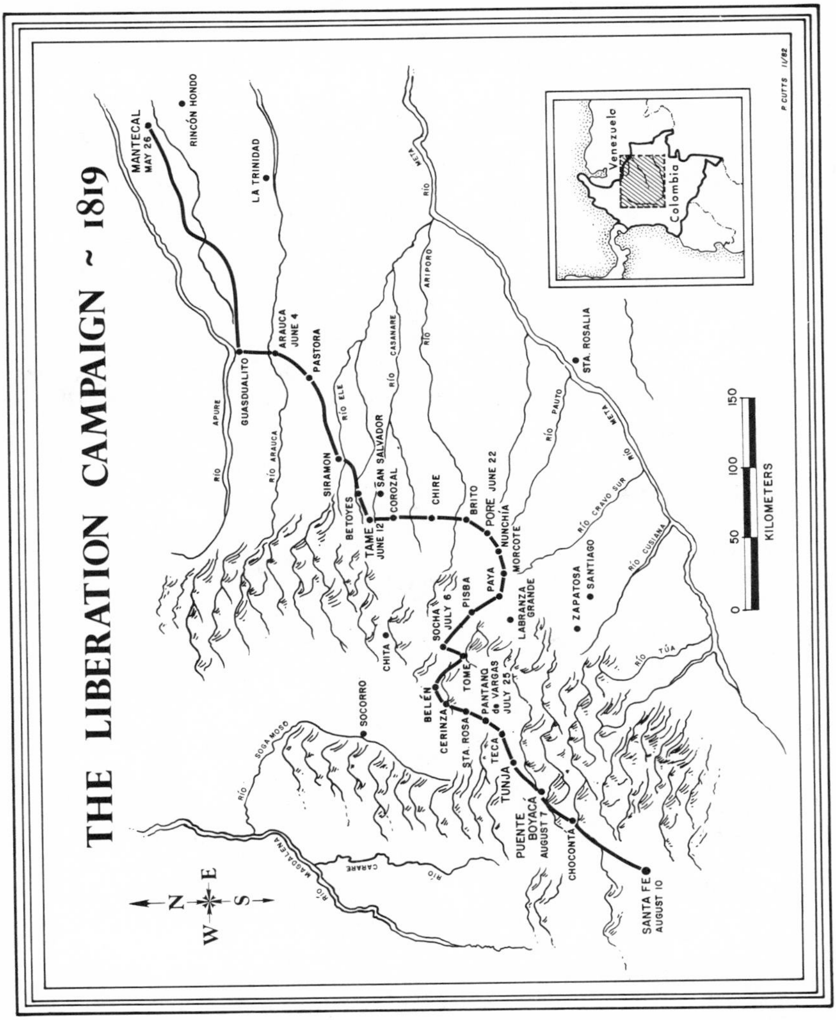

THE LIBERATION CAMPAIGN ~ 1819
N
E
S
W
MANTECAL
MAY 26
RINCÓN HONDO
LA TRINIDAD
RÍO APURE
GUASDUALITO
ARAUCA
JUNE 4
PASTORA
RÍO ARAUCA
SIRAMON
RÍO ELE
BETOYES
SAN SALVADOR
TAME
JUNE 12
COROZAL
RÍO CASANARE
CHIRE
BRITO
PORE JUNE 22
NUNCHÍA
MORCOTE
RÍO ARIPORO
RÍO META
RÍO PAUTO
STA. ROSALIA
CHITA
SOCHA
JULY 6
PISBA
PAYA
LABRANZA GRANDE
ZAPATOSA
SANTIAGO
RÍO CRAVO SUR
RÍO CUSIANA
RÍO TÚA
SOCORRO
RÍO SOGAMOSO
BELÉN
CERINZA
TOME
PANTANO de VARGAS
JULY 25
STA. ROSA
TECA
TUNJA
PUENTE BOYACÁ
AUGUST 7
CHOCONTÁ
SANTA FE
AUGUST 10
RÍO CARARE
RÍO MAGDALENA
Venezuelo
Colombia
0
50
100
150
KILOMETERS
P CUTTS 11/82

whirled over the waters, harassing the wretched soldiers. Many mules and horses were drowned and half of the cattle were already lost.[89]

The sight of Pore, on June 22, brought little respite. Ahead loomed the gigantic Andes—a barrier considered all but insurmountable at this time of year. Bolívar's army consisted almost entirely of men who had lived all their lives in the tropical plains. They had never dreamed that anything like these mountains existed. Their wonder grew with every step. For four days they struggled upward from cliff to cliff, pelted by the incessant rain and shivering from the cold. Many deserted, convinced that only crazy men could keep going at temperatures that benumbed the senses and froze the flesh. Few horses survived, and the dead ones blocked the path. At this point Bolívar's phenomenal leadership was the critical factor. His presence and example, steadfast amidst the hardships, rallied the troops. As O'Leary recalled, "They redoubled their efforts when he spoke to them of the glory that awaited them."[90] Near Paya the advance guard fell upon three hundred royalists, forcing them to retreat. Encouraged by this victory, the soldiers recovered some of their vigor. Bolívar, unable to conceal his movements any longer, issued a proclamation announcing the arrival of the Liberating Army and calling for a general revolt against the Spanish.

The army resumed its march on July 2, taking the road that crossed the Páramo of Pisba, generally believed to be impassable. Huge boulders and fallen trees blocked the way completely at many points. After a terrible night, during which it was impossible to keep a fire going, they struck out across the páramo itself, a bleak and uninviting desert devoid of all vegetation because of its altitude.

> That day the cold, penetrating air proved fatal to many soldiers most of whom were almost naked. During this day's march my attention was drawn to a group of soldiers who had stopped near the place where I had sat down overwhelmed by fatigue. One of them informed me that the wife of a soldier of the Rifles Battalion was in labor. The following morning I saw the same woman with the newborn baby in her arms, and apparently in the best of health, marching along behind the battalion, having already walked two leagues over one of the worst paths of that rugged terrain. The following night was even more horrible than the previous ones, and many soldiers perished as a result of their suffering and privations. . . .[91]

At last this ordeal too came to an end, and the army descended from the páramo. Anzoátegui reached Socha, the first town in Tunja Province, on June 6. The *sochanos* greeted them warmly. They took them into their houses to help them, and the women made shirts and jackets for the soldiers out of their own clothes. Of that day, Anzoátegui wrote to his wife, "This was a miraculous resurrection. Life, courage, and faith came back to us."[92]

Word of their arrival brought little joy to José María Barreiro, quartered in Sogamoso with more than two thousand men. The Spanish commander in chief was amazed that Bolívar had advanced against such odds. Faced with this unexpected challenge, he hoped to avoid a battle until he could muster all available troops. Nevertheless he took a firm stand at Gámeza, and a bloody clash on July 11 resulted in many casualties for royalists and patriots alike.

As Barreiro took refuge in Molinas de Tópaga, Bolívar took control of the valley of Santa Rosa de Viterbo, cutting off communication with Santa Fe. On July 25 he crossed the Sogamoso River and met the Spanish at the place known as Pantano de Vargas. At first the fierce fighting seemed to favor Barreiro. Then, when all but Bolívar despaired of victory, Colonel Juan José Rondón, a Venezuelan, appeared at the head of his llaneros. "Bolívar spoke words of encouragement to them and said to their leader, 'Colonel, save the country.' The latter, followed by his intrepid soldiers, hurled himself against the advancing enemy squadrons and routed them with heavy losses."[93] Inflamed by Rondón's example, the infantry advanced. By nightfall the royalists were in retreat.

Barreiro withdrew to Paipa in order to guard the entrance to Tunja, but on August 5 Bolívar took the city and was given a delirious reception by its inhabitants. Two days later his army surprised the royalists at a bridge sixteen kilometers south of Tunja. The Spanish, still better armed, might have pulled out a victory, but by the end of the day, brilliantly directed by Bolívar, Santander, and Anzoátegui, the patriots won the Battle of Boyacá.

The Battle of Boyacá saw less bloodshed than the earlier encounters at Gámaza and Pantano de Vargas, but it had more decisive consequences for all northern South America. Bolívar took sixteen thousand prisoners, among them Barreiro. He went on to occupy Santa Fe as Sámano, the last Spanish viceroy, fled the country. Boyacá gave reality to the independent republic of Colombia. It placed the initiative in the long war permanently into the hands of Bolívar, and it heralded the defeat of the Spanish in Venezuela, Ecuador, Peru, and Bolivia.[94]

The llaneros from Casanare had enjoyed their finest hour, assuring themselves of a prominent place in histories of New Granada and Colombia, but their role in the war was not yet over. In Venezuela Páez and the Army of Apure were still deadlocked with Morillo's soldiers. Leaving Santander to administer the government in Santa Fe, Bolívar turned his attention to the liberation of his homeland.

Now, just as Venezuela had sustained the republican cause in 1816 and 1817, New Granada became the principal source of men, supplies, and foods for the ongoing struggle. In Casanare Juan Nepomuceno Moreno, replacing José Concha as comandante general, supplied horses and cattle to the highlands and to Páez.[95] The latter, with a firm hold on the llanos of Apure, was reluctant to operate outside this familiar territory. Morillo dominated Caracas and the northern coastal range. Bolívar endeavored to assemble enough troops to fight a decisive war.

In the end events in Spain undermined Morillo's position. The revolt of the army in Cádiz, on January 1, 1820, deprived him of reinforcements. By November he was forced to negotiate a six-month armistice with Bolívar. Morillo retired to Spain in December, leaving his troops dispirited and the less-resolute General La Torre in command.

Bolívar prepared for the final campaign even before the armistice ended. In late April 1821, General José María Bermúdez attacked Caracas from the east and held it briefly. Forced to withdraw, he gave Bolívar time to rally a force of sixty-five hundred, most of whom were New Granadans and many of them veterans of Boyacá.[96] La Torre with five thousand soldiers made his stand on the plains of Carabobo, southwest of Valencia, on the road to the Llanos. On the morning of June 24, Bolívar threatened La Torre's center while Páez led half the army, including the plainsmen and the British Legion, around the enemy's right flank to attack from the rear. The manuever required negotiating a narrow path over difficult terrain. When the army was in place, the fighting was bitter, but ultimately the brave assault by Páez and his llaneros brought victory to the patriots.[97] La Torre retreated to the coastal fortress of Puerto Cabello, and Bolívar reentered Caracas on June 28.

The years between Boyacá and Carabobo also saw the actualization of the Republic of Colombia. At the Congress of Angostura, Bolívar had presented his proposal for a constitution. His decree of September 10, 1819, set up a provisional government in Santa Fe for the Free Provinces of New Granada. In December 1819 Bolívar returned to Angostura, where the congress was still in session. At his behest this body agreed that the Republic of Colombia would include Venezuela, New Granada, and Ecuador, as soon as the latter was liberated. In June 1821 delegates from the first two regions attended the Congress of Cúcuta. There they framed a permanent constitution that was liberal but rigidly centralist. Retaining the capital at Bogotá, the charter divided the territory into a number of departments rather than three large regions. On September 7 the congress chose Bolívar as president and Santander as vice-president.[98]

Between 1818 and 1821 the patriots overcame certain defeat to garner the ultimate spoils of victory—independence from the Spanish and a united republic. By the mid-nineteenth century, historians would compare Bolívar's arduous trek over the Andes with Hannibal's and Napoleon's crossing of the Alps. For their courage, endurance, and unwavering loyalty, the llaneros came to symbolize the essence of Colombian patriotism. In his long essay on Hispanic American society and politics, José María Samper wrote in 1861:

> The Llanero is the Colombian gaucho but a gaucho infinitely more poetic, more accessible, less barbarous. . . . Shepherd of the immense, free herds, rider, bullfighter, celebrated swimmer, fabulous cavalry soldier, poet of the pampas and of savage passions, a gallant artist in his way, the Llanero is the union between civilization and barbarism. . . . The Llanero has never served the cause of oppression nor of any dictatorship. When liberty is in danger, he responds enthusiastically to the first call.[99]

By the twentieth century the image of the the freedom-loving llanero, inseparable from his horse, riding the limitless plains, lance in hand to defend liberty, had become a sacred tenet of Colombian folklore and nationalism, yet early nineteenth-century documents show that the generation that achieved independence took a different view. As we have seen, the creole officers, accustomed to a Europeanized way of life, were appalled by the rudimentary and wretched conditions in the Llanos. A typical reaction is that of Pedro Briceño Méndez who, late in 1819, was sent from Santa Fe to Pore with orders to transfer military equipment deposited there to Guanapalo. On December 3, 1819, Briceño Méndez complained to Santander: "You can imagine how sad and melancholy it makes me—I left only a little while ago the noise and brilliance of the capital . . . to pass suddenly into the inaction, lubricity, and nonexistence of Casanare and particularly of Pore. It is the same as descending from the supreme seat in heaven to the lowest corner of earth, and like being nowhere, so it is that I don't know why I have not died of boredom and weariness, since up to now, I have escaped the pestilence."[100]

Creoles like Briceño Méndez respected the courage of the llaneros, but they disdained their crude habits and feared that their ignorant leaders could not control their rebellious natures. On October 23, 1818, Santander wrote candidly to Bolívar that Galea, Pérez, Moreno, and Arredondo were "four men, ignorant and without resources, who have not feared the anger of the Jefe of Apure. What will happen when they liberate other people less simple and natural *(simples y sencillos)?*"[101] Bolívar himself harbored no illusions about the llaneros. On May 24, 1821, he cautioned Pedro Gual, minister of foreign affairs, that as a creole he could not form a true understanding of the spirit which filled the llaneros:

> These are not the soldiers you know; these are soldiers you have never known. They are men who have fought long and hard, and who, believing that they deserve much, feel thoroughly humiliated and miserable. They are without hope of gathering the fruit of what they have won by the lance. They are obstinate, ignorant Llaneros, who have never regarded themselves as the equal of men who know more or who make a better appearance. I myself, who have always been at their head, still do not know all their capabilities. I treat them with extreme consideration, and yet this consideration is not enough to inspire in them the confidence and frankness that should exist among comrades and fellow-citizens. You can be sure, Gual, that we are over an abyss, or rather, over a volcano that is about to erupt. I fear peace more than war.[102]

The Llaneros preserved the patriot cause at great personal sacrifice. With extraordinary efforts they acquired their own liberty, sustained it, and gave it to their countrymen. By the late nineteenth century there would be national gratitude and recognition. In the 1820s their reward was the devastation of their province and abandonment by the republican government.

8 *The Frontier Transformed, 1819–1831*

The stunning victories at Boyacá and Carabobo confirmed the right of Bolívar, Santander, and Páez to direct the fortunes of the new republic, Gran Colombia.[1] During the next five years, Bolívar waged war against the Spanish in Ecuador, Peru, and Bolivia. In Venezuela Páez ruled as military commander sharing power with the civilian intendant, Carlos Soublette, Santander, as vice-president in Bogotá, tackled the enormous task of putting into operation the government designed by the Congresses of Angostura and Cúcuta. The heavy cost of nine years of fighting was apparent throughout New Granada but especially in the Llanos, where the struggle had disrupted the population, decimated the livestock, depleted the economy, destroyed the missions, created a multitude of discontented and landless veterans, perpetuated lawlessness, and nurtured caudillism. An analysis of these consequences and the largely futile efforts of Gran Colombia leaders to alleviate them helps to explain why the Llanos have remained, throughout the nineteenth and twentieth centuries, a permanent frontier.

The Eastern Cordillera isolated cities, towns, and missions in the Llanos of Casanare, and San Juan and San Martín, for nearly 250 years. Immigrants trickled in from the highlands and Venezuela, but the population grew slowly. The census of 1778 recorded 20,892 inhabitants, of whom only 7 percent were white.[2] Another official count was not taken until 1825, but José Manuel Restrepo put Casanare's population in 1808 at 22,000—an estimate that gives an annual growth rate of .18 percent after 1778, considerably less than the 1.6 percent growth that Jorge Orlando

Table 10. Population of New Granada, Casanare, and the Llanos of San Juan and San Martín, 1779–1851

Year	New Granada	Annual Growth Rate	Casanare	Annual Growth Rate (%)	San Juan and San Martín
1779	785,000	——	20,892	——	——
1808	1,309,000	2.3	22,000	.018	——
1810	1,264,000	1.97	22,000	.018	——
1825[a]	1,129,000	(-0.81)	19,084	(-.078)	——
1825[b]	1,344,000	0.16	22,137	Neg.	——
1827	——	——	——	——	1,782
1832	——	——	——	——	1,530
1835	1,686,038	2.5	15,948	(-2.7)	——
1845	1,931,684	1.82	18,489	1.99	——
1851	2,243,684	2.02	18,573	.06	——

Sources:

1779: Census of 1778. Figures corrected by Melo, "La evolución económica," 138.

1808: Restrepo, *Historia de la revolución,* 1:401.

1810: Felipe Pérez, Geografía general (Bogotá, 1883), 156. Figures corrected by Melo.

1825a: Census of 1825, believed to be undercounted.

1825b: Census of 1825 corrected by Melo.

1827: *Gaceta de Colombia,* October 14, 1827.

1832: Feliciano Montenegro Colón, *Geografía general* (Caracas, 1834), 3: 550.

1835: Census of 1835.

1845: Census of 1845.

1851: Census of 1851.

All official censuses are reprinted in Miguel Urrutia and Mario Arrubla, *Compendio de estadísticas históricas de Colombia* (Bogotá, 1970).

Melo calculates for New Granada overall during the same period (see table 10).[3]

The Llanos took the brunt of the war during the Spanish reconquest. In 1810 the Provisional Junta in Pore sent men to fight in the interior. In 1813 it recruited an army to defend Arauca, but it was not until 1816 that hundreds of rebel soldiers and civilians, fleeing Morillo's advancing troops, sought safety in the plains. In July La Torre took Pore, burned Chire, and executed prominent patriots. Many others emigrated to Venezuela. The hardening of guerrilla resistance and the determination on both sides to show no mercy plunged the province into relentless struggle, while in Apure Casanareños were also fighting and dying with Páez. When Santander arrived in Pore, in November 1818, he raised yet another army, taking the few remaining able-bodied men and boys. Some of these soldiers eventually returned to Casanare. Others died on the march over the Andes, at Boyacá, at Carabobo, or in Bolívar's subsequent campaigns.

Disease took more lives than military action. Health conditions had always been abominable in the Llanos, even for those born there. During the war there was the added problem of acclimatizing highland soldiers to the tropics and llaneros to the cool mountain air.[4] Without money and physicians, it was impossible to provide even rudimentary medical care. On December 3, 1819, Pedro Briceño Méndez urged Santander to regard Casanare as a vast military hospital and to send doctors immediately: "The pestilence has carried off half the population of the province and continues to exterminate the rest. . . . It is pitiful to see men and entire families perishing for want of medical help."[5]

As table 10 reveals, the paucity of accurate census data for the first half of the nineteenth century makes it difficult to determine the demographic loss attributable to war and disease. For New Granada as a whole, the decline did not match that of Venezuela, where the population decreased by 15 percent—from 899,043, in 1810, to 767,100, in 1822.[6] Historians regard the census of 1825 total of 1,129,000 inhabitants for New Granada as undercounted. Basing his calculations on the later, more accurate censuses, Melo suggests that 1,344,000 is more probable for 1825.[7] If Melo is correct, New Granada's population showed an increase of 25,000 over the 1808 estimate of 1,309,000, and 80,000 over the 1810 estimate of 1,264,000. In Casanare the population remained remarkably stable over this period, with 22,137 in 1825 as compared with an estimated 22,000 in 1808 and 1810.

A more striking contrast appears from a comparison of the corrected figures for 1825 with the census of 1835. While the total population of

New Granada grew at an annual rate of 2.5 percent, to reach 1,686,035, Casanare declined by 27 percent, to 15,948. Although the province rallied in 1845 to register a total of 18,498, its growth rate continued to be less than that of the rest of the country. Thus by 1851, when the population of New Granada reached 2,243,730, or nearly three times its size in 1778, Casanare had 18,573 inhabitants, 80 percent of its population of seventy-five years before. These are crude figures with a wide margin of error, but it is clear that the Llanos suffered a disproportionate loss of people between 1810 and 1835. By 1851 Casanare constituted demographically a much smaller segment of the Republic of New Granada than it had of the old viceroyalty.

Equally dramatic and imprecise are estimates of the decline of livestock in the Llanos. Between 1810 and 1819 patriots and royalists alike routinely expropriated cattle for food and horses for the cavalry. Bushnell notes that the most prevalent single variety of military extortion was seizure of animals, and that most llaneros rode horses confiscated from private hatos.[8] Even after Boyáca, the government expected ranchers in Casanare to supply meat to the troops in the highlands and to Páez in Apure. On January 19, 1820, Governor Juan Nepomuceno Moreno pressed Santander to stop taking animals because the province was entirely annihilated and had no other hatos besides those of Guanapalo, San Emigdio, and Arania. He pointed out that ever since the liberation campaign, cattle from Casanare had been slaughtered to feed the troops or sold to buy cloth for their uniforms. The formerly vast herds of Tocaría were so depleted that it took fifty men with five hundred horses two months to find and round up one hundred head. To see cattle one had to travel to Arauca. The governor reminded Santander that the llaneros would sacrifice their lives and property to defend liberty, "but it is necessary, sir, to have some consideration. Cattle is the only industry here, and when this is finished, the province is finished."[9] A month later a petition written by Juan José Molina underscored Moreno's plea. It stated that of the estimated 273,000 cattle and 30,000 horses which had grazed in Casanare in 1814, there were now only 50,000 cattle and 4,000 horses, in a completely wild state.[10]

The textile industry, long the economic mainstay of the towns on the slopes of the Cordillera, was another casualty of the war. Fighting blocked normal trade lines. Conscription of Indian craftsmen dealt the finishing blow to an industry already bested by competition from Socorro. These same conditions crippled agricultural activities. In 1819 Santander tried to encourage planting of crops by releasing soldiers from their military duties to attend to this task.[11] He ordered all Indians who were not drafted to work in their fields.[12] Captured Indian deserters were not to be deprived of their agricultural implements.[13] Despite these measures the inhabitants could not raise enough food for the Army of the Vanguard, and Santander imported supplies from Guayana. By the end of the war, the fields were empty. The province lay in desolation.

Recovery turned on the natural procreation of cattle and horses—a process requiring many years. In Venezuela ranchers who formerly enjoyed a brisk trade in hides and live animals with the Antilles, lobbied for policies which would foster its resumption. Santander resisted their pressure. Faced with the possibility of another Spanish reconquest, he feared that systematic export would extinguish the herds. Instead he taxed hides at 10 percent and prohibited the sale of cattle and mules abroad in 1821 and again in 1824.[14] These steps incurred the wrath of the Venezuelans, for without commercial incentive they could not afford to reinvest capital in their war-ravaged hatos. Páez proved more sensitive to their frustrations and lifted these prohibitions in 1830.[15]

Santander's restrictions did not apply to commerce within New Granada. Ranchers of Casanare had traditionally sent their cattle to Tunja and Sogamoso. Yet the owners found that by the time they drove their steers to the highlands, the price needed to cover their expenses was not competitive with the asking price for animals obtained from other parts of the country. In 1833 Juan Nepomuceno Moreno complained that trade with Boyacá had ended completely and that "no one comes here to buy a single bull."[16] Rather than protecting their cattle in order that they might reproduce, the ranchers found it more lucrative to slaughter them for their hides. In Arauca the herds had not suffered from the war to the same degree, and the ranchers shared the Venezuelan conviction that trade with the Antilles was imperative. They believed that the Llanos had more to gain by being part of Venezuela than by remaining under Bogotá. In 1830 Moreno actually attempted to lead Casanare out of New Granada in order to join Páez. For many reasons, then, cattle raising in the Llanos was not remunerative, and the herds multiplied very slowly. Agustín Codazzi, the Italian-born cartographer, estimated that in 1840 there were 100,000 cattle and 5,000 horses in Casanare, as compared to 400,000 cattle and 60,000 horses in the Venezuelan Llanos.[17]

Santander's fiscal policies contributed to the sluggish economic recovery. The Congress of Cúcuta, eager to scuttle the entire mechanism of colonial taxation, abolished outright internal customs duties and Indian tribute, and it revised the alcabala or sales tax. It validated the state monopolies on tobacco and salt, but opened the distilling industry to anyone who cared to enter it, taxing the liquor produced. To compensate for the loss of former revenues, the congress imposed a levy of 10 percent per year on income generated by land and capital, as well as a series of extraordinary contributions called *subsidios*—forced loans which the government demanded without any pretense of repayment. These reforms provided the Republic of Gran Colombia with more revenue than its colonial predecessor enjoyed, but the income was still inadequate to pay the costs of the war in Peru. Santander raised a loan of £20,000,000 in London, in 1824, to stave off disaster, but by 1826 the expanding national debt had brought the nation to the brink of ruin.[18]

During the viceroyalty Indian tribute was a major source of revenue in the Provincia de los Llanos. The governor had collected it until 1810. The new republican sources of income did not compensate for this loss. The annual report of Faustino Nieto, treasurer of the public hacienda of Casanare, for fiscal year July 1823 to June 1824, indicates that the tax on the manufacture and sale of aguardiente and the subsidios produced the largest provincial revenues, with lesser amounts coming from the salt and tobacco monopolies (see table 11). Salaries of government employees, military officers, and disabled soldiers were the greatest expenditures. The minuscule balance of 39 pesos 2¼ reals, in June 1824, did not long survive. In December Comandante Moreno ordered Nieto to pay state employees and disabled veterans who had not received their salaries for three months, adding that the invalids "absolutely can not help themselves, not even to go out and beg." Some claimants came in person to the treasurer. Nieto showed them the empty coffer and explained that there was not even enough money to pay the commander or to buy food for the troops. Entreating the intendant in Tunja for assistance, Nieto wrote: "This treasury does not have any funds, and expenses increase daily, and all those with complaints direct them against the treasurer as if it were possible to produce miracles. There are only a few reals left and when they are gone, the *caja* (cash box) will be closed."[19] The intendent sent Nieto's letter, with supporting documents, on to the secretary of state and hacienda in Bogota, but no aid materialized. Insolvency plagued the treasury throughout the 1820s.

The production of sugarcane and tobacco to replace cattle raising was not without obstacles. In 1820 Juan José Molina complained that Colonel Antonio Rangel, sent to Casanare to collect cattle for the central government, was requisitioning oxen used to work the sugarcane mills, "making it impossible to produce *aguardiente* which is the principal income of this

Table 11. Treasurer's Report for the Province of Casanare, July 1, 1823 to June 20, 1824

Income	Pesos	Reals	
Balance at the end of June 1823	325	2	1/4
Alcabala (sales tax)	238	1	——
Contribución directa (property tax)	798	7	1/4
Revenue from:			
Aguardiente (liquor tax)	2,595	3	1/2
Tobaccos (tobacco tax)	838	3	3/4
Correos (mail)	173	2	1/2
Papel sello vendido (stamped paper)	628	7	——
Salinas (salt monopoly)	688	7	1/2
Alcance de cuentas (previous year's balance)	553	7	3/4
Subsidio de guerra (forced loans)	1,487	3	1/4
Fábrica de iglesias (fund for church repair)	6	——	——
Manumisión (manumission)	53	4	——
Reintegro (refunds)	500	——	——
Mora común de hacienda (miscellaneous)	46	——	——
Total	8,934	2	3/4
Expenditures			
Salaries:			
Tesorería (treasury office)	1,311	——	1/4
Gobierno (government office)	1,865	7	1/2
Comandante de Armas (military chief)	1,907	2	1/4
Jueces políticos (municipal officers)	1,288	4	——
Militares (soldiers)	511	——	——
Inválides (disabled)	234	2	——
Portes de Correo (postage)	211	4	1/2
Gastos de Oficina (office expenses)	137	2	1/2
Reíntegros (refunds)	6	——	——
Manumisión (manumission)	105	——	——
Suplemento a la Factoria Admon. de Tabaco (Tobacco monopoly supplement)	500	——	——
Mora común de hacienda (miscellaneous)	821	——	1/2
Total	8,894	7	1/2

Comparison:

Income:	8,934	1	3/4
Expenditures:	8,894	7	1/2
Balance:	39	2	1/4

Source: Prepared by Faustino Nieto, Pore, July 1, 1824. AHN, Intendencia de Boyacá, vol. 3, fol. 259.

Province."[20] A law required tobacco growers to sell their crop to the state tobacco factories, but because of the war state funds were diverted to military expenses, and the factories could not compensate the farmers in full or on time for their harvest. On January 29, 1826, the Provincial Junta at Pore sent a manifesto to Bogota, citing the extreme poverty of Casanare and asking that part of the British loan be used to purchase local tobacco "in order to promote agriculture and to increase the income of the Province."[21] Deluged by similar requests from other regions, the congress did not legislate special relief for Casanare.

Santander did endorse two schemes with developmental potential—a proposal to put steamboats on the Orinoco and another to colonize the Llanos with European immigrants. As early as the seventeenth century, the Jesuits had demonstrated the advantages of direct riverine trade to Guiana and the Atlantic. More recently supplies procured in Guiana and shipped along the Orinoco and Meta formed the lifeline of the patriot army. Juan Bernardo Elber's apparent success in initiating steam navigation on the Magdalena, in 1824, prompted entrepreneurs to submit similar projects for the Orinoco. In that year the congress granted the concession to Miguel Palacios, a Venezuelan deputy, and James Hamilton, a Scots businessman, but they failed to get a boat on the river even after the congress extended the time limit by special decree. In 1826 Santander rescinded the contract and fined Hamilton 20,000 pesos for noncompliance with the terms.[22]

The congress was eager to attract immigration, in 1823 it passed the Colonization Law, which designated up to three million *fanegas* (land measure equal to 1.6 acres) of national land for distribution to foreign colonists. This law prompted a spate of contracts, awarded to hastily formed companies that undertook to find settlers in Europe and transport them to Gran Colombia. On October 29, 1823, Jean Baptiste Pierre François d'Esmenard, Paravey and Company, Paris bankers, signed such a contract, securing the right to 120,000 fanegas of land in Magdalena, 40,000 in Neiva, and 40,000 in Casanare. They agreed to begin colonies of French, English, German, or Swiss farmers, artisans, craftsmen, and mechanics on one-fifth of this land within six years, six months.[23] But d'Esmenard and his associates could not carry out the bargain. Like the other companies, they discovered that few immigrants would choose to come to South America as long as land in the United States was readily available. The government canceled the contract after they failed to meet their obligation.[24]

Steam navigation and foreign colonization were impractical in the Llanos at this time, and Santander had neither the resources nor the inclination to look for other kinds of assistance. Recovery was left to the operation of natural forces, which seemed to work against Casanare. As the population and economy steadily declined, Salvador Camacho tendered his resignation as governor, in 1827, with the dire prediction that "This province is going to its ruin. Its population and the little wealth that remains are disappearing. I am sorry in my soul to see this happening and am powerless to remedy it."[25]

The virtual disappearance of the missions heightened the malaise. Since 1661 they had been the principal Spanish device for defending, expanding, and peopling the Llanos frontier. They had weathered attacks by jealous settlers, hostile Indians, and Charles III, with his expulsion of the Jesuits. By 1800, as we have shown, there were some 15,679 Indians living in twenty-eight reductions, operated by Dominicans, Franciscans, and Recoletos. When the Recoletos welcomed Rosillo, Salgar, and Cadena, they could hardly have imagined that within a decade a system that had endured two hundred years would vanish.[26]

Once the patriots declared war, the clergy, even in the remote missions, found it difficult to keep aloof from the struggle. There were some royalists among them, but the creole religious were, in great majority, partisan defenders of the republicans.[27] In 1816 Pablo Morillo imprisioned many priests for their revolutionary attitudes, including members of the hierarchy of the Archdiocese of Santa Fe.[28] He expelled ninety-five seculars and regulars from the capital, some of whom he had deported from the country.

Repression fanned the flame of resistance. Between 1817 and 1821 clerical enthusiasm for independence increased. Everywhere priests served as propagandists and contributed, sometimes under duress, to the war assessments euphemistically described as loans and gifts. A surprising number took up arms; others held posts of major responsibility under the new regime. A common form of personal service was participation in juntas, congresses, and assemblies, because such activities were consistent with the clerical vocation and were often filled by popular elections.[29]

Missionaries in the Llanos conformed to this general pattern. The cordial reception they gave to the ill-fated revolutionaries, in 1810, was fair indication to the crown where their sympathies lay. In 1812 the prefect of the Missions of Cuiloto reported that the Recoletos had deserted the reductions without permission, whether to free themselves from vexations, to emigrate to the highlands, or, as in the case of Fr. Manuel Ordoñez and Fr. Vicente Heredia, to serve as chaplains for the patriots.[30] The most famous of the new breed of warrior-priests was a Dominican, Fr. Ignacio Mariño, whose career during and after the war merits special attention.

Ignacio Mariño was born in Chocontá (Cundinamarca) in 1775. He entered the Dominican convent in Tunja in 1790, receiving ordination seven years later. In 1800 he went as a missionary to Tame, where he remained, officially at least, until 1819. In 1803 he reported that his parish consisted of 1,070 Indians and 6 white and pardo agregados, living in seven capitanías.

Mariño committed himself to the patriot cause very early. In December 1813 he signed the Declaration of Independence of the Province of Tunja. In 1814, holding the rank of colonel, he led six hundred men in Bolívar's asault against Nariño in Santa Fe. When the patriots withdrew to the Llanos, Mariño returned to his parish. Converting himself into a guerrillero, he led the Indians of Tame, Macaguane, and Betoyes against the Spanish garrisons in Cuiloto, Pore, and Chire. In February 1818 he participated in Ramón Nonato Pérez's attack on Fundación de Upía. He acted as mediator between Colonel Pérez and Bolívar, and he attended the Congress of Angostura as an alternate delegate from Casanare. He marched as chaplain with Santander's Army of the Vanguard. After the Battle of Boyacá, he held briefly the post of civil and military head of Sogamoso. He died of natural causes on July 25, 1821.[32]

Despite his military exertions, Mariño persevered as a Dominican. Missionary to Tame until 1819, he served the parishes of Guateque (Boyacá) and Nemoncón (Cundinamarca) in 1820 and 1821. In January 1821 he composed a tract that defended the regular clergy and condemned the routine practice of replacing friars, after they had carved reductions out of the wilderness, with secular priests.[33] When Mariño came to Bogotá, during the war years, he lived in the Dominican convent and performed his religious obligations wearing his habit over his uniform. In *Cartas a un sacerdote católico* (Bogotá, 1857), José Joaquín Ortiz, conservative journalist and poet, recalled the first time he, as a young boy, saw Mariño:

> One day I went to the parish church, and I saw entering a friar dressed in the white sack cloth of Santo Domingo. It was Padre Mariño. Over his hat waved a restless plume, over his shoulders gleamed the epaulets of a colonel, his spurs and long sword rang out against the pavement of the church. He reached the altar, took off his military acoutrements to put on the *alba de los levits* and the other priestly garments and offered to the awful God of the armies, the bloodless sacrifice of health and peace.[34]

A curious blend of soldier and cleric, Marino was one of the most intriguing figures to emerge from the war in Casanare.

Not all clergy aspired to march to battle drums. For missionaries who remained at their posts in the Llanos, coexistence with the patriot junta was far from easy. Documents published by Marcelina Ganuza suggest that between 1810 and 1816 the provincial authorities provided neither financial subsidy nor military protection to the Recoletos and violated with impunity their customary autonomy over the Indians. In 1811, for example, the Junta at Pore decreed unilaterally that whites might own land and live in the missions of Cuiloto, so long as they possessed documents attesting to their good conduct. The law required that two of these individuals assist the priests in teaching the Indians to attend mass, to learn Spanish, and to use agricultural tools. Beyond this stipulation it exempted the settlers from obeying the priest as well as from military service. Fray Agustín Villate in Chire protested against this law, on February 18. For fourteen years, he wrote, he and his colleagues had labored without government aid. In their reduced circumstances, there was no way that they could take on the added burden of caring for Spanish agregados. Moreover, unless concrete help was forthcoming, their work was finished. "In view of what you have resolved, I will resign our mission. . . . I ask you to reflect with the knowledge that you have. Is it possible to live among the Guahibos in these missions without weapons, subsidy, or any protection from assault?"[35]

Governor Andrés Solano provoked a second civil-religious crisis on May 3, 1814, when he ordered the prefect of the Recoleto Missions of Meta, Fr. Pedro de la Santísima Trinidad Cuervo, to hand over the account books of the hatos so that the government might expropriate horses and cattle for the troops. On June 22 he informed Cuervo that he must supply five hundred cattle annually to the government and submit a report of all business related to the hatos. Cuervo went to Pore to argue against this demand. He reminded Solano that the missionaries depended on cattle sales to finance the reductions since they did not receive salaries. The governor was adamant and continued the extraction of livestock. By the end of 1814, five Recoleto towns—Guacacía, Mitimiti, Arimena, Caviuna, and Cavapune—disintegrated. Cuervo fled from Casanare, taking refuge in the convent in Tunja.[36]

During the reconquest Morillo tried to reestablish the missions in the Llanos. On July 16, 1816, he directed the prior of the Candelaria convent in Santa Fe to send the brothers back to their posts. Cuervo returned to Macuco. He served as prefect of the Meta Missions but soon ran afoul of the patriots. In April 1817, Ramón Nonato Pérez imprisoned him in Chire for unknown reasons. Since both Juan Nepomuceno Moreno and Juan José Molina testified on Cuervo's behalf, it is unlikely that he betrayed the revolutionary cause. His incarceration may have been a capricious whim on the part of Pérez, but it illustrates the general atmosphere of insecurity.[37]

Santander, as commander of the Army of the Vanguard in 1818–19, further undermined the missions. The young brigadier general did not hesitate to draft neophytes as soldiers and laborers. On January 18, 1818, he directed the juez mayor of Manare to round up the Indians so that they could build a barracks for the army.[38] On January 29 he told Fr. Ignacio Delgadillo, cura of Betoyes, that he must keep the Indians from fleeing by assuring them that they would serve in the cavalry, not infantry.[39] The reluctant native soldiers deserted whenever possible. Santander frequently reminded his commanders to take precautions to stop them from running away.[40]

Santander continued the practice of confiscating the gold and silver holy objects that graced parish and mission churches. On April 27, 1816, by order of Governor Molina, the Casanare treasury took in 85 *libras* (pounds), 15 *onzas* (ounces), and 4 *ochavas* (eights) of precious metal, collected from the church at Casimena. Similar hauls arrived from Paya, Pisba, Guanapalo, Macuco, and Surimena.[41] Santander had the sacred objects melted down and stamped into coins, at a mint established in Casanare.[42] His drive to leave no potential source of wealth untapped had a grisly side. On learning that the priest in Manare was near death, he ordered the man's property embargoed, except for that which was necessary to bury him.[43]

Early in 1810 Frs. Pedro Cuervo, Hipólito Pino, and José Antonio Jaramillo handed over to Rosillo the weapons stored in the missions to fight Indians. Unable to acquire others, they were helpless against the increasingly aggressive Guahibos, vividly described by Cortés Madariaga as "muscular, tall, dark copper color, of deformed features with a bloody and warlike character."[44] On December 3, 1819, Pedro Briceño Méndez described the situation in Casanare as out of control. Ferocious, "cannibalistic" Guahibos infested the Llanos on both sides of the Meta River. Insolent and daring, they imperiled military communications, raided army camps, and had killed at least twenty soldiers. Briceño urged Santander to order that boats armed with small cannon be built, which could protect the province from the Indian menace by patrolling the Meta.[45]

Clerical support of the patriots, the drafting of recruits and draining of resources by the rebels, and Guahibo raids all jeopardized the mission system. In theory, the Dominicans, Franciscans, and Recoletos were active in the Llanos throughout the war. In practice, by 1821 only four reductions remained—Casimena, Macuco, Surimena, and Guanapalo—all located along the Meta and served by Recoletos. Governor Molina urged that more priests be sent, since without them "the Province will not grow and its towns will be ruined."[46] Republicans in Bogotá believed that the orders should continue to minister to the estimated 200,000 unbaptized Indians living in the back country of Gran Colombia. At the same time, they wanted to alter the legal structure of power and privilege that the Church had enjoyed under the viceroyalty. A wave of anticlericalism crippled mission revitalization in the Llanos in the 1820s.

The Congress of Cúcuta initiated the attack by abolishing the Inquisition. Charging that monastic life was obsolete and parasitic, the legislators closed all convents with fewer than eight members. A law passed in 1826 required that novices be at least twenty-five years old before they might be admitted to a convent or monastery. Religious were forced to contribute to war loans and to pay direct taxes the same as other citizens. Moreover the government sought to reduce clerical income. While not completely eliminating tithes, it exempted Indians from paying parish fees and stated that the public treasury would no longer pay the stipends the priests had received under Spanish rule. Liberal congressmen debated a bill that would have abolished or reduced mortmain, censos (mortgages), and dowries of nuns, but failed to agree on its merits. The measures that were adopted reduced priests who served Indian congregations to living on sporadic alms plus whatever they might receive from tithes and from a complex system of direct assessments levied on the Indians.[47]

These laws notwithstanding, Gran Colombian officials blamed the dissolution of the missions on the general decadence of the religious orders. In 1824 Minister of Interior José Manuel Restrepo charged that the lack of priests had caused many towns in the Orinoco, Meta, and Apure regions to vanish. He called for a new law that would encourage the orders to return to these places.[48] Santander agreed that the missions must play an important role in civilizing the Indians. He frequently requested superiors of various orders to send priests to the Llanos and elsewhere, but they did not have enough men to fill the vacancies. At times those assigned to posts in faraway places deserted en route to their destinations. On July 11, 1823, Santander told the president of the Chamber of Representatives that he wearied of asking the Recoleto provincial for missionaries. "The clergy, in general, show in the capital and great cities, much zeal for religion, but on demanding from them some sacrifice as in missions to the gentile Indians in which their apostolic zeal might have a vast field, they withdraw and do not want to leave their comforts: most of them desire nearby parishes which produce two or three thousand pesos of income. There are very few who want to go to the missions in which they cannot become rich."[49]

The religious communities, of course, saw the problem in an entirely different light. Even in the best of times, conversion of the Indians on the frontier had been fraught with danger. The scorn heaped upon them by the government, the curtailment of financial aid, and the absence of material assistance made what had been difficult work well nigh impossible. In the case of the Recoletos, the law suppressing minor convents left them with a single monastery, in Bogotá. With some missionaries dead, others sick, and all nervous and upset about the new laws, the order could not convert Indians in the Llanos with its former zeal.[50] In 1824 Fr. Francisco Forero de Santo Domingo became *cura reductor* (missionary priest) of Macuco and the missions of Meta. In 1826, as *vicario provincial* (ecclesiastical judge), he reported that the Meta missions were absolutely abandoned, surrounded everywhere by misery and lacking even elementary resources for subsistence.[51] On December 17, 1829, the Recoletos notified the archbishop that there were so few cattle in the Llanos that one missionary had starved to death and others had left their posts to search for food.[52] These documents and others published by Ganuza show that while a few dedicated priests struggled on, the mission system as it existed before the War of Independence had disappeared forever.

Nor could the republicans come up with a feasible replacement. In 1824 the congress passed the Law of July 30, "Methods of Civilizing the Savage Indians," which granted land and tools to any tribe that agreed to settle down to a sedentary existence. The government pledged to supply the new towns with priests and to assign seculars if regulars could not be found.[53] A second law offered the Indians of Casanare full exemption from military service if they would renounce their pagan ways, but nothing much happened.[54] On July 16, 1826 Governor Salvador Camacho disclosed that Ciriaco de Córdoba, a vecino of Chire, had founded two Indian towns, known as San Simón and San Francisco, on the banks of the Meta. The Indians supported themselves by provisioning travelers.[55] Camacho hoped that Córdoba's success would mark the beginning of the extension of civilization, moral principles, and religion to a considerable number of Indians, but no other settlements appeared. Experience proved that civilian populators were no more able than missionaries to win over the Indians without bribing them with tools and food. In 1826 the congress set aside 100,000 pesos annually to cover such expenses, but due to financial difficulties, the funds were never available.[56] The failure to find an alternative way to Hispanicize the Indians explains why Grenadine governments all through the nineteenth century periodically tried to revive the missions in the Llanos.

Under Spanish rule military presence in Casanare consisted of escoltas assigned to the missions. Regular army troops were unknown. The threat of a British invasion in 1797 did not generate enough concern to bring about the creation of a militia company. Townsmen and ranchers relied upon private resources to repel the Guahibos or to capture cattle rustlers.

The situation changed during the Wars of Independence. Out of the peones-vaqueros, Indians, and creoles coalesced a ragtag army that waged guerrilla war for nine years. Sacking, pillage, and plunder were characteristic of its operations, and only quasi-military discipline restrained the troops. Santander dreaded the lawlessness of these llaneros. After the victory at Carabobo, he sent them home on indefinite, unpaid leave. For the next five years, the congress tried to work out a mechanism for honoring their claims for back pay and promised bonuses. The dilemma of what to do with these discontented, unemployed veterans, accustomed to living off the land, was a critical issue in Casanare, but it was especially acute in Venezuela, where early republican policy had created an explosive atmosphere.

We have already noted that the legalization of the export of hides and live animals to the Antilles, in 1789, sparked a boom in cattle production and population in the Llanos of Guárico, Barinas, and Apure. Rosy economic prospects encouraged creoles, peninsulars, and foreign planters fleeing social and political upheaval in the Caribbean to acquire ranches. Slaves escaping from the coastal plantations swelled the large vagabond population of Indians and free blacks who roamed the plains freely, living as outlaws, attacking towns, and stealing cattle. The landowners tried repeatedly to control this group, but the laws they passed proved unenforceable and generated great bitterness.

In 1811 the leaders of the First Republic took firm steps to bring the llaneros to heel. They promulgated the *Ordenanzas de los Llanos,* which protected private property by forbidding anyone to hunt or round up cattle except by written consent from the owner of the land in question. The law sought to reduce llaneros to serf-like status by forcing them to register, to carry identity cards, and to live on ranches, under the rule of a patrón. Men twice convicted of vagrancy faced a year's imprisonment, while rustlers were to be executed.[57] The resentment engendered by this law, which embodied the elitist and class-oriented agrarian philosophy espoused by republican leaders and attacked common rights long enjoyed by the llaneros, accounts for their readiness to fight for the crown under the leadership of such men as Calzada, Puig, Yáñez, and especially Tomás Boves.

José Antonio Páez won over the llaneros to the patriot side by promising them a share of the estates seized from the enemy. A llanero himself, Páez understood that they would not respond to ideology; plunder was the only way to hold them. In 1817 Páez recognized Bolívar's supreme authority on the condition that he would confirm Páez's promise that his men would receive the confiscated royalist lands after the war was over. At Bolívar's prodding the Congress of Angostura extended this offer to the entire army, pledging bonuses in national property ranging from $500 for a common soldier to $25,000 for a general in chief. Since Bolívar could not fulfill this agreement until victory was assured, and since the patriots had no money to pay salaries to the troops, the llaneros lived off the land, taking as booty whatever struck their fancy. Only partially and temporarily subjected to the rule of their officers, they instilled fear in the hearts of all the creoles who had to deal with them.[58]

In Casanare and the Llanos of San Juan and San Martín, there was no economic boom in the last half of the eighteenth century. There were landless peons, but communities of escaped slaves so prevalent in the Venezuelan llanos, were uncommon. During the patria boba the creoles did not pass measures seeking to tie the llaneros to the land. From the beginning the inhabitants of Casanare fought against the royalists advancing from Venezuela.

In 1816, with La Torre's invasion, however, llaneros of New Granada and Venezuela formed a single army under Páez. Almost immediately cultural and protonationalistic antagonisms developed. The Casanareños returned to their homeland as soon as it was militarily feasible. They rejected Páez as a leader in favor of Santander, a fellow Grenadine. Nevertheless the style of fighting adopted by the Venezuelan troops before 1816 characterized battles fought throughout the Llanos, and once the war was over both countries emerged with the problem of an alienated, unpaid mass of veterans. As early as December 1820, when most llaneros were still in active service, Páez warned Bolívar that his men doubted that the government would keep its promise and repay them for their sacrifices.[59]

Bolívar, who confessed to Dr. Pedro Gual that he feared peace more than war, fully shared Páez's apprehension. The Congress of Angostura had stipulated that bonuses and back wages would be paid in *vales* (promissory notes), which the recipients were supposed to use in bidding for state property. The Congress of Cúcuta confirmed the awards, but also provided that national property be distributed to claimants at an assessed value.[60] Neither system was satisfactory. There was not enough desirable land to go around; estates seized from royalists were limited, and national lands were insufficient to meet the demand. But the officers fared better as a group than did the common soldiers. Most of the former received their full bonus, and some were even more fortunate. Páez, for example, obtained an estate worth $200,000 which covered all his past claims and represented a partial advance payment on what he had yet to earn.[61] In Casanare Rafael Urdaneta received the income from the haciendas belonging to the missions of Meta which, somewhat miraculously, still contained thirty thousand cattle and five thousand horses.[62]

When unrest continued the congress passed, in 1823, a special relief measure for the soldiers of Apure and Casanare, whose demands were unsatisfied because of the lack and deterioration of national land. The law set up an extraordinary commission in Apure, empowered to award national property to military claimants on the spot. It stipulated that the veterans must accept a quarter of what was owed them in land and the rest in cattle borrowed from the owners of hatos, at 5 percent interest.[63] The extraordinary commission completed its task mainly through the technique of turning one kind of debt into another. In 1826 an optimistic Santander pronounced the unrest in Apure under control.[64]

The government had defused the bomb, but historians from the vantage point of the twentieth century have branded its methods of paying off the veterans a failure. The llaneros never valued land for its own sake, but rather for the cattle that roamed over it. Ignorant and impoverished ex-soldiers sold their promissory notes to their officers. Of those who actually received small parcels, only a few had the capital to develop them. On the other hand, the officers, many of whom already belonged to the landowner class, saw their holdings increase by the receipt of estates taken from the royalists and by purchase of small properties from the soldiers. The ultimate effect was to accelerate the process of land concentration, a trend which continued throughout the nineteenth century.[65]

Santander had no better luck in reducing banditry and rustling. On September 22, 1819, he instructed Juan Nepomuceno Moreno as governor and comandante of Casanare to work with the civil authorities to stop cattle from being extracted illegally from the province.[66] The infamous *Ordenanzas de los Llanos* adopted in Venezuela in 1811 outlined procedures for branding and rounding up cattle and established jails and patrols of mounted police to apprehend those who violated them. The congress of Gran Colombia elaborated on these laws, extending the death penalty to include thieves and members of outlaw gangs.[67] Another law, passed in 1826, set down guidelines for judges in prosecuting rustlers and vagrants found in cattle regions everywhere in New Granada.[68] Such laws were honored mostly in the breach. Rustling still flourished in the Llanos.

In 1826 Páez rebelled against Santander. Although Bolívar managed to retain his loyalty, the general emerged as virtual dictator of Venezuela. On August 25 he decreed the "Law of Landowners and Ranchers in the Llanos." This measure continued to protect private property, to prohibit transit through estates without permission of the owner or mayordomo, and to make rights over wild cattle dependent on land ownership; but it also recognized the rights of small ranchers over cattle. It did not restrict the personal liberty of the llaneros, nor did it subject them to the degradation of forced labor.[69] Bolívar, as dictator of Gran Colombia, issued a similar law in February 1829 for the Llanos of Casanare and San Martín, recognizing private property, setting penalties for rustling, and prohibiting the crossing of land on foot or on horseback or hunting or fishing without permission of the owner.[70] While in neither Venezuela nor New Granada were llaneros reduced to serfdom in the decade after the Wars of Independence, they remained outside the agrarian property structure. Most lived by their wits. Branded as *cuatreros, bandidos, bandoleros,* and *criminales,* they became, especially in Venezuela, the source of constant unrest in the 1830s and 1840s.[71]

The llaneros commanded little esteem in New Granadan society. The creoles who fought with Páez or in Casanare could not forget the ferocious character of the struggle. Abhorrence of the mixed racial heritage of the plainsmen and a rejection of their barbaric life-style fueled their prejudice. Santander's merciless trial and execution on March 28, 1824, of Colonel Leonard Infante dramatized the clash of cultures.

Infante was a Venezuelan llanero, born in Maturín in 1795. Noted for his bravery during the war, he was one of the 150 heroes at Las Queseras del Medio to be awarded the Order of the Liberators. He covered himself with glory at the Pantano de Vargas and the Battle of Boyacá. Infante came to live in Bogotá, but early in 1824 was accused of murdering another Venezuelan officer, Francisco Perdomo. A war court (consejo de guerra) with a majority of New Granadan judges condemned him to death on the basis of extremely shaky evidence. Irregular legal proceedings punctuated the trial. In the opinion of José Manuel Groot, Infante's conviction resulted not from his crime but from the animosity which his uncouth behavior evoked in the urbane Bogotanos:

> The Colonel was a complete Llanero, and Llaneros have obnoxious habits. . . . He was a Negro of the purest type, a plainsman from Maturín, a fierce cavalryman, robust, well-shaped. . . . With these manners of a plainsman, he annoyed his neighbors and even those whom he knew regarded him with hostility, because a plainsman in a society of educated people is like a bulldog which enters a hall wagging its tail, and even though its owner says that it does not bite they all look at it with hostility and want it thrown out.[72]

Infante was acutely aware of the injustice of his sentence. On the way to the gallows it is said that he looked up at the congress building and, addressing several civilian representatives, exclaimed, "I am the one who put you in those positions." Again, before dying, he shouted to the assembled troops, "This is the payment I am given . . . I am the first, but others will follow me."[73]

The creoles did not distinguish between mestizo New Granadan and mulatto Venezuelan llaneros. Sensitivity to their disdain was a factor in General Juan Nepomuceno Moreno's decision to secede from Gran Colombia and unite his province with Venezuela. In 1833 he told Santander that in contrast to Venezuela, where there was much esteem for the Llanos because of their role in the war, "in New Granada it is rare to find a man that does not speak ill of and hate Casanare . . . which was made very clear to me, so that even in the Convention, there were a great many deputies who when they heard mentioned the Province of Casanare, acted as if someone had insulted them."[74] As long as they had to deal with a genuine llanero who by summoning his so-called barbarians could threaten the very existence of the republic, the elites elaborated no fantasies of gallant, freedom-loving cowboys.

A final legacy of the War of Independence was the growth of caudillism. For three hundred years, Spain ruled the New World with a minimum of military action and without personalism, but the war nurtured both militarism and the personification of the military leader in the caudillo, who drew his power from personal loyalties. John Lynch argues that it was probably an inevitable tendency in time of war to confer absolute power on a strong man who could recruit troops and commandeer resources. The caudillo was originally a war leader, but he also responded to civilian pressure groups of various kinds. Commonly he represented regional interests and defended those interests against the policies of the center. In many instances such caudillos were regional only until they became national leaders—federalists until they became unitarians. In all cases they reflected the weakness of newly formed, unconvincing republican institutions.[75] The Llanos did not escape this trend. The trappings of republican government fell into place but power remained effectively in the hands of one man, Juan Nepomuceno Moreno.

Under the Spanish the Provincia de los Llanos had been one of thirteen *gobiernos,* or provinces, within the jurisdiction of the Audiencia of Santa Fe. The chief executive officer was the governor, a professional bureaucrat appointed by the viceroy.[76] After the scare over Nariño's plotted uprising in 1798, the crown designated the Llanos as a *gobierno politíco y militar,* in which the king rather than the viceroy appointed the governor, who had to be a military officer. Within the province were cities, villas, pueblos, and *lugares.* Each city had a cabildo, or municipal council. The cabildos were bastions of local power. They were often at odds with the governor, who, more likely than not, had been born outside the province.

After the Act of Revolution, on July 20, 1810, Casanare became one of the fifteen United Provinces of New Granada.[77] Morillo toppled this republic in 1816, but Santander restored it again on December 18, 1818, when he declared that the free state of Casanare embodied the military and political powers of the United Provinces until the rest of the territory could be liberated. Santander sent delegates to Angostura, accepting union with Venezuela as a wartime necessity and recognizing Bolívar as president of the Republic of Colombia. After Boyacá he transferred the seat of government from Casanare to Bogotá.

The Congress of Cúcuta reorganized the Colombian territory that had been liberated by 1821 into seven departments: Orinoco, Venezuela, Zulia, Boyacá, Cundinamarca, Cauca, and Magdalena. Each department was subdivided into provinces, cantons, and parroquias (parishes). Casanare became a province within the Department of Boyacá. It had six cantons: Pore, Arauca, Macuco, Nunchía, Chire (with its capital at Tame), and Santiago (with its capital at Taguana). The Llanos of San Martín was a canton of Bogotá Province, within the Department of Cundinamarca. This territorial arrangement remained in force until the breakup of Gran Colombia, in 1830. The Law of June 25, 1824, which incorporated Ecuador did not affect the political status of the New Granadan llanos.[78]

The legislators of Cúcuta adopted the Spanish administrative code under which the chief executive officers in the departments and provinces exercised civil and military functions. Liberals, however, were unhappy, since this system violated the basic principle of the separation of powers. In 1825 they passed a new law, which established distinct civilian, military, judicial and administrative jurisdictions. In each department the *corte superior, intendente,* and *comandante general* had specific duties, just as did the *juez letrado de hacienda,* governor and *comandante de armas,* in each province. The Congress of Cúcuta retained the cabildos on the local level, but limited their power by creating the offices of the *jefe político,* to represent the wishes of the national government, and the *juez letrado,* to serve as the principal judge. In addition Casanare had a provincial council and sent one delegate to the Chamber of Representatives, in Bogotá.[79]

Bushnell points out that the newly created officials seldom enjoyed the traditional respect that had surrounded the colonial civil servant. There was a lack of qualified civilians to serve in public posts, and military men were often appointed to fill the gap. This tendency was especially true in Casanare, where few men possessed a law degree and where appointments to provincial offices had little attraction for the lawyers that abounded in Bogotá. The first three men nominated by Santander to be lieutenant governor declined the honor on the spot, forcing the interim governor, Salvador Camacho, to serve as lieutenant governor as well, not an unusual situation.[80]

Salvador Camacho, an intimate friend of Santander and a native of Casanare, appeared to be an excellent choice for governor. He was born in Chire on July 20, 1791, and went to Santa Fe to study in 1808. In 1810 he enlisted in the urban militia. Pursued by the Spanish, he went into hiding. Camacho took part in the conspiracy guided by Policarpa Salvarrieta. After the Battle of Boyacá, he served as vice-rector of the Colegio de San Bartolomé, and was a member of the Congress of Cucutá before becoming governor, in 1822.

Despite his excellent credentials, weak health and an inclination to be elsewhere limited Camacho's administrative effectiveness. In 1823 he was elected as Casanare's delegate to the Chamber of Representatives, but Santander disallowed the election on the grounds that Camacho could not hold two positions at the same time.[81] On August 12, 1823, the governor requested permission to come to Bogotá to attend to personal business and to recover his health, which the climate in the Llanos had destroyed. Santander acceded but reiterated that Camacho could not attend the congress except as an official observer.[82]

By the end of 1824, Camacho was back in Pore. Two years later, disheartened by the rebellion of Páez, the course of national events, and the economic decline of the Llanos, he tendered his resignation. He then served for a while as governor of the Province of Socorro and went to the Congress of Ocaña, where as a supporter of Santander he opposed the efforts of the Bolivarists to strengthen the central government and the chief executive. Late in 1828, finding himself juez de hacienda of Casanare, he was involved in the persecutions of the Bolivarian dictatorship. He fled to Barinas, returning to attend the Admirable Congress in Socorro (January 1830). In 1831 Camacho actively contributed to organizing the army that General Moreno led from the Llanos to overthrow Urdaneta's dictatorship.[83]

While Camacho served off and on during the 1820s as political head of Casanare, the real caudillo was Juan Nepomuceno Moreno, who occupied the position of comandante de armas. Like Camacho, Moreno was a native Casanareño, born at the site of the old city of La Fragua. However, military prowess was the key to his successful career. Rough and illiterate, he fought against the Spanish in Arauca in 1814 and participated in the battle of Guasdualito on January 31, 1815. Two years later, as governor of Casanare, Moreno refused to submit to Rafael Urdaneta, whom President Fernández Madrid in Santa Fe had appointed to command the patriot troops in the Llanos. He accepted the decision of the Arauca Junta, on July 16, 1816, which elected Santander commander in chief of the army. Retreating with the rest into Venezuela, he followed Páez after his coup on September 16 in Trinidad. Moreno fought at Yagual (October 8, 1816) and Achaguas (October 13, 1816).

In April 1817, after Galea's dispersal of the Spanish in Casanare, Moreno accepted with alacrity Páez's appointment as governor. In November 1818 he welcomed Santander to Guanapalo as his new commander in chief. Santander confirmed Moreno as governor but permitted him to remain with his cavalry. On May 8, 1819, Moreno was promoted to colonel and commander of the first regiment of the lancers. On June 15 he became commander general of the cavalry in the Division of the Vanguard.

After Boyacá Santander kept Moreno on as governor and commander general of Casanare, instructing him in September 1819 to work in harmony with the gobernador político, to reorganize the hato of Tocaría, and to unify the troops in Arauca.[84] In February 1821 Moreno resigned this position to join the army of General Páez. He fought at Carabobo and in the seige against Puerto Cabello, on November 8, 1823. Having achieved a distinguished military record, he returned to Casanare and stayed there until 1830 as comandante de armas.

Moreno has inspired no full length biography, and few descriptions of him appear in the primary sources.[85] He seems to have enjoyed the confidence of Santander. On the other hand Briceño Méndez, in 1819, citing his "natural apathy and indolence," regretted that Casanare was destined to fall into the hands of such men as he.[86] Recounting Moreno's invasion of the highlands in 1831, José Manuel Groot wrote that his bizarre appearance was "worthy of a photograph": "Fat and dark-skinned *(corpulento y renegrido),* with a long, blue frock coat, a white handkerchief worn like a cap and tied under his jaws, and a three-cornered hat trimmed with braid . . . a crude Llanero."[87]

Precisely because he was a "crude Llanero," Moreno represented more consistently than Camacho the interests of Casanare in the 1820s. In letters to Santander he protested policies which confiscated cattle and prohibited their export. He pressed for a tobacco subsidy, missionaries to convert the Indians, and doctors to tend the sick—all to no avail. When Páez revolted in 1826, Moreno was loyal, informing the vice-president of relevant events in Arauca in a letter which he signed "Juan N. El Sostenedor."[88]

After Santander's exile for complicity in the September 25, 1828, plot to assassinate Bolívar, Moreno grew restless. He believed that Casanare could expect better treatment from Venezuela, where Páez was already defying Bolívar's orders and initiating policies more favorable to ranchers in the Llanos. In December 1830 a Venezuelan congress, meeting in Caracas, called for separation from Gran Colombia. While delegates to the Admirable Congress in Bogotá frantically tried to come up with a workable framework for Gran Colombia, Venezuela declared itself independent. Sick at heart, Bolívar resigned on March 1 and prepared to go into exile. On May 4 the congress elected Joaquín Mosquera and Domingo Caicedo to take over as president and vice-president, respectively.[89]

Moreno now made his move. On April 2, 1830, he ordered the assassinations of General Lucas Carvajal and Francisco Segovia, men employed by Rafael Urdaneta to administer the haciendas of the Meta missions, and overthrew the incumbent governor, Luis Fernando Santos.[90] On April 4 vecinos of Pore came out for union with Venezuela. In their manifesto they stated that Casanare had been the first region free from Spain, but that since 1819 the authorities in Bogatá had reduced it to colonial status by appointing officials who did not know the needs of the people and who never even left the highlands because of their fear of the tropical climate. They had awarded the Meta missions to Carvajal and Segovia, unscrupulous men who took cattle that did not belong to them and treated the rightful owners as criminals when they protested. The vecinos declared broken forever "the feudal ties" which linked Casanare to New Granada. They recalled their representative from the congress in Bogotá and arranged for a new election to select a delegate to send to the Venezuelan congress, meeting in Valencia. They proposed that General Moreno should rule until Venezuela might dictate a more appropriate arrangement. The vecinos expressed the hope that, sharing with Venezuela a common climate, topography, and public opinion, Casanare might become part of the representative and popular form of government which that nation would develop. Within days the cantons of Arauca, Nunchía, Macuco, and Santiago endorsed the manifesto, and on April 19 Juan Nepomuceno Hurtado was chosen to represent Casanare at Valencia.[91]

Páez carefully monitored these developments from Caracas. He denied accusations from Bogotá that he had instigated Moreno's insurrection and affirmed that while he had submitted Casanare's request to join Venezuela to the congress, he had not endorsed the petition.[92] The delegates voted against annexation on July 31, after several days of debate. They explained that while they had the warmest regards for Casanare, historically it had never formed part of Venezuela, and New Granada would rightly view its incorporation as an act of war.[93]

The issue lay unresolved during the chaos that followed the breakup of Gran Colombia. On September 5, 1830, General Urdaneta overthrew the government of Mosquera and Caicedo and announced a dictatorship in the name of Bolívar. The lines were now drawn between militarists, who supported Bolívar and civilian Liberals, who looked to the exiled Santander. Throughout the country resistance flared against Urdaneta. José María Obando and José Hilario López raised troops in Cauca. Salvador Córdoba began a revolution in Antioquia, while Juan José Neira led the opposition in Cundinamarca. In March Joaquín Posada Gutiérrez declared in favor of the ousted Mosquera and Caicedo. Cauca, Panama, Magdalena, El Norte, and Casanare were in open revolt. With the country on the brink of civil war, Urdaneta met with some of the opposing generals at the Junta de Apulo near Tocaima (Cundinamarca), on April 28, 1831. Retaining command of the army, he agreed to recognize Caicedo as head of the government until a convention could be called to draft a new constitution.[94]

In the meantime General Moreno, claiming loyalty to Venezuela and backed by Salvador Camacho, rallied support in Casanare to march against Urdaneta. On February 15 Colonel José María Gaitán and Captain José Manuel Lasprial read to an assembly at Pore an *Exposición* urging Casanare to fight against Urdaneta. After some discussion the assembly resolved to send General Juan Nepomuceno Moreno, "our worthy caudillo in whom the people of Casanare have placed all their confidence," with an army of llaneros, to liberate the people of New Granada from their oppressor, in the name of justice and humanity.[95]

In April Moreno set off from Pore with three hundred cavalry and four hundred infantry, armed with guns supplied by Páez. They marched along the Morcote and Paya roads, crossing the Andes over the páramo of Pisba, where the extreme cold caused some deaths among the ill-clothed soldiers. As soon as Moreno reached Socha, on April 23, he wrote to General Justo Briceño and Coronel Reyes Patria, commanders of Urdaneta's army in Sogamoso, demanding their surrender, in the name of liberty.[96] Without awaiting their reply, he continued west, ordering his troops to swim across the Chicamocha River during the night because the bridge had been cut. On the following day he occupied Cerinza.

Briceño and Reyes Patria attacked on April 26. They managed to take the plaza, but a charge by mounted llanero lancers changed the situation within minutes, to give Moreno the victory. When the smoke had cleared, there were one hundred dead on each side. Moreno took prisoners including Reyes and four hundred others, five hundred guns, and many horses, Briceño retreated with four hundred followers to Tunja. He executed four of the enemy officers, one of whom was the son of Francisco de Miranda, the Venezuelan Precursor of Independence.[97]

The battle at Cerinza imperiled the truce just adopted by the opposing generals at Apulo. Opponents of Urdaneta swelled Moreno's ranks as he marched to Zipaquirá. The other leaders feared that he would use this momentum to seize power for himself and to exterminate the Bolivarian party. General José Hilario López acted quickly. He went to Zipaquirá, where he found Moreno ill in bed. Pursuading the llanero to be guided by his orders, López got him to recognize the Apulo agreement.[98] Of this uneasy alliance, he wrote: "General Moreno was a good patriot of excellent intentions; but it would be necessary to watch him closely in order that some of his advisors might not force him to take imprudent and destructive steps."[99]

On May 13 López and Moreno, with an army of four thousand, entered Bogotá. During the next two months partisans of Urdaneta, who went into exile on May 28, and those of Caicedo labored to work out their differences. Several times during the long meetings, López restrained Moreno from seizing power.[100] In the end moderation prevailed. Among other important decisions were two decrees issued by Caicedo. The first, of May 25, called for a constitutional convention to draw up a new government for New Granada. The second, dated June 10, permitted Santander and all those exiled as a result of the conspiracy of September 28, 1828, to return home.[101]

While the generals talked, the llanero soldiers wandered through the streets of the capital, taking what they wanted from stores and houses and harassing the residents. According to Groot, "Everyone feared the band of barbarians since it was known that their chiefs could not subjugate them to military discipline when there was no enemy in front of them"; he added that they would kill a man in cold blood with as little emotion as killing a bull.[102] The bogotanos breathed a sigh of relief when, with the resolution of the crisis, Moreno withdrew with seven hundred men to Tunja, on July 13. In that city too, the plainsmen were unwelcome guests. They caused such a disturbance that General López was obliged to march after them to restore order. On September 26 Moreno issued a proclamation bidding farewell to the highlands and returned with his troops to the Llanos.[103]

Still to be arranged was the reintegration of Casanare with New Granada. On August 16, 1831, Caicedo invited the province to send delegates to the constitutional conventional slated to begin in October.[104] A faction led by Colonel Calisto Molina, son of the former governor Juan José Molina, held out for union with Venezuela. Moreno managed to bring this group into line. An election in November 1831 saw the selection of Molina and Moreno as principal and alternate delegates to the convention.[105] On December 21 an assembly in Pore officially recognized the Caicedo government.[106]

Moreno remained the most popular and influential figure in Casanare until his death, on December 31, 1839. He continued to demand measures that would bring economic relief to the province. In a letter to Santander dated January 4, 1833, he deplored the decline of cattle trade between Casanare and Boyacá, the ban on exports to Venezuela that paralyzed ranching in Arauca, and the high duties collected on imports from Venezuela in the customs houses of Guanapalo and Arauca, but there seemed to be no solutions for these problems.[107]

Discontent in Casanare led to persistent rumors of rebellion. On December 24, 1838, at the behest of the governor, Juan Nepomuceno Gómez, Santander chided Moreno for letting such suspicions circulate and expressed confidence in his loyalty:

> I speak with the frankness of a true friend and an old and constant companion. I know your character; I penetrate your heart, and I know that your patriotism is pure, disinterested, and unstained; for that reason, they do you an injustice, those who say that you will launch a revolution and disturbances which would ruin the country and discredit friends of progressive liberty. Do nothing, my friend. Calm, order, tranquility and respect for the law; firmness and the energy to reclaim in favor of Casanare all the arbitrary acts that the administration may have committed—this is the procedure of good patriots.[108]

A year later Moreno was dead. On his hato, near the site of La Fragua, a settlement named Moreno began to grow. Soon it eclipsed the old capital of Pore to become the most prosperous town in Casanare between 1870 and 1885.[109] By 1907 it also lay in ruins, its moment in history, like that of its namesake, all too fleeting and soon forgotten.[110]

The Wars of Independence transformed the economy and society of the Llanos and their relationship with the highlands. The struggle brought about a drastic decline of population and livestock. It broke the economy, triggered the collapse of the missions, and generated lawlessness. From a modestly self-sufficient region within the viceroyalty, Casanare became a tropical desert.

Discontent with this inglorious fate enhanced the popularity of Juan Nepomuceno Moreno, who defended the interests of the Llanos throughout the war. In the critical year of 1831, Moreno repeated Bolívar's feat of leading an army over the Andes. Fighting with the same ferocity as the Army of the Vanguard, his llanero lancers easily defeated the highland troops. With New Granada in turmoil, Moreno might have gone on to proclaim himself dictator, as Páez had done in Venezuela, but the highland elite, civilian and military, were determined that this was not to be. General López diplomatically restrained Moreno's ambitions. When the llanero returned with his troops to Casanare, republican institutions had triumphed over caudillism, establishing a pattern that would make New Granada unique among South American nations.[111]

Familiarity breeds contempt. More than anything else, events of the early years of independence instilled in the creoles a revulsion for what they thought of as the barbarian llaneros. Restrepo described the incompatibility of the two cultures well when he wrote that in September 1831 the llaneros went back to Casanare because they could not adapt to Bogotá, where there were no facilities for killing cattle and they could not eat meat whenever they liked. "The inhabitants of the Cordillera, tired of the disorders committed by such annoying auxiliaries, prayed to Heaven that they might never need them again."[112] After 1831 the leaders of New Granada made sure that no need arose by reducing Casanare to abject political and economic dependency. The Llanos saw hard, vicious fighting during the War of a Thousand Days (1899–1901) and the Violencia (1948–52), but no army of plainsmen again invaded the highlands.

9 *The Llanos Frontier in Comparative Perspective*

Civilization versus barbarism has been one of the most durable themes in Latin American literature since Domingo Sarmiento first immortalized the clash between Europeanized Buenos Aires and the savage, untamed pampas in *Facundo. Life in the Argentine Republic in the Days of the Tyrants* (1845). Eighty years later the encounter of urban culture with the grasslands of northern South America inspired two brilliant novels that addressed this same theme. In *La vorágine* (Bogotá, 1929), by José Eustasio Rivera, the poet protagonist, Arturo Cova, is in turn fascinated, repelled, and destroyed by the tropical plains and jungles of Colombia. In *Doña Bárbara* (Caracas, 1929), by Rómulo Gallegos, the hero, Santos Luzardo, is an educated city man who becomes a rancher and eventually tames the barbaric Venezuelan plains by imposing fences and the rule of law.[1]

The Llanos make up a substantial part of the territory of Colombia and Venezuela, yet as frontier regions they functioned quite differently in the colonial and independence eras. By the end of the nineteenth century, Bogotá had abandoned the Llanos as a land of the future, while Caracas still struggled to subdue the caudillos of the plains very much as Sarmiento had fought against Facundo Quiroga. A comparison of the development of these two regions identifies some important contrasts and helps to place the llanos frontier of New Granada within the broader context of frontiers in Latin American history.

The area which the Spanish came to call the Llanos of San Juan and San Martín, Casanare, and the Airico de Macaguane form the western third of the natural grasslands that cut across northern South America and extend from the Eastern Cordillera to the Orinoco delta and from the Coastal Range in the north to the Guaviare and Orinoco rivers in the south. Due to their low altitude, equatorial location, and pattern of trade winds, the Llanos present a climate of great extremes. Temperatures range between 70‘ and 110°F. There are nine months of heavy rain, between March and November, followed by three months of unrelieved drought. The Meta, Casanare, and other fast-flowing rivers cut through the plains to feed into the Orinoco. The predominant vegetation is tropical bunch grass, but along the Cordillera slopes and the river banks are strips of gallery and rain forest.

In precontact times the infertility of the open grasslands forced Indian cultivators to settle in the foothills of the llanos arriba and along the rivers. The Achagua, Betoy, Jirara, Tunebo, Guayupe, and Sae lived in small, kin-based hamlets. They used slash-and-burn agriculture to raise subsistence crops and hunted and fished to supplement this diet. Only foragers could adapt to the meager resources afforded by the grasslands of the llanos abajo. The Guahibo had no dwellings of any kind. They traveled in kin-based bands from place to place, hunting animals, gathering the fruit of the palm trees, and trapping fish and turtles in the rivers. The total aboriginal population is unknown, but anthropologists theorize that the Llanos were occupied to the limits of their potential, given the exploitative techniques available to the cultivators and foragers.

In the precontact world, the Eastern Cordillera rose as a great wall, separating the tropical lowlands from the highlands, where the Chibchas had built their empire. There were commercial and cultural exchanges between the Chibchas and the llanos cultivators, and the Tunebos and Saes paid allegiance to the Andean chiefdom. Yet the principal direction of trade was east, along the rivers. The people of the Llanos traded and fought with each other and their neighbors in the Guiana highlands and the Amazon basin. Robert and Nancy Morey have argued that the grasslands served as a conduit for cultural contacts, diffusion, and migration between mountains and the Caribbean coast, the Amazon basin and the Guiana hills.[2]

The Spanish conquest of the Chibchas, in 1538, had momentous consequences for the Llanos. Fixing their capital at Santa Fe de Bogotá, the Spanish proceeded to exploit the obvious sources of wealth. They raised crops and bred cattle in the highland plains and valleys with the aid of Indian labor. By the end of the sixteenth century, their attention fastened upon the rich gold deposits of Antioquia. With the emergence of Cartagena and Santa Marta as major Caribbean ports, the Magdalena River became the principal commercial route between the Andean interior and the coast. Meanwhile, driven on by the legend of El Dorado, conquistadors from Santa Fe and Tunja made their tortuous way over the Eastern Cordillera to claim the Llanos for New Granada.

To some extent the ensuing cultural clash between Europeans and Indians followed the precontact pattern. The sedentary peoples who had traded with the Chibchas fell under Spanish domination, while nomads of the grasslands maintained their contacts with the Caribbean, Guayana, and the Amazon. Throughout the colonial era, there were influences from the east, such as the explorations undertaken by the Welsers from Coro, the slave trade instigated by the Dutch, Venezuelan immigration into Arauca, and the threat of military invasion via the Orinoco. During the Wars of Independence, the patriots unified the llanos of New Granada and Venezuela, while the royalists held the highlands. Nevertheless, the Spanish in the Andes, unlike the Chibchas, actively sought to expand their control over the Llanos and to integrate the Indians into their empire by converting them to Christianity and by establishing Spanish political and economic institutions. In this sense the precontact relationship was reversed, and the plains, especially the foothill areas, became an eastern frontier of a colony whose heartland lay in the Andes. After 1538, the major thrust for change came from the west.

Between 1531 and 1810 conquistadors, founders of towns, encomenderos, crown officials, ranchers, and missionaries, coming from Santa Fe, Tunja, and Sogamoso, spread and sustained Spanish rule in the Llanos.[3] The conquistadors explored vast areas still unknown today, but failed to find the mythical kingdom of El Dorado. One of them, Juan de Avellaneda, returned to the foothills south of the Meta River in 1556 to begin the first permanent city, San Juan. For twenty years San Juan flourished as a mining community, but the alluvial gold extracted from the Ariari River was all too quickly exhausted. Afterwards the city and the surrounding Llanos of San Juan and San Martín became an isolated backwater, attractive primarily to slavers, who captured Indians to work in obrajes farther to the north.

On the Cordillera slopes east of Tunja, leading to Casanare, the Spanish found relatively dense populations of sedentary people who had paid tribute to the Chibchas. By the 1560s they reduced these Indians and assigned them to encomenderos. The Indians raised cotton, which they spun into thread and cloth. In 1588 Santiago de las Atalayas was founded and became a center of this activity. By the end of the sixteenth century, cattle and horses, introduced somewhat earlier, began to master the brutal environment. Wild herds multiplied despite the cycles of flood and drought, insects, and unpalatable grass. The Indians were slow to take advantage of this new source of food, but the Spanish founded hatos around Santiago de las Atalayas. By 1620 the city was the administrative capital of the Provincia de los Llanos and was sending pigs, cattle, cotton, and textiles to Tunja and Sogamoso.

Despite this promising beginning, Spanish settlement languished. Reduction of Indians into encomiendas continued during the seventeenth century, but the number of natives was small, and only a few encomenderos benefited. The hope of El Dorado slowly faded. The plains had few agricultural possibilities. From his base in Santiago, Governor Adriano de Vargas founded San José de Pore and Santa Bárbara de Cravo before 1649, and Chire was begun in 1672. These so-called cities remained tiny metropolitan outposts in the grassy wilderness. Few Spanish tackled the hazardous journey over the Eastern Cordillera in order to dwell in a region offering so many hardships and so few rewards.

In the absence of white colonists, missionaries played a dominant role after 1650. Dominicans and Jesuits were active in the 1620s but activities increased in 1662, when the Junta de Propaganda Fide divided the Llanos between the Dominicans, Franciscans, Augustinians, Recoletos, and Jesuits. Between 1662 and 1767 the five orders carried out their assignments with varying success and enthusiasm. The Recoletos and Franciscans established missions in San Juan and Casanare. The Augustinians controlled ten textile-producing towns around Santiago and Pore in the foothills, balanced demographically by eleven cattle-based reductions administered by the Jesuits in western Casanare and along the Meta. The Jesuits also operated eight haciendas and hatos, with a combined herd in 1767 of 44,066 cattle. By 1760 there were approximately 14,838 Indians living in thirty-one missions throughout the Llanos.

The mission remained the most important imperial institution even after the secularization of the Augustinian towns and the expulsion of the Jesuits. In the second half of the eighteenth century, Dominicans, Capuchins, Franciscans, and Recoletos continued to convert the Indians. Lack of royal support, internal weaknesses, insufficient funds, and native resistance soon paralyzed the Capuchins and handicapped the other orders to some degree. Nevertheless by 1810 there were 15,679 Indians living in thirty-one missions, a gain of 5 percent over the total in 1760. The Franciscans made solid progress in the Llanos of San Juan and San Martín, but the Recoletos were the true heirs of the Jesuits. Penetrating into Arauca and along the Meta River, their reductions rivaled those of the ousted Jesuits in size and organization. By the end of the period, the nine Recoleto hatos had 104,400 cattle, more than twice the herd managed by the Jesuits.

The Llanos frontier crystalized quickly. Town, encomienda, corregimiento, mission, and ranch—the typical institutions of Spanish frontier rule—were introduced before 1650, except for the mission they saw little change in the next two hundred years. They depended largely on the incorporation of the Indian. Notwithstanding the hard core of resistance put up by the Guahibos outside the line of Spanish settlement, the frontier was one of inclusion, or assimilation, and not one of exclusion, such as those found in the United States, Australia, and South Africa, where Europeans peopled the frontier and sought to destroy the natives beyond it.[4]

As elsewhere in their empire, the Spanish attempted to segregate the races by establishing Indian and Spanish towns. The first Indian towns of Chita, Pauto, and La Sal date from the 1560s. Támara, Paya, Pisba, Labranzagrande, and Morcote appeared before 1630; Ten, Manare, and Tame appeared by 1671. The two largest towns, Támara and Paya, each had over two thousand residents in 1778. The Indians paid tithes, taxes, and fees to the civil and religious authorities of their towns, and most were involved in some aspect of the textile industry.

The Spanish cities were more transitory. Many were abandoned for want of an economic base or because of Indian hostility, and on various occasions the vecinos of Pore, Cravo, Chire, and Santiago moved their towns to healthier sites. Only two new cities were added in the eighteenth century—Nunchía in 1770, made up of mestizos, and Arauca, founded by Venezuelans and Indians in 1780. According to the census of 1778, all supposedly Spanish cities had ample components of mestizos and Indians. Of the 1,535 whites in the entire Provincia de los Llanos, 670 resided in Iximena, officially still designated a mission, and 492 lived in Santiago, the capital. Pore had 129. At the other end of the scale were Chire, San Juan, and San Martín with scarcely more than 50 vecinos.

Small as they were, the cities were centers of Spanish rule and home for the encomenderos, officials, and ranchers. The vecinos energetically competed for the handful of municipal offices. There was also rivalry between cities. By the beginning of the nineteenth century, Pore dominated Casanare and San Martín was the principal city in the Llanos south of the Meta. San Juan had already disappeared, and Santiago lay on the verge of extinction.

María Teresa Molino García has shown that the encomienda reached a greater development and endured longer in the highlands between Santa Fe and Tunja than anywhere else in New Granada.[5] Introduced in 1544, the encomiendas in the Llanos formed a subunit of this highland district. By the seventeenth century they were administered in four geographic zones: those in the Llanos of San Juan and San Martín, about which little is known, and the partidos of the Ciudad de Tunja, Tasas de los Llanos, and Santiago de las Atalayas. In 1603 there were seven private and two royal grants, with a total of 2,113 tributaries in these three partidos. By 1653 the rolls listed thirteen private grants and 1,422 tributaries, revealing a decline of Indians in the highland towns as well as a 30 percent increase in the grants based in Santiago de las Atalayas, as unbaptized Indians were incorporated into the system. The number of tributaries grew to 1,819 by 1690. Smaller than the encomiendas based in Tunja and Santa Fe, those in Casanare were of relative importance and long duration. The system disappeared in most of New Granada after 1750. Of four encomiendas that survived until 1806, one included tributaries in Támara, Morcote, and its agregado of Yunao, Ten, Manare, Pisba, and Paya.[6]

The chief administrative officer in the Llanos was the governor, who resided in Santiago de las Atalayas. Equally important were the corregidors, officials who managed local government in rural districts, or corregimientos, populated by Indians. In the eighteenth century the corregidor of Cáqueza had responsibility for the Indian towns in the Llanos of San Juan and San Martín. Within the Provincia de los Llanos there were the Corregimiento of Meta, which included Guanapalo, Iximena, Surimena, and Macuco; the Corregimiento of Támara, which included Morcote, Ten, Paipa, and Pisba; and the Corregimiento of Casanare, which included Tame, Betoyes, Macaguane, and Patute.[7] The corregidor had great power over the Indians, for he served as tax collector, policeman, and magistrate. Appointed by the viceroy or the Audiencia for two or three years, he had no particular training for his duties. The corregidors often engaged in illegal practices to augment their small salaries, but from an administrative point of view they were the only royal officials who could counterbalance the influence of the missionaries and the encomenderos in the rural areas. This study has not attempted to analyze the role of the corregidor, but the numerous clashes between them and the missionaries suggest that they made their influence felt on the llanos frontier.

The organization of the llanos missions varied according to the religious order and the nature of the Indians being evangelized. Before 1767 the Jesuit reductions were the largest and most elaborately structured. Tame, Macaguane, and Betoyes each had over one thousand Indians. The neophytes built their houses on streets laid at right angles from the central plaza, around which stood the church, government house, public granaries, and the residence of the priests. They learned crafts along with Christian doctrine and raised subsistence crops or worked on the cattle haciendas. On the other hand, the Franciscan missions rarely had more than two hundred Indians and often less than sixty. The churches were small, thatched huts. The neophytes lived in scattered hamlets and traveled to the mission to perform their religious obligations. The population fluctuated daily. The sites of the mission were constantly changed, and the standard of living seldom rose above the barest survival level. Between these extremes fell the Recoleto, Capuchin, and Dominican missions. For all the missionaries, however, the goal was the same: to teach the Indians Catholicism, Hispanic civilization, and political government, in order to transform them into copies of the town-loving Spaniards.[8]

The presidio, or garrison, a familiar sight on the Spanish borderlands of the United States and the Argentine pampas, did not appear on the llanos frontier. Military presence was limited to the escoltas, which the crown first allotted to the Jesuits in Guayana in 1681. The escolta consisted of a captain, a sergeant, and from six to forty-eight soldiers. Under the direction of the missionaries they repelled Indian attacks, prevented neophytes from escaping, and assisted in entradas. The soldiers were badly paid and poorly equipped. Frequently they deserted, but despite their disreputability, the missionaries valued them as the best way to protect their towns from attacks by the Guahibos.

The ranches in the Llanos were called hatos. Originally this word meant herd, and the first cattle operations amounted to rounding up a few wild animals and killing them for their meat or hides. Gradually the hato came to be an estate that included a house for the mayordomo, a bunkhouse for the vaqueros, corrals, and a garden. By the eighteenth century most of the privately owned hatos lay within a one-hundred-mile zone along the Andes between the Pauto and Arauca rivers, and from there, in increasing density, northward into the Venezuelan llanos.[9] The owners were generally absentees who hired mayordomos to supervise the work force, made up of tributary Indians, free whites, and mestizos. These peons, concertados, and vaqueros attended to the daily tasks of the ranch. They rounded up the cattle, slaughtering them for their hides or driving them up to the highlands over one of the rough trails of the Cordillera.

Many cofradías, Indian parishes, and churches owned their own herds. The Jesuits and Recoletos systematically founded hatos to support each mission, and the biggest estates in the Llanos were the five Jesuit haciendas in Casanare, each of which consisted of several hatos administered as a single unit. At Caribabare and Tocaría, black slaves planted and harvested sugarcane. Caribabare's herd of 10,606 cattle in 1767 ranked second in size among Grenadine ranches to Hacienda Doyma in the Magdalena Valley, with 14,229 cattle. After the expulsion of the Jesuits, the Junta de Temporalidades sold the haciendas to private citizens, and while their herds dwindled, their value actually increased by the end of the eighteenth century.

Frederick Jackson Turner argued that the most distinctive theme of the history of the United States was the continuous advance of settlement westward into a series of geographical zones across the North American continent, until by 1890 the frontier had been closed. Elaborating on Turner's theory, comparative historians have categorized frontiers in various parts of the world as static or dynamic, depending upon whether colonization is or is not checked by environmental, technological, or human barriers.[10] It is clear from the above summary that the llanos frontier was not dynamic. No waves of settlers invaded zone after zone of wilderness to carry Spanish rule to the Venezuelan border. Yet the term *static* is misleading, for changes did take place. Transformation of Indian cultures and mestizaje were certainly dynamic social processes that modified the frontier over the course of three centuries.

The arrival of the Spanish in the Llanos was an unmitigated disaster for the Indians. The intruders brought new sources of food, iron tools, and weapons, but their insatiable demand for slaves, workers, and Christian converts wreaked havoc on the native societies. Violence marked all phases of the cultural contact. Indians captured by slavers, reduced into encomiendas, or cajoled into missions sacrificed much of their original way of life in order to survive within the new system. Whether in encomienda or mission, whole villages were forced to relocate. The Indians were restricted in their freedom to hunt and fish. They were routinely exposed to disease. Some groups disappeared before the end of the sixteenth century. Others fled beyond the line of Spanish control.

Even the peoples outside the reach of the Spanish experienced radical change. By the seventeenth century the Caribs, who inhabited Guiana and the Orinoco Delta, were conveying large amounts of European goods, especially iron tools and small trinkets, to regional native markets and demanding slaves in return. Pressured by the Caribs and their French and Dutch allies, the nomadic Guahibo also soon turned to this avenue for gain. Relentlessly they pursued the Achagua and Sáliva, their former trade partners and close associates, capturing their children to be sold as slaves.[11] Defenseless against their onslaught, many cultivators lost control of their ancestral lands, which disrupted the balance of power among the native societies.

The decimation of the Indian population was slower in the Llanos than in the highlands and more devastating for the cultivators than the foragers. It is not known when the first epidemics reached the plains, but by the seventeenth century disease, along with the shock of conquest, dislocation, and exploitation, had nearly exterminated the Guayupe and other cultivating groups who lived near the Eastern Cordillera. Reports of epidemics multiplied in the eighteenth century when many tribes were only small remnants of their former size.[12] Within the area under Spanish control, Indians continued to make up 73 percent of the population. Outside the line, except for a few villages, the entire region was dominated by the Guahibo, whose mobility and small band size enabled them to escape the worst effects of contact.

Mestizaje contributed to the Indian decline. The Spanish who enslaved the men took the women as concubines and servants. It was not uncommon for a man to have as many as five or six wives living within a single household. In 1733 Rivero reported that there was no mestizo in the Llanos, however poor, who did not have an Achagua slave; by 1770 the cura of Morcote was complaining that mestizos were taking over many towns reserved for Indians. The census of 1778 bore out this assertion. Mestizos made up 19 percent of the population of the Provincia de los Llanos. They were present in all but three of the Spanish and Indian towns and constituted a majority in Chire, Pore, Nunchía, Labranzagrande, and Aguariva.

The impact of mestizaje can be seen in the amalgamation of Spanish and Indian ways that came to characterize frontier life. The Spanish imposed their political organization, language, forms of labor, and religion on the Indians, but in order to survive in the Llanos they adopted native techniques. The Indians showed them how to construct houses out of palm leaves, how to build boats, and how to navigate the rivers. They taught them how to raise yuca, plátanos, and corn, and to gather food from the forest. The Spanish learned to hunt deer, jaguars, and tapirs with pointed sticks, bows and arrows, and lances. They adopted many Indian words into their language. Indian religious beliefs worked their way into Catholic forms of worship. Even the frequent relocation of missions and towns reflected the nomadic instincts of the natives.

Cultural and racial syncretism is nowhere more evident than in the emergence of the cowboy llaneros. Everywhere the Spanish went in the

New World they introduced the livestock and ranching methods developed by medieval Iberians, such as the constant use of the horse, periodic rodeos, branding, and overland drives.[13] Unlike the Indians of Chile, Argentina, and northern Mexico, who became horseriding, cattle-hunting people, the llanos societies were slow to avail themselves of these new animal resources. By the eighteenth century, however, Indian parishes as well as missions maintained herds of cattle, and Guahibos on horseback were attacking travelers and ranches. The vaqueros learned from the Indians how to be at ease on the rivers. Since flooding often required them to swim with their cattle, they replaced boots, which would weigh them down, with light *alpargatas* (sandals), or went barefoot. They wore light cotton clothes, sombreros called *peloeguamas,* and ponchos called *bayetónes.* They slept in hammocks fashioned out of *moriche* and *cumare* palms. They supplemented their diet of beef with fish and crops grown in gardens.[14] By the eighteenth century these mestizo vaqueros could be found on ranches throughout the Llanos. For the most part, they were not social outcasts living in communities beyond the frontier, and rarely were blacks, free or slave, found among them.

Between 1531 and 1810 the Spanish in highland New Granada extended their rule over the western portion of the Llanos by conquering the Indians and establishing towns, encomiendas, corregimientos, missions, and ranches. After 1650 the line of settlement remained fairly stationary, but within the frontier zone the transformation of the native culture and mestizaje produced a distinctive way of life. For three hundred years the Provincia de los Llanos was a political unit within the Presidency of the New Kingdom of Granada (1563–1719) and later within the viceroyalty. Despite the fact that less than 2 percent of the population of New Granada lived east of the Andes, the Llanos frontier had a role to play in the development of the colony.

New Granada was a conglomeration of four semi-independent regions, isolated from each other by three branches of the Andes, jungles, and rivers. The most important cities—Bogotá, Honda, Tunja, and Socorro—lay in the eastern belt, which produced food crops, cattle, cotton, and textiles. To the south and west lay the agricultural and pastoral areas of Popayán and the Cauca Valley, together with the mining zone on the Pacific slopes of the Andes. On the northern coast were fertile plains for livestock and the seaports of Cartagena and Santa Marta. Between the coast and the Cauca Valley lay Antioquia, the source of minerals which were the chief asset of the colony. While self-sufficiency and intense regionalism characterized New Granada, there was a degree of economic integration and an active internal trade.[15]

The Llanos, as a remote hinterland of Tunja, were a subregion of the eastern belt. Soon after the conquest, Tunja became the principal center for textile manufacture and distribution in the colony. Encomenderos in that city and in Santiago de las Atalayas employed their tributaries to grow cotton and spin cloth. Blankets, handkerchiefs, banners, and other cloth items, as well as pottery and articles of wood and straw made in the Llanos, were valued items of commerce throughout the highlands. Even after Socorro surpassed Tunja as the leading producer of textiles, the industry in the Provincia de los Llanos continued to have more than regional importance. In addition cattle raised in the Llanos were regularly driven to Tunja, Sogamoso, and Velez.

Further expansion was prevented by the mountain barrier which made highland markets inaccessible, and by monopolistic regulations. The most natural direction for trade, as the Jesuits had demonstrated, was to the west, with Guayana and the Atlantic, using the Meta, Casanare, and Orinoco rivers. There was some contraband traffic along this route, but suggestions to legalize trade were opposed by merchants in Cartagena and were regarded by most officials as impractical, given the long distances involved and the presence of Spain's enemies in Guayana and the Orinoco delta.

In any event the president and viceroys were more interested in the defense of the eastern border and the conversion of the Indians than in economic development. The conquistadors had revealed the ease by which an enemy might penetrate the heartland of New Granada by dispatching an army from the Atlantic down the Orinoco. The uproars in Santa Fe caused by Lope de Aguirre's rampage through Venezuela in 1561 and the revolt of Diego de Torres, Cacique de Turmeque, twenty years later showed that fear of an invasion of the Andes from the eastern plains was realistic and widespread. To prevent such a disaster, the authorities relied on missionaries who, along with spreading the faith, were expected to occupy the far-flung frontiers and to repel foreign aggressors. The crown subsidized their efforts by paying stipends and providing them with escoltas. Before 1767 the Franciscans, in the Llanos of San Juan and San Martín, and the Augustinians, Jesuits, and Recoletos, in Casanare and on the Meta, had built up a defensive network of missions. After 1767 the Recoletos extended the line westward, along the Meta and into Arauca.

By mid-eighteenth century internal and external threats alerted the viceroys that missions alone might be insufficient to secure the Llanos. Casanare's participation in the Comunero Revolt of 1781 prompted Caballero y Góngora to commission Captain Antonio de la Torre to reconnoiter the territory between Sogamoso and Macuco on the Meta and from there to Guiana, in order to determine which points should be fortified to prevent a possible enemy attack from the east. After the dreaded British invasion from Trinidad failed to materialize in 1797, Mendinueta reconstituted the Provincia de los Llanos as a gobierno politico y militar and appointed a military officer as governor. He recommended stationing a militia unit in Casanare as well, but his successor, Amar y Borbón, was not sufficiently alarmed to carry out this proposal. Thus when Rosillo, Cadena, and Salgar exposed the vulnerability of Spanish rule by raising the standard of independence, in 1810, the viceroy sent an army from Santa Fe to suppress their revolt, just as Caballero y Góngora had done in dealing with the Comunero Javier Mendoza.

In his analysis of the Spanish borderlands of the United States, Charles Gibson has written that "it should not be forgotten that the borderland was a frontier. What made it a frontier was precisely the reduced intensity of Spanish concern with it, and in this sense it paralleled other frontiers such as southern Chile and southern Argentina, where Indians were sparse and hostile and where the Spaniards found no mines to work."[16] In New Granada the apparent invincibility of the Eastern Cordillera reinforced this natural lack of concern; by walling off the heartland from the plains, it nourished the most fantastic ideas about the unknown wilderness. The missionaries, settlers, and officials, who lived in Casanare, saw possibilities for development despite the environmental disadvantages. For example, when the corregidor del Meta asked Regent Gutiérrez de Piñeres, in 1782, to pay the salaries of the local escolta, he asserted that "in this immensity of land . . . if people were sent here and cattle raised they could supply the whole world without exaggeration . . . if populated by the surplus people of the Kingdom and if general commerce were opened by the Meta River, although it might not be more than the hides that are produced here, the trade to outside areas would be admirable, and the Llanos would produce cotton, sugar, tobacco, cacao, coffee and everything that one might desire."[17]

Highlanders, however, persisted in associating the Llanos with El Dorado. In 1789 Silvestre Sánchez wrote that "it was by the Llanos that efforts were made at various time to discover El Dorado, more the product of deceit and avarice than of reality, which the greedy still wish to believe in spite of the sad and tragic disillusionment of the first ones who tried to find it."[18] The skeptical Silvestre continued that "if gold and silver had been taken from their rich mines and the natural wealth of the land developed, there is no doubt that it would have been not only El Dorado but many mountains of gold. But it is necessary to leave these ideas to the poets."[19]

In 1810 the collapse of the colonial regime forced the discrete worlds of metropolis and frontier to come together. The drive for independence broke down the isolation of the plains from two directions. During the First Republic (1810–16), the inhabitants of Casanare kept the royalist army in Venezuela from engulfing New Granada. José Nonato Pérez, Juan Nepomuceno Moreno, and Fr. Ignacio Mariño transformed Indians and vaqueros into cavalrymen and became powerful caudillos. The fighting in Arauca between 1812 and 1815 and the union of llaneros from Venezuela and New Granada under Páez transplanted to Casanare the violent guerrilla warfare that was ubiquitous in Apure, Guárico, and Barinas.

During the Spanish Reconquest (1816–19), patriot soldiers and hundreds of civilians found safety in the Llanos. Military exigency required the creoles to adopt the life-style of the frontier and a mode of fighting which they regarded as barbaric. Nevertheless, Bolívar and Santander soon realized that as long as the Spanish dominated the highlands, the only road to victory lay in creating a new army from the creole refugees, British volunteers, and llaneros, in the plains of Venezuela and New Granada.

Perhaps the ability of the patriot officers to adapt to conditions in the Llanos reflects the molding of a new American identity in the crucible of the plains, for the Spanish could not make the adjustment. In 1817 General LaTorre took the cities in Casanare, but he could not command the countryside. A year later Morillo conceded the Llanos to the patriots and redoubled his defense of the passes to the highlands. General Barreiro's disastrous invasion of Casanare, in April 1819, demonstrated once and for all the helplessness of peninsular troops when required to fight in the tropical plains. In surmounting the Cordillera, Bolívar's Liberation Campaign made real the nightmare that had plagued the Spanish for three hundred years. The forces of the frontier overwhelmed those of the metropolis at Boyacá, and the llaneros enjoyed their hour of glory.

Once the creole leaders were firmly installed in Bogotá, they turned their backs on the plains. The war disrupted the population, decimated the livestock, depleted the economy, destroyed the missions, left many discontented and unemployed veterans, perpetuated lawlessness ,and fostered caudillism. The efforts of Santander to alleviate these conditions were negligible, and his associates did not hide their scorn for the crude half-breeds from the Llanos. Unhappy with the status quo, Juan Nepomuceno Moreno, still the most powerful man in Casanare, looked to union with Páez's Venezuela as the solution. Amid the political turmoil that surrounded the collapse of Gran Colombia, he repeated Bolívar's feat and led an army over the Cordillera to topple Urdaneta's dictatorship. Many highland officers supported Moreno's action, but they were determined that the llanero should not direct their republic. With diplomacy and force, they convinced Moreno to return to the plains. After 1831 they made sure that Casanare would never again be a threat by reducing it to abject political and economic dependency.

For three hundred years the Llanos formed a strangely inflexible frontier to Spanish civilization in the highlands. Like the Argentine pampas and the grasslands of northern Mexico, they produced a rudimentary cattle industry and a cowboy subculture, but unlike those other plains regions, they showed little capacity for territorial expansion. No waves of settlers appeared, and the institutions introduced before 1650 underwent little change. Since the pampas and the Mexican grasslands lie in temperate zones, it might be plausible to ascribe the lack of dynamism in the Llanos to the tropical climate, the extreme cycles of flood and drought, and the infertility of the soil, but a review of the Venezuelan portion of the region reveals that those grasslands were densely populated and vital politically and economically to the development of the captaincy general and the independent nation during the nineteenth century. A comparison of the history of the two sections of the same region suggests that the difference lay not in the frontier environment but in the geopolitical arrangement of Spanish settlement in the highlands and the nature of the mountain barrier that separated metropolis from frontier.

The Venezuelan llanos cover 300,000 square kilometers or 35 percent of the present area of the republic (see map 8). They are delineated on the south and east by the Orinoco, on the north by the Coastal Range, and on the west they merge with the llanos of Arauca and Casanare. Like the Colombian llanos, the region consists of rolling grassland, with occasional clumps of trees and palm groves. The Orinoco and its tributaries cut through the tropical savannas, which endure the same long rainy season from April to October, when steady downpours cause severe flooding in the lower altitudes, and the same fierce dry season, when the blazing sun dries up the water and turns the lakes into deserts. The temperatures are extremely hot; the average annual temperature at Calabozo is the highest in Venezuela, after Maracaibo.

Unlike the Colombian llanos, which lie at the periphery of the highland-

The PHYSIOGRAPHY of NORTHERN SOUTH AMERICA

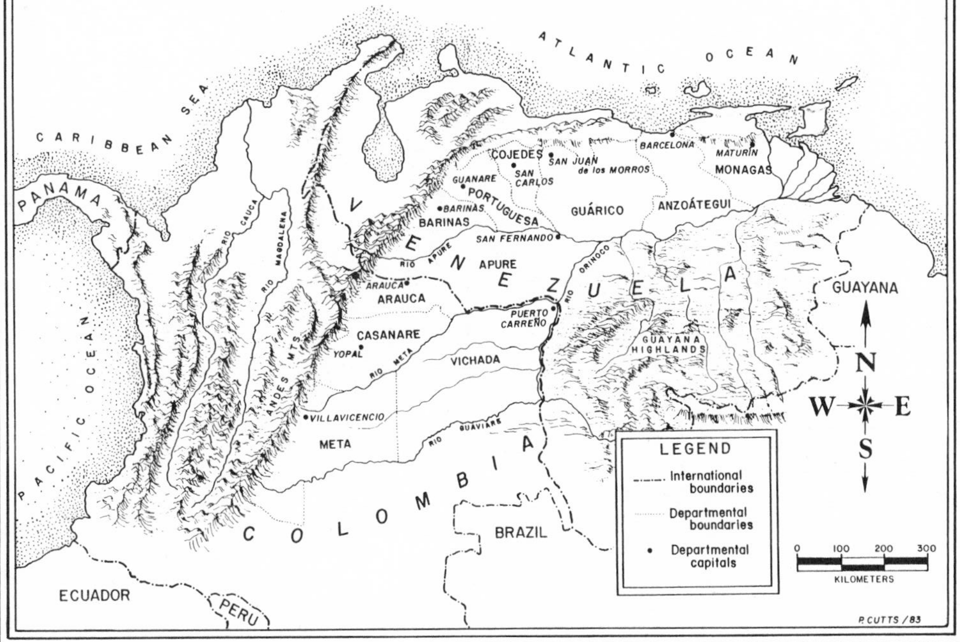

coastal core, these plains run the length of the country from east to west for fifteen hundred miles, to form the geographical heartland of Venezuela. The eastern llanos are contained in the present states of Anzoátegui and Monagas, while the central and western llanos make up Guárico, Apure, and parts of Barinas, Portugesa, and Cojedes.[20] Since precontact times the bulk of the population has preferred to live on the narrow coastal strip or in the mountain valleys, but the crests of the Coastal Range (averaging between 7,000 and 9,000 feet) do not constitute the formidable barrier posed by the Eastern Cordillera. Convenient passes through the mountains enable migrants to reach the plains with little difficulty, to the south the Orinoco offers a direct entry from the Atlantic.

The Venezuelan llanos break into three physiographic zones as they descend in altitude away from the mountains. The forested piedmont zone is situated at 400 meters of altitude, the alto llanos is an area of transition, where the forest begins to give way to plains, at less than 100 meters are the bajo llanos, or open grasslands, with only scattered palm groves to break the monotony of the landscape. As in precontact New Granada, Caquetío, Cuyba, Otomaco, Achagua, and Jirara cultivators occupied the fertile valleys at higher elevations and the forested river banks, while the Guahibos wrested their existence from the bajo llanos. Other groups such as the Guayquerí and Guamo, not found in New Granada, concentrated exclusively on fishing. Turtle beaches and fish markets along the Orinoco, Guaviare, and Cojedes rivers were important aboriginal trade centers.[21]

Spanish and German seekers of El Dorado were the first to explore the plains, traveling up the Orinoco and overland south from Coro. After Charles V revoked the Welser grant in the 1540s, the conquest began in earnest. By the last two decades of the seventeenth century, the Spanish broke the back of Indian resistance in the highlands, causing many groups to retreat to the Llanos. They established the first towns in the piedmont zone—Barinas, 1572, San Sebastian de los Reyes, 1584, Pedraza la Vieja and Guanare, 1591—and divided up the remaining natives into encomiendas. Farms sprang up on the fertile land around Barinas. In 1606 a royal cedula designated this district as the only place within the captaincy general where tobacco might be grown, a measure designed to control contraband and facilitate administration of the tobacco monopoly. The crown lifted this prohibition six years later, but Barinas continued to be the center of high-quality tobacco production. Settlers brought Indians from the mountains to grow the leaf for export, in addition to cotton, indigo, and maize.[22]

The Spanish did not venture far beyond the piedmont zone during the next fifty years, but in the alto and bajo llanos spontaneous changes were taking place. Cattle, first introduced in the mid-sixteenth century, began to multiply after the founding of permanent towns. By 1610 there were hatos around Barinas. By the second half of the seventeenth century, llanos towns and villages were sending steers, hides, and tallow to the settlements on the coast and central valleys of Caracas Province.[23]

Meanwhile the grasslands beyond Spanish control were becoming a haven for Indians fleeing assimilation, as well as for all those people who for very different reasons had left the agricultural north—black slaves from plantations, Indians and mestizos who did not want to work for the Spanish, and people of various colors made marginal by repressive legislation.[24] These fugitives captured the wild horses to use as mounts. They hunted cattle for food and sold the hides as contraband. Some worked as vaqueros on ranches. Others lived in palenques called *puntas de monte*. In contrast to New Granada, there appeared here very early an identifiable llanero subculture encompassing mestizos, Indians and blacks regarded as outlaws by Spanish vecinos. In 1702 a royal cedula ordered the captain general to take steps to control these people, who "were living and dying like savages in the wilderness."[25]

As in New Granada the mission was a primary institution for extending the frontier, but in Venezuela white immigration and the spread of organized ranching reinforced the work of four religious orders. The Dominicans founded some twenty towns in Apure and Barinas. The Jesuits, from their base in Casanare, established their Guayana reductions and haciendas around the confluence of the Meta and Orinoco rivers. In 1767 they relinquished these towns to the Franciscans who moved on into the llanos of Barcelona and the far reaches of the Orinoco. The most energetic group was the Capuchins, whose efforts outstripped even those of the Jesuits in New Granada. Between 1648 and 1810 they founded 107 reductions in the central llanos and 45 towns in the eastern plains between Cumaná and the Orinoco.[26]

The Venezuelan missions were distinctive in three ways. First, the personnel of the most influential order, the Capuchins, was drawn almost entirely from peninsulars, a factor that probably contributed to the strong royalist allegiance in the Llanos after 1811. Second, regulars administered the missions throughout the eighteenth century, because of a shortage of secular priests. Third, because the Capuchins found that they were constantly competing with whites for control over the Indians and that it was difficult to keep the neophytes from running away to join the llaneros in the wilderness, they received permission from the Council of the Indies, in 1692, to conduct entradas against rebellious and apostate Indians and to distribute those captured among the vecinos of the neighboring towns. The law permitted settlers to exploit the labor of the Indians for three days a week during the first ten years they were living in the mission. It stated that Indians who submitted voluntarily could not be enslaved, but there was a tendency to ignore fine distinctions. As a result missionaries and settlers cooperated in the reduction of Indians, and serfdom was rooted in the Llanos with an official sanction absent in New Granada.[27]

The willingness of the religious to work with the vecinos is an indication that large numbers of Spanish were immigrating to the Llanos by the eighteenth century. Many settled in or around the missions and engaged in the commerce of cattle, mules, and horses. San Fernando de Apure, San Carlos de Cojedes, San Felipe, Calabozo, Ocumari del Tuy, Acarigua, Araure, Santa Rosa, and Tucupido all began as missions and later became Spanish towns, achieving an economic importance and political permanency that escaped the white towns in the llanos of New Granada.[28]

A boom in cattle raising after 1690 brought the incorporation of most of the territory of the central llanos into private ranches by 1748. In Caracas Province Brito Figueroa calculates that there were 137,688 cattle, divided among fifteen ranches, in herds ranging from 2,000 to 30,000 head. The ranches were owned by some of the most prominent families in the capital. In the llanos of Guárico, Apure, and Cojedes, seventy hatos controlled 600,000 hectares of land and 301,780 cattle. There were 50,000 cattle in the llanos of Barcelona, by 1784 these herds had increased to 74,792.[29]

Demographic and economic growth peaked in the first decade of the nineteenth century. Bolstered by innoculation against smallpox and immigration from the Antilles, the population of Barinas Province doubled between 1800 and 1807 and grew substantially in Cojedes, Guárico, and Apure. By 1810 over a quarter of the 785,000 inhabitants of the captaincy general lived in the Llanos. The cattle region covered 150 leagues, from El Pau (Cumaná) in the east to Mérida in the west, and 40 leagues from north to south. In 1806 DePons estimated that there were 1,200,000 cattle, 180,000 horses, 90,000 mules, and a large number of sheep grazing throughout this territory.[30]

The plains were broadly integrated into the economic and political life of the highlands and the coast. John Lynch has described eighteenth century Venezuela as "part plantation, part ranch," with people and production concentrated in the valleys of the coast and the Llanos of the south.[31]

Making up 60 percent of the total exports was cacao produced on large estates in the coastal zone and the southern slopes of the Cordillera by slaves, debt peons, and freedmen. Tobacco, cotton, and coffee, grown on plantations in Barinas, the valley of Aragua, and the Andean provinces, along with hides, live animals, and animal extracts from the Llanos, accounted for another 30 percent. The ranches in the plains and the coastal plantations traded with one another within three regional subsystems. The Llanos south of the Venezuelan Andean spur to Coro, south of the central valleys of Caracas and Araure, and south of the eastern periphery, composed of Cumaná and Barcelona, funneled hides, meat, and animals to the ports of Maracaibo and Coro, Caracas-La Guaira, and Cumaná or Barcelona.[32] The tie between frontier and metropolis was further strengthened by the fact that most of the owners of ranches in the Llanos lived in the highland cities. For example, 1.5 percent of the population of Caracas monopolized all cultivable and grazing land in the province.

In New Granada the viceroy's main concern with the Llanos was that the line of missions prevent an enemy from penetrating the Andes. In Venezuela the captain general wanted to foster cattle ranching and to repress the twenty-four thousand llaneros, who by 1789 were living as fugitives in the plains. Social control was a perennial issue in a colony where whites were scarcely 20 percent of a population numerically dominated by blacks and pardos. The white landed aristocracy, or mantuanos, felt a deep class consciousness, born of their close clan ties and sharpened by conflicts with Spaniards, on one hand, and their scorn of the racially mixed pardos, on the other. They strove to maintain their privileged position from encroachment by the pardos, who were not a class but "an indeterminate, unstable and intermediary mass blurring at the edges downwards and upwards."[33] The pardos were especially noticeable in the towns, places of acute tension, where in the daily collision of castes, oppression stirred their profound and implacable hatred.

Social frustration was also high in the llanos, where the mantuanos were determined to defend their interests against real or imaginary dangers posed by Indians and llaneros. In the second half of the eighteenth century, they moved unilaterally against the former by attacking villages and missions near their ranches and burning them to the ground. In 1771 a delegation of ranchers requested the governor in Caracas to give them better protection against the llaneros, who were living in the forests with their women and children and raiding the ranches and towns at will. The marquis de la Torre responded with the Ordenanzas of 1772, a series of regulations which required all inhabitants of the Llanos to reside in towns, where they would be under the control of municipal authorities. The laws prohibited killing or transferring cattle. They created the position of juez general de los Llanos, whose salary would be paid by the vecinos and who would rule on cases regarding slaughter and theft of animals, contraband, and the pusuit and punishment of rustlers. A decree issued in 1786 created five additional judges, each with a cuadrilla de ronda, or squadron, of twelve soldiers to apprehend outlaws.[34]

Both Miguel Izard and Manuel Luceno Salmoral, who have analyzed the behavior of the llaneros in the eighteenth century, conclude that they stole from the towns and ranches primarily to secure enough food and supplies to stay alive. They participated in contraband trade, but they were not a criminal organization and represented no threat either to the ranchers or the colony. Nevertheless, after 1788 the cuadrillas de ronda attacked their settlements, burning houses, killing the men, and moving women and children into towns. This relentless persecution escalated resentment between landowner and the landless and prepared the way for the violence that surfaced after 1811. On the eve of independence the Llanos were a powder keg of social tensions.[35]

The spark that ignited this explosive mixture was not the creole proclamation of the First Republic, in 1811, but the adoption in the same year of new *Ordenanzas de los Llanos,* which expanded upon the principles set down in 1772, to require llaneros to register with local authorities, to carry an identity card, and to belong to a ranch on pain of imprisonment or death. The llaneros were prepared to resist this undisguised attempt to reduce them to serfdom. Calzada, Puig, Yáñez, and Boves opportunely emerged to turn their hatred against the mantuanos into a willingness to fight for the king. "The Llaneros rode into battle because they expected to gain from the spoils of war, because their caudillos led them there, and because the alternatives were less attractive."[36] They were phenomenally successful as guerrilla warriors, bringing down the Second Republic on June 15, 1814, but the death of Boves left them without a leader. By 1816 Páez had won them over to the patriot side, by promising them plunder and land after the war and by winning victories in the llanos of Apure.

When it defeated the Spanish at Boyacá, the llanero army enabled a creole regime to take power in Bogotá, a regime strong enough in 1831 to turn back Juan Nepomuceno Moreno's bid for power. In Venezuela, the triumph at Carabobo meant that a plainsman, José Antonio Páez, would shape the future of republican Venezuela, yet Páez dealt with the unruly llanero veterans as firmly as Santander, and in the aftermath of war, he enforced the two-class system of landowner and landless.

Before 1810 the large hatos that had dominated the economy of the Llanos controlled only a fraction of the usable land. The rest was covered by small, scattered properties without precise limits. No one used fences, and it was customary to consider grazing as collective property. Cattle, not land, meant wealth in the Llanos. During ten years of fighting, confiscation of animals took place on a grand scale. By the end of the war, the remaining herds were converted into public property. Thousands of beasts without brands wandered in the plains, and the veterans who returned to their homes with empty hands saw in the free access to cattle their just compensation.

The leaders of Gran Colombia attempted to resolve this problem by giving Páez, on January 18, 1821, special power to distribute national land to pay off the claims of the soldiers. As was the case in New Granada, this law and later ones, passed in 1823 and 1826, failed to create a class of small land holders. The llaneros did not value land. When they received it from the government, they sold it to their officers, accelerating the process of land concentration that had begun in the seventeenth century.[37] On August 25, 1812 Páez decreed a Law of Landowners and Ranchers in the Llanos that vindicated private property by making rights over wild cattle depend on ownership of land. Expressed in more moderate terms than that of 1811, the law promoted the demarcation and fencing of small properties, granting privileges to owners if they complied. These measures had some success, at least in Barinas, where the expansion of small properties after the war was visible, but Barinas was the exception rather than the rule. The law of 1828 did not subject the llaneros to the degradation of forced labor or restriction of personal liberty, but their aspirations to cattle ownership went unfulfilled and, as vaqueros and peons, they depended upon the ranchers for employment. In general the large-scale transfer of land that occurred in the 1820s created a new latifundist class without significantly modifying the colonial social structure.[38]

After Venezuela seceded from Gran Colombia, modest prosperity returned to the Llanos together with social unrest. In 1830 Páez authorized exports of live cattle and cattle products, enabling many landowners to revive their hatos.[39] Cattle increased from 2.5 million in 1833 to 5.5 million in 1847, reaching an all-time high of 12 million in 1858.[40] In 1839 some 390,000 persons, or 40 percent of the Venezuelan population, lived in the Llanos.

The plains continued to attract refugees from the highlands, fleeing repressive legislation that favored the landowner and merchant elite.[41] As Páez became associated with the mantuanos of Caracas, discontent grew among his former llanero colleagues. The government branded the guerrillas who roamed the plains cuatreros, bandoleros, and criminales, but the series of laws passed in the 1830s to control them did not succeed in reducing violence and rustling.[42]

Throughout the nineteenth century, the Llanos were a breeding ground for caudillism. The llaneros became pawns in the struggle of their leaders to gain national power. Revolts broke out in 1830, 1844, 1846–47, and 1848–49, culminating in the Federalist Wars of 1856–63. The Monagas dynasty (1847–58) drew its wealth and prestige from the Llanos. Juan Falcón (1863–68) and Antonio Guzmán Blanco (1870–88), although they lived elsewhere, based their ascendancy in part upon the plainsmen. Joaquín Crespo (1892–98) was a son of the great plains, and many an insurgent used the region as a base of operations.[43] It remained for Juan Vicente Gómez (1908–35) to transform the system of caudillism into a centralized personal despotism, taming the frontier by installing a draconian peace and an irresponsible absolutism of authority.[44] Given this century-long clash between highlands and plains, it is not surprising that the idealistic Rómulo Gallegos, writing in 1929, predicted that civilization, personified by Caraqueño Santos Luzardo, would eventually conquer the barbarism symbolized by the plains and insure the future of a modern, integrated Venezuela.

To summarize, during the colonial era, the Spanish established similar institutions in the llanos of New Granada and Venezuela, but the relationship of the frontiers to their respective metropolises was very different. Easily accessible from the highlands, the Venezuelan plains were a refuge for marginal people of all races; in the eighteenth century they experienced rapid demographic and economic growth as the Bourbon reforms stimulated the development of Caracas as a commercial port and opened up new markets for the products of the Llanos. During the Wars of Independence, the llaneros fought first for the royalists and then for the patriots. At Carabobo they managed to impose their leader upon the metropolis. Although the mantuanos coopted Páez, caudillos from the Llanos were a major component in national politics throughout the nineteenth century.

These features of the Venezuelan frontier experience have more in common with the history of the Argentine pampas in the eighteenth and nineteenth centuries than with that of the llanos of New Granada. In Argentina there was no physical barrier at all to separate the pampas from the port of Buenos Aires. The temperate grasslands were an ideal environment for livestock which, after its introduction in the seventeenth century, quickly proliferated into vast, wild herds. The pampas nurtured a class of vagabond, outlaw cattle hunters, or gauchos, who like the Venezuelan llaneros existed as a separate entity in Argentine society between 1775 and 1875. When Bourbon political and commercial reforms freed Buenos Aires from the domination of Upper Peru by designating it the capital of the Viceroyalty of Rio de la Plata, in 1776, the city drew the domestic production of the pampa hinterland into its economic sphere. The introduction of the *saladero* (factory for salting beef) at the end of the century increased the value of cattle on the pampas. Since early hunting expeditions were already depleting the wild stock, formal cattle-breeding ranches multiplied in order to control production. The estancia came to be the chief social and economic unit in the countryside.

The gauchos, like the llaneros, were a major factor in the patriot victory in the Wars of Independence; in the aftermath one of their leaders, Juan Manuel de Rosas, ruled over the Argentine Federation with the support of conservative ranchers. The civil wars prevalent in Venezuela in the early national period also characterized Argentina, as rival caudillos from the pampas jockeyed for power. The analogy breaks down in the last half of the nineteenth century, when modernization, which brought barbed wire fences, railroads, improved cattle breeds, and thousands of European immigrants to the pampas, did not similarly transform the Venezuelan plains.[45]

The location of the llanos of San Juan and San Martín and Casanare on the periphery of the New Granadan heartland and the reinforcement of their isolation by the Eastern Cordillera prevented them from developing in a fashion paralleling the Venezuelan plains and the Argentine pampas. If this thesis is valid, it follows that the frontiers that will present features most like those of the New Granadan llanos are not grasslands, but rather the eastern border valleys of the Andes and adjacent Amazon lowlands that make up the eastern portions of Bolivia, Peru, and Ecuador. Like the Llanos these regions have been occupied by white settlers since the sixteenth century, but have never been effectively incorporated into their respective nations. Also like the Llanos, they are so cut off from the rest of the world by mountain barriers on one side and the distance from ocean ports on the other that they remained so-called lands of the future in the twentieth century.[46]

In 1923 the Peruvian thinker Victor Andrés Belaunde considered the lack of development of these regions within the framework of the Turner thesis. Pointing out that the Andes Mountains had prevented Colombia, Ecuador, Peru, and Bolivia from expanding into the Amazon basin in the way the United States had moved into the Mississippi Valley, he concluded that these "most typical Hispanic countries" lacked the characteristics of frontier nations—"the youthful growth, the fluidity and the constant transformation in the social organism," because "the frontier such as we conceive it is the free land, the land within the reach of property and human effort; that free land does not exist in these countries."[47]

Since Belaunde's time the concept of frontier has broadened considerably from the narrow focus ascribed to it by Turner. Historians who study the Amazon regions of Bolivia, Peru, and Ecuador today may find that the Hispanic institutions established there functioned very much like those in the Llanos. They may also discover that these frontiers have played a greater role in national formation than has previously been conceded.[48] In 1962 Jaime Jaramillo Uribe argued that because the Andean region had molded the "personality" of Colombia, the Llanos and ranching society had little impact upon that country's history; yet we have seen that the plains provided a stage for some of the most dramatic events of the colonial era: the search for El Dorado, the conquest and reduction of Indians into encomiendas, and their conversion and settlement into missions.[49] The expulsion of the Jesuits probably had a greater impact on the Llanos than on any other region in the country. Comuneros and Indians from Casanare took part in the Revolt of 1781, which convulsed the colony. The patriots preserved the cause of independence in the Llanos, and plainsmen alongside creoles and British volunteers defeated the Spanish at Boyacá. The ability of the highland elite to repress caudillism emanating from Casanare contributed, in part at least, to the formation of the New Granadan civilian political system, contrasting sharply with the militarism that dominated many Spanish American states in the nineteenth century.

After surveying the role of the frontier in Latin American history, Alistair Hennessy concluded that in contrast to the United States, the frontier experience in Latin America gave birth to no myths.[50] It is probably more accurate to say that while there is no unified frontier myth, as was the case in the United States, the geographic diversity of the continent spawned many myths rooted in particular regions. Certainly the Llanos of New Granada have generated myths. Throughout the colonial era, the belief that El Dorado lay in the eastern plains mesmerized the minds of restless adventurers in the highlands. In the nineteenth century, the legendary heroism of the plainsmen in the Wars of Independence gave rise to the myth of the romantic, picturesque llanero, "half-Spanish, half-Indian, wild, brave, restless, devil-may-care cowboy, Cossack of the Colombian steppes and boastful Tartar full of poetic fire."[51] In the early twentieth century, Rivera's *La vorágine* popularized a more horrifying myth, the Llanos as devourer of men ("devoradora de hombres"), and those few who traveled to the region in the 1930s were motivated by the desire to appear to be heroes and to return to the highlands with frightening stories of cannibals, beasts, and poisonous snakes.[52]

Since World War II the myth of the so-called eastern lands of promise or a soon-to-arise Civilization of the Plains, likewise articulated by Rivero and later promoted by an over-enthusiastic press, has captured the imagination of the public. Hundreds of thousands of Colombians have descended from the Cordillera to seek their fortunes in the Department of Meta, formerly known as the Llanos of San Juan and San Martín, taking advantage of the only road, an all-weather highway that connects Bogotá to Villavicencio, capital of Meta and the so-called Gateway to the Llanos. This region today is among the most active pioneer settlement and colonization zones in Latin America, yet Dieter Brunnschweiler, after a careful study of the growth that has occurred in the last two decades, cautions that as in colonial times, the trans-Andean frontier remains physically separated from the core areas of a country whose development is not dependent on progress in the Llanos.[53] Like New Granada, Colombia still does not move eastward behind its eastern tropical plains frontier.

Abbreviations

ACHSC	*Anuario Colombiano de Historia Social y de la Cultura*
AHN	Archivo Histórico Nacional, Bogotá
Armando	Ramón Armando Rodríguez, *Diccionario biográfico, geográfico e histórico de Venezuela.* Madrid, 1957.
AS	*Archivo Santander.* 24 vols. Bogotá, 1913–32.
AS-Bogotá, 194?	*Archivo Santander.* 1 vol. Bogotá, 194?.
BHA	*Boletín de Historia y Antigüedades.*
Cartas y mensajes	*Cartas y mensajes del General Santander.* Ed. by Roberto Cortázar. 10 vols. Bogotá, 1953–56.
CDI	*Colección de documentos inéditos.* Comp. by Antonio B. Cuervo. 4 vols. Bogotá, 1891–94.
Corresp.	*Correspondencia dirigido al General Santander.* Ed. by Roberto Cortázar. 14 vols. Bogotá, 1964–67.
Handbook	*Handbook of South American Indians,* vol. 4. *The Circum-Caribbean Tribes.* Ed. by Julian H. Steward. New York, 1963.
Lecuna	Vicente Lecuna and Harold Bierck, *Selected Writings of Bolívar.* 2 vols. 2nd ed. New York, 1951.
Ospina	Joaquín Ospina, *Diccionario biográfico y bibliográfico de Colombia.* 3 vols. Bogotá, 1937.
Scarpetta	M. Leonidas Scarpetta y Saturnino Vergara, *Diccionario biográfico de los campeones de la libertad.* Bogotá, 1879.

Notes

Preface

1. See George Rogers Taylor, *The Turner Thesis Concerning the Role of the Frontier in American History,* 3rd ed. (Boston, 1972) and Ray Allen Billington, *The American Frontier Thesis: Attack and Defense* (Washington, D.C., 1973).

2. Walter Prescott Webb, *The Great Frontier* (Cambridge, 1952), 411–12. Silvio Zavala, "The Frontiers of Hispanic America," in W. D. Wyman and C. B. Kroeber, eds., *The Frontier in Perspective* (Madison, 1957), 35–58; José Honório Rodrigues, "Webb's Great Frontier and the Interpretation of Modern History," in A. Lewis and T. McGann, eds., *The New World Looks at its History* (Austin, 1963), 155–64.

3. Alistair Hennessy, *The Frontier in Latin American History* (Albuquerque, 1978), 2–3.

4. Dieter Brunnschweiler, *The Llanos Frontier of Colombia. Environment and Changing Use in Meta* (East Lansing, 1972), 62.

5. Jorge Orlando Melo, "Los estudio históricos en Colombia, situación actual y tendencias predominantes," in Dario Jaramillo Agudelo, ed., *La nueva historia de Colombia* (Bogotá, 1978), 34. Jaime Jaramillo Uribe, "Algunos aspectos de la personalidad histórica de Colombia," in *La personalidad histórica de Colombia y otros ensayos* (Bogotá, 1977); 152–53, Julio Londoño, *Integración del territorio colombiano* (Bogotá, 1967), 16; Gerardo Reichel Dolmatoff, *Colombia* (New York, 1965), p. 29.

When a frontier model has been used to interpret some aspect of Colombian history, the results have been impressive. See Hermes Tovar Pinzón, *Grandes empresas agrícolas y ganaderas* (Bogotá, 1980); William Frederick Sharp, *Slavery on the Spanish Frontier: The Colombian Chocó, 1680–1810* (Norman, Okla. 1976); and

James J. Parsons, *Antioqueño Colonization in Western Colombia,* rev. ed. (Berkeley and Los Angeles, 1968).

6. María Teresa Cobos, "Guía Bibliográfica para los Llanos Orientales de Colombia," *Boletín Cultural y Bibliográfica* 8, no. 12 (1965):1888–1935. Of the handful of works by historians, Juan M. Pacheco, *Los jesuítas en Colombia* (Bogotá, 1959–62), and E. Ortega Ricaurte, *Villavicencio (1842–1942): Monografía histórica* (Bogotá, 1943), are particularly valuable.

7. Brunnschweiler, *The Llanos Frontier of Colombia,* 64; Robert V. Morey, "Ecology and Culture Change among the Colombian Guahibo," Ph.D. diss. (University of Pittsburgh, 1977), 12.

8. One example is Guillermo Ramírez's essay, "San Luis de Palenque: El Llanero y su Presente," *Económica Colombiana,* 2 (August 1954):21–38, which assesses the impact on the Llanos of "La Violencia," the undeclared civil war that took thousands of lives in Colombia from the late 1940s to the mid-1960s. Ramírez writes (pp. 36–37): "All knowledge about the Llanos today is fragmentary, exaggerated, and the product of supposition. . . . To study the llanero, his disposition, traditions, his folklore, to delve into his beliefs and superstitions, to improve his health and to develop his mind, to train him vocationally for creative activities suited to the Llanos are imperatives of the government."

9. Billington, *The American Frontier Thesis,* 18.

10. Richard M. Morse, *The Bandeirantes: Historical Role of the Brazilian Pathfinders* (New York, 1965), 30.

11. Hennessy, *The Frontier in Latin American History,* 3.

12. This terminology is adapted from the model proposed by Leonard Thompson and Howard Lamar in *The Frontier in History: North America and Southern Africa Compared* (New Haven and London, 1981), 7–9.

13. Charles Gibson, *Spain in America* (New York, 1966), 200.

Chapter One

1. Ernst Röthlisberger, *El Dorado* (Bogotá, 1963), 228–29.

2. For example, in 1733 the Jesuit Juan Rivero wrote that "The splendor and magnificence of the Llanos can not be understood without seeing them. The pen is impotent, words and phrases are inadequate, and all descriptions too pallid to make known this immense territory which, similar to the calm sea, extends beyond where the eyes can see, and loses itself in the blue firmament of the horizon", *Historia de las misiones de los llanos de Casanare y los ríos Orinoco y Meta* (Bogotá, 1956), 1. For first impressions of other travelers, see Emiliano Restrepo, *Una excursión al territorio de San Martín en diciembre de 1869* (Bogotá, 1957), 35; Ramón Guerra Azuela, "Apuntamientos de Viaje," *Boletín de Historia y Antigüedades* (hereinafter cited as *BHA),* 4 (January 1907):421; H.L. Mozans, *Up the Orinoco and down the Magdalena* (New York, 1910), 202; Hamilton Rice, "Further Exploration in the Northwest Amazon Basin," *Geographical Journal* 44 (August 1914):138.

3. Robert C. West, "The Geography of Colombia," in A. Curtis Wilgus, ed., *The Caribbean. Contemporary Colombia* (Gainesville, 1962), 19.

4. The Instituto Geográfico A. Codazzi's *Diccionario geográfico de Colombia,* 2 vols., edited by Eduardo Acevedo Latorre (Bogotá, 1971), gives the area of the present four political units in the Llanos as follows. Department of Meta, 85,770 km^2; Intendencia of Arauca, 23,490 km^2; Intendencia of Casanare, 44,300 km^2; and the Comisaría of Vichada, 98,970 km^2. The total area of Colombia is 1,138,914 km^2.

5. Brunnschweiler, *The Llanos Frontier,* 3.

6. West, "The Geography of Colombia," 19.

7. Marston Bates, "Climate and Vegetation in the Villavicencio Region of Eastern Colombia," *Geographical Review* 38 (October 1948):569.

8. F. J. Vergara y Velasco, *Nueva geografía de Colombia* (Bogotá, 1901–2), 683.

9. Bates, "Climate and Vegetation," 569.

10. Brunnschweiler, *The Llanos Frontier,* 10.

11. J. S. Beard, "The Savanna Vegetation of Northern Tropical America," *Ecological Monographs* 23 (1953):189.

12. Bates, "Climate and Vegetation," 566–88. Bates, who studied the epidemiology of sylvatic yellow fever in the Llanos for several years, adds that the surales, esteros, and marshes are excellent breeding places for the mosquitoes, which are present in "incredible numbers."

13. Brunnschweiler, *The Llanos Frontier,* 13.

14. Bates, "Climate and Vegetation," 557–58.

15. Brunnschweiler, *The Llanos Frontier,* 13.

16. Joaquín Díaz Escobar, *Bosquejo estadístico de la región oriental de Colombia* (Bogotá, 1879), 15.

17. Brunnschweiler, *The Llanos Frontier,* 15.

18. Ibid. See also Beard, "The Savanna Vegetation," 203. Some scholars have suggested that for several thousand years, vegetation in the Llanos has fluctuated between forest and savanna because of the felling and burning of the forest by humans. For that view see T. A. Wijmstra and T. Van Der Hammen, "Palynological Data on the History of Tropical Savannas in Northern South America," *Leidse Geologische Mededelingen,* 38 (1966):71–90.

19. Brunnschweiler, *The Llanos Frontier,* 16–17.

20. Costly exploration for oil yielded only negative results until 1978, when exploitable deposits were found around Caño Garza, Trinidad, and Tocaría. At a conference held in Yopal in February 1983, Rodolfo Segovia, president of ECOPETROL, stated that the government petroleum corporation in collaboration with foreign companies, planned to extract five thousand barrels daily from Casanare by 1984. Nevertheless, he warned that the reserves were not large enough to constitute anything like a bonanza for the Intendency. See *El Tiempo,* February 13, 1983. By contrast, there is a vigorous petroleum industry in the eastern Venezuelan Llanos state of Anzoátegui. See James J. Parsons, "Europeanization of the

Savanna Lands of Northern South America," in David R. Harris, ed., *Human Ecology in Savanna Environments* (London, 1980), 267–89.

21. José Eustacio Rivera, *The Vortex,* trans. Earle K. James (New York, 1935), 26.

22. Ibid., 29.

23. Jean Franco, *The Modern Culture of Latin America,* rev. ed. (Middlesex, 1970), 141.

24. Rivera, *The Vortex,* 231.

25. Franco, *Modern Culture,* 141.

26. Bates, "Climate and Vegetation," 558.

27. Gerardo Reichel Dolmatoff, *Colombia* (New York, 1965), 25–26.

28. Robert Morey, "Ecology and Culture Change among the Colombian Guahibo," Ph.D. diss. (University of Pittsburgh, 1977), 202.

29. Irving Rouse and José M. Cruxent, *Venezuelan Archaeology* (New Haven, 1963), 28.

30. Ibid., 51–54. Gerardo Reichel Dolmatoff, "Momíl. A formative Sequence from the Sinú Valley, Colombia," *American Antiquity* 22 (1957):233–34.

31. Carl O. Sauer, *Agricultural Origins and Dispersals* (New York, 1952).

32. R. Morey, "Ecology and Culture Change," 202.

33. Donald Lathrap, "The Hunting Economies of the Tropical Forest Zone of South America: An Attempt at Historical Perspective," in Daniel R. Gross, ed., *Peoples and Cultures of Native South America* (New York, 1975), 94. An excellent review of the theories of Steward, Lathrap, and others as they apply to cultural development in Amazonia can be found in Anna Curtenius Roosevelt, *Parmana: Prehistoric Maize and Manioc Subsistence along the Amazon and Orinoco* (New York, 1980).

34. Paul Kirchhoff, "The Guayupé and the Sae," in Julian E. Steward, ed., *Handbook of South American Indians* (Hereinafter cited as *Handbook)* (Washington, 1946–50), 4:385.

35. Sven Lovén, "The Orinoco in Old Indian Times," *Atti del XXII Congresso Internazionale degli Americanisti* (Rome, 1926) 2:725.

36. Robert V. Morey and Nancy C. Morey, "Relaciones comerciales en el pasado en los Llanos de Colombia y Venezuela," *Montalban* 4 (Caracas, 1975): 533–38.

37. Explorers and missionaries left detailed descriptions of these Indians. Thirty years ago Paul Kirchhoff and Gregorio Hernández de Alba synthesized these materials with the knowledge gleaned by anthropologists in essays they prepared for the Smithsonian Institution's monumental *Handbook of South American Indians.* A more recent and comprehensive study is Nancy C. Morey's unpublished Ph.D. dissertation, "Ethnohistory of the Colombian and Venezuelan Llanos" (University of Utah, 1975). Morey classifies the Indians as cultivators, fishers, and foragers, but since all the fishers were in the Venezuelan llanos, they have been omitted from this survey.

38. Gregorio Hernández de Alba, "The Achagua and their Neighbors," *Hand-*

book 4:399–412; N. Morey, "Ethnohistory," 38, 122–130. The Llanos Indians cultivated many varieties of bitter and sweet yuca, or manioc *(Manihot utilissima)*. It is a slow-growing root crop, not to be confused with the flowering plant called yucca, the state flower of New Mexico. From the root the Indians produced flour, which they made into unleavened bread called cassava, or in Spanish, *casabe*.

39. Julian Steward and Louis C. Faron, *Native Peoples of South America* (New York, 1959), 356.

40. N. Morey, "Ethnohistory," 128.

41. Hernández de Alba, "The Achagua," 403.

42. N. Morey, "Ethnohistory," 128–129.

43. Ibid., 269.

44. Julian H. Steward, "The Circum-Caribbean Tribes. An Introduction," *Handbook,* 4:37.

45. N. Morey, "Ethnohistory," 298; Steward and Faron, *Native Peoples,* 357.

46. Gregorio Hernández de Alba, "The Betoi and their Neighbors," in *Handbook* 4:393–98; N. Morey, "Ethnohistory," 34–35.

47. N. Morey, "Ethnohistory," 34–35.

48. Steward, "The Circum-Caribbean Tribes," 35; N. Morey, "Ethnohistory," 154.

49. N. Morey, "Ethnohistory," 386; Hernández de Alba, "The Betoi," 398.

50. Steward and Faron, *Native Peoples,* 355; Paul Kirchhoff, "The Guayupé and the Sae," in *Handbook* 4:385–91; N. Morey, "Ethnohistory," 130–32.

51. N. Morey, "Ethnohistory," 130.

52. Steward and Faron, *Native Peoples,* 355.

53. Kirchhoff, "The Guayupé," 385.

54. Steward and Faron, *Native Peoples,* 356; N. Morey, "Ethnohistory," 280.

55. Kirchoff regards the Guahibo and the Chiricoa as two tribes which were culturally indistinguishable, but which may have spoken different dialects of the same language. Morey states that the sixteenth-century accounts used the two names interchangeably and that the Guahibo and the Chiricoas were the same people. See Paul Kirchhoff, "Food-Gathering Tribes of the Venezuelan Llanos," *Handbook* 4:446–48; N. Morey, "Ethnohistory," 218–28.

56. Baron Alexander von Humboldt, in N. Morey, "Ethnohistory," 219.

57. Joseph Gumilla, *El Orinoco ilustrado* (Bogotá, 1955), 169. This work was written in the 1730s and was originally published in 1741.

58. N. Morey, "Ethnohistory," 218.

59. Kirchhoff, "Food-Gathering Tribes," 452.

60. N. Morey, "Ethnohistory," 300. By the nineteenth century the Guahibo themselves had altered considerably. They settled down to a more sedentary life, having absorbed remnants of other decimated groups. Yet even into the twentieth century, they remained the terror of the Llanos, regularly attacking white and mestizo colonists. For a study of the modern Guahibo see R. Morey, "Ecology and Culture Change."

61. Jaime Jaramillo Uribe, "La población indígena de Colombia en el momento de la conquista y sus transformaciones posteriores," *Anuario Colombiano de Historia Social y de la Cultura* (hereinafter cited as *ACHSC)* 1 (1964):239–93.

62. The census which Jaramillo cites was published by José Manuel Groot in *Historia eclesiástica y civil* (Bogotá, 1953) 2:658. The total of 8,077 includes only the Indians in the Meta Missions and omits the Indians in the Provincia de los Llanos, which numbered more than 15,000 at that time.

63. Jaramillo, "La población indígena," 284. The Candelario historian Marcelino Ganuza is more willing to accept Rivero's statements at face value. "It seems to us very risky to affirm that Casanare never nor at any time was very populated. The statistics do not exist and for that reason we accept the most authoritative testimony which for us is that of the earliest witnesses." *Monografía de las misiones vivas de agustinos recoletos (candelarios) en Colombia,* 2 vols. (Bogotá, 1921), 1:133.

64. William M. Denevan, "The Aboriginal Population of Western Amazonia in Relation to Habitat and Subsistence," *Revista Geográfica* 72 (June 1970):62.

65. Denevan first presented his theory at the 37th International Congress of Americanists, Mar del Plata (Argentina), September 1966. In the paper which he published in the *Revista Geográfica* he estimated an average population density for all of Greater Amazonia of .59 people per square kilometer, which based on an area of 9,714,000 square kilometers gave a total of 5,750,000 people. Subsequently Denevan revised his essay for publication in a book that he edited, *The Native Population of the Americas in 1492* (Madison, 1976). In the 1976 version he raised the average density to .7 and the total area of Greater Amazonia to 9,769,000, to produce a population estimate of 6,800,000. In both the 1970 and 1976 essays, the calculations for the Colombian and Venezuelan llanos are the same.

66. Denevan, *The Native Population,* 230. Multiplying the density of 1.3 people per square kilometer by 253,000 square kilometers of Colombian llanos gives 328,900 people. This figure appears to be too high. It is likely that Denevan would not consider all 253,000 square kilometers as his lowland savanna.

67. N. Morey, "Ethnohistory," 324. See Paul T. Baker and William T. Sanders, "Demographic Studies in Anthropology," *Annual Review of Anthropology* 1 (1972): 151–78.

68. N. Morey, "Ethnohistory," 304.

69. José Caicedo, Provincia de los Llanos: "Padrón formado en el año de 1778." Morcote, October 14, 1778. Archivo Histórico Nacional, Bogotá (hereinafter cited as AHN).

70. Manuel Zapata Olivella, *El hombre colombiano* (Bogotá, 1974), 355.

71. John Blydenstein, "Tropical Savanna Vegetation of the Llanos of Colombia," *Ecology* 48 (Winter 1967):13.

Chapter Two

1. Irving Leonard, *Books of the Brave* (New York, 1964), 12.

2. Joaguín Piñeros Corpas, *The New Kingdom Book. A Vision of Colombia* (Bogotá, 1966), 8.

3. Juan Friede, "Geographical Ideas and the Conquest of Venezuela," *The Americas,* 16 (October 1959):152.

4. Ibid., 153.

5. Lucas Fernández de Piedrahita, *Historia general de las conquistas del Nuevo Reino de Granada* (Bogotá, 1881 [1688]), 4.

6. Friede, "Geographical Ideas," 149.

7. Ibid., 151.

8. Guillermo Morón, *Historia de Venezuela,* 5th ed., (Caracas, 1970), 82.

9. Juan Friede, *Los Welser en la conquista de Venezuela* (Caracas, 1961), 13. For a negative assessment see Germán Arciniegas, *Germans in the Conquest of America* (New York, 1943).

10. Joaquín Acosta, *Historia de la Nueva Granada* (Bogotá, 1971 [1848]), 187.

11. Raquel Angel Flórez, *Conozcamos al Departamento del Meta* (Bogotá, 1963), 1:83.

12. Walker Chapman, *The Golden Dream—Seekers of El Dorado* (Indianapolis, 1967), 77. The most complete account of Federman's career is Juan Friede, *Vida y viajes de Nicolás Federman, conquistador, poblador y confundador de Bogotá* (Bogotá, 1960).

13. Chapman, *The Golden Dream,* 186; Fernández de Piedrahita, *Historia general,* 266–70.

14. M. M. Lacas, "A Sixteenth-Century German Colonizing Venture in Venezuela," *The Americas* 9 (1953):288.

15. Chapman, *The Golden Dream,* 270.

16. Jesús María Henao and Gerardo Arrubla, *Historia de Colombia,* 5th ed. (Bogotá, 1929), 110–11.

17. Fernández de Piedrahita, *Historia General,* 242–45; Joseph Gumilla, *El Orinoco ilustrado* (Bogotá, 1955 [1741]), 221.

18. Henao and Arrubla, *Historia de Colombia,* 111.

19. José Manuel Groot, *Historia eclesiástica y civil de Nueva Granada* (Bogotá 1953), 1:201.

20. Ibid.

21. Chapman, *The Golden Dream,* 270.

22. Acosta, *Historia de la Nueva Granada,* 387.

23. Chapman, *The Golden Dream,* 284.

24. Germán Arciniegas, *The Knight of El Dorado* (New York, 1943), 238. For a scholar's synthesis of the life of Quesada based on a careful review of archival sources, see Juan Friede, *El Adelantado Don Gonzalo Jiménez de Quesada,* 2 vols. (Bogotá, 1979).

25. Acosta, *Historia de la Nueva Granada,* 389.

26. Chapman, *The Golden Dream,* 284.

27. Morón, *Historia de Venezuela,* 93.

28. Juan Rodríguez Fresle, *El carnero. Conquista y descubrimiento del Nuevo Reino de Granada que comprende hasta el año de 1638* (Bogotá, 1955), 10.

29. Governments in Bogotá from the days of Santander until the present have steadily proclaimed that the Llanos are a region of untold wealth and resources, which within a few short years would become the heartland of Colombian prosperity. Typical is the following statement from a report prepared for the Senate, dated September 29, 1892: "The Llanos of Casanare and San Martín, by their topography, by the fertility of their soil, and by the abundance and wealth of their natural products, are called to be in the more or less distant future, the center of a civilization more advanced perhaps than that which the now occupied interior regions will reach." *Anales del Senado,* 21 (Sept. 29, 1892):167.

30. Pedro Aguado, *Recopilación historial* (Bogotá, 1956), 569–81. Fernández de Piedrahita, *Historia general,* 355–57.

31. Alejandro Carranza B., "San Juan de los Llanos," *BHA* 24 (August 1937): 493–96.

32. Acosta, *Historia de la Nueva Granada,* 387. Acosta adds that it is singular that Aguilar committed his wealth to this enterprise, "the difficulties of which, as a resident of the Llanos, he should have been more aware of than anyone else."

33. Aguado, *Recopilación historial,* 614–38.

34. Rodríguez Fresle listed all cities, villas, and *lugares* under the authority of the Archdiocese of Santa Fe and the Audiencia that had been founded by 1638 under the heading, "Catalogue of the Cities that are Subject to this Holy Metropolitan Church, also the Villas and *Lugares* and the Captains which Populated Them" *(El carnero,* 350–51). Only the king, not the Audiencia, could bestow the titles of city or villa. There was no substantive difference between the two categories as administrative entities, but cities enjoyed more prestige. Thus, even though the white settlements in the Llanos had small populations, they continued to rank among the so-called cities of New Granada. See Germán Colmenares, "La economía y la sociedad conyugales, 1550–1800," in *Manual de historia de Colombia,* 3 vols. (Bogatá, 1978–80), 1:285.

35. Basilio Vicente de Oviedo, *Cualidades y riquezas del Nuevo Reino de Granada* (Bogotá, 1930 [1761]), 233; Manuel M. Zamora, *Guía de la República de Colombia* (Bogotá, 1907), 381.

36. Ganuza, *Monografía de las misiones vivas,* 1:171–72.

37. "Acta de fundación de la ciudad de Santiago de las Atalayas," *Revista del Archivo Nacional,* 6 (1944):45–47.

38. Ganuza, *Monografía de las misiones vivas,* 1:174–76. Speculating on why the crown designated Santiago the provincial capital, a city founded by Daza rather than one of the towns within Jiménez de Quesada's encomienda, Ganuza concludes that this decision reflected the disfavor incurred by the adelantado and Berrio, both of whom failed to discover El Dorado and wasted their energies in that pursuit rather than in fostering permanent settlements.

39. Ganuza reprints this report word for word *(Monografía de las misiones vivas,* 1:176–78). The original is in AHN, Encomiendas, vol. 24, fols. 821–22.
40. Ibid.
41. Zamora, *Guía,* 140; Juan M. Pacheco, *Los jesuítas en Colombia,* 2 vols. (Bogotá, 1959–62), 2:397.
42. Richard M. Morse, "Some Characteristics of Latin American Urban History," *American Historical Review* 67 (1962):327.
43. The geographer Dieter Brunnschweiler notes that these perambulations, combined with the hopeless inaccuracy of colonial cartography, make accurate reconstruction of early settlement patterns very difficult. *The Llanos Frontier,* 18.
44. Pacheco, *Los jesuítas,* 2:346.
45. Alfred W. Crosby, Jr., *The Colombian Exchange: Biological and Cultural Consequences of 1492* (Westport, 1972), 85, 89.
46. Pablo Vila, "La iniciación de la ganadería llanera," *El Farol* 22 (Caracas, 1961):2–7.
47. Crosby, *Colombian Exchange,* 89.
48. Germán Colmenares, *Las haciendas de los jesuítas en el Nuevo Reino de Granada* (Bogotá, 1969), 113.
49. John Rouse, *The Criollo. Spanish Cattle in the Americas* (Norman, Okla., 1977), 141, 159.
50. Brunnschweiler, *The Llanos Frontier,* 43.
51. C. Langdon White, "Cattle Raising. A Way of Life in the Venezuelan Llanos," *Scientific Monthly* 83 (September 1956):124; Rouse, *The Criollo,* 164.
52. Alexander von Humboldt, *Personal Narrative of Travels to the Equinoctial Regions of the New Continent during the Years 1799–1804* (New York, 1966 [1806]), 4:394.
53. Ibid.
54. AHN, Caciques e Indios, vol. 18, fols. 279–82.
55. N. Morey, "Ethnohistory," 56.
56. AHN, Resguardos de Boyacá, vol. 2, fols. 320–328.
57. R. Morey, "Ecology and Culture Change," 44.
58. Germán Colmenares, *La Provincia de Tunja en el Nuevo Reino de Granada: Ensayo de historia social 1539–1800* (Bogotá, 1970), 25.
59. Pacheco, *Los jesuítas,* 2:344.
60. José Mojica Silva, *Relación de visitas coloniales* (Tunja, 1946), 12.
61. Pacheco, *Los jesuítas,* 2:344.
62. Mojica Silva, *Relación,* 12–16.
63. Colmenares, *La Provincia de Tunja,* 43. From Fernando de la Hoz y Berrio and Martín de Mendoza de la Hoz Berrio y Quesada, the encomienda passed in 1707 to Nicolás Dávila Maldonada. In 1761 it went to the daughter of Nicolás Dávila and in 1763 to José Antonio Maldonado. Ibid., 216.
64. For example, Rodrigo Zapata's comprehensive listing in 1653 of enco-

miendas, encomenderos, and tributary Indians in the provinces of Santa Fe, Tunja, Vélez, Pamplona, Antioquia, Huila, and part of the Atlantic Coast, includes the following note. "Of the encomiendas of the Gobierno de San Juan de los Llanos and el Caguan, nothing is known because they have not been inspected nor taxed." *ACHSC* 1 (1964):530.

65. Juan Friede, "Algunas consideraciones sobre la evolución demográfica en la Provincia de Tunja," *ACHSC* 2 (1965):11. Colmenares, *La Provincia de Tunja,* 68.

66. Colmenares, *La Provincia de Tunja,* 68.

67. Ibid., 57.

68. N. Morey, "Ethnohistory," 313.

69. Ganuza, *Monografía,* 1:177.

70. Ibid.

71. Juan Rivero, *Historia de las misiones de los Llanos de Casanare y los ríos Orinoco y Meta* (Bogotá, 1956), 24.

72. Ibid., 25–26.

73. AHN, Caciques e Indios, vol. 29, fols. 897–1043; vol. 10, fols. 411–12.

74. Rivero, *Historia de las misiones,* 27–30.

75. AHN, Caciques e Indios, vol. 25, fols. 732–39.

76. R. Morey, "Ecology and Culture Change," 24.

77. N. Morey, "Ethnohistory," 319.

78. Raymond E. Crist, *Etude geographique des Llanos du Venezuela occidental* (Grenoble, 1937), 76.

79. Rivero, *Historia de las misiones,* 33.

80. Pacheco, *Los jesuítas,* 2:345.

81. Mojica Silva, *Relación,* 11.

82. Ibid., 80.

83. Ibid., 198.

84. Pacheco, *Los jesuítas,* 1:379.

85. José Pérez Gómez, *Los apuntes históricos de las misiones agustinianas en Colombia* (Bogotá, 1924), 126.

86. Ibid., 123.

87. "Encomiendas, encomenderos e indígenas tributarios del Nuevo Reino de Granada en la primera mitad del siglo XVII," *ACHSC,* 1 (1964):441–49.

88. Colmenares, "La Provincia de Tunja," 16–17.

89. Ibid., 44.

90. Ibid., 43.

91. Mojica Silva, *Relación,* 11–16.

92. Rivero, *Historia de las misiones,* 26–27, 32.

93. Pacheco, *Los jesuítas,* 1:378–80.

94. Indalecio Liévano Aguirre, *Los grandes conflictos sociales y económicos de nuestra historia* (Bogotá, 1964), 304.

95. Pacheco, *Los jesuítas,* 1:383. Missionaries had varied religious and academic

training. A *bachiller* had completed the first university degree and was eligible for further study in the faculties of theology and canon law. A *presbitero* was an ordained priest.

96. Pacheco stresses this point because historians have traditionally attributed the Jesuit failure to resistance by the encomenderos and merchants as well as by the secular clergy. See Groot, *Historia eclesiástica y civil,* 1:270.

97. Pacheco, *Los jesuítas,* 1:390.

98. Ibid., 1:392.

99. Groot, *Historia eclesiástica y civil,* 1:424.

100. Alonso de Zamora, O. P., *Historia de la provincia de San Antonio del Nuevo Reino de Granada* (Caracas, 1930 [1701]), 381.

101. Ibid.

102. Ibid., 383.

103. Groot, *Historia eclesiástica y civil,* I, p. 361. A brief summary of Aguirre's violent career can be found in Bernard Moses, *The Spanish Dependencies in South America* (New York, 1965), I, pp. 285–88.

104. Rodríguez Fresle, *El carnero,* 182; Henao and Arrubla, *Historia de Colombia,* 187. Diego de Torres (1549–90) was the son of a conquistador, Juan de Torres, and Catalina de Moyachoque, a sister of the cacique of Turmequé. After inheriting the title of cacique from his uncle, in 1570, Torres was the object of numerous efforts to deprive him of jurisdiction over the Indians and repeated attempts to convict him of fomenting rebellion among them. He was acquitted of all major charges in 1587. See Ulises Rojas, *El Cacique de Turmequé y su época* (Tunja, 1965).

Chapter Three

1. Herbert Eugene Bolton, "The Mission as a Frontier Institution in the Spanish American Colonies," in John Francis Bannon, ed., *Bolton and the Spanish Borderlands* (Norman, Okla., 1964), 211.

2. The crown elevated the presidency of New Granada to a viceroyalty with jurisdiction over Ecuador, Panama, and Venezuela, as well as New Granada, on two occasions. The first experiment lasted between 1719 and 1723. In 1739 the crown reconstituted the Viceroyalty of the New Kingdom of Granada, and this arrangement endured until the Wars of Independence.

3. Basilio Vicente de Oviedo, *Cualidades y riquezas,* 222.

4. Ibid., 234.

5. "Noticia positiva sobre el curso y navegación del río Ariari, ya solo, ya incorporado con el Guayabero," in Antonio B. Cuervo, ed., *Colección de documentos inéditos* (hereinafter cited as *CDI)* 4 vols. (Bogotá, 1891–94), 3:107.

6. Oviedo, *Cualidades y riquezas,* 202–21.

7. Brunnschweiler, *The Llanos Frontier,* 43.

8. Julian Bautista Ruíz Rivera, *Fuentes para la demografía histórica de Nueva Granada* (Sevilla, 1972), 132.

9. Antonine Tibesar, O. F. M., "The Franciscan Doctrinero versus the Franciscan Misionero in Seventeenth-Century Peru," *The Americas* 14 (1957–58):118.

10. Sergio Elías Ortiz, *Nuevo Reino de Granada: Presidentes de capa y espada 1654–1719* (Bogotá, 1966), pt. 2, 118.

11. Juan Manuel Pacheco, *Historia eclesiástica: La consolidación de la iglesia—siglo XVII* (Bogotá, 1975), 2:656.

12. J. J. Borda, *Historia de la Companía de Jesus en Nueva Granada* (Paris, 1970), 2:127.

13. Bolton, "The Mission," p. 195. Tibesar points out that this money was not always paid, and even if it had been, it was not sufficient to meet the multiple needs of the missions. ("The Franciscan Doctrinero," p. 119.)

14. Pacheco, *Historia eclesiástica,* 2:656.

15. José Pérez Gómez, *Apuntes históricos de las misiones agustinianas en Colombia* (Bogotá, 1924), 100.

16. Pacheco, *Los jesuítas,* 1:378.

17. Pérez Gómez, *Apuntes históricos,* 105.

18. Ibid., 73; Pacheco, *Historia eclesiástica,* 2:658.

19. The lack of Dominican interest in the Llanos of San Juan and San Martín was offset by their intensive involvement in the Llanos of Apure and Barinas, where they founded more than a dozen missions.

20. In 1860 the archive of the Franciscan Province of New Granada was mercilessly sacked. Other primary sources remain in the Archivo Histórico Nacional, in Rome, and in Spain. Gregorio Arcila Robledo reprints many documents in *Las misiones franciscanas en Colombia* (Bogotá, 1950), a basic source that has recently been supplemented by the publication of Luis Carlos Mantilla Ruíz, *Actividad misionera de los Franciscanos en Colombia durante los siglos XVII y XVIII—Fuentes documentales* (Bogota, 1980). The most comprehensive history of the Recoletos is Marcelino Ganuza, *Monografía de las misiones vivas,* which also includes many relevant documents.

21. Arcila Robledo, *Las misiones franciscanas,* 250–51.

22. Ibid., 246. La Macarena is a unique mountain range in the Llanos of San Juan and San Martín, detached from the Andes, with altitudes reaching 2,000 meters. A rugged wilderness, it has remained virtually unexplored in the twentieth century and was declared a national park by the Colombian government in 1948.

23. Ibid., 256. Despite the small size of the missions, Arcila Robledo regards them as the "perennial glory" of the Franciscan Province in New Granada because of the great obstacles which the order faced there (ibid., 227).

24. Pacheco, *Historia eclesiástica,* 2:656; Fray Eugenio Ayape, "Missiones de Casanare," *BHA* 28 (1949):772. Ayape states that Iximena was founded in 1668.

25. Ganuza, *Monografía de las misiones vivas,* 1:224.

26. Charles Joseph Fleener, "The Expulsion of the Jesuits from the Viceroyalty of New Granada, 1767," Ph.D. Diss. (University of Florida, 1969), 46. The general superior of the Society of Jesus resides in Rome. The worldwide order is divided into provinces, and to each province the general superior nominates a provincial superior, who serves from three to five years. Each province is made up of houses, or colleges, which are in the charge of local superiors, usually called rectors. All these officers have small councils of advisors, but the final decisions are the responsibility of the superiors alone.

27. Liévano Aguirre, *Los grandes conflictos,* 326.

28. Pacheco, *Los jesuítas,* 2:248.

29. Ibid., 2:362–75; Germán Colmenares, *Las haciendas de los jesuítas en el Nuevo Reino de Granada* (Bogotá, 1969), 54.

30. Ruíz Rivera, *Fuentes,* 132; Pacheco, *Los jesuítas,* 2:398.

31. Pacheco, *Los jesuítas,* 2:383–401.

32. *CDI* 4:192–98.

33. José del Rey, "Estudio preliminar," in Joseph Gumilla, *Escritos varios* (Caracas, 1970), xx.

34. Eugenio de Alvarado, *Informe reservado* (1767) in *CDI* 3:124. Alvarado did not list the mission at Güicán, near Chita, but it was mentioned by Viceroy Solís in his *Relación de mando* of 1760; E. Posada and P. M. Ibáñez, *Relaciones de mando,* 2 vols. (Bogotá, 1910), 1:76.

35. Rivero's book *Historia de las misiones de los Llanos de Casanare y los ríos Orinoco y Meta,* first published in 1746, is more than a history of the missions, for it contains valuable data on the exploitation of Indians by encomenderos and officials as well as on ethnography and environment. Rivero was born in Toledo, Spain, in 1681. He joined the Jesuits, came to New Granada, and was sent to Casanare in 1720. He died in 1736.

36. The Recoletos gave the Jesuits permission to move Surimena and Casimena into territory granted them by the Junta de Propaganda Fide. Ganuza, *Monografía de las misiones vivas,* 2:44.

37. Alvarado, *Informe reservado,* 125. In 1755 P. Antonio Salillas founded Concepción de Iraca, near Apiay. The Jesuits later abandoned the town because the Franciscans claimed it was in their territory. Ibid., 122.

38. Liévano Aguirre, *Los grandes conflictos,* 325.

39. An earlier report to the king on the best way to check the Caribs and Dutch is found in *CDI* 3:483–97.

40. Del Rey, "Estudio preliminar," xxvi–xxx.

41. Alvarado, *Informe reservado,* 127.

42. One consequence was the introduction of coffee in Cauca. In 1732 some Jesuits traveled to Popayán via the Orinoco and brought with them the first coffee seeds grown on one of Gumilla's farm plots in the Orinoco missions. Daniel Restrepo, *La Compañía de Jesús en Colombia* (Bogotá, 1940), 107.

43. Gumilla, *El Orinoco ilustrado,* 209.

44. Ibid.
45. Arcila Robledo, *Las misiones franciscanas,* 245–47.
46. Pacheco, *Los jesuítas,* 2:356.
47. Ibid., 2:398.
48. Ibid., 2:360–61.
49. Ibid., 2:367.
50. Pacheco, *Historia eclesiástica,* 2:662.
51. Mantilla Ruíz, *Actividad misionera,* 137.
52. Pacheco, *Historia eclesiástica,* 2:677.
53. Rivero, *Historia de las misiones,* 149.
54. Pacheco, *Los jesuítas,* 2:380–81.
55. N. Morey, "Ethnohistory," 291–95.
56. Restrepo, *La Compañía de Jesús,* 86.
57. Bernard Moses, *Spain's Declining Power in South America. 1730–1806* (Berkeley, 1919), 146.
58. Alvarado, *Informe reservado,* 140–44.
59. Arcila Robledo, *Las misiones franciscanas,* 227.
60. Pacheco, *Los jesuítas,* 2:419.
61. Alvarado, *Informe reservado,* 151.
62. Baron von Humboldt, cited in R. Morey, "Ecology and Culture Change," 30.
63. N. Morey, "Ethnohistory," 230–32.
64. Rivero, *Historia de las misiones,* 420.
65. Liévano Aguirre, *Los grandes conflictos,* 320.
66. Arcila Robledo, *Las misiones franciscanas,* 247.
67. Rivero, *Historia de las misiones,* 388.
68. Ibid., 250.
69. Alvarado, *Informe reservado,* 144–47.
70. Rivero, *Historia de las misiones,* 256–57.
71. Pacheco, *Los jesuítas,* 2:396.
72. Gumilla, cited in Liévano Aguirre, *Los grandes conflictos,* 321.
73. Oviedo, *Cualidades y riquezas,* 226–27.
74. Liévano Aguirre, *Los grandes conflictos,* 319.
75. Tibesar, "The Franciscan Doctrinero," 119. Tibesar notes that in Peru this policy rendered a well-planned program of expansion and development out of the question. The state was unable to pay the Franciscan stipends regularly, and free-will offerings were only occasionally forthcoming. "The result was that when money was available, the Franciscan missions tended to leap forward spasmodically and to fall back in the same abrupt fashion" (ibid., 119).
76. Arcila Robledo, *Las misiones franciscanas,* 249.
77. Pacheco, *Los jesuítas,* 2:397.
78. Oviedo, *Cualidades y riquezas,* 234.

79. Ibid., 226.

80. Liévano Aguirre, for one, maintains that the Jesuits made a division of work between their mission zones. The reductions in Casanare specialized in the production of textiles which came to dominate the commerce of New Granada, those in Meta produced meat, and the Orinoco missions produced cacao, vanilla, and other tropical products, *Los grandes conflictos,* 320. Other sources show that the Casanare missions, like those in Meta, were primarily involved in the raising of cattle and horses.

81. Fleener, "Expulsion," 76.

82. R. P. F. D. Delgado, *Excursiones por Casanare* (Bogotá, 1910), p. 166; Liévano Aguirre, *Los grandes conflictos,* p. 324. The most complete description of hacienda management is that of Alvarado, *Informe reservado,* 132–35.

83. AHN, Temporalidades, vol. 5, fols. 635–66; Colmenares, *Las haciendas,* 95.

84. Colmenares, *Las haciendas,* 128.

85. Groot, *Historia eclesiástica y civil,* 2:567.

86. Alvarado, *Informe reservado,* 135.

87. Colmenares, *Las haciendas,* 109.

88. Ibid., 114.

89. Ibid., 16.

90. Liévano Aguirre, *Los grandes conflictos,* 322. Another example is Hipólito Jérez, *Los jesuítas en Casanare* (Bogotá, 1952), who writes that "besides teaching the Indians to cultivate yuca and sugar and developing the small industries of the proletariat, the Jesuits improved the existence of the savage's life as they adorned it with the gentle customs of civilization and Christianity. How those ranches might have proliferated! What farms with rows of furrows like a handsome chess board might have developed! Then Casanare might have grown green and produced a most beautiful ideal: a Chirstian Democracy" (ibid., 226).

91. Sergio Elías Ortiz, *Nuevo Reino de Granada. El virreinato, período de 1753–1810* (Bogotá, 1970), 2:58.

92. Demetrio Ramos, "Apuntes para la biografía del Virrey de Nueva Granada, D. José Solís," *BHA* 24 (1947):139.

93. Ibid., 141.

94. *CDI* 3:360–61.

95. Alvarado to Solís, July 1, 1759, *CDI* 3:355–56.

96. *CDI* 3:329–33.

97. Alvarado, *Informe reservado,* 188.

98. Ramos, "Apuntes para la biografía," 147.

99. José Morales to Solís, San Martín, October 16, 1759, *CDI* 3:303–5.

100. Alvarado to Solís, Santa Fe, November 20, 1759, *CDI* 3:399–402. In another letter, of December 15, 1759, Alvardo expanded the plan to suggest that officials send vagabonds from Santa Fe, Zipaquirá, Ubate, Chipaque, and Cáqueza as well.

101. Posada and Ibáñez, *Relaciones de mando,* 1:82. Of the thirty thousand pesos to be paid in October, only six thousand were actually collected—four thousand from the royal treasury and two thousand from the Casa de Moneda.

102. Ibid., 84–85.

103. Solís to Alvarado, Santa Fe, January 7, 1760, *CDI* 3:385.

104. Posada and Ibáñez, *Relaciones de mando,* 1:76.

105. CDI 3:301–2.

106. Posada and Ibáñez, *Relaciones de mando,* 1:88.

107. Ramos, "Apuntes para la biografía," 149.

108. *CDI* 3:271–81.

109. Ortiz, *Nuevo Reino de Granada,* 61.

Chapter Four

1. Alvarado, *Informe reservado,* 169.

2. Ibid., 166.

3. Ibid., 154.

4. Ibid., 170.

5. Ibid., 188.

6. Gibson, *Spain in America,* 82.

7. John Lynch, *The Spanish-American Revolutions 1808–1826* (New York, 1973), 9–10.

8. Henao and Arrubla, *Historia de Colombia,* 244.

9. Ortiz, *Nuevo Reino de Granada: El virreinato,* 2:139–43, Fleener, "The Expulsion of the Jesuits," 48.

10. Groot, *Historia eclesiástica y civil,* 2:123.

11. Colmenares, *Las haciendas,* 132; Fleener, "The Expulsion of the the Jesuits," 169.

12. AHN, Temporalidades, vol. 29, fol. 846.

13. Colmenares, *Las haciendas,* 137.

14. AHN, Temporalidades, vol. 5, fols. 610–14.

15. Ibid., vol. 5, fol. 76.

16. Ibid., vol. 5, fol. 184.

17. Groot, *Historia eclesiástica y civil,* 2:284, 577.

18. Fleener, "The Expulsion of the Jesuits," 194.

19. Ortiz, *Nuevo Reino de Granada: El virreinato,* 2:149.

20. Henao and Arrubla, *Historia de Colombia,* 244.

21. José A. Plaza, *Memorias para la historia de la Nueva Granada* (Bogotá, 1849), 368; J. J. Borda, *Historia de la Compañía,* 142–43; Jerez, *Los jesuítas en Casanare,* 299–303; Groot, *Historia eclesiástica y civil,* 2:123; Liévano Aguirre, *Los grandes conflictos,* 375; Eduardo Carranza, *El Tiempo,* June 28, 1974.

22. R. A. Humphreys and John Lynch, *The Origins of the Latin American Revolutions, 1808–1826* (New York, 1965), 16.

23. Lynch, *The Spanish-American Revolutions,* p. 231.

24. John L. Phelan, *The People and the King* (Madison, 1978), xviii.

25. The complete text of the *Capitulaciones* is reprinted in Pablo E. Cárdenas Acosta, *El movimiento comunal de 1781 en el Nuevo Reino de Granada,* 2 vols. (Bogotá, 1960), 2:18–29 and analyzed in Phelan, *The People and the King,* 156–86.

26. Manuel Briceño, *Los comuneros* (Bogotá, 1977), 115–24.

27. Phelan evaluates earlier interpretations on pp. 151–55 and in the accompanying footnotes. Examples of the reformist position are Lynch, *The Spanish-American Revolutions,* and Armando Gómez Latorre, *Enfoque social de la revolución comunera* (Bogotá, 1973). Of those who see the movement as a precursor to independence, the most important are Cárdenas Acosta, *El movimiento comunal,* Briceño, *Los comuneros,* and Horacio Rodríguez Plata, *Los comuneros* (Bogotá, 1950). For the aborted social revolution thesis see Liévano Aguirre, *Los grandes conflictos,* Germán Arciniegas, *Los comuneros* (México, 1951), and Luis Torres Almeyda, *La rebellión de Galán, el comunero* (Bucaramanga, 1961).

28. Of the major works dealing with the Comunero Revolt, Cárdenas Acosta, Phelan and Arciniegas give partial accounts of the conflict in Casanare. Other sources quote from Arciniegas as in the case of Torres Almeyda, *La rebellión de Galán,* 212–13, or dismiss this phase of the revolt with a passing reference.

The principal unpublished sources are in the Archivo Histórico Nacional, Bogotá, Los Comuneros (hereafter cited as AHN, LC) vol. 6, fol. 49–62. They consist of the correspondence between officials and rebels in Casanare and the Comunero Captains in Socorro—Salvador Plata, Ramón Ramírez, Antonio José Monsalve and Francisco Rosillo. See also Cárdenas Acosta, *El movimiento comunal,* 1:251–56; Phelan, *The People and the King,* 104–6.

29. Cárdenas Acosta, *El movimiento comunal,* 1:252.

30. Común of Cocuy to Captains and Lieutenants of the Towns of Támara, Ten, and Manare, Cocuy, May 23, 1781, AHN, Los Comuneros, vol. 6, fol. 49.

31. José Tapia to Salvador Plata, Morcote, July 10, 1781, AHN, Los Comuneros, vol. 6, fols. 53–56.

32. José Caicedo to Salvador Plata, Antonio Monsalve, Francisco Rosillo, and Ramón Ramírez, Socotá, June 21, 1781, AHN, Los Comuneros, vol. 6, fols. 56–60. The authorship of the Cocuy letter has been the subject of considerable controversy. Phelan has postulated that Berbeo himself may have planted it in the remote village in order to intimidate royal authorities into accepting moderate creole demands. This thesis is partially substantiated by the fact that Caicedo, in the letter cited above, states that even before May 19 Mendoza had received several unsigned papers purporting to be orders from the Inca that he had made public. On the other hand, both Tapia, who enclosed a copy of the Cocuy document with his letter to the War Council, and Caicedo emphatically maintained that in Casanare it was common knowledge that the document had been written in Pore in the name of the Común of Cocuy as a way to trick the Indians into obeying the orders it contained. See also José Caicedo to Salvador Plata, Antonio Monsalve,

Francisco Rosillo, and Ramón Ramírez, Socotá, July 28, 1781, AHN, Los Comuneros, vol. 6, fols. 60–62.

33. Tapia to Plata, Morcote, July 10, 1781, AHN, Los Comuneros, vol. 6, fols. 56–60.

34. Ibid.

35. Ibid.

36. Caicedo to Plata, Monsalve, Rosillo, and Ramírez, Socotá, June 21, 1781, AHN, Los Comuneros, vol. 6, fols. 56–60.

37. Salvador Plata, Ramón Ramírez, Antonio José Monsalve, and Francisco Rosillo to Javier de Mendoza, Socorro, July 17, 1781, AHN, Los Comuneros, vol. 6, fol. 52.

38. Cárdenas Acosta, *El movimiento comunal,* 1:254.

39. Ibid., 2:116–17; a patacón was a silver coin weighing one ounce.

40. José Antonio Villalonga to Charles III, Bogotá, June 28, 1784, in Eduardo Posada, *Los comuneros* (Bogotá, 1905), 45.

41. Plata, Ramírez, Monsalve, and Rosillo to Mendoza, Socorro, July 17, 1781, AHN, Los Comuneros, vol. 6, fol. 52.

42. For sympathetic views of the stormy career of Lozano de Peralta, see Raimundo Rivas, "El Marqués de San Jorge," *BHA* 6 (May 1911):721–50, and Ortiz, *Nuevo Reino de Granada: El virreinato,* 2:271.

43. Posada, *Los comuneros,* 427.

44. José Caicedo to Salvador Plata, Antonio José Monsalve, Francisco Rosillo, and Ramón Ramírez, Socotá, July 28, 1781, AHN, Los Comuneros, vol. 6, fols. 60–62.

45. José Caicedo to Salvador Plata and Francisco Rosillo, Socotá, August 13, 1781, AHN, Los Comuneros, vol. 6, fol. 62.

46. Posada, *Los comuneros,* 428; José Francisco Méndez to Salvador Plata, Pore, Sept. 28, 1781, AHN, Los Comuneros, vol. 6, fols. 52–53.

47. Posada, *Los comuneros,* 430.

48. José Caicedo, Provincia de los Llanos: Padrón formado en el año de 1778, Morcote, October 14, 1778, AHN.

49. Phelan, *The People and the King,* 41.

50. Arcila Robledo, *Las misiones franciscanas,* 219–20.

51. Pérez Gómez, *Los apuntes históricos,* 105.

52. Groot, *Historia eclesiástica y civil,* 2:122–23; Ganuza, *Monografía de las misiones vivas,* 2:44.

53. Colmenares, *La Provincia de Tunja,* 44; Oviedo, *Cualidades y riquezas,* 226.

54. Luis Ospina Vásquez, *Industria y protección en Colombia 1810–1930* (Medellín, 1955), 62.

55. Phelan, *The People and the King,* 173.

56. Francisco Antonio Moreno y Escandón, "Estado del Virreinato de Santa Fe, Nuevo Reino de Granada Año 1772," *BHA* 23 (Sept.–Oct. 1936):587–88.

57. Posada and Ibáñez, *Relaciones de mando,* 1:145.

58. Briceño, *Los comuneros,* 2–4.

59. Cárdenas Acosta, *El movimiento comunal,* 2:21.

60. Ibid., 1:106–7.

61. Ortiz, *Nuevo Reino de Granada: El virreinato,* 2:239.

62. The People of Támara to Javier de Mendoza, Támara, July 16, 1781, AHN, Los Comuneros, vol. 6, fol. 49.

63. Caicedo to Plata, Monsalve, Rosillo and Ramírez, Socotá, June 21, 1781, AHN, Los Comuneros, vol. 6, fols. 56–60.

64. Phelan, *The People and the King,* 170.

65. Arciniegas, *Los comuneros,* 228, Arciniegas does not indicate the location of this document.

66. The Officials of Pore to the Captains and Jefes of Socorro, Pore, June 1, 1781, AHN, Los Comuneros, vol. 6,l fols. 49–50.

67. AHN, Temporalidades, vol. 7, fol. 428.

68. Angel Comacho Baños, *Sublevación de comuneros en el virreinato de Nueva Granada en 1781* (Seville, 1925), 49.

69. Briceño, *Los comuneros,* 104.

70. The Officials of Pore to the Captains and Jefes of Socorro, Pore, June 1, 1781, ANH, Los Comuneros, vol. 6, fols. 49–50.

71. Caicedo to Plata, Monsalve, Rosillo, and Ramírez, Socotá, June 21, 1781, AHN, Los Comuneros, vol. 6, fols. 56–60.

72. Ibid.

73. Cárdenas Acosta, *El movimiento comunal,* 1:255.

74. Francisco Javier de Mendoza to the Captains General, Pore, July 17, 1781, AHN, Los Comuneros, vol. 6, fols. 50–51.

75. Set in the context of the ongoing debate over the significance of the Comunero movement in the history of New Granada, the events which occurred in Casanare provide grist for every mill. The creole-Indian demands for relief from unfair taxes and local abuses of power vindicate the so-called reformist historians, who argue that the revolt was primarily against specific injustices in the colonial regime. Those who view the Comuneros as precursors to independence take heart in the defiant behavior of Javier de Mendoza. Proponents of the aborted-social-revolution theory will stress that it was the elite members of the War Council in Socorro, Comuneros themselves, who cooperated with Archbishop Caballero y Góngora and José Antonio Villalonga in crushing one of the most broadly based and radical manifestations of the protest. Finally these developments do not disprove Phelan's central thesis, based on a textual analysis of the *Capitulaciones,* that the movement was fundamentally a profound political and constitutional crisis in which the Socorro leaders challenged the arbitrary policies of Gutiérrez de Piñeres and demanded a return to "the unwritten constitution" by which an informal decision-making process had been worked out with the authorities by creole elites and nonelites alike. See Phelan, *The People and the King,* 41.

76. Briceño, *Los comuneros,* 115–24.

77. Humboldt, *Personal Narrative,* 4:547–48; José Cortés Madariaga, "Viaje de Cortés Madariaga," *BHA* 3 (Nov. 1905):446.

78. Enrique Otero d'Costa, "La Revolución de Casanare en 1809," *BHA* 17 (April 1928):535.

Chapter Five

1. Allan J. Kuethe, *Military Reform and Society in New Granada, 1773–1808* (Gainesville, 1978), 130.
2. Moreno y Escandon, "Estado del Virreinato de Santa Fe," 560.
3. Francisco Silvestre Sánchez, *Descripción del Reino de Santa Fe de Bogotá* (Bogotá, 1950 [1789]), 44.
4. Posada and Ibáñez, *Relaciones de mando,* 1:318.
5. Stanley Payne, *A History of Spain and Portugal,* 2 vols. (Madison, 1976), 2:377.
6. Andres Mesanza, O. P., *Apuntes y documentos sobre la orden dominicana en Colombia (de 1680 a 1930)* (Caracas, 1929), 86.
7. Nicholas P. Cushner, *Lords of the Land. Sugar, Wine and Jesuit Estates of Coastal Peru, 1600–1767* (Albany, 1980), 5–6.
8. Groot, *Historia eclesiástica y civil,* 2:147.
9. R. Morey, "Ecology and Culture Change," 42.
10. Groot, *Historia eclesiástica y civil,* 2:581.
11. Posada and Ibáñez, *Relaciones de mando,* 2:447.
12. Pérez Gómez, *Los apuntes historicos,* 105.
13. José M. Pérez Ayala, *Antonio Caballero y Góngora, Virrey y Arzobispo de Santa Fé (1723–1796)* (Bogotá, 1951), 315.
14. Groot, *Historia eclesiástica y civil,* 2:149.
15. Ibid., 2:581.
16. Ibid., 2:147.
17. Posada and Ibáñez, *Relaciones de mando,* 2:441.
18. Groot, *Historia eclesiástica y civil,* 2:589.
19. Phelan, *The People and the King,* 212. It is interesting to note that Capuchins founded over one hundred towns in the Llanos of Venezuela. See John Lombardi, *Venezuela: The Search for Order, The Dream of Progress* (New York 1982), 89.
20. Gabriel Giraldo Jaramillo, *Relaciones de mando de los virreyes de la Nueva Granada: Memorias económicas* (Bogotá, 1954), 155. Groot states that the viceroy's request that the Dominicans take over the Cuiloto missions was never communicated to them, *Historia eclesiástica y civil,* 2:284.
21. Groot, *Historia eclesiástica y civil,* 2:257.
22. Ganuza, *Monografía de las misiones vivas,* 2:92.
23. Posada and Ibáñez, *Relaciones de mando,* 2:306; Groot, *Historia eclesiástica y civil,* 2:357.

24. Groot, *Historia eclesiástica y civil,* 2:362.
25. Alvarado, *Informe reservado,* 125.
26. Mesanza, *Apuntes y documentos,* p. 85; Posada y Ibáñez, *Relaciones de mando,* 2:441.
27. Arcila Robledo, *Las misiones franciscanas,* 219–20.
28. Ibid., 259–61. The Amarizanas were a subgroup of the Achaguas.
29. Ibid., 249.
30. Ibid., 248.
31. Ibid.
32. Ibid., 257.
33. Ibid., 259–61.
34. Ibid., 263.
35. Ibid., 267.
36. Oviedo, *Cualidades y riquezas,* 230.
37. Ganuza, *Monografía de las misiones vivas,* 2:64.
38. Posada and Ibáñez, *Relaciones de mando,* 1:308.
39. Ganuza, *Monografía de las misiones vivas,* 2:99. Groot presents a similar census, taken in 1810, in which the figures for individual missions vary slightly and the total number of Indians comes to 8,077; *Historia eclesiástica y civil,* 2:658.
40. Daniel Delgado, *Excursiones por Casanare* (Bogotá, 1910), 167.
41. Posada and Ibáñez, *Relaciones de mando,* 1:315.
42. Ganuza, *Monografía de las misiones vivas,* 2:57.
43. Ibid., 2:61–66.
44. Ibid.
45. Ibid., 2:71.
46. Ibid.
47. Ibid., 2:77.
48. Ibid., 2:83.
49. José Cortés Madariaga, "Viaje de Cortés Madariaga," *BHA* 3 (Nov. 1905): 446–47.
50. Ganuza, *Monografía de las misiones vivas,* 2:98.
51. Ibid., 2:102.
52. Ibid., 2:99.
53. *CDI,* 4:415.
54. Ibid., 417.
55. Ganuza, *Monografía de las misiones vivas,* 2:114.
56. Ibid., 2:118.
57. Posada and Ibáñez, *Relaciones de mando,* 2:418–21.
58. Captain Diego Ruíz Maldonado, who in 1638 led an expedition from Santa Fe across the Llanos to recover Santo Tomé, in Guayana, from the Dutch, was an early advocate of travel on the Meta and Orinoco. Antonio Arellano Moreno has published his 1642 report in *Relaciones geográficas de Venezuela* (Caracas, 1964), 331–60.

59. In the fondo Contrabandos of the Archivo Histórico Nacional, there are documents relating to five smuggling cases in the Llanos during the eighteenth century. In 1743 the crown investigated alleged smuggling in Puerto de Casanare by two Dutchmen, Sebastian and Christian, in partnership with Juan Pablo de la Cruz, born in Curaçao but a resident of Chire (vol. 5, fols. 48–113). In 1767 the Lieutenant-governor of the Llanos, Juan Herrera de Tejada, confiscated illegal French merchandise that had been sent along the Meta to Cravo (vol. 12, fols. 958–1029). In 1783 authorities detained Pedro Buitrago in Tegua with illegal merchandise he was taking to the Llanos (vol. 18, fols. 54–60). In 1786 Isidro Arguello, *asentista* (contractor) of the alcabala of the Partido de Chita, denounced the contraband trade in the towns that made up his partido (vol. 24, fols. 696–803). In 1804, Cristóbal Barragan, alcalde of Pore, investigated alleged smuggling activities of Gabriel Gutiérrez on the Meta River (vol. 16, fols. 189–247).

60. Alvarado, *Informe reservado,* 97–98.

61. Silvestre Sánchez, *Descripción,* 44.

62. Pérez Ayala, *Antonio Caballero y Góngora,* 359.

63. Francisco DePons, *Travels in South America during the Years 1801, 1802, 1803, and 1804,* 2 vols. (London, 1807), 2:63.

64. Humboldt, *Personal Narrative,* 4:364–366. Another proponent of commercial development of the Meta was José Cortés Madariaga, whose travels have already been cited with reference to the Recoleto missions. Madariaga was the Venezuelan diplomat who signed a treaty of alliance between Caracas and Cundinamarca, in 1811, and sought to cement this agreement by finding a better road from Bogotá to the Meta, which in turn led to the Orinoco, "the only route that can assure the prosperity of the states of Cundinamarca and Venezuela." His plan was to avoid the passes through the páramos of Labranzagrande, Toca, and Chita, which regularly claimed the lives of men, burros, and cattle. While he did not discover such a route, his account of his return to Caracas via Casanare and the Meta and Orinoco rivers is a valuable source of information. See Madariaga, "Viaje de Cortés Madariaga," 437–38.

65. AHN, Mejoras Materiales, vol. 24, fols. 745–73.

66. Posada and Ibáñez, *Relaciones de mando,* 1:401.

67. AHN, Caciques e Indios, vol. 20, fols. 770–80.

68. AHN, Poblaciones Varias, vol. 8, fols. 127–34.

69. Arcila Robledo, *Las misionas franciscanas,* 264.

70. Ganuza, *Monografía de las misiones vivas,* 2:108.

71. AHN, Caciques e Indios, vol. 102, fols. 324–28.

72. Kuethe, *Military Reform and Society,* 147; Posada y Ibáñez, *Relaciones de mando,* 1:228.

73. Posada and Ibáñez, *Relaciones de mando,* 2:445.

74. Camacho Baños, *Sublevación de comuneros,* 71.

75. Kuethe, *Military Reform and Society,* 173.

76. José Manuel Pérez Sarmiento and Luis Martínez Delgado, *Causas celebres a los precursores,* 2 vols. (Bogotá, 1939), 1:170–73.

77. Thomas Blossom, *Nariño: Hero of Colombian Independence* (Tucson, 1967), 44.

78. Posada and Ibáñez, *Relaciones de mando,* 2:570.

79. Lynch, *The Spanish-American Revolutions,* 238.

80. Oswaldo Díaz Díaz, *La reconquista española,* 2 vols., (Bogotá, 1964–67), 1:185.

81. Enrique Otero d'Costa, "La Revolución de Casanare en 1809," *BHA* 17 (1928):530–46. This essay summarizes the events of the revolution of 1809 as presented in the primary documents found in AHN, Historia Civil, vol. 10, fols. 224–381. The discussion that follows is based on Otero's interpretation.

82. Salgar joined the patriot army and was killed in battle, in 1816.

83. Otero d'Costa, "La Revolución," 545; Sergio Elías Ortiz, *Genesis de la Revolucion del 20 de julio de 1810* (Bogotá, 1960), 101.

84. Ganuza, *Monografía de las misiones vivas,* 2:209.

85. AHN, Historia Civil, vol. 10, fols. 238, 242.

86. Caldas, quoted by Otero d'Costa, "La Revolución," 545–46. Another eyewitness was José María Caballero, who recorded the event in his diary, *La patria boba* (Bogotá, 1902), 121.

Chapter Six

1. Oviedo, *Cualidades y riquezas,* 220–22.

2. *CDI* 4:288.

3. Brunnschweiler, *The Llanos Frontier,* 66.

4. AHN, Temporalidades, vol. 4, fols. 334–39.

5. AHN, Temporalidades, vol. 26, fols. 1–69.

6. AHN, Temporalidades, vol. 28, fol. 94.

7. AHN, Temporalidades, vol. 5, fols. 12–32. Originally there was a seventh hato, Carichana. Indians destroyed it after 1767, leaving only the ruins of the buildings constructed by the Jesuits.

8. AHN, Temporalidades, vol. 5, fols. 635–66.

9. AHN, Temporalidades, vol. 26, fols. 476–78.

10. Hermes Tovar Pinzón, *Grandes empresas agrícolas y ganaderas* (Bogotá, 1980), 75.

11. AHN, Temporalidades, vol. 26, fols. 476–78.

12. Tovar Pinzón, *Grandes empresas,* 73, 91.

13. AHN, Temporalidades, vol. 6, fol. 145.

14. AHN, Temporalidades, vol. 20, fols. 334–39.

15. AHN, Temporalidades, vol. 23, fols. 400–43.

16. Ibid.

17. AHN, Juicios Criminales, vol. 138, fol. 660.

18. AHN, Caciques e Indios, vol. 26, fols. 914–32.
19. Ibid.
20. AHN, Juicios Criminales, vol. 171, fols. 289–324.
21. AHN, Juicios Criminales, vol. 97, fols. 451–55.
22. AHN, Juicios Criminales, vol. 181, fols. 924–27.
23. AHN, Juicios Criminales, vol. 174, fols. 280–82.
24. AHN, Temporalidades, vol. 29, fol. 846.
25. AHN, Temporalidades, vol. 6, fols. 145, 164.
26. AHN, Temporalidades, vol. 5, fol. 184.
27. Ibid.
28. Gary W. Graff, "Spanish Parishes in Colonial New Granada: Their Role in Town-Building on the Spanish-American Frontier," *The Americas* 33 (1976–77):336.
29. Phelan, *The People and the King,* 40.
30. Germán Colmenares, "La economía y la sociedad conyugales, 1550–1800," 285.
31. William P. McGreevey, *An Economic History of Colombia, 1845–1930* (Cambridge, 1971), 22.
32. *CDI,* 4:388.
33. AHN, Poblaciones de Boyacá, vol. 2, fols. 845–901.
34. Ibid.
35. Rogerio Guáqueta Gallardo, "La Fundación de Arauca," Bogotá (Jan. 1976): 14–15; Delgado, *Excursiones por Casanare,* 282.
36. AHN, Poblaciones de Boyacá, vol. 1, fols. 529–44. Cabildos existed only in the cities and villas. They consisted of a *justicia mayor,* who served as presiding officer, and the regidores, who bought their positions. Cabildos were in charge of the welfare of their districts and of the economic and political government of the towns. Their most important function was to elect, annually on January 1, the alcaldes ordinarios and other judges who administered municipal justice. The alcaldes pedáneos or de partido, elected also by the cabildos, administered justice in their parroquías, but only in matters of little importance. *Corregidores de indios* exercised this role in the Indian towns. See José María Restrepo, *Historia de la revolución de Colombia,* 6 vols. (Medellín, 1974 [1858]), 1:27.
37. AHN, Poblaciones de Boyacá, vol. 1, fols. 529–44.
38. Ibid.
39. AHN, Poblaciones de Boyacá, vol. 2, fol. 671.
40. AHN, Poblaciones de Boyacá, vol. 2, fols. 758–66.
41. Ibid.
42. AHN, Poblaciones de Boyacá, vol. 2, fol. 823.
43. AHN, Poblaciones de Boyacá, vol. 1 bis, fols. 259–93.
44. AHN, Poblaciones Varias, vol. 8, fols. 127–34. Previous reference was made to this case in the discussion of Bourbon policy and the escoltas, in chapter 5.

45. Ibid.
46. AHN, Negros y Esclavos de Boyacá, vol. 2, fols. 392–424.
47. AHN, Poblaciones Varias, vol. 11, fols. 875–907.
48. Alejandro Carranza B., "San Juan de los Llanos," *BHA* 24 (August 1937):494.
49. Jaime Jaramillo Uribe, "Mestizaje y diferenciacion social en el Nuevo Reino de Granada en la segunda mitad del siglo XVIII," in *Ensayos sobre historia social colombiana* (Bogotá, 1968), 167.
50. Jaime Jaramillo Uribe, "La controversia jurídica y filosófica librada en la Nueva Granada en torno a la liberación de los esclavos y la importancia económica y social de la esclavitud en el siglo XIX," in *Ensayos sobre historia social colombiano,* 235.
51. Colmenares, "La economía y la sociedad conyugales, 1550–1800," 282.
52. There are no scholarly studies of the Colombian llanero. M. T. Cobas, "Guía bibliográfica para los llanos orientales de Colombia," *Boletín Cultural y Bibliográfica* 8 (1965):1888–1935, is an excellent guide to published sources. Manuel Zapata Olivella, *El hombre colombiana* (Bogotá, 1974), includes a helpful chapter, "Grupo llanero u oriental," 351–56. "La raza llanera," by Rogerio Guáqueta Gallardo (Bogotá, 1978) synthesizes the Indian contribution to Llanero culture. For the Venezuelan llanero, Raymond E. Crist, *Etude geographique du Venezuela occidental* (Grenoble, 1937) and Rafael Bolívar Coronado, *El llanero* (Madrid, 1919) are still useful, but sadly outdated. Miquel Izard's "Ni cuatreros ni montoneros, llaneros," *Boletín Americanista* (Barcelona) 23 (1981):83–142 is the best survey available. For a comparative view see Jane M. Loy, "Horsemen of the Tropics. A Comparative View of the Llaneros in the History of Venezuela and Colombia," *Boletín Americanista* 23 (1981):159–71.
53. Miquel Izard, *El miedo a la revolución: La lucha por la libertad en Venezuela 1777–1830* (Madrid, 1979), 51.
54. Frederico Brito Figueroa, *La estructura económica de Venezuela colonial* (Caracas, 1978), 191.
55. Leonard V. Dalton, *Venezuela* (New York, 1912), 247.
56. Manuel Lucena Salmoral, "El sistema de Cuadrilla de Ronda para la seguridad de los llanos a fines del periódo colonial," *Memoria del Tercer Congreso Venezolano de Historia* (Caracas, 1979), 1:191–225.
57. Alexander von Humboldt, *Voyage aux Régions Equinoxiales du noveau continent fait en 1799, 1800, 1801, 1802, 1803 et 1804* (Paris, 1815), book 3, chapter 6, p. 29.
58. Alexander von Humboldt, *Personal Narrative of Travels to the Equinoctial Regions of the New Continent during the Years 1799–1804* (London, 1814–29, reprinted New York, 1966, in 6 vols.), 4:319.
59. Zapata Olivella, *El hombre colombiano,* 362.
60. Aguado, *Recopilación historial,* 617.
61. Jorge Palacios, "La esclavitud y la sociedad esclavista," in *Manual de historia,* 1:310.

62. Zapata Olivella, *El hombre colombiano,* 363.
63. Flórez, *Conozcamos al Departamento del Meta,* 1:60.
64. AHN, Negros y Esclavos de Boyacá, vol. 2, fols. 182–85.
65. AHN, Negros y Esclavos de Boyacá, vol. 2, fols. 392–424.
66. AHN, Temporalidades, vol. 26, fols. 12–32. It is interesting to note that coffee, a dietary staple for the llanero in the nineteenth century, had not yet been introduced to Casanare.
67. AHN, Temporalidades, vol. 5, fols. 12–32.
68. *CDI* 3:332–33.
69. Zapata Olivella, *El hombre colombiano,* 356–60.
70. Restrepo, *Historia de la revolución,* 1:43.

Chapter Seven

1. Fabio Lozano y Lozano, "De Casanare a Boyacá," in *Curso superior de historia de Colombia (1781–1830),* 6 vols. (Bogotá, 1951–53), 2:130.
2. Lynch, *The Spanish-American Revolutions,* 239.
3. Juan José Molina, "Instrucción que el gobierno de la Provincia de Casanare forma de todos los puntos," Pore, February 28, 1820, in Enrique Ortega Ricaurte, *Villavicencio 1842–1942: Monografía histórica* (Bogotá, 1943), 50–51. (The original is in AHN, Salón de la República, Gobernación de Casanare, vol. 1, fol. 647). Cayo Leonidas Peñuela, *Album de Boyacá,* 2nd ed., 2 vols. (Tunja, 1969), 1:41.
4. Restrepo, *Historia de la revolución,* 2:116.
5. Stephen K. Stoan, *Pablo Morillo and Venezuela, 1815–1820* (Columbus, 1974), 29.
6. Lynch, *The Spanish-American Revolutions,* 205; Izard, *El miedo a la revolución,* 132. It is estimated that over half of the white population had lost their lives by 1815.
7. Stoan, *Pablo Morillo,* 51.
8. Germán Carrera Damas, *Boves: Aspectos socioeconómicos de la guerra de independencia,* 3rd ed. (Caracas, 1972), 248.
9. Molina, "Instrucción que el gobierno," 51.
10. Joaquín Ospina, *Diccionario biográfico y bibliográfico de Colombia* (hereinafter cited as Ospina), 3 vols. (Bogotá, 1937) 2:136. There is disagreement about the early life of Olmedilla. Ramón Armando Rodríguez, in *Diccionario biográfico, geográfico e histórico de Venezuela,* (hereinafter cited as Armando) (Madrid, 1957), states that he was born in Barinas and was one of the first to take arms there in support of the revolt in Caracas, in 1810. He commanded the cavalry raised by Governor Manuel Antonio Pullido and "in the difficult days of 1813 was one of the chiefs who recognized Bolívar as the true leader of emancipation and the supreme military commander" (p. 535).
11. Peñuela, *Album de Boyacá,* 1:42–43.

12. José Antonio Páez, *Autobiografía del General José Antonio Páez* (New York, 1867, reprinted Caracas, 1975, in 2 vols.), 1:59–66.
13. Ospina, 3.566.
14. Peñuela, *Album de Boyacá,* 1:43; Rafael Villamizar, "Los llanos de Casanare y Apure," *BHA* 25 (April 1938):205.
15. Lynch, *The Spanish-American Revolutions,* 213.
16. Páez, *Autobiografía,* 1:54.
17. Villamizar, "Los llanos de Casanare y Apure," 207.
18. Restrepo, *Historia de la revolución,* 2:126.
19. Ganuza, *Monografía de las misiones vivas,* 2:227. Ospina adds that the Spanish took Olmedillo to Pore where they shot him on October 25, 1816, quartering his body (Ospina 2:137). In his *Autobiografía* Páez maintains that Olmedilla escaped from the Spanish by interning himself in the Llanos, where he suffered such bodily miseries that "he was obliged to eat the body of his young son in order to satisfy the hunger that pressed him." Páez, *Autobiografía* (1:66). Armando Rodríguez states that he was living among the Indians in Casanare under great privations when death ended his life in 1816 (Armando, 536).
20. Javier O'Campo López, "El proceso político, military y social de la independencia," *Manual de historia,* 1:131.
21. Lynch, *The Spanish-American Revolutions,* 242.
22. Restrepo, *Historia de la revolución,* 2:143.
23. Lynch, *The Spanish-American Revolutions,* 213.
24. Restrepo, *Historia de la revolución,* 2:266.
25. Peñuela, *Album de Boyacá,* 1:50.
26. Villamizar, "Los llanos de Casanare y Apure," 211; Lozano y Lozano, "De Casanare a Boyacá," 137.
27. Alfonso Zawadsky, "La guerra de la independencia en los llanos," *BHA* 9 (March, April, May, June 1917):429.
28. Páez, *Autobiografía,* 1:85; Peñuela, *Album de Boyacá,* 1:55.
29. Raymond C. Crist, "Desarrollo político y orígen de caudillismo en Venezuela," *Revista Geográfica Americana* 7 (1937):266.
30. José Antonio Páez, cited by Lynch, *The Spanish-American Revolutions,* 213.
31. Lozano y Lozano, "De Casanare a Boyacá," 147.
32. Francisco de Paula Santander, *Apuntamientos para las memorias sobre Colombia y la Nueva Granada* (Paris, 1869, reprinted Bogotá, 1973), 48.
33. Páez, *Autobiografía,* 1:89, 113; R. B. Cunningham Graham, *José Antonio Páez* (New York, 1970 [1929]), 108.
34. Villamizar, "Los llanos de Casanare y Apure," 218; Santander, *Apuntamientos,* 49.
35. Lynch, *The Spanish-American Revolutions,* 212.
36. Restrepo, *Historia de la revolución,* 2:163.
37. Peñuela, *Album de Boyacá,* 1:467–68.

38. Ibid., 65–71; Restrepo, *Historia de la revolución,* 2:165; Páez, *Autobiografía,* 1:113.

39. Oswaldo Díaz Díaz, *La reconquista espanola,* 2 vols. (Bogotá, 1964–67), 1:267.

40. Ibid., 1:290.

41. Ibid., 1:359, James D. Henderson and Linda Roddy Henderson, *Ten Notable Women of Latin America* (Chicago, 1978), 119.

42. Henao and Arrubla, *Historia de Colombia,* 442–44. Henderson and Henderson add that La Pola has been transformed into a symbol of all women patriots of the resistance: "She is revered not so much for her own qualities and dramatic bravery, but because she alone, among the women who supported the underground with their deeds and sometimes their lives, had a national audience at the moment of death" *(Ten Notable Women,* 120). For more information about Salvarrieta see Enriqueta Montoya de Umaña, *La criolla Policarpa Salavarrieta* (Bogotá, 1969) and Eduardo Posada, *Apuntes sobre la Pola* (Tunja, 1917).

43. Díaz Díaz, *La reconquista española,* 2:117. See also Oswaldo Díaz Díaz, *Los Almeydas: Episodios de las resistencia patriota contra el ejército pacificador de Tierra Firme* (Bogotá, 1962).

44. Lynch, *The Spanish-American Revolutions,* 242.

45. Restrepo, *Historia de la revolución,* 2:172.

46. These documents and the petition are reprinted in Roberto María Tisnes J., *Fray Ignacio Mariño, O. P.* (Bogotá, 1963), 237–56. The originals are in AHN, Secretaría de Guerra y Marina, vol. 323, fols. 23–25 and 38–59. See also the biographical sketch of Pérez in Peñuela, *Album de Boyacá,* 2:149–65.

47. Tisnes J., *Fray Ignacio Mariño,* 237.

48. Ibid., 240.

49. Ibid., 127.

50. Santander to Simón Bolívar, Guanapalo, December 8, 1818, in *Archivo Santander* (Bogotá, 194?) (hereinafter cited as *AS*-Bogotá, 194?), 192–93; Camilo Riaño, *La campaña libertadora de 1819* (Bogotá, 1969), 29.

51. Peñuela, *Album de Boyacá,* 1:72.

52. Restrepo, *Historia de la revolución,* 2:112.

53. Santander to José Antonio Páez, Angostura, July 22, 1818, in Roberto Cortázar, ed., *Cartas y mensajes del General Santander* (hereinafter cited as *Cartas y mensajes),* 10 vols. (Bogotá, 1953–56), 1:77–84.

54. Páez to Santander, Achaguas, October 30, 1818, in *Archivo Santander,* 24 vols. (Bogotá, 1913–32) (hereinafter cited as *AS),* 1:367.

55. Lynch, *The Spanish-American Revolutions,* 216.

56. *AS* 1:363–64.

57. Manuel Cedeño to Santander, Guayana, August 13, 1818, *AS* 1:361–62.

58. Daniel Florencio O'Leary, *Memorias* (Caracas, 1879–88), in *AS* 1:339.

59. Páez, *Autobiografía,* 1:154–55.

60. "Proclama de Páez," November 1, 1818, in *AS* 1:366.

61. Santander to Bolívar, Guanapalo, December 8, 1818, *AS*-Bogotá, 194?, 192–95.

62. Santander to Bolívar, Guanapalo, December 2, 1818, *AS*-Bogotá, 194?, 179–80.

63. Antonio Arredondo to Santander, Zapatosa, November 28, 1818, *AS*-Bogotá, 194?, 173–74.

64. Santander, *Apuntamientos,* 51.

65. Enrique Otero d'Costa, "Fundación de la Gran Colombia," in *Curso superior de historia,* 2:225.

66. Santander to Governador de la Provincia, Guanapalo, December 8, 1818, *AS* 1:191.

67. Santander to Ignacio Castro, La Laguna, February 13, 1819, *Cartas y mensajes,* 1:198–99.

68. Santander to Bolívar, La Trinidad, January 14, 1818, AS-Bogotá, 194?, 238–39.

69. Santander to Bolívar, La Laguna, March 30, 1819, *AS* 2:96–97.

70. Santander to Captain Leal, La Laguna, December 18, 1818, *Cartas y mensajes,* 1: p. 198.

71. Peñuela, *Album de Boyacá,* 1:160.

72. Santander to Jacinto Lara, Curimina, December 20, 1818, *AS*-Bogotá, 194?, 206–7.

73. Santander to Comandante Ortega, Trinidad, January 30, 1819, *AS*-Bogotá, 194?, 82.

74. Santander to Fray Ignacio Delgadillo, Trinidad, January 29, 1819, *AS*-Bogotá, 194?, 280.

75. Santander to Bolívar, Pore, February 13, 1819, *AS* 2:68–69.

76. *AS* 2:87.

77. *AS* 2:360–61.

78. Restrepo, *Historia de la revolución,* 2:186.

79. Santander, *Apuntamientos,* 52.

80. Riaño, *La campaña libertadora,* 56.

81. Gerhard Masur, *Simón Bolívar* (Albuquerque, 1948), 360.

82. Daniel Florencio O'Leary, *Bolívar and the War of Independence,* trans. and ed. by Robert F. McNerney, Jr. (Austin, 1970), 143. This is an abridged version of the *Memorias del General Daniel Florencio O'Leary, Narración* (Caracas, 1952).

83. Páez, *Autobiografía,* 1:165; Riaño, *La campaña libertadora,* 103.

84. O'Campo, "El Proceso Político," 121.

85. Simón Bolívar, cited in Lynch, *The Spanish-American Revolutions,* 215.

86. Masur, *Simón Bolívar,* 371.

87. José Anzoátegui to Teresa Anzoátegui, Bogotá, August 28, 1819, in Francisco de Paula Santander, *Libro de órdenes generales del ejército de operaciones de la Nueva Granada, 1819* (Bogotá, 1969), 19.

88. M. Leonidas Scarpetta y Saturnino Vergara, *Diccionario biográfico de los campeones de la libertad* (hereinafter cited as Scarpetta) (Bogotá, 1879), 109.

89. Masur, *Simón Bolívar,* 372.

90. O'Leary, *Bolívar and the War of Independence,* 158.

91. Ibid., 158–59.

92. Anzoátegui to Teresa Anzoátegui, Bogotá, August 28, 1819, 20.

93. O'Leary, *Bolívar and the War of Independence,* 161.

94. Riaño, *La campaña libertadora,* 293.

95. Ortega Ricaurte, *Villavicencio 1842–1942,* 59.

96. Stoan, *Pablo Morillo and Venezuela,* 204; Peñuela, *Album de Boyacá,* 1:356.

97. O'Leary, *Bolívar and the War of Independence,* p. 194; Páez, *Autobiografía,* 1:183–87.

98. David Bushnell, *The Santander Regime in Gran Colombia* (Newark, 1954), 20.

99. José María Samper, *Ensayo sobre las revoluciones políticas y la condición social de las repúblicas Colombianas* (Paris, 1861), 91–93.

100. Pedro Briceño Méndez to Santander, Pore, December 3, 1819, in Roberto Cortázar, ed., *Correspondencia dirigida al General Santander,* 14 vols. (hereinafter cited as *Corresp.)* (Bogotá, 1964–67), 2:169–71.

101. Santander to Bolívar, Caribena en Orinoco, October 23, 1818, in *Cartas y Mensajes,* 1:93.

102. Bolívar to Pedro Gual, Guanare, May 23, 1821, in Vicente Lecuna and Harold Bierck, *Selected Writings of Bolívar,* 2nd ed., 2 vols. (New York, 1951), 1:266.

Chapter Eight

1. The Congress of Angostura created the Republic of Colombia, which included portions of Venezuela, Colombia, Ecuador, and Panama. Historians commonly refer to this nation as Gran Colombia, in order to distinguish it from the modern Republic of Colombia, established in 1886.

2. José Caicedo, Provincia de los Llanos: Padrón formado en el año de 1778, Morcote, October 14, 1778, AHN.

3. Restrepo, *Historia de la revolución,* 1:401; Jorge Orlando Melo, "La evolución economica de Colombia, 1830–1900," *Manual de Historia de Colombia* 3 vols. (Bogotá, 1978–80), 2:138. The total population of New Granada in 1779 was 785,000. Melo estimates that by 1810 it had increased to 1,264,000.

4. Bushnell, *The Santander Regime,* 252.

5. Pedro Briceño Méndez to Santander, Pore, December 3, 1819, *Corresp.,* 2:169.

6. Frederico Brito Figueroa, *Historia económica y social de Venezuela,* 2 vols. (Caracas, 1966), 1:259.

7. Melo argues that comparison of the original 1825 census total of 1,129,000 with the 1835 census total of 1,686,038 indicates that the population increased in that ten-year period at an annual rate of 3.51 percent, mathematically unlikely given the much lower growth rate of other periods. Restrepo also believed that the 1825 census was undercounted because many people hid from the census takers, fearing that they would be drafted into the army; *Historia de la revolución,* 4:630.

8. Bushnell, *The Santander Regime,* 255.

9. Juan Nepomuceno Moreno to Santander, Pore, January 19, 1820, *AS* 4:64–66.

10. Juan José Molina, "Instrucción que el gobierno," 54.

11. Santander to Capitán Leal, Laguna, December 18, 1818, *Cartas y mensajes,* 1:117–18.

12. Santander, "Instrucción para el Coronel Jacinto Lara," Curimena, December 20, 1818, *AS*-Bogotá, 194?, 206–7.

13. Santander al Juez Mayor del Meta, Guanapalo, December 8, 1818, *Cartas y mensajes,* 1:109–10.

14. Izard, *El miedo a la revolución,* 87.

15. Páez, *Autobiografía,* 2:28.

16. Moreno to Santander, Pore, January 4, 1833, *Corresp.,* 8:269.

17. Agustín Codazzi, *Geografía y política de las provincias de la Nueva Granada* (Bogotá, Archivo de la Economía Nacional, no. 24, 1959 [1856]), 376.

18. Bushnell, *The Santander Regime,* 124.

19. AHN, Intendencia de Boyacá, vol. 3, fol. 173.

20. Molina, "Instrucción que el gobierno," 55.

21. *Gaceta de Colombia,* January 29, 1826.

22. Ibid., March 5, 1826.

23. Ibid., April 10, 1825.

24. Bushnell, *The Santander Regime,* p. 146.

25. Salvador Camacho to Santander, Nunchía, January 25, 1827, *AS* 16:189.

26. Ganuza, *Monografía de las misiones vivas,* 2:222.

27. Tisnes, *Fray Ignacio Mariño, O.P.,* 100.

28. Leandro Tormo and Pilar Gonzalbo Aizpuru, *La iglesia en la crisis de la independencia* (Bogotá, 1961), 47.

29. Bushnell, *The Santander Regime,* 199.

30. Ganuza, *Monografía de las misiones vivas,* 2:221.

31. Tisnes, *Fray Ignacio Mariño, O.P.,* 41.

32. Ibid., 91. Fray Humberto Molano, O.P., "El muy reverendo Padre Fray Ignacio Mariño y Torres," *Repertorio Boyacense* 68 (June 1924):994.

33. Bushnell, *The Santander Regime,* 202. The text of this tract is reprinted in Tisnes, *Fray Ignacio Mariño, O.P.,* 257–62.

34. Quoted by Molano, "El muy reverendo," 1011.

35. Ganuza, *Monografía de las misiones vivas,* 2:213.

36. Ibid., 2:222–23.

37. Ibid., 238–39.

38. Santander to Capitán Leal, Trinidad, January 18, 1819, *Cartas y mensajes,* 1:147–48.

39. Santander to M.R.P. Fray Ignacio Delgadillo, Trinidad, January 29, 1819, *Cartas y mensajes,* 1:140.

40. Santander to Comandante Ortega, Trinidad, January 30, 1819, *Cartas y mensajes,* 1:211, Santander to Capitan Feliciano Gómez, Trinidad, January 13, 1819, *Cartas y mensajes,* 1:140.

41. Ganuza, *Monografía de las misiones vivas,* 2:242–43.

42. Santander to Tesorero, Laguna, February 15, 1819, *Cartas y mensajes,* 1:251.

43. Santander to Juez Mayor de Occidente, Trinidad, January 18, 1819, *Cartas y mensajes,* 1:149.

44. Cortés Madariaga, "Viaje de Cortés Madariaga," 445.

45. Briceño Méndez to Santander, Pore, December 3, 1819, *Corresp.,* 2:170.

46. Molina, "Instrucción que el gobierno," 56.

47. Bushnell, *The Santander Regime,* 227.

48. José Manuel Restrepo, *Exposición que el secretario de estado del despacho del interior de la república de Colombia hizo al congreso de 1824* (Bogotá, 1827), 14–15.

49. Santander to President of the Cámara de Representantes, Bogotá, July 11, 1823, *AS* 4:206.

50. Ganuza, *Monografía de las misiones vivas,* 2:279.

51. Ibid., 253.

52. Ibid., 261.

53. *Gaceta de Colombia,* August 15, 1824.

54. Bushnell, *The Santander Regime,* 179.

55. *Gaceta de Colombia,* July 16, 1826.

56. Bushnell, *The Santander Regime,* 179.

57. Lynch, *The Spanish-American Revolutions,* 206.

58. Bushnell, *The Santander Regime,* 276.

59. Ibid., 279.

60. Izard, *El miedo a la revolución,* 158.

61. Bushnell, *The Santander Regime,* 277.

62. Restrepo, *Historia de la revolución,* 6:317.

63. *Gaceta de Colombia,* August 3, 1825.

64. Bushnell, *The Santander Regime,* 281.

65. Izard, *El miedo a la revolución,* 158–62; See also Izard, "Ni cuatreros ni montoneros, llaneros," *Boletín Americanista* 13 (1981), 83–142; Eduardo Arcila Farías, "El régimen de la propiedad territorial en Hispanoamérica," in *Comisión de historia de la propiedad territorial agraria en Venezuela* (Caracas, 1968), 10–49; Germán Carrera Damas, "Algunas consideraciones históricas sobre la cuestión agraria en Venezuela," in *Temas de historia social y de las ideas* (Caracas, 1969), 134–35.

66. Ortega Ricaurte, *Villavicencio 1842–1942,* 59–60.

67. Robert Paul Mathews, *Violencia rural en Venezuela 1840–1858: Antecedentes socioeconómicos de la guerra federal* (Caracas, 1977), 82–83.

68. Miguel Izard, "Tanto pelear para terminar conversando, el caudillismo en Venezuela," *Nova Americana* 2 (1979):53.

69. Lynch, *The Spanish-American Revolutions,* 223.

70. *Codificación nacional de todos las leyes de Colombia desde el año de 1821* (Bogota, 1924), 4:25–31.

71. Mathews, *Violencia rural,* 61–92.

72. Groot, *Historia eclesiástica y civil,* 5:15–16.

73. Ibid., 5.30; see also Pedro M. Ibáñez, "El Coronel Leonardo Infante," *BHA* 3 (December 1905):449–66 and 3 (January 1906):513–32; Anthony P. Maingot, "Social Structure, Social Status, and Civil-Military Conflict in Urban Colombia 1810–1858," in Stephen Thernstrom and Richard Sennett, eds., *Nineteenth Century Cities* (New York, 1969), 297–355.

74. Juan Nepomuceno Moreno to Santander, Pore, January 4, 1833, *Corresp.,* 8:272. The convention to which Moreno is referring was called in 1831 to draw up a constitution for the Republic of New Granada (1832–58).

75. Lynch, *The Spanish-American Revolutions,* 344.

76. Londoño, *Integración del territorio colombiano,* 162. The administrative unit was variously known as Provincia de los Llanos, Gobierno de Los Llanos, and Santiago de las Atalayas.

77. Between 1811 and 1814 Cundinamarca set up a rival government, but was brought under submission by Bolívar.

78. José Miguel Pinto, "División política de la República de Colombia de 1819 a 1905," *BHA* 5 (January 1908):241. The Law of June 25, 1824, did establish Apure as a separate department.

79. Bushnell, *The Santander Regime,* 26–31; *Gaceta de Colombia,* January 29, 1826. Representation in the Chamber of Representatives was proportional to provincial population.

80. Bushnell, *The Santander Regime,* 37.

81. *Gaceta de Colombia,* May 4, 1823.

82. Santander to President of the Chamber of Representatives, *AS* 4:466–67.

83. The most comprehensive biographical sketch of Camacho is in Scarpetta, 79–80. The authors note that although Camacho opposed Bolívar's dictatorship, at the Admirable Congress he proposed that the lifelong pension awarded to the Liberator in 1823 be continued, a motion that was passed unanimously by the Congress. Between 1843 and 1852 he was a member of the senate of the Republic of New Granada (1832–58). He died in 1860. His son, Salvador Camacho Roldán (1827–1900) was a prominent Liberal statesman, economist, and writer, who served as secretary of *hacienda y fomento* and secretary of the treasury in the 1870s.

84. Ortega Ricaurte, *Villavicencio. 1842–1942,* 59.

85. Ospina, 2:828–29; Scarpetta, 359–60; Peñuela, *Album de Boyacá,* 2:310–11.

For a man who played such an important role in Casanare and New Granada, these biographical sketches are vague and incomplete.

86. Briceño Méndez to Santander, Pore, December 3, 1819, *Corresp.*, 2:170.

87. Groot, *Historia eclesiástica y civil,* 5:506.

88. Moreno to Santander, Pore, December 1, 1826, *AS* 16:30–31; in *Corresp.*, 8:266–67, the same letter is reprinted but with the signature "Juan N. Moreno."

89. Henao and Arrubla, *Historia de Colombia,* 560–63. The Admirable Congress met from January 20 to May 10, during which time it promulgated the constitution of 1830. This constitution was suppressed by Urdaneta the following September.

90. Rafael Urdaneta, *Memorias del General Rafael Urdaneta* (Caracas. 1888), 455–56.

91. Gustavo Arboleda, *Historia contemporánea de Colombia,* 3 vols., 2nd ed. (Cali, 1933), 1:42; Restrepo, *Historia de la revolución,* 6:317–18.

92. Páez, *Autobiografía,* 2:74–75.

93. Arboleda, *Historia contemporánea,* 1:47.

94. Henao y Arrubla, *Historia de Colombia,* 583–86; Carlos Restrepo Canal, *La Nueva Granada,* 2 vols., (Bogotá, 1971), provides the most complete discussion of these events in his first volume, which deals with the period between 1831 and 1840.

95. *Gaceta de Colombia,* July 10, 1831.

96. Ibid., June 24, 1831. In this letter Moreno described Urdaneta as "that colossus that terrorizes these unfortunate peoples," but denied any personal ambition in trying to bring him down.

97. Arboleda, *Historia contemporánea,* 1:92; Groot, *Historia eclesiástica y civil,* 5:501.

98. José Hilario López, *Memorias,* 2 vols. (Bogotá, 1942), 2:132–34; Groot, *Historia eclesiástica y civil,* 5:503; Restrepo, *Historia de la revolucion,* 6:541.

99. López, *Memorias,* 2:133–34.

100. Ibid., 147–58.

101. Restrepo Canal, *La Nueva Granada,* 1:191.

102. Groot, *Historia eclesiástica y civil,* 5:509.

103. Arboleda, *Historia contemporánea,* 1:103.

104. *Gaceta de Colombia,* August 2, 1831.

105. Francisco Soto to Santander, Bogotá, November 1, 1831, *AS* 19:83.

106. Vicente Azuero to Santander, Bogotá, January 7, 1832, *AS* 19:153.

107. Moreno to Santander, Pore, January 4, 1833, *Corresp.*, 8:269–73.

108. Santander to Moreno, Bogotá, December 24, 1838, *AS* 24:81.

109. Eugenio Ayape, "Misiones de Casanare," *BHA* 28 (Sept.–Oct. 1941):794. Delgado in *Excursiones por Casanare* (Bogotá, 1910), states that Moreno had thatched buildings on straight and wide streets and an elegant structure to house the government offices, on the north side of the plaza next to the church (p. 30).

110. Hiram Bingham, *Journal of an Expedition across Venezuela and Colombia, 1909* (New Haven, 1909), 159.

111. Maingot, "Social Structure, Social Status and Civil-Military Conflict," 328.

112. Restrepo, *Historia de la revolución,* 6:570.

Chapter Nine

1. In comparing these two novels, Jean Franco adds that both Rivera and Gallegos brought a fresh vision of national reality to the literary circles of their respective countries; Franco, *The Modern Culture of Latin America,* 99. Raymond Crist offers a geographer's assessment of the two works in "Some Aspects of Human Geography in Latin American Literature," *American Journal of Economics and Sociology,* 21 (October 1962):407–12.

2. R. Morey and N. Morey, "Relaciones comerciales en el pasado," 534.

3. Turner argued that the North American frontier expanded by an orderly procession of fur trappers, hunters, cattle raisers, and farmers marching westward. Later historians have found the migration process more complex, but they still tend to classify frontiers by the occupations of the intruders, such as missionaries, traders, administrators, soldiers, and so on.

4. Marvin W. Mikesell distinguishes between frontiers of "inclusion" and "exclusion" in a review essay, "Comparative Studies in Frontier History," *Annals of the Association of American Geographers* 50 (1960), 65. Alistair Hennessy argues that both types of frontiers occurred in Latin America. *(The Frontier in Latin American History,* 166).

5. María Teresa Molino García, *La encomienda en el Nuevo Reino de Granada durante el siglo XVIII* (Sevilla, 1976), 54.

6. Ibid., 57.

7. CDI 4:423.

8. A. S. Tibesar, "Mission in Colonial America, I (Spanish Missions)," *New Catholic Encyclopedia* (New York, 1967), 9:946.

9. Brunnschweiler, *The Llanos Frontier,* 43.

10. Dietrich Gerhard, "The Frontier in Comparative View," *Comparative Studies in Society and History* 1 (March, 1959), 206.

11. N. Morey, "Ethnohistory," 290.

12. Ibid., 299.

13. Crosby, *The Colombian Exchange,* 85–86.

14. Zapata Olivella, *El hombre colombiano,* 361; Rogerio Guáqueta Gallardo, "La raza llanera," (unpub. 1978), 12.

15. Lynch, *The Spanish-American Revolutions,* 228. Germán Colmenares provides an excellent survey of the colonial economy of New Granada in "La economía y la sociedad colonial, 1550–1800," in *Manual de historia,* 1:225–98.

16. Gibson, *Spain in America,* 200.
17. AHN, Caciques e Indios, vol. 29, fol. 773.
18. Silvestre Sánchez, *Descripción,* 24.
19. Ibid.
20. Izard, "Ni cuatreros, ni montoneros," 85–87. For geographic background see Marco-Aurelio Vila, *Geoeconomía de Venezuela,* 3 vols. (Caracas, n.d.) and *Por los espacios llaneros* (Caracas, 1967).
21. N. Morey describes the fishing cultures at length in "Ethnohistory," 195–250.
22. Parsons, "Europeanization of the Savanna Lands," 273.
23. Pablo Vila, "La iniciación de la ganadería," 9; Brito Figueroa, *La estructura económica,* 191.
24. Izard, "Ni cuatreros, ni montoneros," 112.
25. Ibid.
26. John Lombardi, *Venezuela: The Search for Order, the Dream of Progress* (New York, 1982), 85–92.
27. Izard, "Ni cuatreros, ni montoneros," p. 111; Brito Figueroa, *La estructura económica,* 293.
28. J. L. Salcedo Bastardo, *Historia fundamental de Venezuela,* 9th ed. (Caracas, 1982), 120. For an excellent history of one of these towns, see J. A. de Armas Chitty, *Tucupido: Formación de un pueblo del llano* (Caracas, 1961).
29. Brito Figueroa, *La estructura económica,* 191.
30. DePons, cited by Brito Figueroa, *La estructura económica,* 196.
31. Lynch, *The Spanish-American Revolutions,* 189–90.
32. Lombardi, *Venezuela,* 77.
33. Lynch, *The Spanish-American Revolutions,* 190.
34. Lucena Salmoral, "El sistema de cuadrilla de ronda," 198–205.
35. Ibid., 208, Izard, "Ni cuatreros, ni montoneros," 119; Izard, *El miedo a la revolución,* 162–63.
36. Lombardi, *Venezuela,* 132.
37. Mathews, *Violencia rural,* 63.
38. Ibid.; Lynch, *The Spanish-American Revolutions,* 223.
39. Izard, *El miedo a la revolución,* 162–63.
40. White, "Cattle Raising. A Way of Life," 122.
41. Mathews, *Violencia rural,* 64.
42. Izard, "Tanto pelear," 52.
43. J. Fred Rippy, "Dictators of Venezuela," in A. Curtis Wilgus, ed., *South American Dictators during the First Century of Independence* (Washington, D.C., 1937), 394.
44. Robert L. Gilmore, *Caudillism and Militarism in Venezuela, 1810–1910* (Athens, Ohio, 1964), 60.
45. Much has been written about the Argentine pampas and the gaucho. A good place to start is Jonathan C. Brown, *A Socioeconomic History of Argentina,*

1776–1860 (Cambridge, 1979). Brown argues that the expanding external market for Argentine cattle provided the major impetus for the development of organized ranching on the pampas in the eighteenth century. James R. Scobie, *Argentina: A City and a Nation,* 2nd ed. (Oxford, 1971), is another helpful introduction. The standard sources on the gaucho are Ricardo Rodríguez Molas, *Historia social del gaucho* (Buenos Aires, 1968); Emilio A. Coni, *El gaucho: Argentina-Brasil-Uruguay* (Buenos Aires, 1945); and Madaline Nichols, *The Gaucho* (New York, 1968). Two essays by Venezuelans that compare the gaucho with the llanero are "El gaucho y el llanero," *Cultura Venezolana* 71 (1926):41–55, by José E. Machado, and "Gauchos y llaneros," *Cultura Venezolana* 70 (1926):177–94, by Achelpohl (Luis Urbaneja).

46. Raye R. Platt, "Opportunities for Agricultural Colonization in the Eastern Border Valleys of the Andes," in *Pioneer Settlement,* American Geographical Society Special Publication 14 (New York, 1932):107.

47. Victor Andrés Belaunde, "The Frontier in Hispanic America," *Rice Institute Pamphlet* 10 (October, 1923):208.

48. Most of the scholarly work on these frontiers has been done by geographers and focuses on the twentieth century. Two such studies are Raymond E. Crist and Charles M. Nissly, *East from the Andes: Pioneer Settlements in the South American Heartland* (Gainesville, 1973), and Edmund Edward Hegen, *Highways into the Upper Amazon Basin* (Gainesville, 1966). One exception is John L. Phelan, *The Kingdom of Quito in the Seventeenth Century* (Madison, 1967), which includes a chapter entitled "Thrust to the Amazon: Success and Failure." In sketching the colonial history of the Ecuadorean Amazon, Phelan notes that the Province of Quijos, after the initial conquest, languished in poverty and that the Spanish relied on Jesuit missionaries to explore and defend Mainas. He concludes that local conditions were more decisive in determining the developments on the frontier than they were in the major centers of Spanish settlement, where imperial bureaucratic control was usually more influential (p. 42).

49. Jaime Jaramillo Uribe, "Algunos aspectos de la personalidad histórica," 153.

50. Hennessy, *The Frontier in Latin American History,* 13.

51. Phanor James Eder, *Colombia* (New York, 1913), 235.

52. "Los colonizadores del llano," *Revista Pan* (Bogotá) 15 August, 1937):145. Eduardo Zuleta Angel, *El Presidente López* (Madellín, 1966):225–26; see also L. E. Nieto Caballero, *Vuelo al Orinoco* (Bogotá, 1935).

53. Brunnschweiler, *The Llanos Frontier,* 62.

Glossary

Two excellent guides to llanero vocabulary in the twentieth century are José Antonio de Armas Chitty, *Vocabulario del hato* (Caracas, 1966) and María Teresa Cobos, "Del habla popular en el llano," *Boletín Cultural y Bibliográfico* 4 (1966): 949–81.

agregado: tenant farmer
aguardiente: raw liquor distilled from sugarcane
alcabala: sales tax
alcalde: town magistrate
aposenta: room in a ranch house
arroba: unit of weight equivalent to about 25 pounds
bahareque: wall construction using sticks interwoven with reeds and covered with mud
bayetón: large poncho made of wool
cabildo: municipal council
cabildo abierto: open town meeting held in an emergency
caney: house without walls, shed
caporal: foreman on a roundup
carga: unit of weight equivalent to about 40 pounds
casabe: unleavened bread made from yuca flour
caudillo: leader
cofradía: sodality; lay brotherhood supporting ecclesiastical functions
concertado: contract laborer
corral: an enclosed cattle yard

corraleja: corral immediately next to the large corral where tame cattle are kept
corregidor: district magistrate and judge set over Indian settlements
corregimiento: district of a corregidor or magistrate
cura: parish priest
curato: parish
chozo: pike made out of palm wood
doctrina: Indian parish
encomienda: grant of Indians to a Spanish settler; the Indians worked and paid tribute to the recipient, who was called an encomendero
entrada: expedition into wilderness not under Spanish domination
escolta: a group of soldiers assigned to protect a mission
escopeta: shotgun
fanega: land measure equal to 1.6 acres
fique: fiber from the agave (maguey) plant, woven into a rough material; it is used for bagging and transporting products
fuste: wooden saddletree
guayuco: loin cloth worn by Indians
hacienda: large estate
hato: ranch
juez: judge
mantuano: Venezuelan term for a creole who owns a large estate
mayordomo: overseer of an hato or hacienda
novillo: steer
obraje: textile factory
oidor: appeals judge, member of an audiencia
palenque: community of runaway slaves
palo y paja: wall construction using sticks interwoven with grass or reeds
panela: unrefined brown sugar in large pieces
páramo: desert, wilderness
pardo: Venezuelan term for a person of mixed blood
peloeguama: classic, wide-brimmed hat of the llanero, made of dark, velvet-like felt
peón: day laborer on an hato or hacienda
plátano: plantain, a variety of banana with fruit larger, less sweet, and more starchy than the ordinary banana
punta de monte: community of runaway slaves, palenque
puntero: peón who leads a herd of cattle
quiripa: strings of shell disks used by Indians for money and ornamentation
ramada: house without walls often used as a bunkhouse for cowboys

reducción: town of Indians converted to Christianity
remuda: spare horses taken on a roundup or drive
resguardo: land reserved for Indians
ruana: square, heavy poncho made from wool
saca: roundup or cattle drive
sala: room, parlor
saladero: factory for salting beef
serranía: ridge of mountains, mountainous country
sínodo: stipend paid by the crown to missionary clergy
tijeras de trasquilar: sheep shears
trabuco: blunderbuss
trapiche: sugarhouse mill powered by animals
vaquería: roundup
vaquero: cowboy
vara: unit of measure equivalent to about one yard
vecino: full citizen of a town
visita: inspection
yegua: mare
yuca: Manihot utilissima, a starchy root crop grown widely in the Llanos
zambo: a person of Indian and African descent

Bibliography

Archival Materials Consulted

ARCHIVO HISTÓRICO NATIONAL, BOGOTÁ

Established in 1868, this archive is a major repository for manuscripts from the sixteenth through the nineteenth centuries. Both the Sección Colonial and the Sección de la República have substantial amounts of material concerning the Llanos. The documents are bound into volumes arranged in *fondos,* or collections according to subject matter. Each document is indicated by fondo, volume, and folio number. The following fondos proved to be of greatest value for this study:

Seccion Colonial

- Caciques e Indios
- Contrabandos
- Historia Civil
- Juicios Criminales
- Los Comuneros
- Mejoras Materiales
- Negros y Esclavos
- Poblaciones de Boyacá
- Poblaciones Varias
- Resguardos de Boyacá
- Temporalidades
- Tierras de Boyacá

Sección de la República

- Gobernación de Bogotá y Casanare (1819–1822)
- Gobernación de Casanare (1830–1857)
- Gobernación de Bogotá (1832–1857)
- Intendencia de Bogotá (1824–1827)

ARCHIVO DEL CONGRESO, BOGOTÁ

This archive contains manuscripts concerning the activities of the Colombian congress from 1819 to the present. The materials for each year are divided into two categories, Senado and Cámara, and are bound into separate volumes under the headings of Proyectos Pendientes, Peticiones, Informes de Comisión, etc. Most of the data I collected here deal with the second half of the nineteenth century and were not included in this study.

Published Documents

Many documents relating to the history of the Llanos have been published. Of particular importance for the colonial era are the four volumes of unedited materials compiled by Antonio B. Cuervo. Also available in printed form are documents concerning encomiendas, the Comunero Revolt, and the viceregal *relaciones de mando,* compiled by E. Posada and P. M. Ibáñez. The studies by Marcelino Ganuza and Gregorio Arcila Robledo contain a large number of documents pertaining to the work of the missionaries. Published documents for the republican era include decrees and laws, reports of government officials, congressional records, the official newspapers, censuses, and correspondence of key figures. Both the Biblioteca Nacional and the Biblioteca Luis Angel Arango have fine collections of these materials, but the catalogue and retrieval system are more efficient at the latter. The library of the Ministry of Government also makes accessible to the public a complete collection of national and department laws, reports of government ministers, and official periodicals.

COLONIAL ERA

"Acta de fundacion de la Ciudad de Santiago de Las Atalayas." *Revista del Archivo National* (Bogotá) 6 (1944):45–47.

Arcila Robledo, Gregorio. *Las misiones franciscanas en Colombia*. Bogotá, 1910.

Cárdenas Acosta, Pablo E. *El movimiento comunal de 1781 en el Nuevo Reino de Granada*. 2 vols. Bogotá, 1960.

Cuervo, Antonio B., comp. *Colección de documentos inéditos sobre la geografía y la historia de Colombia*. 4 vols. Bogotá, 1891–94.

"Encomiendas, encomenderos e indigenas tributarios del Nuevo Reino de Granada en la primera mitad del siglo XVII." *ACHSC* 1, no. 2 (1964):410–530.

Ganuza, Marcelino. *Monografía de las misiones vivas de Agustinos Recoletos (Candelarios) en Colombia*. 2 vols. Bogotá, 1921.

Giraldo Jaramillo, Gabriel. *Relaciones de mando de los virreyes de la Nueva Granada: Memorias económicas*. Bogotá, 1954.

Mantilla Ruíz, Luis Carlos. *Actividad misionera de los Franciscanos en Colombia durante los siglos XVII y XVIII—Fuentes documentales*. Bogotá, 1980.

Mensanza, Andres. *Apuntes y documentos sobre la orden dominicana en Colombia (de 1680 a 1930): Apuntes o narración*. Caracas, 1929.

Mojica Silva, José. *Relación de visitas coloniales*. Tunja, 1946.

Posada, Eduardo, ed. *Los Comuneros*. Bogotá, 1905.

Posada, E. and P. M. Ibáñez, comps. *Relaciones de mando*. Bogotá, 1910.

Ruíz Rivera, Julian Bautista. *Fuentes para la demografía histórica de Nueva Granada*. Sevilla, 1972.

GRAN COLOMBIA ERA

Archivo Santander, 24 vols. Bogotá, 1913–32.

Codificación nacional de todas las leyes de Colombia desde el año de 1821. Bogotá, 1924.

Colección de decretos dados por el poder ejecutivo de Colombia en los años de 1821 a 1826. Bogotá, 1933.

Cortázar, Roberto, ed. *Cartas y mensajes del General Santander,* 10 vols. Bogotá, 1953–56.

———. *Correspondencia dirigida al General Santander*. 14 vols. Bogotá, 1964–67.

Gaceta de Colombia, 1821–32.

Lecuna, Vicente, and Harold Bierck, eds. *Selected Writings of Bolívar*. 2nd ed. 2 vols. Bogotá, 1951.

Ministerio de Gobierno, *Memorias,* 1823, 1824, 1831, 1834, 1839.

Ministerio de Hacienda, *Memorias,* 1833, 1834, 1835.

Otero d'Costa, Enrique, and L. A. Cuervo, ed. *Archivo Santander*. Bogotá, 194?.

Santander, Francisco de Paula. *Libro de órdenes generales del ejército de operaciones de la Nueva Granada, 1819*. Bogotá, 1969.

Urrutia M., Miguel, and Mario Arrubula. *Compendio de estadísticas históricas de Colombia*. Bogotá, 1970.

Chronicles, Diaries, Memoirs, and Travel Accounts

Aguado, Pedro de. *Recopilación historial*. 4 vols. Bogotá, 1956.

Bingham, Hiram. *Journal of an Expedition across Venezuela and Colombia*. New Haven, 1909.

Caballero, J. M. *La patria boba*. Bogotá, 1902.

Cortés Madariaga, José. "Viaje de Cortés Madariaga," *BHA* 3 (Nov. 1908):437–48, 475–89.

Dalton, Leonard V. *Venezuela*. New York, 1912.

Delgado, Daniel. *Excursiones por Casanare*. Bogotá, 1910.

DePons, Francisco. *Travels in South America during the Years 1801, 1802, 1803, and 1804*. 2 vols. London, 1807.

Eder, Phanor James. *Colombia*. New York, 1913.

Fernández de Piedrahita, Lucas. *Historia general de las conquistas del Nuevo Reino de Granada*. Bogotá, 1981.

Guerra Azuela, Ramón. "Apuntamientos de Viaje." *BHA* 4 (Jan. 1907):416–29.

Gumilla, Joseph. *El Orinoco ilustrado*. Bogotá, 1955.

———. *Escritos varios*. Estudio preliminar y compilación del José del Rey. Caracas, 1970.

Humboldt, Alexander de. *Voyage aux régions équinoxiales du Nouveau Continent fait en 1799, 1800, 1801, 1802, 1803 et 1804*. Paris, 1815.

———. *Personal Narrative of Travels to the Equinoctial Regions of the New Continent, during the Years 1799–1804*. Trans. by Helen María Williams. 7 vols. New York, 1966.

López, José Hilario. *Memorias*. 2 vols. Bogotá, 1942.

Moreno y Escandón, Francisco Antonio. "Estado del Virreinato de Santafé, Nuevo Reino de Granada año 1772." *BHA* 23 (Sept.–Oct. 1936):547–616.

Mozans, H. J. *Up the Orinoco and down the Magdalena*. New York, 1910.

Nieto Caballero, Luis Eduardo. *Vuelo al Orinoco*. Bogotá, 1935.

O'Leary, Daniel Florencio. *Bolívar and the War of Independence*. Trans. and ed. by Robert F. McNerney, Jr. Austin, 1970.

Oviedo, Basilio Vicente de. *Cualidades y riquezas del Nuevo Reino de Granada*. Bogotá, 1930.

Páez, José Antonio. *Autobiografía del General Páez*. 2 vols. Caracas, 1975.

Plaza, José A. *Memorias para la historia de la Nueva Granada*. Bogotá, 1850.

Restrepo, Emiliano. *Una excursión al Territorio de San Martin*. Bogotá, 1957.

Restrepo, José M. *Historia de la revolución de la República de Colombia en la América Meridional*. 6 vols. Medellín, 1974.

Rivero, Juan. *Historia de las misiones de los llanos de Casanare y los Ríos Orinoco y Meta*. Bogotá, 1956.

Rodríguez Fresle, Juan. *El carnero: Conquista y descubrimiento del Nuevo Reino de Granada que comprende hasta el año de 1638*. Bogotá, 1955.

Röthlisberger, Ernst. *El Dorado*. Trans. by Antonio de Zubiaurre. Bogotá, 1963.

Ruiz Maldonado, Diego. "Viaje por los Ríos Casanare, Meta y Orinoco." In *Relaciones geográficas de Venezuela*. Ed. by Antonio Arellano Moreno, 331–60. Caracas, 1964.

Samper, José M. *Ensayo sobre las revoluciones políticas y la condición social de las repúblicas Colombianas (Hispano-Americanas)*. Paris, 1861.

Santander, Francisco de Paula. *Memorias del General Santander*. Bogotá, 1973.

Silvestre Sánchez, Francisco. *Descripción del Reino de Santafé de Bogotá*. Bogotá, 1950.

Simón, Pedro. *Noticias historiales de las conquistas de Tierra Firme en las Indias Occidentales*. 5 vols. Bogotá, 1882–92.

Urdaneta, Rafael. *Memorias del General Rafael Urdaneta*. Caracas, 1888.

Zamora, Alonso de. *Historia de la Provincia de San Antonio del Nuevo Reino de Granada*. Caracas, 1930.

Atlases and Biographical Dictionaries

Acevedo Latorre, Eduardo. *Atlas de mapas antiguos de Colombia—Siglo XVI a XIX*. Bogotá, 1971.

———. *Diccionario geográfico de Colombia*. 2 vols. Bogotá, 1971.

Armando Rodríguez, Ramón. *Diccionario biográfico, geográfico e histórica de Venezuela*. Madrid, 1957.

Ospina, Joaquín. *Diccionario biográfico y bibliográfico de Colombia*. 3 vols. Bogotá, 1937.

Scarpetta, M. Leonidas, and Saturnino Vergara. *Diccionario biográfico de los campeones de la libertad*. Bogotá, 1879.

Zamora, Manuel M. *Guía de la Repúbica de Colombia*. Bogotá, 1907.

Books

Acosta, Joaquín. *Historia de la Nueva Granada*. Medellín, 1971.

Arboleda, Gustavo. *Historia contemporánea de Colombia*. 6 vols. Bogotá, Popayán, and Cali, 1918–35.

Arciniegas, Germán. *Germans in the Conquest of America*. Trans. by Angel Flores. New York, 1943.

———. *The Knight of El Dorado*. New York, 1943.

———. *Los comuneros*. México, 1951.

Bannon, John. *Bolton and the Spanish Borderlands*. Norman, Okla., 1964.

Billington, Ray Allen. *The American Frontier Thesis: Attack and Defense*. Washington, D.C., 1973.

Bolívar Coronado, Rafael. *El llanero: Estudio de sociología venezolano*. Madrid, 1919.

Borda, J. J. *Historia de la Compañía de Jesús en Nueva Granada*. Paris, 1870.

Briceño, Manuel. *Los comuneros*. Bogotá, 1977.

Brito Figueroa, Frederico. *Historia económica y social de Venezuela*. 2 vols. Caracas, 1966.

———. *La estructura economica de Venezuela colonial*. Caracas, 1978.

Brown, Jonathan C. *A Socioeconomic History of Argentina*. Cambridge, Eng., 1979.

Brunnschweiler, Dieter. *The Llanos Frontier of Colombia: Environment and Changing Land Use in Meta*. East Lansing, Mich., 1972.

Bushnell, David. *The Santander Regime in Gran Colombia*. Newark, 1954.

Camacho Baños, Angel. *Sublevación de comuneros en el virreinato de Nueva Granada in 1781*. Sevilla, 1925.

Chapman, Walker. *The Golden Dream—Seekers of El Dorado*. Indianapolis, 1967.

Carrera Damas, Germán. *Boves: Aspectos socioeconómicos de la guerra de independencia*. 3rd ed. Caracas, 1972.

Codazzi, Agustin. *Geografía física y política de las provincias de la Nueva Granada*. Bogotá, 1959.

Colmenares, Germán. *Las haciendas de los jesuítas en el Nuevo Reino de Granada*. Bogotá, 1969.

———. *La Provincia de Tunja en el Nuevo Reino de Granada: Ensayo de historia social 1539–1800*. Bogotá, 1970.

Coni, Emilio. *Historia de las vaquerías del Río de la Plata, 1555–1750*. 2nd ed. Madrid, 1930.

Crist, Raymond E. *Etude geographique des Llanos du Venezuela occidental*. Grenoble, 1937.

——— and Charles M. Nissly. *East from the Andes: Pioneer Settlements in the South American Heartland*. Gainesville, 1973.

Crosby, Alfred. *The Columbian Exchange: Biological and Cultural Consequences of 1492*. Westport, 1972.

Cushner, Nicholas P. *Lords of the Land: Sugar, Wine, and Jesuit Estates of Coastal Peru, 1600–1767*. Albany, 1980.

Denevan, William. *The Native Population of the Americas in 1492*. Madison, 1976.

Díaz Díaz, Oswaldo. *La reconquista española*. 2 vols. Bogotá, 1964–67.

———. *Los Almeydas: Episodios de la resistencia patriota contra el ejército pacificador de Tierra Firme*. Bogotá, 1962.

Díaz Escobar, J. *Bosquejo estadístico de la región oriental de Colombia y medios económicos para su conquista*. Bogotá, 1879.

Fleener, Charles J. "The Expulsion of the Jesuits from the Viceroyalty of New Granada, 1767." Ph.D. diss., University of Florida, 1969.

Flórez, Raquel Angel de. *Conozcamos al Departamento del Meta*. 2 vols. Bogotá, 1963.

Franco, Jean. *The Modern Culture of Latin America*. Rev. ed. Middlesex, Eng., 1970.

Friede, Juan. *El Adelantado Don Gonzalo Jiménez de Quesada*. 2 vols. Bogotá, 1979.

———. *Los Welser en la conquista de Venezuela*. Caracas, 1961.

———. *Vida y viajes de Nicolas Federman, conquistador, poblador y confundador de Bogotá*. Bogotá, 1960.

Gibson, Charles. *Spain in America*. New York, 1966.

Gilmore, Robert. *Caudillism and Militarism in Venezuela 1810–1910*. Athens, Ohio, 1964.

Gómez Latorre, Armando. *Enfoque social de la revolución comunera*. Bogotá, 1973.

Groot, José Manuel. *Historia eclesiástica y civil de Nueva Granada*. 5 vols. Bogotá, 1953.

Hegen, Edmund Edward. *Highways into the Upper Amazon Basin: Pioneer Lands in Southern Colombia, Ecuador and Northern Peru*. Gainesville, 1964.

Henao, Jesús María, and Gerardo Arrubla. *Historia de Colombia*. 5th ed. Bogotá, 1929.

Henderson, James, and Linda Roddy Henderson. *Ten Notable Women of Latin America*. Chicago, 1978.

Hennessy, Alistair. *The Frontier in Latin American History*. Albuquerque, 1978.

Humphreys, R. A., and John Lynch. *The Origins of the Latin American Revolutions 1808–1826*. New York, 1965.

Izard, Miquel. *El miedo a la revolución: La lucha por la libertad en Venezuela (1777–1830)*. Madrid, 1979.

Jaramillo Uribe, Jaime. *Ensayos sobre historia social Colombiana*. Bogotá, 1968.

———. *La personalidad histórica de Colombia y otros ensayos*. Bogotá, 1977.

Jerez, Hipólito. *Los jesuítas en Casanare*. Bogotá, 1952.

Kuethe, Allan J. *Military Reform and Society in New Granada, 1773–1808*. Gainesville, 1978.

Lamar, Howard, and Leonard Thompson. *The Frontier in History: North America and Southern Africa Compared*. New Haven, 1981.

Leonard, Irving A. *Books of the Brave*. New York, 1964.

Liévano Aguirre, Indalecio. *Los grandes conflictos sociales y económicos de nuestra historia*. Bogotá, 1964.

Lombardi, John. *Venezuela: The Search for Order, the Dream of Progress*. New York, 1982.

Londoño, Julio. *Integración del territorio colombiano*. Bogotá, 1967.

Lynch, John. *The Spanish-American Revolutions, 1808–1826*. New York, 1973.

McGreevey, William P. *An Economic History of Colombia, 1845–1930*. Cambridge, Eng., 1971.

Masur, Gerhard. *Simón Bolívar*. Albuquerque, 1948.

Mathews, Robert Paul. *Violencia rural en Venezuela 1840–1858: antecedentes socio-económicos de la guerra federal*. Caracas, 1977.

Molino Garcia, María Teresa. *La encomienda en el Nuevo Reino de Granada durante el siglo XVIII*. Sevilla, 1976.

Montoya de Umaña, Enriqueta. *La criolla Policarpa Salvarrieta*. Bogotá, 1969.

Morey, Nancy Kathleen Creswick. "Ethnohistory of the Colombian and Venezuelan Llanos." Ph.D. diss., University of Utah, 1975.

Morey, Robert V. "Ecology and Culture Change among the Colombian Guahibo." Ph.D. diss., University of Pittsburgh, 1970.

Morón, Guillermo. *Historia de Venezuela*. 5th ed. Caracas, 1970.

Morse, Richard M. *The Bandeirantes: Historical Role of the Brazilian Pathfinders*. New York, 1965.

Moses, Bernard. *Spain's Declining Power in South America 1730–1806*. Berkeley, 1919.

———. *The Spanish Dependencies in South America*. 2 vols. New York, 1965.

Nicholas, Madeline Wallis. *The Gaucho: Cattle Hunter, Cavalryman, Ideal of Romance*. New York, 1968.

Ortega Ricaurte, Enrique. *Villavicencio (1842–1942)—Monografía histórica*. Bogotá, 1943.

Ortiz, Serio Elías. *Génesis de la revolución del 20 de julio de 1810*. Bogotá, 1960.

———. *Nuevo Reino de Granada: El virreinato-período de 1753–1810*. Bogotá, 1970.

———. *Presidentes de capa y espada (1654–1719)*. Bogotá, 1966.

Ospina Vásquez, Luis. *Industría y protección en Colombia 1810–1930.* Medellín, 1955.
Pacheco, Juan Manuel. *La consolidación de la iglesia. Siglo XVII.* Bogotá, 1975.
———. *Los jesuítas en Colombia.* 2 vols. Bogotá, 1959–1962.
Parsons, James J. *Antioqueño Colonization in Western Colombia.* Rev. ed. Berkeley, 1968.
Payne, Stanley. *A History of Spain and Portugal.* 2 vols. Madison, 1976.
Peñuela, Cayo Leonidas. *Album de Boyacá.* 2 vols. 2nd ed. Tunja, 1969.
Pérez, Felipe. *Geografía general, física y política de los Estados Unidos de Colombia.* Bogotá, 1883.
Pérez Ayala, José M. *Antonio Caballero y Góngora, virrey y arzobispo de Santa Fe (1723–1796).* Bogotá, 1951.
Pérez Gómez, José. *Apuntes históricos de las misiones agustinianas en Colombia.* Bogotá, 1924.
Pérez Sarmiento, José Manuel, and Luis Martínez Delgado. *Causes célebres a los precusores.* 2 vols. Bogotá, 1939.
Phelan, John L. *The Kingdom of Quito in the Seventeenth Century.* Madison, 1967.
———. *The People and the King.* Madison, 1978.
Piñeros Corpas, Joaquín. *The New Kingdom Book: A Vision of Colombia.* Bogotá, 1966.
Posada, Eduardo. *Apuntes sobre la Pola.* Tunja, 1917.
Reichel Dolmatoff, Gerardo. *Colombia.* New York, 1965.
Restrepo, Daniel. *La Compañía de Jesús en Colombia: Compendio historial y galería de ilustres varones.* Bogotá, 1940
Restrepo Canal, Carlos. *La Nueva Granada: 1831–1840.* Bogotá, 1971.
Riaño, Camilo. *La campaña libertadora de 1819.* Bogotá, 1969.
Rivera, José Estacio. *La vorágine.* Buenos Aires, 1945.
———. *The Vortex.* Trans. by Earle K. James. New York, 1935.
Rodríguez Molas, Ricardo. *Historia social del gaucho.* Buenos Aires, 1968.
Rojas, Ulises. *El cacique de Turmequé y su época.* Tunja, 1965.
Roosevelt, Anna Curtenius. *Parmana: Pre-historic Maize and Manioc Subsistence along the Amazon and Orinoco.* New York, 1980.
Rouse, Irving and Cruxent, José M. *Venezuelan Archeology.* New Haven, 1963.
Rouse, John. *The Criollo: Spanish Cattle in the Americas.* Norman, Okla., 1977.
Salcedo-Bastardo, J. L. *Historia fundamental de Venezuela.* 9th ed. Caracas, 1982.
Sarmiento, D. F. *Life in the Argentine Republic in the Days of the Tyrants.* Trans. by Mrs. Horace Mann. New York, 1961.
Sauer, Carl O. *Agricultural Origins and Dispersals.* New York, 1952.
Scobie, James. *Argentina: A City and a Nation.* 2nd ed. New York, 1971.
Sharp, William Frederick. *Slavery on the Spanish Frontier: The Colombian Chocó 1680–1810.* Norman, Okla., 1976.
Steward, Julian, and Louis C. Faron. *Native Peoples of South America.* New York, 1959.
Stoan, Stephen. *Pablo Morillo and Venezuela, 1815–1820.* Columbus, Ohio, 1975.

Taylor, George Rogers, ed. *The Turner Thesis Concerning the Role of the Frontier in American History*. 3rd ed. Boston, 1977.
Tisnes J., Roberto María. *Fray Ignacio Mariño, O. P.: Capellán general del Ejercito Libertador*. Bogotá, 1963.
Tormo, Leandro, and Pilar Gonzalbo Aizpuru,. *La iglesia en la crisis de la independencia*. Bogotá, 1961.
Torres Almeyda, Luis. *La rebelión de Galan, el comunero*. Bucaramanga, 1961.
Tovar Pinzón, Hermes. *Grandes empresas agrícolas y ganaderas: Su desarollo en siglo XVIII*. Bogotá, 1980.
Vergara y Velasco, F. J. *Nueva geografía de Colombia*. Bogotá, 1901–2.
Vila, Marco-Aurelio. *Geoeconomía de Venezuela,* 3 vols. Caracas, n.d.
———. *Por los espacios llaneros*. Caracas, 1967.
Webb, Walter Prescott. *The Great Plains*. Boston, 1931.
Zapata Olivella, Manuel. *El hombre colombiano*. Bogotá, 1974.
Zuleta Angel, Eduardo. *El Presidente López*. Medellín, 1966.

Articles

Achelpohl (Luis Urbaneja). "Gauchos y llaneros." *Cultura Venezolana* 70 (1926): 177–94.
Arcila Farías, Eduardo. "El régimen de la propiedad territorial en Hispanoamérica." In *Comisión de historia de la propiedad territorial agraria en Venezuela,* 10–49. Caracas, 1968.
Ayape, Eugenio. "Missiones de Casanare." *BHA* 28 (1944):769–98; 36 (1949): 650–80.
Baker, Paul T., and William T. Sanders. "Demographic Studies in Anthropology. *Annual Review of Anthropology* 1 (1972):151–78.
Bates, Marston. "Climate and Vegetation in the Villavicencio Region of Eastern Colombia." *Geographical Review* 38 (Oct. 1948):555–74.
Beard, J. S. "The Savanna Vegetation of Northern Tropical America." *Ecological Monographs* 23 (1953):149–215.
Belaunde, Victor Andrés. "The Frontier in Hispanic America." *Rice Institute Pamphlets* 10 (Oct. 1923):202–13.
Blydenstein, J. "Tropical Savanna Vegetation of the Llanos of Colombia." *Ecology* 48 (1967):1–14.
Carranza B., Alejandro. "San Juan de los Llanos." *BHA* 24 (Aug. 1937):493–96.
Carrera Damas, Germán. "Algunas consideraciones históricas sobre la cuestión agraria en Venezuela." In *Temas de historia social y de las ideas,* 134–35. Caracas, 1969.
Cobos, M. T. "Guía bibliográfica para los llanos orientales de Colombia." *Boletín Cultural y Bibliográfico* 8 (1965):1888–1935.
Colmenares, Germán. "La economía y la sociedad conyugales, 1550–1800." In *Manual de historia de Colombia,* 1:225–300. Bogotá, 1978–80.

Crist, Raymond E. "Desarrollo político y orígen de caudillismo en Venezuela." *Revista Geográfica Americana* 7 (1937):253–70.

———. "Some Aspects of Human Geography in Latin American Literature." *The American Journal of Economics and Sociology* 21 (Oct. 1962):407–12.

Denevan, William M. "The Aboriginal Population of Western Amazonia in Relation to Habitat and Subsistence." *Revista Geográfica* (Rio de Janeiro) 72 (June 1970):61–86.

Friede, Juan. "Algunas consideraciones sobre la evolución demográfica en la Provincia de Tunja." *ACHSC* 2 (1965):5–19.

———. "Geographical Ideas and the Conquest of Venezuela." *The Americas* 16 (Oct. 1959):145–59.

Gerhard, Dietrich. "The Frontier in Comparative View." *Comparative Studies in Society and History* 1 (March 1959):205–29.

Graff, Gary W. "Spanish Parishes in Colonial New Granada: Their Role in Town Building on the Spanish American Frontier." *The Americas* 33 (1976–77):336–51.

Guáqueta Gallardo, Rogerio. "La fundación de Arauca." Bogotá, 1976.

———. "La raza llanera." Bogotá, 1978.

Hernández de Alba, Gregorio. "The Achagua and Their Neighbors." In Julian H. Steward, ed. *Handbook of South American Indians,* 4:399–412. New York, 1963.

———. "The Betoi and Their Neighbors." In Julian H. Steward, ed. *Handbook of South American Indians,* 4:393–98. New York, 1963.

Ibáñez, Pedro M. "El Coronel Leonardo Infante." *BHA* 3 (Dec. 1905):449–66; (Jan. 1906):513–33; (April 1906):577–602.

Izard, Miquel. "Ni cuatreros ni montoneros, llaneros." *Boletín Americanista* (Barcelona) 13 (1981):83–142.

———. "Tanto pelear para terminar conversando, el caudillismo en Venezuela." *Nova Americana* (Turin) (1979):37–81.

Kirchoff, Paul. "Food-Gathering Tribes of the Venezuelan Llanos." In Julian H. Steward, ed., *Handbook of South American Indians,* 4:445–68. New York, 1963.

———. "The Guayupe and the Sae." In Julian H. Steward, ed., *Handbook of South American Indians,* 4:385–91. New York, 1963.

Lacas, M. M. "A Sixteenth-Century German Colonizing Venture in Venezuela." *The Americas* 9 (1953):275–90.

Lathrap, Donald. "The Hunting Economies of the Tropical Forest Zone of South America. An Attempt at Historical Perspective." In Daniel R. Gross, ed., *Peoples and Cultures of Native South America,* 83–95. New York, 1975.

"Los colonizadores del llano." *Revista Pan* (Bogotá) 15 (August 1937), 145ff.

Lovén, Sven. "The Orinoco in Old Indian Times." *Atti del XXII Congresso Internazionale degli Americanisti* (Rome) 2 (1928):711–25.

Loy, Jane M. "Horsemen of the Tropics: A Comparative View of the Llaneros in the History of Venezuela and Colombia." *Boletín Americanista* (Barcelona) 13 (1981):159–71.

Lozano y Lozano, Fabio. "De Casanare a Boyacá." In *Curso superior de historia de Colombia (1492–1830),* 2:123–54. Bogotá, 1950.

Lucena Salmoral, Manuel. "El sistema de cuadrillas de ronda para la seguridad de los llanos a fines del período colonial: Los antecedentes de las Ordenanzas de Llanos de 1811." In *Memoria del Tercer Congreso Venezolano de Historia,* 2:189–225. Caracas, 1977.

Machado, José E. "El gaucho y el llanero." *Cultura Venezolana* 71 (1926):41–55.

Maingot, Anthony P. "Social Structure, Social Status, and Civil-Military Conflict in Urban Colombia 1810–1858." In Stephen Thernstrom and Richard Sennett, eds., *Nineteenth Century Cities,* 297–355. New York, 1969.

Melo, Jorge Orlando. "La evolución económica de Colombia, 1830–1900." In *Manual de historia de Colombia,* 2:135–207. Bogotá, 1978–80.

———. "Los estudios históricos en Colombia, situación actual y tendencias predominantes." In Dario Jaramillo Agudelo, ed., *La nueva historia de Colombia,* 25–65. Bogotá, 1976.

Mikesell, Marvin. "Comparative Studies in Frontier History." *Annals of the Association of American Geographers* 50 (1960):62–74.

Morey, Nancy C., and Robert V. Morey. "Relaciones comerciales en el pasado en los llanos de Colombia y Venezuela." *Montalban* (Caracas) 4 (1975):5–36.

Morse, Richard M. "Some Characteristics of Latin American Urban History." *American Historical Review* 67 (1962):317–38.

Ocampo López, Javier. "El proceso político, militar, y social de la independencia." In *Manual de historia de Colombia,* 2:16–132. Bogotá, 1978–80.

Otero d'Costa, Enrique. "Fundación de la Gran Colombia." In *Curso superior de historia de Colombia,* 2:189–244. Bogotá, 1950.

———. "La revolución de Casanare en 1809." *BHA* 17 (1928):530–46.

Palacios Preciado, Jorge. "La esclavitud y la sociedad esclavista." In *Manual de historia de Colombia,* 1:303–46. Bogotá, 1978–80.

Parsons, James J. "Europeanization of the Savanna Lands of Northern South America." In David R. Harris, ed., *Human Ecology in Savanna Environments,* 267–89. London, 1980.

Pinto, José Miguel. "División política de la república de Colombia de 1819 a 1905." *BHA* 5 (1908):240–44.

Platt, Raye. "Opportunities for Agricultural Colonization in the Eastern Border Valleys of the Andes." In *Pioneer Settlement,* American Geographical Society Special Publication 14, 80–107. New York, 1932.

Ramírez A., Guillermo. "San Luis de Palenque, el llanero y su presente." *Económica Colombiana* 2 (August, 1954):21–38.

Ramos, Demetrio. "Apuntes para la biografía del virrey de Nueva Granada, D. José Solís." *BHA* 34 (1947):124–49.

Reichel Dolmatoff, Gerardo. "Momíl. A Formative Sequence from the Sinú Valley, Colombia." *American Antiquity* 22 (1957):233–34.

Rice, Hamilton A. "Further Explorations in the Northwest Amazon Basin." *Geographical Journal* 58 (Nov. 1921):321–44.

Rippy, J. Fred. "Dictators of Venezuela." In A. Curtis Wilgus, ed., *South American Dictators during the First Century of Independence,* 391–426. Washington, D.C., 1937.

Rivas, Raimundo. "El marqués de San Jorge." BHA 6 (May 1911):721–50.

Rodrigues, José Honório. "Webb's Great Frontier and the Interpretation of Modern History." In Archibald R. Lewis and Thomas F. McGann, eds., *The New World Looks at its History,* 155–64. Austin, 1963.

Rodríguez Plata, Horacio. "Quién fué Salvador Plata?" *BHA* 44 (1957):366–79.

Steward, Julian H. "The Circum-Caribbean Tribes. An Introduction." In Julian H. Steward, ed. *Handbook of South American Indians,* 4:1–43. New York, 1963.

Tibesar, Antonine S. "The Franciscan *Doctrinero* versus the Franciscan *Misionero* in Seventeenth-Century Peru." *The Americas* 14 (1957–58):115–24.

Vila, Pablo. "La iniciación de la ganadería llanera." *El Farol* (Caracas) 24 (1961): 2–7.

Villamizar, Rafael. "Los llanos de Casanare y del Apure." *BHA* 25 (April 1938): 201–25.

West, Robert C. "The Geography of Colombia." In A. Curtis Wilgus, ed., *The Caribbean. Contemporary Colombia,* 3–21. Gainesville, 1962.

White, C. Langdon. "Cattle Raising. A Way of Life in the Venezuelan Llanos." *The Scientific Monthly* 83 (Sept. 1956):122–29.

Zavala, Silvio. "The Frontiers of Hispanic America." In W. D. Wyman and C. B. Kroeber, *The Frontier in Perspective,* 35–58. Madison, 1957.

Zawadsky, Alfonso. "La guerra de la independencia en los llanos." *BHA* 11 (1917):306–14, 353–63, 428–34, 482–511.

Index